LINCOLN CHRISTIAN UNIVERSITY

D0906914

Bible and Cinema

This volume is a comprehensive introduction to the ways in which the Bible has been used and represented in mainstream cinema. Adele Reinhartz considers the pervasive use of the Bible in feature films, and the medium of film as part of the Bible's reception history. The book examines how films draw on the Old and New Testament and the figure of Jesus Christ in various direct and indirect ways to develop their plots, characters, and themes. As well as movies that set out explicitly to retell biblical stories in their ancient context, the book explores the ways in which contemporary, fictional feature films make use of biblical narrative. Topics covered include:

- how filmmakers make use of scripture to address and reflect their own time and place.
- the Bible as a vehicle through which films can address social and political issues, reflect human experiences and emotions, explore existential issues such as evil and death, and express themes such as destruction and redemption.
- the role of the Bible as a source of ethics and morality, and how this connection is both perpetuated and undermined in a range of contemporary Hollywood films.
- films that create an experience of transcendence, and the ways in which the Bible figures in that experience.

Reinhartz offers insightful analysis of numerous films including *The Ten Commandments* and *The Shawshank Redemption*, paying attention to visual and aural elements as well as plot, character, and dialog. Students will find this an invaluable guide to a growing field.

Adele Reinhartz is Professor in the Department of Classics and Religious Studies at the University of Ottawa, Canada. She has authored a number of books on the intersection of Bible and film, including *Scripture on the Silver Screen* (2003), *Jesus of Hollywood* (2007), and *Bible and Cinema: Fifty Key Films* (2012).

"Reinhartz is the leading interpreter of the use of the Bible in film. In this volume she provides readers with a helpful overview of the subject, raising a host of significant questions and unpacking a wide variety of relevant movies. It is a must-read book for anyone interested in the field."

Robert K. Johnston, *Fuller Theological Seminary,*
USA and author of Reel Spirituality

"Reinhartz deftly shows how cinematic representations of the Bible always reflect the values of the times in which the films are made, as she examines how gender, race, class, and other ideological constructs influence the adaptation of the Bible onto the screen. Through a wide range of examples from biblical epics to modern comedies, her analysis suggests that these films tell us more about contemporary society than about biblical times, as we see how films have used the Bible to validate American exceptionalism, and to structure modern ideas about redemption, morality, apocalyptic, and transcendence."

John Lyden, *Liberal Arts Core Director,*
Grand View University, USA

Bible and Cinema

An introduction

Adele Reinhartz

Routledge
Taylor & Francis Group

LONDON AND NEW YORK

First published in 2013
by Routledge
2 Park Square, Milton Park, Abingdon, Oxon OX14 4RN

and by Routledge
711 Third Avenue, New York, NY 10017

Routledge is an imprint of the Taylor & Francis Group, an informa business

© 2013 Adele Reinhartz

The right of Adele Reinhartz to be identified as author of this work has been asserted by her in accordance with sections 77 and 78 of the Copyright, Designs and Patents Act 1988.

All rights reserved. No part of this book may be reprinted or reproduced or utilized in any form or by any electronic, mechanical, or other means, now known or hereafter invented, including photocopying and recording, or in any information storage or retrieval system, without permission in writing from the publishers.

Trademark notice: Product or corporate names may be trademarks or registered trademarks, and are used only for identification and explanation without intent to infringe.

British Library Cataloguing in Publication Data
A catalogue record for this book is available from the British Library

Library of Congress Cataloging in Publication Data

Reinhartz, Adele, 1953–
Bible and cinema: an introduction/Adele Reinhartz.
pages cm
1. Bible–In motion pictures. 2. Motion pictures–Religious aspects. I. Title.
PN1995.9.B53R45 2013
791.43'6822–dc23
2013015803

ISBN: 978-0-415-77947-0 (hbk)
ISBN: 978-0-415-77948-7 (pbk)
ISBN: 978-1-315-88566-7 (ebk)

Typeset in BemboMTStd
by Cenveo Publisher Services

For Norbert Reinhartz
(1924–2011)

פֿאַר מײַן טײַערן טאַטאַ

איך וועל דיך שטענדיק

ליב האָבן

131171

Contents

10 Conclusion: "My heart is glad, and my soul rejoices": Cinema

List of figures

Acknowledgments

The first draft of this book was written in 2011–12, when I had the privilege of being a member of the School of Historical Studies at the Institute for Advanced Study in Princeton, New Jersey. Like many Canadian academics I visit the United States frequently. But it was only during this year-long sojourn that I began to perceive the profound cultural differences between the United States and Canada, and the ways in which Hollywood movies, including but not limited to the biblical epics of the 1950s and 1960s, express, reflect, and perhaps even perpetuate particular elements of American identity. I am particularly indebted to the work of Sacvan Bercovitch, a fellow Canadian (and lover of Yiddish literature) who has lived and worked in the United States for most of his career, for a glimmer of understanding about the role of the Bible in public life and discourse.[1]

I have benefited greatly from the resources at several libraries, in particular, the Morisset Library at the University of Ottawa, the Firestone Library and the Marquand Art Library at Princeton University, and the Humanities and Social Sciences Library at the Institute for Advanced Study in Princeton. I also greatly appreciated the assistance of Terrie Bramley, at the School of Historical Studies, and the Humanities and Social Sciences Library staff, especially Kirstie Venanzi, Karen Downing, and Marcia Tucker. My thanks to the Hetty Goldman Membership Fund for the generous support which made possible my year at the Institute. I wish also to express my gratitude to the Social Sciences and Humanities Research Council of Canada, which supported this project through a Standard Research Grant, and to the Faculty of Arts at the University of Ottawa for release time.

This book, like my other work on Bible and film, was developed in the classroom. I am grateful to have had the opportunity to talk about movies with the many students in SRS 4107 at the University of Ottawa over the years. My current students in this course (Winter 2013) have not only discussed these movies with me but have also read through the draft chapters of this book, and I wish in particular to thank Hannah Barr and Kiara Morissey, who provided me with their written comments on the chapters. I also wish to thank Duke University (Durham, NC), Flagler College (St. Augustine, FL),

Carleton University (Ottawa, ON) and elsewhere, for providing the opportunity to lecture on Bible and film to broader audiences.

Many individuals provided much-needed assistance at various stages of the
project. My thanks to William R. Telford and Barry Walfish for reading and
commenting on the entire manuscript, to Kim Shier for commenting and
fact-checking, to Natalie Neill for indexing, to Jason Shim, Andrew
Thompson, and Simcha Walfish for technical assistance, and to Lesley Riddle,
Katherine Ong, Emma Hudson, Jaya Dalal, and many others at Routledge
for encouragement and assistance throughout the process. Many friends and
family members have been my conversation partners with regard to the phenomenon of Bible and film. In particular, I wish to thank Barry Walfish, with
whom I have watched most of these films, and Simcha Walfish, with whom I
have discussed several of them, as well as the rest of my family for their love
and support in this project as in everything else.

It was with my parents that I first encountered the magic of cinema, and
among the many things I have missed in recent years is the fun of talking
about movies with them both. I dedicate this book with love and longing to
my father, who died after a lengthy illness when this book was in its earliest
stages. May his memory be for a blessing.

Unless otherwise noted, all transcriptions of film dialog are my own.

Unless otherwise noted, all scripture quotations are from the *Common Bible:
New Revised Standard Version*, © 1989 National Council of the Churches of
Christ in the United States of America. Used by permission. All rights
reserved.

Portions of Adele Reinhartz, *Jesus of Hollywood* (2007) are used in chapters
1–4 by permission of Oxford University Press, USA.

Chapter 5 draws on Adele Reinhartz, "Playing with Paradigms: The
Christ-Figure Genre in Contemporary Film." *Australian Religious Studies
Review* 21, no. 3 (2008): 298–317, © Equinox Publishing Ltd, 2008.

Portions of Chapters 4 and 5 draw upon Adele Reinhartz, "Jesus and
Christ-Figures." In *The Routledge Companion to Religion and Film*, edited by
John Lyden, 421–39. London: Routledge, 2009.

A section of Adele Reinhartz, "History and Pseudo-History in the Jesus Film
Genre." *Biblical Interpretation* 14 (2006): 1–17. Special Issue: *The Bible in Film –
The Bible and Film* is used in chapter 8, by permission of Koninklijke Brill NV.

Notes

1 See especially Sacvan Bercovitch, "The Biblical Basis of the American Myth," in
 The Bible and American Arts and Letters, edited by Giles B. Gunn (Philadelphia, PA;
 Chico, CA: Fortress Press; Scholars Press, 1983), 219–29; Sacvan Bercovitch, *The
 Puritan Origins of the American Self* (New Haven, CT: Yale University Press, 1975),
 and Sacvan Bercovitch, *The Rites of Assent: Transformations in the Symbolic Con-
 struction of America* (New York: Routledge, 1993).

1 Introduction

"Seeking a vision": Bible movies as film genre

On 22 November 1897, a person seeking novelty and entertainment in the city of Philadelphia could wander over to the American Academy of Music at Broad and Locust Streets and plunk down 50 cents for the premiere of a new "moving picture," *The Horitz Passion Play*.[1] The evening featured "scenes in the life of Christ and the crucifixion and the resurrection," supplemented by slide pictures of "local points of interest in the town of Horitz, Austria" and rounded out by an "explanatory lecture" delivered by Professor Ernest Lacy.[2] The slides, lecture, organ music, and hymns stretched the five-minute moving picture sequence to an hour and a half of lively entertainment. The next morning, the reviewer for the *Philadelphia Inquirer* enthused about the "moving picture" experience (if not necessarily its theatrical content):

> Without the life-like movement of these views it would have been impossible to have appreciated anywhere near to the full the unquestioning, credulous simplicity of this theatrical representation. In these pictures, however, we actually see the half-naked Adam and Eve running about in a quaint little Garden of Eden, with invading devils lurking under the Tree of Life, and an odd-looking Serpent of Evil leaning its flat head out of the boughs....
>
> (*Philadelphia Inquirer*, 23 November 1897, p. 6).[3]

Thus began the Bible's long and illustrious movie career. Some 115 years after this debut, the Bible – Old Testament and New – remains a fixture of the American and world cinema, readily available in numerous versions, in whole or in part, on screens large and small.[4]

Nowadays, we associate "Bible movies" not so much with the quaint simplicity of the early Passion Play films as with the extravagance and melodrama of the Hollywood epics of the 1950s and early 1960s. Like other epics, these Bible films engage the fundamental human emotions in direct and uncomplicated ways. The glamorous stars, beautiful clothing, dramatic scenery, and romantic orchestral music befitted the Bible's broad sweep, and the majesty of the all-powerful God who created the world and oversees its affairs. How can one not thrill to the passion of King David and the ravishing Bathsheba, the

fierce rivalry between the brooding Moses and the exotic Ramses, the spectacular battles, the plagues, and, of course, the parting of the Red Sea?

Appealing and popular as they were, however, Bible epics abruptly disappeared from the American big screen in the mid-1960s. In the years since
1965 only a small number of Bible-based feature films – notably, Bruce
Beresford's *King David* (1985), Martin Scorsese's *Last Temptation of Christ*
(1988), the animated film *The Prince of Egypt* (1998), Mel Gibson's *The Passion
of the Christ* (2004) – have made it to the local Cineplex. To be sure, the Bible
is alive and well on Christian television, in the occasional studio or cable
mini series, and in children's video series such as *Veggie Tales*. But full-blown
epic treatments of the lives and loves of Moses, David, Solomon, or Jesus are
now few and far between.

The decline of the Bible epic, however, did not cause the scriptures to
disappear from the silver screen. On the contrary, numerous fictional feature
films that are not about the Bible make ample use of biblical quotations,
allusions, paradigms, themes, images, and narratives, as well as Bibles themselves. The Bible's role in such films did not begin suddenly in the mid-1960s;
earlier films, such as Charlie Chaplin's *The Great Dictator* (1940), and Elia
Kazan's *East of Eden* (1955), explicitly drew upon biblical stories and verses in
their narrative structure, characterization, and dialog. But the phenomenon
increased rapidly in the latter part of the twentieth century and continues
unabated today. *Being There* (1979) draws upon Jesus' parables; *Crimes and
Misdemeanors* (1989) recalls the Joseph saga in the book of Genesis; *Independence Day* (1996) makes ample use of the Book of Revelation.[5] In *Magnolia*
(1999), a veritable plague of frogs afflicts a neighborhood in the San Fernando
Valley – rubber frogs, as it turns out, some 7,900 of them (according to the
Internet Movie Database [IMDb], no real frogs were hurt in the making of
this film).[6] In some cases, the use of the Bible reflects the scriptures' canonical
status in Judaism and Christianity. Hollywood's Bibles often appear in churches (*Gran Torino*, 2008) and synagogues (*A Serious Man*, 2009), or in the
hands of preachers (*The Apostle*, 1997) and Bible-sellers (*O Brother, Where Art
Thou?*, 2000). But in many other films, it is the Bible as such – removed from
any religious institution or functionary – that is woven into a film's plot,
characters, dialog, and visual imagery. It would be only a slight exaggeration
to say that, whether we are aware of it or not, we encounter scripture in
almost every film we view.

The study of Bible and film

The cinema's attraction to the Bible has not gone unnoticed. Among the
Bible epics, the Jesus-movies, Moses movies, and "sword-and-sandal" films
have garnered special attention.[7] Some subgenres of more recent Bible-related
movies, especially apocalyptic films and so-called Christ-figure films, have also
been scrutinized.[8] Indeed, Bible and film is a growing subfield within biblical
studies, with numerous essays and articles published each year. Many

universities, colleges, and seminaries offer courses in Bible and film, and numerous instructors use feature films in their introductory and advanced biblical studies courses. The annual conferences of academic organizations such as the Society for Biblical Literature routinely devote sessions to Bible and film, and specialized conferences, symposia, and workshops are frequent.

Missing from the Bible and film bookshelf, however, is any comprehensive look at the "Bible and film" phenomenon as such. The plethora of writings and courses suggests that this absence is not due to a lack of interest or expertise. Why then the gap? The reason, I believe, lies in the unwieldy and ever-expanding nature of the cinematic corpus as such. For scholars trained to master all of the relevant primary sources before embarking on any broad-ranging study, the impossibility of viewing, let alone analyzing, every poten-tially relevant movie, is a major deterrent. Any hypothesis or generalization risks being overturned by those who have seen more or different movies, as well as by future, unpredictable directions of cinema itself.

This point is well illustrated by a 1999 book that predicted that the 1989 film *Jesus of Montreal* had brought the Jesus-movie genre to an end. This film, it claimed,

> brings us to the end of things, and, indeed, to the end of the possibility of the Christian metanarrative. [...] The world that constructed the Jesus film is at an end because, in a certain sense, the humanist culture that assembled an image called "Jesus Christ" has disappeared.[9]

A few short years later, Philip Saville (*The Gospel of John*, 2003) and, more famously, Mel Gibson (*The Passion of the Christ*, 2004) would prove this pro-phecy wrong. Even as I write these words, several new Bible movies are in the works – on Noah (Darren Aronofsky), Moses (Steven Spielberg, Ridley Scott), and Jesus (Paul Verhoeven) – and rumors of even more – on Cain and Abel (Will Smith), David and Goliath (Scott Derrickson), and Pontius Pilate (starring Brad Pitt) – which may yet revive the epic genre, and require a thorough revision of the historical account I have just presented.[10]

The danger – one might say, the likelihood – that new information or new perspectives will overturn one's favorite hypotheses inheres in any broad study, and the benefits are well worth the risk. Bible and film can be studied from several different disciplinary perspectives. Within religious studies, Bible and film is a subset of "religion and film," and can contribute to the under-standing of religion and contemporary culture.[11] Bible and film can also be seen as a branch of "theology and film,"[12] or indeed as an aspect of film stu-dies per se.[13]

From the perspective of my primary field, biblical studies, it has been sug-gested that the study of Bible movies can illuminate the Bible itself, in a process that has been called "reversing the hermeneutical flow."[14] My own study of Bible and film – and therefore this book – focuses on two other areas: the Bible's reception history, that is, the varied ways in which individuals and communities through the centuries have reflected upon, interpreted or come to grips with the Bible; and the Bible in the public square.

Bible, film, and reception history

Since the end of the nineteenth century, film has taken its place alongside literature, music, art, drama, exegesis, liturgy, and theology as a medium for thinking about and interpreting the Bible. Film not only stands alongside these vehicles of biblical reception, however, but makes abundant and creative use of these other media in the course of creating their own Bible-related narratives.

This use is most apparent in filmmakers' attempts to fill the many gaps that the biblical stories leave to our imaginations. In the prolog to his 1956 *The Ten Commandments*, Cecil B. DeMille states that he drew on the writings of first-century writers such as Philo of Alexandria and Flavius Josephus, to fill in the gaps in the biblical account, for example, with regard to Moses' youth in the Pharaoh's court. The most recent film of the Exodus story, *The Prince of Egypt*, makes ample use of rabbinic midrash for the same purpose. Some of the Jesus films draw on apocryphal sources such as the Infancy Gospel of James to describe Jesus' childhood. Filmmakers often model the visual elements of their movies (costumes, settings, scene composition) on famous works of art, such as Michelangelo's *Pietà* and Leonardo's *Last Supper*, and draw attention to major dramatic moments, such as the Raising of Lazarus, with orchestral renditions of famous music such as the Hallelujah Chorus from Handel's *Messiah*. The cinema's use of ancient sources as well as medieval and modern artistic, theological, and other reflections demonstrates that film is an active participant in a long and highly developed tradition of interpretation of sacred stories.

The Bible in the public square

The Bible's starring role in cinema is part of another, larger story: the Bible's role in society, culture, politics, and public discourse.[15] Feature films dramatize, quote from, allude to, and otherwise make use of the Bible to tell their own biblical and non-biblical stories, to reflect upon central social, cultural, and political issues, to describe human experiences and emotions, and, most important, to reflect on, or perhaps even to create and perpetuate, national identity. As many have noted, the Bible epics say more about mid-twentieth-century America than about ancient Israel.[16]

Aims

The present study will focus on both of these issues: film as an aspect of the Bible's reception history, and the cinematic use of the Bible to express identity. With regard to reception history, the study will document amply, though not exhaustively, the movies' use of both the Bible and other modes of biblical reception. It will argue that film, perhaps more than any other medium, testifies to the thick fabric that artistic, liturgical, theological, exegetical, and historical representations and interpretations have woven around the Bible as such, to the point where one is hard-pressed to distinguish between the source and the reception. The cinema's numerous blond-haired, blue-eyed Jesuses – products of European art rather than Jesus' own Middle-Eastern provenance – testify to this very point. On the Bible's cinematic role in the expression of identity, this study will document some of the different ways in which movies make use of scripture to address, express, reflect, or question the anxieties, norms, values, social structures, worldviews of the eras in which they were made.

Underlying these two issues, and, indeed, the study of Bible and film as a whole, is an even more fundamental question: why has the Bible achieved and maintained stardom over such a long period of time, and across virtually all film genres?

Several answers suggest themselves immediately. One lies in both the familiarity and the popularity of the Bible in America in the late nineteenth and early twentieth centuries. Through the efforts of the American Bible Society and other groups, many American households had a Bible on their bookshelf. Americans not only owned Bibles, and meticulously recorded their family histories within them, but also placed themselves figuratively within its narrative.[17] Fictional adaptations as well as vivid historical or quasi-historical accounts helped create a sense of immediacy.[18] But moving pictures! These were more compelling than any novel or illustrated Bible could be. While many would never have the opportunity to view a Passion Play, the movies were within everyone's means.[19] Furthermore, because of their sacred subject matter, Bible movies helped to counteract the strong concerns voiced by clergy and other leaders about the immorality of film as a mode of popular entertainment.[20]

Another reason lies in the economics of the movie industry. Not all Bible movies have been box office hits. Notable commercial failures include films that became iconic after dismal theater runs, such as Griffith's *Intolerance* (1916), and George Stevens' *The Greatest Story Ever Told* (1965). On the whole, however, the Bible movie has been a highly lucrative genre. In 1907, the Passion Play movie produced by the French company, Pathé Brothers, was the most popular film in North America and Europe.[21] Other megahits have been DeMille's 1927 Jesus-movie, *The King of Kings* and, most recently, Mel Gibson's *The Passion of the Christ* (2004).[22] One may well speculate that the spate of Bible movies now in various stages of production is not unrelated to the tremendous financial success of Gibson's blockbuster.

Another measure of the centrality of Bible movies to the cinema is their role in the development of film technology itself. Passion Play films as well as Old Testament movies such as Vitagraph's *The Life of Moses* (1910) and D. W. Griffith's *Judith of Bethulia* (Biography film company, 1913–14), were among the pioneers of multi-reel film and paved the way for the feature film as we know it today.[23] Griffith's *Intolerance* was the first film to weave together different narratives from different historical eras; one of these was a "Judean story" that dramatized incidents from the life of Jesus. Some decades later, *The Robe* was the first feature film to make use of widescreen technology, known as CinemaScope.[24]

The Bible movie genre

Another factor that comes into play is the epic genre's establishment of firm conventions for the use of the Bible. These epic conventions became so deeply entrenched in Hollywood narrative style that they spilled over into other movie genres, and continue to be used in a broad range of films, to the point where the use of the Bible as such has become conventional in many genres. The establishment of genre conventions in this manner is not unique to the use of the Bible *per se*, but a widespread phenomenon. For example, the iconic chariot race in *Ben-Hur* (1959) has influenced numerous races, car chases, and other similar movie scenes. *Ben-Hur* was not the first to use the motif of the chariot race – it appears, for example, in *Quo Vadis?* (1951) as well as in DeMille's 1956 *The Ten Commandments* – but it quickly became the most famous version and recurs not only in films but in live re-enactments.[25]

Movie genres depend upon conventions that are repeated from film to film and thereby become familiar to viewers. Film theorist Thomas Schatz comments that

> Movies are not produced in creative or cultural isolation, nor are they consumed that way. Individual movies may affect each one of us powerfully and somewhat differently, but essentially they are all generated by a collective production system which honors certain narrative traditions (or conventions) in designing for a mass market.[26]

Conventions not only convey meaning but also generate enjoyment; as Linda Hutcheon notes, some of the pleasure of film-watching "comes simply from repetition with variation, from the comfort of ritual combined with the piquancy of surprise."[27]

These observations undergird what is known as the genre theory. According to Schatz, the genre approach involves several assumptions and propositions:

> (1) It assumes that filmmaking is a *commercial* art, and hence that its creators rely on proven formulas to economize and systematize production; (2) it recognizes the cinema's close contact with its *audience*, whose response to individual films has affected the gradual development of story formulas and standard production practices; (3) it treats the cinema as primarily a *narrative* (storytelling) medium, one whose familiar stories involve dramatic conflicts, which are themselves based upon ongoing

cultural conflicts; (4) it establishes a context in which cinematic *artistry* is evaluated in terms of our filmmakers' capacity to re-invent established formal and narrative conventions [italics in original].[28]

Genres can therefore be identified through their conventions. This is not to say that every film in a given genre will make use of all the conventions associated with that genre. Rather, as Schatz notes, a genre

> represents a *range of expression* for filmmakers and a *range of experience* for viewers. Both filmmakers and viewers are sensitive to a genre's range of expression because of previous experiences with the genre that have coalesced into a system of value-laden narrative conventions. It is this system of conventions – familiar characters performing familiar actions which celebrate familiar values – that represents the genre's narrative context, its meaningful cultural community.[29]

Due to its longstanding popularity, the Bible is a godsend (so to speak) for filmmakers, for whom it provides a ready-made set of "familiar characters performing familiar actions which celebrate familiar values" already ripe for appropriation and adaptation to the demands of other cinematic genres beyond the epic Bible movie as such.

Yet it is unlikely that the convention of drawing on the Bible would have taken hold in genres other than the epics had the Bible not served some fundamental narrative, thematic, or other cinematic goals. This book will argue that the ongoing importance of Bible-related conventions can be attributed to two aspects of the Bible itself, or at least, of the way it is popularly conceived. One is the belief, grounded in the Bible's canonical status, that although the Bible tells of things that occurred long ago and far away, its truths – however one understands that term – remain relevant to the present day. The second is the Bible's presumed connection to the divine, a view that is also grounded in its canonical status. Presenting Bibles on the screen, quoting from its texts, or explicitly modeling characters or plot elements on biblical stories, adds depth and heft to the film's overall story and message by tying the specific narratives and characters to the larger story of humankind and even the cosmos. Underlying this attempt to account for the Bible's presence and role in cinema is the assumption that film is not "merely" entertainment but that it is deeply entangled with social and cultural issues, and even more fundamentally, with identity – personal, social, national – in many and complex ways.[30]

Scope

In principle, the entanglement of film, Bible, and identity could apply to the cinema of any country in which filmmakers incorporate the Bible into their movies. In practice, however, the present study will focus primarily, though not exclusively, on "Hollywood." "Hollywood" has become synonymous with American cinema, including films not actually made in Hollywood. Allen Scott notes that

> in one sense, Hollywood is a very specific place in Southern California, and, more to the point, a particular locale-bound nexus of production relationships and local labour market activities. In another sense, Hollywood is everywhere, and in its realization as a disembodied assortment of images and narratives, its presence is felt across the entire globe. These local and global manifestations of Hollywood are linked together by a complex machinery of distribution and marketing.[31]

To some extent, the decision to focus largely on American feature films is pragmatic. To attempt an account of the global use of the Bible in film would require a much larger canvas than I have at my disposal. But there is also a scholarly justification for focusing on "Hollywood." First, mainstream, commercial cinema – the two-hour (more or less) feature film – was developed and reached its maturity in the United States, and most, though not all, of the well-known Bible-related movies are American, in the sense that they are produced in the first instance for the American market by filmmakers whose careers are based primarily in America. Second, Hollywood movies do not stay in Hollywood but travel throughout the world.[32] Through global distribution and the enormous international popularity of American films, Hollywood genres and their cinematic conventions and norms are familiar to viewers the world over, and have even been absorbed to a greater or lesser extent into the national cinemas of other countries. "Foreign" films are themselves often produced for international, including American, distribution, and for that reason will often use American norms in order to appeal to American tastes.[33] This tendency toward homogeneity is further reinforced by the increasing number of international co-productions.[34] There will be occasion, however, to take note of the distinctively American elements of Hollywood films, and the obviously non-American aspects of films made in other countries.

Film analysis

Bible scholars who spend their waking hours pondering the Bible and the history of its interpretation and reception can easily document the cinematic use of the Bible; they can catch the biblical quotations and allusions, and comment on how they are used (cleverly or naively; appropriately or wrongly; extensively or slightly), when they occur (throughout the entire history of cinema), and in which movie genres (almost all of them).[35] But to account for the Bible's popularity at the movies, one must go beyond documentation to analysis.

A natural first step in the analysis of Bible movies is to compare the movie's plot and characters to the biblical account itself; in the analysis of the Bible in fictional feature films, the tendency is often to focus on dialog. But film analysis requires close attention not only to plot, character, and dialog but also to the visual and aural elements in film.[36] Color, camera angles, mise-en-scène (composition of the frame, including the placement of objects, people, and other elements), setting, costuming, indeed, everything we see on the screen can contribute considerably to our understanding of the use of the Bible in film. The same is true of sound. The presence, and absence, of musical soundtrack, ambient sound, and other aural effects shapes our understanding of and emotional responses to movies, even if we are not at all aware of them. Editing – the juxtaposition of images, sounds, characters, and scenes, the speed and mode of the transitions between one cut and the next, and between one scene and the next – affects our perceptions and interpretations of a film, its characters, its message, and, yes, its use of the Bible.

The structure of this book

Part I: Bible on film

Section One of this book will examine the Bible *on* film, that is, movies that set out explicitly to retell biblical stories in their ancient contexts. Most of the films discussed in these chapters belong to the epic genre, and indeed they are epic in every respect. The biblical epics have attracted attention from film scholars and critics, not all of it positive. Epics are often viewed as significantly inferior to other dramas and therefore unworthy of serious critical attention. Paul Schrader, Martin Scorsese's screenwriter for *Taxi Driver*, *Raging Bull*, and *The Last Temptation of Christ*, and a director in his own right, scorns the biblical epics as "ersatz religious cinema" whose extravagance prevents any true encounter with the divine.[37] Rudolf Arnheim decries the epic as a static genre that "neither deals with a problem nor offers a solution."[38]

Not all scholars, however, dismiss the epics out of hand. Vivian Sobchack argues that the "surge and splendor and extravagance" of the genre should not be deplored, but rather acknowledged as central to their essential function as positing a continuity between the biblical or classical past and the American post-war present. These films participated in a "then as now" discursive field in which American audiences – largely male, white, and middle-class – could experience their own social and political context in the post-war decades.[39] Sobchack draws particular attention to the role of the Hollywood historical film in addressing the perennial and quintessentially human question of "how to comprehend ourselves in time." In constructing the past to reflect the present, epics diminish or even erase the historical distance between ancient times and places and the physical, chronological, and social location of the viewer.[40]

Bruce Babington and Peter Evans too argue for the genre's value both as film and as a subject of serious criticism. While they agree with Schrader's point that epic films do not deliver a transcendental religious experience, they suggest that the epics dramatize "the encounter of religion and secularism in twentieth-century America." For this reason, epics "have a sub-textual rich-ness that emerges from the expression of secular concerns in the context of religious ideology, and vice versa." Even if most epics were far from aesthetic masterpieces, they are often worthy of study as social-historical documents.[41]

On this basis, we will focus primarily on what Sobchack refers to as the "then as now" element of these films: the ways in which filmmakers use the biblical narrative to address and reflect their own time and place.

Chapter 2 will consider movies of famous stories and characters in the Hebrew Bible, such as the Exodus, featuring Moses as liberator and lawgiver, and the sagas of Samson, Ruth, David, and Solomon. As we will see, these films retell biblical stories from an American, Protestant Christian perspective, quite transparently equating biblical Israel with an idealized America as God's chosen people that frees itself from Egyptian and other foreign domination and champions freedom for others. For that reason, we will refer to them not as Hebrew Bible movies, but as Old Testament movies. Like the Old Testa-ment itself, which from a Christian perspective is viewed as a precursor and forerunner of the New Testament, the Old Testament movies almost always include references or allusions to Jesus, or, to be more precise, an idealized and Americanized version of Jesus, as the one who will eventually come to provide the salvation for which biblical Israel strives.

Of course, Jesus himself features prominently in a subgenre all his own: the Jesus-movies. These films will be the subject of Chapter 3. The Jesus-movies portray Jesus as the one who is sent by God to save Israel from Roman domination. But in contrast to Old Testament movies, in which Moses, David, and Solomon really do save their people, at least temporarily, Jesus-movies cannot show Jesus in this same political role, first, because that would be inconsistent with the Gospel accounts that most movies use as primary sources, and second, because of the simple fact that Rome continued to dominate Israel for centuries after Jesus. Despite these obstacles, Jesus-movies proclaim that with Jesus' coming, the world order has been transformed.

Chapter 4 looks at a fictional variation of the Bible movie: so-called "sword-and-sandal" or "peplum" films, such as *Ben-Hur* and *Quo Vadis?* Old Testament and Jesus-movies tell their biblical stories more or less chron-ologically, though with considerable embellishment. Sword-and-sandal movies, by contrast, weave snippets of Jesus' story into a broader fictional narrative about the fate of sincere Christian believers within the ruthless, materialistic, pagan Roman empire. Yet all biblical epics, whether based on the Old Testament, the New Testament, or the experience of the early church, are complicit in validating and protecting a certain status quo with regard to gender relationships, race, class, politics, American Christianity, and the American Way.

The analogy between past and present that is implicit in the "then and now" dimension of these films is made explicit in films that juxtapose biblical stories with modern narratives. Chapter 5 will consider two types of such stories: those that set the two stories side-by-side, and those that embed a biblical story in a modern frame narrative. These films straddle the categories of "Bible on film" and "Bible in film," as they include both an explicit retelling of biblical narratives, as well as one or more stories from times and places far removed from the Bible, in which the biblical stories, characters, and themes are played out.

Part II: Bible in film

Section Two of the book will focus on the ways in which contemporary, fictional feature films make use of the Bible. Though the use of the Bible *in* film is quite different from the portrayal of the Bible *on* film, there are historical and generic connections between them. As the chapters in Section One will point out, Bible epics not only drew upon the conventions of the epic genre as a whole but also established some unique conventions with regard to the use of, quotation from, and allusion to the Bible, and to the drawing of an ancient, Middle Eastern – "biblical" – setting. These conventions included the use of Bible stories as narrative paradigms, the patterning of fictional characters after recognizably biblical characters, and the use of explicit biblical quotation and allusion. Furthermore, Bible movies established and played on iconographic elements pertaining to the Bible: a person standing with outstretched arms immediately evoked the figure of Christ, as did a person who walked on or in a body of water. Bibles as objects – books or scrolls – were present on screen or called to mind by "Bible-like" fonts for biblical or non-biblical texts. Finally, the Bible was directly and positively associated with ethics and a divinely sanctioned social and moral order. These conventions made their way into fictional feature films, though the ends to which they were put often differed sharply from the messages espoused by the Bible epics themselves. Whereas many Bible epics celebrated and perpetuated the view of America as a "light unto the nations," more recent films are often critical of this worldview and its religious and biblical foundations. Unlike the Bible epics, these fictional films do not comprise a homogeneous, easily described, corpus.

Feature films that make use of the Bible span all genres: comedy (*The Truman Show*, 1998), drama (*Gran Torino*, 2008) horror (*Frankenstein*, 1931), science fiction (*The Matrix*, 1999), spy (*The Good Shepherd*, 2006), paranormal (*The Sixth Sense*, 1999), westerns (*Pale Rider*, 1985), and prison films (*The Shawshank Redemption*, 1994). The presence of the Bible in these films is sometimes obvious, as when the movie's title itself is a biblical quotation – *The Good Shepherd* (John 10: 1–9), *Babel* (Genesis 11), or *The Tree of Life* (Genesis 2) – or when there are obvious parallels with biblical characters and stories, such as Moses (*The Lion King*), Jesus (*The Shawshank Redemption*), or Job (*A Serious Man*). In other films, the biblical elements may be apparent only to those with prior familiarity with the Bible (or, to be more precise, with its cultural interpretation), as when a young woman in *Pleasantville* takes a bite out of an apple (Gen. 3:17) and looks seductively at the camera, or when one character refers to another as a "fisher of men" (Matt. 4:19) as in *The Guardian*.

The pervasive use of the Bible in feature films means that North American audiences encounter some aspect of the Bible almost every time they watch a movie. Because movie going, from its inception, was inexpensive and therefore accessible to the general public, regardless of socioeconomic bracket, education, heritage, or knowledge level, film's influence is not limited to a particular class or group, but extends to virtually all segments of society.[42] For this reason, the biblical presence on the silver screen has a potential impact on a large segment of the American population, and, through worldwide distribution patterns, on millions of viewers in other parts of the world. Film is also one medium through which immigrants, often from non-Christian cultures, can be socialized into the norms, values, and foundational stories of "western" (North American, European) society, including its privileging of the Bible. The global marketing of these films means that films that rely on the Bible are increasingly being consumed not only in North America and Europe but throughout the world, to the point that biblical, usually specifically Christian, images are evident in non-Christian national cinemas, as in India (*Karunamayudu*, 1978) and Israel (e.g., *Walk on Water*, 2004).

Due to their very popularity, films "have the potential to reinforce, to challenge, to overturn, or to crystalize religious perspectives, ideological assumptions, and fundamental values. Films bolster and challenge our society's norms, guiding narratives, and accepted truths"[43] and are a "pervasive means" through which the public receives "representations of identity and diversity, relationships, and social arrangements and institutions."[44] If so, the use of the Bible in film should both reflect and shape value systems, worldviews, perceptions, and assumptions about many aspects of society and religion. Even a preliminary survey indicates that the Bible is a vehicle through which films explore numerous political and social issues, such as capital punishment (*Dead Man Walking*, 1995), the environment (*Children of Men*, 2006), racism (*Pleasantville*, 1998), and war (*Passchendaele*, 2008), and basic human emotions such as love and hate (*Cape Fear*, 1991). The Bible also provides a verbal and visual vocabulary for addressing existential issues, such as good and evil (*The Good Shepherd*, 2006), presence and absence (*Sling Blade*, 1996), or life and death (*Magnolia*, 1999).

The chapters in this section will show how the principal Bible-related conventions established in the Bible movie genre – the Bible *on* film – persist in and indeed are integral to films that make use of the Bible to tell other sorts of stories – the Bible *in* film. Chapter 6 will focus on films which make use of the Old Testament in various direct and indirect ways to develop their plots, characters, and themes. Chapter 7 will do the same with regard to films that make use of the New Testament, with particular emphasis on the story of Jesus. Of special interest will be so-called Christ-figure films, in which one or sometimes more than one character is portrayed in a way that directly alludes to Jesus, especially in his role as the savior who must die so that others will live. Chapter 8 will look at the role of the Bible as a source of ethics and morality, and how this connection is both perpetuated and undermined in a range of contemporary Hollywood films. Chapter 9 in turn will examine the use of the Bible in the expression of themes such as destruction and redemption. Finally, the conclusion will consider films that create, at least for some, an experience of transcendence, and the ways in which the Bible figures in that experience.

Notes

1 Ticket prices for such exhibitions ran from 50 cents to a dollar, the same as for a "legitimate play." Sheldon Hall, *Epics, Spectacles, and Blockbusters: A Hollywood History*, Contemporary Approaches to Film and Television Series (Detroit, MI: Wayne State University Press, 2010), 12.
2 *New York Times* review, 23 November 1897. Quoted at http://encyclopedia.jrank. org/articles/pages/1960/The-Horitz-Passion-Play.html (accessed 12 May 2013). The town of Horitz is now in the Czech Republic.
3 Ibid.
4 The term "Bible" will generally be used to refer to the Christian Bible, which is the primary set of scriptures upon which filmmakers draw. As we shall see in chapter 2, even movies that focus on stories from the Hebrew Bible evoke the New Testament, especially the Gospels and the figure of Jesus.
5 For analyses of these films and many more, see the essays in Adele Reinhartz, ed., *The Bible and Cinema: Fifty Key Films* (New York: Routledge, 2012).
6 www.imdb.com/title/tt0175880/trivia (accessed 12 May 2013).
7 For analysis of films in this genre, see Maria Wyke, *Projecting the Past: Ancient Rome, Cinema, and History*, The New Ancient World (New York: Routledge, 1997); Jon Solomon, *The Ancient World in the Cinema* (New Haven, CT: Yale University Press, 2001); Melanie Jane Wright, *Moses in America: The Cultural Uses of Biblical Narrative*, American Academy of Religion Cultural Criticism Series (Oxford; New York: Oxford University Press, 2003); Margaret Malamud, "Swords-and-Scandals: Hollywood's Rome during the Great Depression," *Arethusa* 41, no. 1 (2008): 157–83; Michael G. Cornelius, *Of Muscles and Men: Essays on the Sword and Sandal Film* (Jefferson, NC: McFarland & Company, Inc. Publishers, 2011).
8 See, for example, Lloyd Baugh, *Imaging the Divine: Jesus and Christ-Figures in Film*, Communication, Culture & Theology (Kansas City, MO: Sheed & Ward, 1997); Conrad Ostwalt, "Apocalyptic," in *The Routledge Companion to Religion and Film*, ed. John Lyden (London; New York: Routledge, 2009), 368–83; Mary Ann Beavis, "Pseudapocrypha: Invented Scripture in Apocalyptic Horror Films," in *Reel Revelations*, ed. John Walliss and Lee Quinby (Sheffield: Phoenix, 2010), 75–90; Alice Bach, *Biblical Glamour and Hollywood Glitz* (Atlanta, GA: Scholars Press, 1996); J. Cheryl Exum, ed., *The Bible in Film – the Bible and Film* (Leiden; Boston, MA: Brill, 2006); J. Cheryl Exum, *Retellings: The Bible in Literature, Music, Art and Film* (Leiden; Boston, MA: Brill, 2007); David Shepherd, ed., *Images of the Word: Hollywood's Bible and Beyond* (Atlanta, GA: Society of Biblical Literature, 2008). See also the film reviews and analytical essays in *The Journal of Religion and Film*, http://digitalcommons.uno maha.edu/jrf (accessed 12 May 2013), and *The Journal of Religion and Popular Culture*, www.utpjournals.com/Journal-of-Religion-and-Popular-Culture.html (accessed 12 May 2013).
9 Richard C. Stern, Clayton N. Jefford, and Guerric DeBona, *Savior on the Silver Screen* (New York: Paulist Press, 1999), 332.
10 Although television is beyond the purview of this book, the ongoing interest in the Bible is evidenced by a new television series, *The Bible*, which is currently

(March 2013) showing on the History Channel. See Robert Everett-Green, "How Survivor's Mark Burnett Gathered Believers for His Epic Bible Miniseries," *The Globe and Mail*, http://globeandmail.tumblr.com/post/44278962176/how-survivors-mark-burnett-gathered-believers-for-his (accessed 1 March 2013). The rumored films were mentioned in John Harlow, "Biblical Films May Spark Epic Controversy." *The Ottawa Citizen*. Ottawa, Canada, 12 March 2013, sec. Arts & Life, p. C7.

11 See, for example, Margaret R. Miles, *Seeing and Believing: Religion and Values in the Movies* (Boston, MA: Beacon Press, 1996), and the essays in John Lyden, *The Routledge Companion to Religion and Film* (London; New York: Routledge, 2009).

12 See, for example, Clive Marsh, *Cinema and Sentiment: Film's Challenge to Theology* (Milton Keynes [England]; Waynesboro, GA.: Paternoster Press, 2004) and, Eric S. Christianson, Peter Francis, and William R. Telford, ed., *Cinéma Divinité: Religion, Theology and the Bible in Film* (London: SCM, 2005).

13 See Bruce Babington and Peter William Evans, *Biblical Epics: Sacred Narrative in the Hollywood Cinema* (Manchester; New York: Manchester University Press; St. Martin's Press, 1993).

14 See especially the work of L. Joseph Kreitzer, *The New Testament in Fiction and Film: On Reversing the Hermeneutical Flow* (Sheffield: JSOT Press, 1993); L. Joseph Kreitzer, *The Old Testament in Fiction and Film: On Reversing the Hermeneutical Flow* (Sheffield: Sheffield Academic Press, 1994); L. Joseph Kreitzer, *Pauline Images in Fiction and Film: On Reversing the Hermeneutical Flow* (Sheffield: Sheffield Academic Press, 1999); L. Joseph Kreitzer, *Gospel Images in Fiction and Film: On Reversing the Hermeneutical Flow* (London; New York: Sheffield Academic Press, 2002). See also Bruce C. Birch, "The Arts, Midrash, and Biblical Teaching," *Teaching Theology and Religion* 8, no. 2 (2005): 114–22.

15 In biblical studies, see Allene Phy-Olsen, *The Bible and Popular Culture in America* (Philadelphia, PA; Chico, CA: Fortress Press; Scholars Press, 1985); Elaine Mary Wainwright and Philip Leroy Culbertson, eds, *The Bible In/and Popular Culture: Creative Encounter*, Society of Biblical Literature Semeia Studies (Leiden; Boston, MA: Brill, 2010); Dan Clanton, "'Here, There, and Everywhere': Images of Jesus in American Popular Culture," in *The Bible In/and Popular Culture: Creative Encounter*, ed. Elaine Mary Wainwright and Philip Leroy Culbertson, Society of Biblical Literature Semeia Studies (Leiden; Boston, MA: Brill, 2010), 41–60.

16 For an eloquent discourse on cinema's role in creating America, Michael Wood, *America in the Movies: Or, "Santa Maria, It Had Slipped My Mind"* (New York: Basic Books, 1975), 23 and passim.

17 Paul C. Gutjahr, *An American Bible: A History of the Good Book in the United States, 1777–1880* (Stanford, CA: Stanford University Press, 1999), 146.

18 Ibid., 147.

19 Robert Sklar, *Movie-Made America: A Cultural History of American Movies* (New York: Vintage Books, 1994), 4–5.

20 Steven J. Ross, *Working-class Hollywood: Silent Film and the Shaping of Class in America* (Princeton, NJ: Princeton University Press, 1999), 27–30.

21 Roberta A. Pearson, "Biblical Movies," in *Encyclopedia of Early Cinema*, ed. Richard Abel (London: Taylor & Francis, 2005), 69.

22 DeMille's film was the most widely viewed film for five decades after its release, according to W. Barnes Tatum, *Jesus at the Movies: A Guide to the First Hundred Years and Beyond*, 3rd ed. (Santa Rosa, CA: Polebridge Press, 2013), 49. Gibson's film was one of the highest grossing movies of all time. Tatum, *Jesus at the Movies*, 268.

23 Pearson, "Biblical Movies," 69.

24 Peter Lev, *Transforming the Screen, 1950–1959* (Berkeley and Los Angeles, CA: University of California Press, 2006), 118–19.

25 Recent re-enactments include London, summer of 2009, Sydney (Australia), October 2011, and a lego chariot race, by robots, by the students at the

University of Florida in July 2010. The scenes also call to mind the chase scenes in American Westerns, which take place in a similar desert and mountain landscape, and involve galloping horses, high emotion, and stirring music. But perhaps the closest equivalent is the car chase scene that is a convention of thrillers and police movies. http://news.ufl.edu/2010/07/27/robot-race (accessed 10 June 2011). See Scott Von Doviak, *Hick Flicks: The Rise and Fall of Redneck Cinema* (Jefferson, NC: McFarland, 2005), 119. Comparisons have also been made to the Star Wars pod racing scene; cf. e.g., www.youtube.com/watch?v=HwgyCmSYI9Q (accessed 9 May 2013). I am grateful to William Telford for this observation.

26 Thomas Schatz, *Hollywood Genres: Formulas, Filmmaking, and the Studio System* (Philadelphia, PA: Temple University Press, 1981), vii.
27 Linda Hutcheon, *A Theory of Adaptation* (New York: Routledge, 2006), 4.
28 Schatz, *Hollywood Genres*, vii–viii.
29 Ibid., 22.
30 John Belton, "Introduction," in John Belton, *Movies and Mass Culture*, Rutgers Depth of Field Series (New Brunswick, NJ: Rutgers University Press, 1996), 1.
31 Allen J. Scott, "Hollywood and the World: The Geography of Motion-Picture Distribution and Marketing," *Review of International Political Economy* 11, no. 1 (2004): 33.
32 Due to global marketing and distribution, Hollywood shapes our understanding of cinema on the one hand and America on the other hand, even in countries such as India with robust national cinemas of their own. According to Paul Monaco, *A History of American Movies: A Film-by-Film Look at the Art, Craft, and Business of Cinema* (Lanham, MD: Scarecrow Press, 2010), 195–216, 335, Hollywood's hold on global cinema only slipped twice: once in the 1920s and once in the 1960s. The 1960s low point for Hollywood led, in turn, to the rise of massive Hollywood conglomerations, run like businesses. Kerry Segrave argues that the American dominance of the international film markets is part of a national – and government-assisted – attempt to create a cinematic cartel, and in doing so also creates a global American "Hollywood monoculture." Kerry Segrave, *American Films Abroad: Hollywood's Domination of the World's Movie Screens from the 1890s to the Present* (Jefferson, NC: McFarland, 1997), 280–82.
33 The cinematic use of the Bible is an international phenomenon, not limited to so-called "Christian" countries but apparent also in other national cinemas. For Jesus in Indian film, see Freek L. Bakker, *The Challenge of the Silver Screen: An Analysis of the Cinematic Portraits of Jesus, Rama, Buddha and Muhammad*, Studies in Religion and the Arts, v. 1 (Leiden; Boston, MA: Brill, 2009), 13–77. For biblical and Christian elements in Israeli film, see Amy Kronish and Costel Safirman, *Israeli Film: A Reference Guide* (Westport, CT: Praeger, 2003), 27–30.
34 Gorham Anders Kindem, *The International Movie Industry* (Carbondale, IL: Southern Illinois University Press, 2000), 285.
35 C. R. Deacy, "Reflections on the Uncritical Appropriation of Cinematic Christ-Figures: Holy Other or Wholly Inadequate?" *Journal of Religion and Popular Culture* 13, no. 1, http://utpjournals.metapress.com/content/m033q25567093k82/?p=44d efd2357804dd18d19ca19a8200488&pi=0 (accessed 9 May 2013).
36 Visual elements are at least as important, if not more so, than the dialog itself. See Erwin Panofsky, "Style and Medium in the Motion Pictures," in *Film Theory and Criticism: Introductory Readings*, ed. Gerald Mast and Marshall Cohen (New York: Oxford University Press, 1974), 151–69.
37 Paul Schrader, *Transcendental Style in Film: Ozu, Bresson, Dreyer* (Berkeley, CA: University of California Press, 1972), 16.
38 Rudolf Arnheim, *Film Essays and Criticism* (Madison, WI: University of Wisconsin Press, 1997), 79.

39 Vivian Sobchack, "'Surge and Splendor': A Phenomenology of the Hollywood Historical Epic," *Representations* 29, Winter (1990): 29.
40 Ibid., 26–27.
41 Babington and Evans, *Biblical Epics*, 15–16.
42 Sklar, *Movie-Made America*, 14.
43 Joel W. Martin and Conrad Eugene Ostwalt, *Screening the Sacred: Religion, Myth, and Ideology in Popular American Film* (Boulder, CO: Westview Press, 1995), vii.
44 Miles, *Seeing and Believing*, 3.

Part I
The Bible *on* film

2 "As it has been written"

The Old Testament epics

In 1951, the breathless trailer to *David and Bathsheba* promised filmgoers a "Goliath of a motion picture" featuring unforgettable spectacles including: "The Instant Doom of Anyone Who Dared Touch the Ark of the Covenant!" "The Stoning of The Unfaithful Wife!" "The Ravishing Dance of the Heathen Temptress!" "The Heavens Open in Blinding Anger!" "The Raging Mob Demand 'The Adulteress, Bathsheba!'" and "The Most Tempestuous and Forbidden of the World's Great Love Stories!"[1]

The grand romance between David and Bathsheba is only one of many epic episodes in the Old Testament. Indeed, the Hebrew scriptures are a veritable treasure trove of material for filmmakers, replete with fierce struggles between superpowers; passionate romance in the upper echelons of society; and stunning displays of superhuman strength. Patriarchs, kings, and warriors with spectacular moral failings act out their lives in the context of the tumultuous relationship between a stubborn nation and its opinionated, powerful, loving, vengeful, and forgiving God, in an ancient and exotic time and place that inspire the creativity of cinematographers and costume designers alike. In the "golden age" of epic film, the grand sagas of the Old Testament were superb vehicles for exploring, addressing, and preaching about the big issues, such as the Cold War and the "Red Menace," that preoccupied America and Hollywood in the mid-twentieth century.

Although the earliest Bible movies focused on Jesus, films about the great figures of ancient Israel followed very shortly thereafter. Among the first Old Testament films were *La Vie de Moïse* [The Life of Moses] (1905) and *Moïse sauvé des eaux* [The Infancy of Moses] (1911), both by Pathé, and the much more ambitious, five-reel spectacular, *The Life of Moses* (1909–10), by Vitagraph, which covered Moses' life "from the bulrushes to Mount Pisgah."[2] Filmmakers soon broadened their horizons to other stories, such as *Adam and Eve* (1912), and *Joseph in the Land of Egypt* (1914).

These films helped to usher in the epic genre, which first flourished in the early decades of cinema, particularly in the late teens and early twenties of the twentieth century. Popular films included *The Chosen Prince*, also known as *The Friendship of David and Jonathan* (1917); *Samson and Delilah* (1922); and *Noah's Ark* (1929). The best known Old Testament epic film from the silent era, however, was Cecil B. DeMille's first version of *The Ten Commandments* (1923), which juxtaposed a slow-moving and unremarkable portrayal of the Exodus story with an entertaining modern story about law, morality, and religion. The early years of the "talkies" also saw a number of films based on the Old Testament, including *Lot in Sodom* (1933) and, perhaps the most unusual film for this era, *The Green Pastures* (1936), a retelling of several Old Testament stories, based on a stage production of the same name, that had an entirely African American cast but white directors.

The genre experienced a decline in the 1930s and 1940s, largely for economic reasons: the era of the depression and Second World War did not permit the luxury of spending so much money on creating large spectacles about the past.[3] The genre experienced a resurgence in the late 1940s, as the American post-war economy boomed. The first significant epic of the post-war era was *Samson and Delilah* (1949); other popular films included *Adam and Eve* (1956), *Noah and the Flood* (1965), *Esther and the King* (1960), and a variety of films about David, his ancestry, and his progeny, including *The Story of Ruth* (1960), *David and Bathsheba* (1951), *A Story of David* (1960), *Solomon and Sheba* (1959), and *The Bible...In the Beginning* (1966).[4]

Perhaps the most famous and influential Old Testament epic of all time, however, is Cecil DeMille's iconic 1956 film, *The Ten Commandments*. This film is still broadcast widely on television networks during the Passover/Easter period, constituting a widespread cultural ritual in its own right,[5] and it remains for many viewers their main source of knowledge of the Exodus story.[6] Since the epic era, there have been very few Old Testament feature films produced for commercial theater release. Instead, production has shifted to home video (e.g., the TNT Bible Collection), television (e.g., *Samson and Delilah*, 1984, *The Storykeepers*) and especially children's television and video series, such as the *Veggie Tales* and *Friends and Heroes*.[7] Exceptions include the poorly received *King David* (1985), the highly successful animated film *The Prince of Egypt* (1998) and a clumsy rendition of the Esther story, *One Night with the King* (2006).

In addition to the economic boom of the post-war era, social factors also contributed to the epics' popularity. Perhaps the most important factor was the Cold War. Bible epics were conscripted in the battle against the Red Menace; Hollywood was shaken by the anti-communist investigations undertaken by the House Un-American Activities Committee which, in its efforts to flush out Hollywood producers and directors who were sympathetic to the communist cause, often pitted major Hollywood figures against one another.[8] Epics, including Bible epics, had a very powerful impact on Cold War movie audiences. As Jonathan Herzog notes,

> When it came to the sacralization of popular culture, no medium outshined the American film industry. In the early Cold War, America was a nation of moviegoers, and Hollywood a seat of concentrated power. In B-grade science fiction and biblical epics, in G-man thrillers and martyrs'

biographies, Americans received an anti-communist religious education as cinemas became Cold War classrooms.[9]

Another social factor may have been the growing interest in and sympathy for Jews and Israel in the aftermath of the Holocaust and the founding of the state of Israel, which, some argue, led to the production of films about biblical figures and stories that portrayed ancient Israel and Israelites in a positive light.[10] Babington and Evans connect this point to the major role played by Jews in the studio system and suggest that the Old Testament epic may have been a vehicle for displaying ethnic pride.[11] This connection, however, is difficult to gauge; although most of the major studio owners were Jewish, the directors and other members of the creative teams were not.[12] Also important in the revival of the epic genre may have been the perceived need to compete with television by providing a thrilling and large-scale Technicolor experience that was not available on small black and white television screens.[13] Finally, one may speculate that during the era of movie censorship, the epics provided one vehicle for displays of sexuality, nudity, and violence that were otherwise not permitted in mainstream Hollywood films.[14]

The golden era of the epics waned in the mid-1960s. Two factors were surely the escalating costs of large-scale productions and the ever-increasing popularity of television.[15] The lifting of the Hollywood censorship code broadened the opportunities for the explicit portrayal of violence and sexuality, which then no longer had to be contextualized in terms of ancient war and exotic spectacle.[16] Furthermore, the fragmentation of American society in the face of the Vietnam war and the civil rights and feminist movements, stood in some tension with the highly patriotic and positivistic vision of history conveyed by the epics.[17]

Bible movies were affected by an important additional factor: declining biblical literacy. The popularity of epic Bible movies in the mid-twentieth century depended not only upon the knowledge base of the filmmakers but also upon the knowledge and receptiveness of its audiences.[18] In an era when American society was often described as "Judeo-Christian," it was reasonable to assume both broad and also relatively deep familiarity with the major stories of the Bible, especially the Exodus and Jesus narratives.[19] Biblical literacy – in the simple sense of familiarity with biblical content – declined in North America and perhaps more broadly in the latter half of the twentieth century. This decline can be attributed to factors such as substantial immigration to North American from non-Christian regions of the world, as well as legal decisions that put an end to the widespread reading and teaching of the Christian Bible in American public schools.[20] One might therefore have expected the use of the Bible in film to decline or even disappear in the latter part of the twentieth century, especially given the fact that young people – less biblically literate than their forebears – constitute the majority of movie viewers.[21] Instead, the Bible has remained a cinema staple but, as we shall see in Part II of this book, in a fragmented form that is also decoupled from the epic genre as such.[22]

This chapter will describe briefly the conventions that govern the Old Testament film particularly in the epic era, consider how these movies address the social and cultural issues of their time, and finally, reflect on what they tell us about the prevailing understanding of and attitude toward the Bible in Hollywood of the 1950s and 1960s.

Conventions

Size, scope, and scale

The Old Testament epics share numerous conventions with other epic films, such as *Gone with the Wind* (1939), *Spartacus* (1960), and *Lawrence of Arabia* (1962). The biblical sagas that made their way to the silver screen generally included wars, requiring numerous extras as soldiers, and marriage, requiring many overwrought declarations of love and expressions of jealousy. The spectacle scenes tied easily enough into the film's story line; the story of the Golden Calf in Exodus 32 provides one of several spectacular opportunities in both of DeMille's renditions of *The Ten Commandments* (1923; 1956). More imaginative was King Vidor's *Solomon and Sheba*, which lingered over the spectacle of an orgiastic festival in honor of the god Ragon, orchestrated by the wily and beautiful Sheba to bind Solomon closer to her. At a time when the production code forbade the explicit portrayal of sex, spectacle scenes were the only way to offer audiences the human body and sexuality on the screen. Such scenes conveyed an ambivalent message, however. Within the plot lines of these films, the spectacles were associated with the "bad guys": the immoral pagans whose presence in Israel's midst threatened the morality, piety, and wellbeing of God's chosen people. Nevertheless, the camera, and the viewer, relished these scenes, conveyed prurient delight in their brazen excess.

Like all other movies of this genre, Old Testament epics were "big" in every way. The cinematography emphasized the vastness of space, with pans across deserts, mountains, and skies. Many epics recreated the drought-prone land of the Israelites in the borderlands of Arizona and Mexico or various locations in Spain, Egypt, or southern California.[23] The use of American locations in Old Testament movies points to the influence of the "Western" movie genre in the conceptualization and execution of these films, which supported the identification between early America and ancient Israel that is an important subtext throughout this set of Bible films.[24]

Casting and costuming

The casting is also typical of the epic genre, featuring big-name Hollywood stars, such as Gregory Peck and Susan Hayward, who play David and

Bathsheba in the 1951 film, and Charlton Heston, who famously played Moses in *The Ten Commandments* (1956). The all-American heartthrob appearance and hairstyles of these stars were charmingly at odds with their "biblical" garb. Many films spiced up their offerings by including at least one "exotic" star with a darkly sexy appearance and deliciously exotic accent – Yul Brynner as Pharaoh in *The Ten Commandments* and as Solomon, in *Solomon and Sheba*, where his leading lady was the ravishing Gina Lollobrigida – and the occasional "authentic" middle eastern star, such as Elana Eden, the Israeli who played a sultry Moabite priestess in the title role in *The Story of Ruth* (1960). The use of well-known American and imported stars enhanced the box office potential of these films but also helped to bridge the distance in time and space between the story and the viewer.[25] The celebrity casting also acted as a subtle commentary on the biblical stories themselves, implying that Moses and the Pharaoh, Solomon, Sheba, Ruth, and others were the "stars" of the Bible, and of biblical history, just as Heston, Brynner, and the rest were "stars" in mid-twentieth-century America.

The exotic costuming not only added color and liveliness to these films but also contributed to the historical illusion that they aimed to create. With the exception of the priestly and high priestly vestments, the Bible provides few clues about the styles, fabrics, and colors of the clothing worn by the dramatis personae of the biblical books.[26] To fill this gap, costume designers drew on a variety of artistic and popular sources, in which most ancient Israelites are clothed in robes and sandals. The outfits of the royal, powerful, and wealthy featured rich fabrics, jewels, and elaborate embroidery while those of the lowly, weak, and poor peasants and slaves were simple, rough, and often torn and dirtied. Perhaps in keeping with the American sense of biblical morality, the cinematic Israelites were dressed modestly in comparison with pagan men, who often went topless (see Ramses and the youthful Moses in DeMille's epic) and women, who wore long, low-cut, close-fitting, and elaborate gowns that would not have been out of place on the red carpet on Oscar night.

"Allusionism"

This mode of costuming is an example of a convention known as "allusionism," found not only in Bible and other epic movies but in Hollywood films more generally. The term refers to the fact that many films allude visually and aurally to external sources – paintings, plays, music, and, especially, other movies – that are presumed to be familiar to audiences before they walk into the movie theater. Biblical epics made extensive use of the 1866 English Bible illustrated by Gustave Doré (1832–83), as well as the Bible drawings of James Tissot (1836–1902), both of which were very well known to Americans by the early twentieth century.[27] In the original trailer for his 1956 *The Ten Commandments*, DeMille referred to the Doré drawings, and there are numerous scenes in this film, and many others from the first six decades of the twentieth century, that borrowed their mise-en-scène from the Tissot Bible.[28] Allusions to famous Bible illustrations and other works of religious art created the illusion of authenticity and situated the Old Testament epics within the long tradition of visual interpretation as well as within the context of contemporary renditions such as the famous drawings by the Scottish artist David Roberts (1796–1864).[29]

Even more important than art, however, were allusions to other movies. Film is a notoriously self-referential medium, and the Old Testament films were no exception.[30] One fine example is provided by the 1959 film *Solomon and Sheba*, which quotes a line made famous by DeMille's 1956 *The Ten Commandments*. In the 1956 film, the young Ramses (Yul Brynner), smarting at the favoritism that his father, the old Pharaoh Sethi, showed towards Moses, prophesies: "The city that he [Moses] builds shall bear my name; the woman that he loves shall bear my child. So it shall be written, so it shall be done." The sentence "So it shall be written, so it shall be done" reappears as a scrolling text beneath the image of the restored tablets of the Decalogue, immediately preceding the final credits. Fast forward three years to King Vidor's 1959 *Solomon and Sheba*, in which the elderly King David declares, "As it is written, so let it be done," immediately prior to anointing Solomon (also played by Yul Brynner) the next king of Israel instead of Solomon's brother Adonijah.[31]

Mise-en-scène also links these two films: toward the end of *Solomon and Sheba*, the Pharaoh's troops fall over the side of a cliff into the gorge below, blinded by the shiny shields of the Israelites whom they are attacking. Their plight evokes the destruction of the Pharaoh's army in the famous scene of the parting of the Red Sea in *The Ten Commandments*. "Allusionism" can even occur on the level of camera angle and shots.[32] For example, the final scene of *Solomon and Sheba*, in which Sheba walks slowly toward the camera and away from her beloved Solomon, recalls the well-known final segment of Koster's 1953 epic, *The Robe*, in which the heroes, Marcellus Gallio (Richard Burton) and Diana (Jean Simmons) walk toward the camera and their martyrdom.

But above all else it is extravagance – in matters of budget, aesthetics, casting, indeed, in all elements of the final product – that characterizes the Bible movie in the epic era, and thereby both created and fulfilled specific and familiar genre-related expectations for the audience. In doing so, however, these conventions also affirmed a particular set of views about the Old Testament, its formative role in American history and society, and its ongoing prescriptive primacy for the contemporary viewer. For these meanings to be apparent to the viewer, the film's relationship to the Bible had to be obvious and transparent. This transparency was achieved by means of a number of explicit and implicit devices. At the same time, these films made use of conventions that stood in tension with these markers of authenticity but that situated the Old Testament epics firmly within the Hollywood context of celebrity, entertainment, and box office appeal.

Markers of (biblical and historical) authenticity

Titles and trailers

Old Testament movies were most obviously connected to the Bible through their titles. These titles refer either to iconic biblical concepts or objects, or, more often, the names of biblical characters. Even viewers who have only a rudimentary knowledge of the Old Testament will likely have heard of the Ten Commandments and will know that Adam, Eve, Ruth, David, Bathsheba, and Solomon are biblical figures. Also important for creating advance interest and publicity are trailers which were, and still are, shown as advertisements in the movie theater, on television, and, now, on the internet. Some trailers, such as DeMille's lengthy and pedantic mini-documentary on the historical background to his 1956 Exodus movie, were meant to educate the audience about the Bible, its historical context, and its reception in art. Most, however, like the sensationalist trailer for *David and Bathsheba*, omitted the word "Bible" altogether and were patently meant to appeal to the emotions rather than the intellect of potential moviegoers.

Movie titles and trailers both reveal and obscure the Old Testament connection: they reveal the biblical source to those who know the Bible and therefore might be attracted to films that revolve around biblical figures, but they often also obscure the biblical connection to those who are unfamiliar with the Bible and/or might be deterred from viewing a film with overtly biblical content. (Presumably those who are familiar with the Bible but dislike biblical movies will avoid these films altogether.) Most important, titles, trailers, and other marketing devices were designed to bring the Bible movie audiences into the theater, where any coyness around the biblical connection vanished.

Scrolling texts and voice-over narrations

Many Bible movies make explicit claims to historical and biblical authenticity from the very first frames. Often this is achieved by means of an opening scrolling text, or, alternatively, through an opening voice-over narration. The point can also be made more subtly, through the use of fonts and other graphics that are culturally and historically associated with the Bible. Most often, the fonts are in the Gothic typeface often associated with old and venerable books, especially the King James Version (KJV) of the Bible, which was the version most often used for family Bibles. The opening credits in *David and Bathsheba* imitate the font and lavish illustration of an illuminated Bible, with the first letters of the principle words in red and decorated with flourishes, thereby recalling the family Bibles that had pride of place in many homes in America and throughout the English-speaking world.[33]

Not only the appearance but also the content of opening scrolling texts makes the biblical connection explicit. These texts often establish the era, context, and setting, as, for example, in *David and Bathsheba*, in which the opening text informs us of the time period ("three thousand years ago"), the political context (when David was king over the "united tribes of Israel"), the biblical source (the Second Book of Samuel), the situation (war between the kingdoms of Israel and Ammon), an important character (Joab, the commander of the Israelite army), and the location (Rabbah, the Ammonite stronghold). This opening text and the attendant military-style music provide a commentary on the opening visuals, which show the armies of King David gathering to fight the Ammonites.

Some recent films, however, are careful to refrain from historical claims. The scrolling text that introduces *The Prince of Egypt* distances the film from any attributions of historicity and explicitly describes it as "an adaptation of the Exodus story." The text acknowledges that the film has taken artistic and historical liberties with the Bible, but nevertheless claims that the film is "true to the essence, values and integrity" of the Exodus story. The filmmakers can thereby sidestep the charge of infidelity often levelled at Bible movie makers, while nevertheless asserting their film's essential truth. In doing so they also refrain from imputing any authority, biblical or otherwise, to their film, and to the Bible itself, even as they acknowledge the moral and spiritual authority that "millions of people worldwide" ascribe to the book of Exodus. Finally, in omitting any reference to Judaism and Christianity, the film's opening tacitly acknowledges that other traditions – perhaps alluding to Islam – also pay some attention to Moses and the Exodus narrative. Even more subtly, the statement provides some visual distance between "the motion picture," which is mentioned in the first sentence, and the phrases "biblical story of Moses" and "the book of Exodus," subject of the final sentence. While it is too much to expect film audiences to remember the precise wording and multiple messages of an opening scrolling text, the visual distance between the references to the motion picture and its biblical source in this opening text may weaken the expectation of fidelity that many viewers bring to any historical film.[34]

The difference between the scrolling texts of the mid-twentieth century and those of the late twentieth century testifies to the changes in American society and in American movie audiences. No longer can it be expected that most viewers will be primarily from communities, Christian or Jewish, in which the "Old Testament" or "Jewish Scriptures" are canonical; instead, diversity and pluralism are not only expected but also valued positively, at least in theory.

Voice-over narrations serve much the same purpose as scrolled texts but they do so more emphatically; as aural rather than written texts, they are usually accompanied by visual images or even entire scenes. And because the voice-over is most often intoned by a deep, masculine "voice of God," it imputes to itself a traditionally coded authority – an authority, it is implied, of universal, even cosmic dimensions – beyond what can be conveyed in a scrolled text.[35] The *Story of Ruth* provides a good example; as the camera pans across a barren hot landscape, the narrator describes Bethlehem, the city of

Naomi, as "a city whose name will one day be known in the far places of the earth...." and looks ahead to a time far in the future when "its star shall rise in the East." A lone man, simply dressed, his head lifted up, is the implied speaker; the references to the city and the star of Bethlehem connect this Old Testament film to the Gospel account and the birth of Jesus.

Biblical quotations

Biblical references are not limited to introductory texts and voice-overs. Bible movies quote from and refer to their biblical sources in numerous and diverse ways from beginning to end. One example will illustrate the widespread use of direct quotation. In the *Story of Ruth*, Naomi's daughter-in-law, Ruth, gently and lovingly defies Naomi's request that she return to her people and resolves to accompany Naomi on her return to Bethlehem from Moab by a rather literal translation of Ruth 1:16: "Where you go I will go, where you lodge, I will lodge; your people shall be my people, and your God, my God," though it takes the film almost an hour to arrive at this point, in contrast to a mere 15 verses in the biblical book.

Old Testament movies typically quote not only from the biblical story that they are retelling but also from many other passages in both Testaments. For the kings of Israel, these other quotations often come from the biblical books traditionally attributed to them. In *David and Bathsheba*, King David sings a plaintive psalm at his lover's request as he accompanies himself on the harp. In *Solomon and Sheba*, King Solomon quotes frequently from the books of Proverbs, Ecclesiastes, and the Song of Songs.

Most biblical quotations are taken from the King James Version; the archaic language, especially the "thees" and "thous," lends an aura of authenticity due to the iconic role of the KJV in the cultural history of English-speaking societies.[36] In films that aim for a more modern tone, the KJV is modified but still recognizable. Some films also make use of Hebrew, perhaps to appeal to Jewish viewers but certainly in order to add to the aura of authenticity; even viewers unfamiliar with the Hebrew language would likely realize that Hebrew is the original language of the Old Testament. The opening credits of *The Story of Ruth*, for example, are superimposed on a background of a Hebrew scroll of the biblical book; the letters are clearly discernible.

Jewish liturgy

For those viewers familiar with Jewish practice, this opening image from *The Story of Ruth* evokes not only the Bible but also its liturgical context as a synagogue reading during the Feast of Weeks. Jewish liturgical practice is also implied in *Solomon and Sheba*, in which a trained male cantorial voice intones the traditional prayer for recovery from illness in David's deathbed scene, and, later, chants the traditional mourning prayer at Abigail's funeral. This aural device is anachronistic. There is no evidence that these prayers were recited in the biblical period; their melodies reflect a cantorial tradition that was born in Europe and brought to the United States by Jewish immigrants in the nineteenth and twentieth centuries.[37] Even as the presence of Hebrew lends these scenes an air of authenticity, the pronunciation of the biblical names ("Bathsheeba" instead of "Bathsheva"; "A-don-i-jah" instead of "A-don-ee-yah") is a constant reminder that the religious world of the Old Testament epic is distinctly English-speaking.

Ambient sound

The ambient sound as well as the soundtracks of these films also convey a sense of historical and religious authenticity. Most striking is the blast of the ram's horn, often heard in association with a prophetic event. The blasts are heard in the opening frames of *The Story of Ruth*, in which a voice-over explains how the story connects to the sweep of biblical history as the visuals focus on a lone prophet surveying the barren landscape. The blasts return later on in the story, heralding the return of the prophet who assures Naomi that the story of Ruth will end well for Ruth, for the people of Israel, and, by implication, for all humankind after Jesus' birth in Naomi's home town of Bethlehem. The blasts of the ram's horn link the film with the biblical remarks about the ram's horn – in Hebrew, the *shofar* – which was heard from the cloud on Mount Sinai at the giving of the Ten Commandments to Moses (Exodus 19:19). The *shofar* was used on the New Year (Lev. 23:24; Num. 29:1), and on the day of proclamation of the Jubilee year (Lev. 25:9) and other important ritual and national occasions.[38]

Perhaps even more evocative, however, are the large orchestral and choral musical scores that accompany the biblical epics, as they do with other epic films. Often this majestic sound and the main musical motifs of the score are established in the opening credits, and function to establish a tone of reverence by associating the film with classical religious and church music. The full orchestral sound matches the large scale of the epic film in its visual and casting dimensions as well.[39]

Art

DeMille was the director perhaps most committed to authenticity, not historicity *per se* but an aura of authenticity that would appeal to the viewer. He made skilful use of allusionism by drawing on elements that would have been familiar to many audiences. For example, the visual design of the 1956 version of *The Ten Commandments* was deliberately conceived to recall the colors and images employed by pre-Raphaelite painters in their reformulation of medieval painting. This association is created by the use of red, green, and blue, and the overall pageantry and detail of the setting and costumes. Especially influential were the works of Dante Gabriel Rossetti (1828–82), which also provided a source for some of the mise-en-scène, and the American painter Arnold Friberg (1913–2010), well-known for his biblical illustrations, who was part of the original creative team for the film.[40] Also important, however, was ancient Egyptian design, evident in the detail on the costumes, the jewellery, architecture, and décor.[41]

Adapting the Bible to film

Markers of biblical inauthenticity

The aura of scriptural fidelity and historical authenticity generated by these various techniques is called into question not only by the film medium itself but also by the actual treatment of narrative and character in these films. Old Testament movies both supplement and contradict their biblical sources; at the same time as filmmakers implicitly claim that their films are "authentic," they subvert that claim by the very act of adapting scripture for the cinema. This paradox is not a criticism of the genre; indeed, it might be seen as its hallmark, the one point that all Bible films, from the earliest silent movies to the most recent made-for-TV specials, have in common.

Every cinematic book adaptation differs in significant ways from its source. Story lines must be shortened, simplified, amplified, or rearranged; sounds, music, settings, actors, props, costumes, and numerous other elements must be added; scenes must be shot and edited. Adaptations of the Old Testament must also contend with their source's terse story-telling style and with characters whose motivations are left to the imagination.[42] The gaps are filled not only by the filmmakers' original ideas but also, in keeping with the practice of allusionism, from a broad range of artistic, musical, dramatic, and popular cultural sources, some related to the subject matter (e.g., illustrated Bibles), and some quite foreign to it (e.g., allusions to other movies).

Adding and subtracting from biblical narratives

Old Testament films vary considerably with regard to their adherence to the plot and narrative sequence of their biblical sources. *David and Bathsheba* follows 2 Samuel fairly closely, in its main contours as well as some of its subplots, such as Absalom's rebellion against his father, King David (2 Sam. 13–20). At times, the film creates a new backstory for elements in the biblical story. Whereas 2 Samuel 13 gives his brother's rape of their half-sister Tamar as the reason for Absalom's rebellion, the film suggests that Absalom was put up to it by David's jealous first wife, Michal.

Other Old Testament movies create new characters and plotlines, even when they claim not to. In the prolog to his 1956 version of *The Ten Commandments*, Cecil B. DeMille explains that in order to fill in the 30-year gap that the Exodus narrative leaves in the life of Moses, he has turned to "ancient historians such as Philo and Josephus" who lived at approximately the same time and "had access to documents long since destroyed, or perhaps lost, like the Dead Sea Scrolls." This sounds reassuring, until we recall that while the Hellenistic Jewish philosopher wrote a treatise on the life of Moses, he did not provide any historical information about the decades that the Bible omits.[43] As for Josephus, this first-century historian did make use of written sources, and he may have known some extra-biblical legendary material, but its historical accuracy cannot be verified.[44] Whether Philo or Josephus had access to the Dead Sea Scrolls, the earliest of which were discovered less than a decade before the movie was filmed, is unclear; in any case, the scrolls themselves do not shed any light on Moses' biography.[45]

Bible films also exploit the silence of the primary sources in order to add plot elements that heighten the drama and develop the characters. The biblical book of Ruth, for example, covers a period of several years in the first five verses: a family moves from Bethlehem to Moab to escape a famine; the sons marry; the father and sons die, and the mother, Naomi, is left alone with her two daughters-in-law (Ruth 1:1–5). To this point there is not a word about Ruth's own background, though she becomes a central player in the story immediately after this introduction. Into this biblical vacuum the 1960 film *The Story of Ruth* inserts a lengthy backstory that endows the beautiful Moabite with a childhood, youthful aspirations, and a feisty personality. In Henry Koster's version of the story, Ruth was a young Moabite girl chosen on account of her beauty and purity to be sacrificed as an unblemished virgin to the Moabite god Chemosh. Just when she was about to enter the period of preparation, she developed a sudden and mysterious skin rash that, to her great distress, disqualified her from taking on this sacred role. Instead, she became a priestess charged with preparing other young girls to serve as sacrifices to Chemosh. In the course of her duties, she met the Judean goldsmith Mahlon, son of Naomi and Elimelech. Mahlon had the distasteful task of fashioning the gold crown that the chosen maiden was to wear on the day of her sacrifice. Mahlon and Ruth fell in love and pledged their troth, but he died before their marriage could be consummated (thereby ensuring that Ruth was a virgin when she later married Boaz). This lengthy backstory fills in the gap between the first verse of Ruth, in which Naomi, her husband and two sons leave Bethlehem for Moab, and the fifth verse, when Naomi decides to return to Bethlehem. As in the Bible, Ruth follows Naomi to Bethlehem and eventually marries Naomi's kinsman Boaz, but the path to that happy ending is filled with numerous non-biblical dramas, love triangles, false accusations, military battles, and high emotion.

In the case of *Solomon and Sheba* (1959), the director has created a feature film from a mere ten verses. The story in 1 Kings 10:1–10 (repeated in 2 Chronicles 9:1–12) simply recounts that the Queen of Sheba heard of Solomon and came with a great retinue to test his wisdom. When he passed with flying colors, she gave him bountiful gifts, and departed. End of story. From this sparse tale, the director King Vidor and his team created a 139 minute film, in which Sheba has become a land traditionally ruled by women, devoted to the worship of the god Ragon and politically allied with Egypt against Israel. The queen, named Sheba, is beautiful, wily, wanton, and ambitious. She and the Pharaoh of Egypt scheme to bring about Israel's downfall: Sheba will seduce the king Solomon and then betray him to the Pharaoh. The inevitable ensues: Sheba falls in love with Solomon and turns from her life of hedonistic idolatry to the austere worship of the true God of Israel.

Add romance and stir

Few films today satisfy Hollywood's romantic imperative as grandiosely as these epics of the 1950s, leaving us sighing at the fulfilment of love that comes at the end of a steady build-up of red-hot but chaste romance between an impossibly attractive, shapely and often exotic woman, and her handsome, well-built, charming suitor.

As they fill out the narrative gaps in the biblical stories, *The Story of Ruth* and *Solomon and Sheba*, and most other Old Testament epics, create opportunity for romances about which their sources are all but silent. Like most other Hollywood movies from the 1950s and 1960s, Old Testament movies present romantic love as a powerful force in the lives of heroes and villains alike. But simple love is not enough. Rather, the dramatic tension must be increased either by the forbidden nature of the love, as when the beloved is an idolater, married to another, plagued by a rival, or, often, suffers from two or more of these conditions at once.

The love triangle subplot has a number of variations. In *The Story of Ruth*, the beautiful Moabite priestess is sought out by the lascivious King of Moab, but she is in love with Mahlon and risks her life to save him. Later, in Bethlehem, the young widow falls in love with Boaz, but a closer kinsman, Tob, aggressively seeks her hand. All ends well, with Boaz and Ruth safely married, to Naomi's delight.

In *David and Bathsheba*, Ruth's descendant David is enmeshed in a more distressing – and ethically problematic – situation. David is in love with Bathsheba, the girl next door, but Bathsheba is already married to the soldier Uriah who is presently away fighting David's war against the Ammonites. Uriah is a neglectful and unloving husband who values the army and the military life far above Bathsheba and his marriage. Nevertheless, Bathsheba's marital status is a problem. Only by orchestrating Uriah's death can David have his beloved, who by now is pregnant with his child.

This aspect of David and Bathsheba's story in 2 Samuel 11 is juicy enough to be adapted without very much imaginative embellishment. The film, however, adds a second deadly love triangle. David's first wife, Michal, the former king Saul's daughter, is furious with David for consorting with other women, and she is particularly jealous of the captivating Bathsheba. Michal plots her revenge by enlisting David's son Absalom to join her in bringing charges of adultery against David and Bathsheba. Their false testimony is enough to convict Bathsheba to death by stoning; according to biblical law the testimony of two suffices in the case of a capital crime such as adultery (Deut. 19:15).[46] The starkness of the sentence corresponds to the drought in the land which, it is implied, is an expression of God's anger with David for his violation of the prohibitions against adultery and murder. At the eleventh hour, David repents of his sins and saves the day. God forgives David, Bathsheba lives, the drought ends.

Even the great prophet Moses has a triangulated romantic entanglement – completely absent from the biblical account – foisted upon him. In *The Ten Commandments* (1956), both Moses and his brother Ramses II are in love with the (fictional) princess Nefretiri. But Moses, in contrast to the later Israelite kings David and Solomon, has the ability to set aside his feelings in order to pursue higher goals. Initially he leaves Nefretiri when he must escape Egypt before he is caught and punished for killing an Egyptian. Later, he refuses her advances because he is married to Zipporah, and, even more important, he has dedicated himself to the liberation of his people.

Then as now

The romantic elements in the Old Testament epics fulfilled the expectations of movie audiences in the mid-twentieth century era, and thereby also the conventions of the epic movie genre. In other respects too, Old Testament movies address the concerns and express the norms of the eras in which they were made, even as they tell tales of long ago and far away.[47] In doing so, they construct the past as an analogy to the present – describe "then" as "now."[48] This construction is most apparent in their explicit representations of gender roles, and their implicit reflections on American national identity.

Gender

The Old Testament epics were made in the aftermath of the Second World War, as America welcomed back the soldiers who returned from the war and the American household embraced the wives and mothers who returned from the factories. Both men and women resumed their pre-war roles – men as breadwinners and women as wives, mothers, and homemakers. But women did not quickly forget the autonomy, the sense of purpose, and the financial independence that came with work outside the home and with contributing economically to the war effort.[49]

These social changes provided the immediate context for the portrayal of gender and male–female relationships in the Old Testament epics. Gender relationships in the Old Testament movies parallel those found in mid-twentieth-century situation comedies, advertisements for household products, and non-biblical movies of the same era, and mirror the ideals and values of America in the immediate post-war decades.[50] But the hierarchical relationships between handsome, protective, and dominant men and their beautiful, delicate, and submissive women are subtly infused with other messages: female rebellion against oppression, strength in the face of injustice, and morality and common sense in the face of their men's emotion-, ego-, and testosterone-driven impulses and behaviors. As a result, Old Testament films simultaneously elevate and debase their female protagonists. This dynamic is illustrated well by the figure of Bathsheba in the Bible and in epic film.

Women, men, and morality

In the biblical account, Bathsheba first appears in 2 Samuel 11, a literary masterpiece in the laconic style of biblical literature. The era is the reign of King David, the time of year, spring, "the time when kings go out to battle" (2 Samuel 11:1). David dispatches his officers and soldiers, under the leadership of Joab; the army ravaged the Ammonites and besieged Rabbah, "but David remained at Jerusalem." Perhaps the king suffered from spring fever, or perhaps he just had too much time on his hands, for "it happened, late one afternoon, when David rose from his couch and was walking about on the roof of the king's house, that he saw from the roof a woman bathing; the woman was very beautiful" (11:2). He learned that she was Bathsheba, daughter of Eliam, the wife of Uriah the Hittite. David sent messengers to her; she arrived, and "he lay with her." At this point, the biblical narrator confides that she was fertile, having just purified herself after her period. David may have been surprised to learn of her pregnancy, but readers are not (11:2–5).

The narration conceals Bathsheba's feelings and motivations in what must have been a rather tumultuous series of events within the story world. As Meir Sternberg has shown, the story is told in a way that raises questions at each point, prompting the reader to formulate hypotheses that are then confirmed or discarded as the reading proceeds. Why does David stay home during the season that kings go out to war? Does Bathsheba know that David can see her from his rooftop? Is she complicit in the affair or politically powerless to reject the king's illicit advances? What is the outcome that she hopes, fears, or expects when she sends word of her pregnancy to David?[51]

It is a gaze that sets the epic events in motion: David "saw from the roof a woman bathing; the woman was very beautiful" (11:2). The king did not merely glance at Bathsheba. No, he looked at her long enough to register her beauty, to feel his own desire, and to act accordingly, consequences be damned. The notion of "the gaze" has been much discussed in feminist film criticism. Laura Mulvey argues that "the way film reflects, reveals and even plays on the straight, socially established interpretation of sexual difference which controls images, erotic ways of looking and spectacle."[52] The gaze generates desire, in the cinematic character, to be sure, but also in the viewer who gazes at films in which men and women gaze at one another. Mulvey notes that "there are three different looks associated with cinema: that of the camera as it records the pro-filmic event, that of the audience as it watches the final product, and that of the characters at each other within the screen illusion."[53] David gazes at Bathsheba; she is aware of his gaze – if not at the time then certainly once he sends for her; as we read the story or watch the film, we also gaze at her, through David's eyes, our gaze enhanced by our awareness of his interest in this woman who is forbidden to him by biblical law.[54]

The biblical story refers only to David staring at Bathsheba; the film, however, makes the gaze mutual. Not only was David watching Bathsheba, but Bathsheba was also watching David, flirtatiously, perhaps dangerously, looking over her shoulder and staring directly into the camera. And while David's desire is aroused for the first time on this lazy spring afternoon in the season when kings go out to war, Bathsheba lets the king know that her desire has long preceded his. David Gunn comments that the bathing scene typifies "the ambiguities of the film, the genre, and the social order of the early fifties as it related to women." He notes that her own gaze is ambiguous. As she turns toward the camera, she appears to look straight at us, but is she perhaps gazing at David, whose point of view is now our own? Or is she looking nowhere at all?[55] But perhaps it is not so much the gaze that is ambiguous; after all, any uncertainty about Bathsheba's feelings is resolved by her declaration of love for David. Rather, it is the ethical underpinnings of the film that are ambiguous, or rather, ambivalent. Bathsheba's behavior reflects America's ambivalence with regard to women's roles and the social order in the immediate post-war era. Bathsheba is both beautiful seductress and moral agent. She is successful – if dangerous – in the first role, less so in the second, and in the end both fall to the side as she is fully domesticated into the role of loving wife and mother. David too is an ambiguous figure. He ostensibly holds the balance of power in this relationship; not only is he Bathsheba's man, but he is also her king. Yet he is weak, for he allows love and lust to overcome his rational and moral self.

The moral ambiguity of its heroes extends to the film as a whole. For David and Bathsheba, romantic love trumps the Ten Commandments. Adultery and murder are sins, of course, but understandable, almost excusable, when there is no love between man and wife. This, at least, is what we glean from the pivotal confrontation between Uriah and David. As in 2 Samuel 11:6–13, David has called Uriah back from the front to provide him with the opportunity to sleep with his wife and thereby claim paternity of the unborn child. In the film, David is both surprised and relieved when the soldier refuses to pay a conjugal visit to his lovely wife; he soon learns that Uriah does not love his wife nor does he treat her well. He provides Uriah with husbandly advice that reflects a mid-twentieth century ethos: a husband should spend time with his wife, talk with her, and be sensitive to her needs. (Michal, David's jealous and vengeful first wife, would be the first to point out that David had not followed this advice himself, but the film excuses David's indifference to Michal on the grounds that he does not really love her as he does Bathsheba, whom he showers with affection and attention.) As a neglectful workaholic, Uriah does not deserve his beautiful wife. Perhaps he does not deserve to die the death that David orchestrates for him, but even so, it is hard to mourn for him. In identifying with the dashing and passionate king, we become complicit, at least in spirit, in David's violation of the sixth commandment, "thou shalt not kill." Nor do we applaud the figures within the story who are bothered by David's violation of the commandments against adultery and murder, for they, like Uriah, are portrayed as unsympathetic and unlikable, not holy so much as holier-than-thou. In presenting a confused morality, the film anticipates both the changes in social expectations and norms and the resistance to those changes that will come in the 1960s, especially around gender and sexual behavior.[56]

To later viewers, the romantic relationships in these films may come across as blatantly sexist and outdated. The couples are invariably white, heterosexual, extraordinarily beautiful, rich, and passionately in love. Yet even if we have become accustomed to a more varied representation of couples and a more nuanced and perhaps more realistic portrayal of human relationships, the 1950s-style romance both inspires and satisfies longings for a perfect love with the perfect lover, and a happy ever after in which love conquers all and viewers can feel as beautiful, beloved, and wealthy as the heroes on the screen.

Women as leaders

Similar ambivalence attends the portrayal of women in public life. Old Testament epics subtly acknowledge that women, like men, can be political and military leaders. This role, however, is most often portrayed as provisional, secondary, or as insufficient in some way. Moses' and Aaron's sister Miriam, for example, is not entirely ignored in DeMille's 1956 *The Ten Commandments*, but neither does she take her place as a leader and prophet alongside her brothers to nearly the same extent as she does in the Pentateuch and Jewish tradition.[57] Vidor's Sheba may rule over an ancient matriarchy yet she too is domesticated, as she falls in love with Solomon, gives up idolatry to worship the God of Israel, and carries Solomon's baby home in her womb to be the first king of Sheba. The transformation of the land of Sheba from a matriarchy to a patriarchy is seen as a positive outcome, presumably because it also entails a move from polytheism to monotheism. Yet it is the male gender of the future ruler that apparently normalizes the nation of Sheba in the eyes of God, the filmmaker, and perhaps also movie audiences.[58]

At the same time, women characters, while secondary to the mighty men who face off against each other in the typical Bible epic, can be important in other ways. Gary Smith notes that DeMille often "preferred to use a female character as the catalyst who sparks off the dramatic chain of events. Consequently, the leading lady roles in DeMille films are usually far better defined than those of the leading men."[59] The example he cites is Nefretiri in *The Ten Commandments*, one of the few main characters who undergoes any change or development over the course of the film.[60]

National (American) identity

The 1950s Old Testament epics mirror not only an idealized romantic life, but also an idealized American identity. It is perhaps no accident that the Exodus is the most popular biblical event in American epic cinema. Even Bible movies that are not directly about the Exodus evoke this central event by portraying the Egyptian Pharaoh as a reluctant and hostile ally of Israel (*David and Bathsheba*) or as an ongoing and powerful enemy of Israel (*Solomon and Sheba*). Each film illustrates the victory of God's "team": the misguided heroes who were born into idolatry (Ruth, Sheba) or who were temporarily led astray into adultery, murder, and idolatry (David, Solomon) are incorporated or reincorporated into the covenant people; Israel's enemies are vanquished.

Liberty

The first major Old Testament epic film of the golden era was released in 1949, a year after the creation of the state of Israel, an event which, like the Exodus, is often told as the story of escape from bondage.[61] It is not surprising, then, that this event is obliquely reflected in some of the epics. The film *Solomon and Sheba* begins with a deep masculine and uncredited "voice of God" that situates its subject matter in the broad sweep of history by referring to the borderland between Egypt and Israel that was filled with spies and "ablaze with the fire of hatred and conflict" in the millennium before Jesus' birth as it is "today".[62] For 1950s viewers, this opening would surely call to mind the war that broke out immediately upon the United Nations' declaration of the founding of the state of Israel. The same situation is evoked later on in the film. When the Egyptian Pharaoh enlists Sheba's aid in bringing about the downfall of Solomon, it is to help him regain dominance over the young upstart state that is threatening the northern borders of his own country. Pharoah and his allies declare that they must "trample Israel into the dust" and "drive them into the sea," echoing the language used in the Israeli–Arab conflict.[63] These films draw a parallel between the American self-understanding as a country that successfully liberated itself from an oppressive empire (England) and the founding of Israel, which, for some, represented Jewish liberation from an oppressive regime (Nazi Germany) and which fought successfully against its enemies who attempted to thwart its striving for an independent and democratic state of its own.[64]

In American culture itself, however, the Exodus resonates in two rather different ways. For the Puritans who had a profound and ongoing impact on the political, social, and cultural origins of the United States as a national entity, the Exodus was a metaphor for their journey from British oppression to New World freedom.[65] For African Americans, the Exodus is a paradigm for their own enslavement and subsequent liberation as a consequence of the Civil War, and the continuing struggle for equality in American law and society.[66] Both paradigms are reflected in the Old Testament epics. These films link ancient Israel with post–Second World War America and imply that America, like ancient Israel, is a divinely guided democratic nation struggling to free the world from oppression.[67] America's role as the champion of liberty for the oppressed people of the world is hinted at in the final frames of *The Ten Commandments*, which portray Moses as Lady Liberty, standing proud and high above the Jordan River and looking toward the land of Israel just like the Statue of Liberty stands high above the New York Harbor and looks toward the eastern shoreline of the United States.[68]

The most immediate analogy, however, is to the Cold War and America's opposition to communism, both within its borders and globally. DeMille makes this connection explicit in the prolog to the film, in which he steps out from behind the curtain to declare that "the theme of this picture is whether men ought to be ruled by God's law or whether they ought to be ruled by the whims of a dictator like Ramses. Are men the property of the State or are they free souls under God? This same battle continues throughout the world today."[69] As Jonathan Herzog notes,

> Americans were not simply watching a three-thousand year-old biblical tale. They flocked by the millions, perhaps unknowingly, to a modern-day morality play. They were the inheritors of an ancient wisdom, handed down from God to his surrogates. This God-given freedom could rescue modern-day slaves around the world from the thralldom of communism as it had freed the Israelites from Egyptian servitude millennia ago. Armed with this sacred justification, the "free souls under God" were destined to triumph.[70]

The identification of ancient Israel and America, and America's opposition to communism is explicit in DeMille's film. Moses' (Charlton Heston's) indisputably American accent is apparent in his pronunciation of the vowels as well as in the general rhythm and cadence of his speech. The "old" Pharaoh, Sethi (played by the well-known British actor Sir Cedric Hardwicke) who is a pagan but a fair-minded and not unsympathetic leader, has a British accent, whereas the true villain of the piece, his son Ramses, played by Yul Brynner, has an indeterminate but vaguely sinister European accent. Many film viewers do not consciously think about accents, perhaps assuming that actors deploy the accents of their native lands, but in fact, voice and accents are important markers of character, personality, and role, and movie actors are generally adept at speaking in whatever accent their roles require. Moses' American accent is therefore not incidental to his redemptive identity and role in the film, but essential to it. By depicting the "bad guy" not as British but simply as foreign, DeMille is in effect declaring that the enemies of America in the twentieth century were not the British, who are foreign but basically okay. Rather, America must beware of the Eastern Europeans among whom communism has taken root, lest these latter day Egyptians attempt to enslave the true Israel once more.

Civil rights

If America is a beacon for the oppressed of other lands, surely it must also hold out the promise of liberty and equality for the oppressed within its own borders.[71] Hints of this theme can be detected – if only faintly – in *The Ten Commandments*; when Jethro offers to help Moses, Moses asks if he is sure he wants to do that, for "It is death to give sanctuary to a runaway slave." In the biblical context, it is unlikely that Moses, who at this point (Exod. 2:15) is not a runaway slave but an escaped murderer, would have been pursued beyond the borders of Egypt, but in an American context his statement recalls the Fugitive Slave Act of 1793, which made it illegal to help runaway slaves. The theme of civil rights is overshadowed, however, by the focus on America's perceived struggle against foreign authoritarian regimes. This is not surprising perhaps at a time when the Cold War was front and center in American, and Hollywood, consciousness, and the Civil Rights Movement had yet to spawn widely known and revered leaders such as Martin Luther King Jr.[72]

DeMille's representation of Sephora, Moses' wife, is another missed opportunity to address this theme directly. According to Exodus, Sephora, or Zipporah as she is more commonly referred to (Exod. 2:21), is the daughter of a Midianite priest (Exod. 2:16). Numbers 12:1, however, refers to Moses' wife as a Cushite, the biblical term for Ethiopian, in other words, as black. In the context of biblical society it is plausible that Moses had a Cushite wife in addition to the Midianite Zipporah, but later sources, imagining Moses as monogamous, identify Zipporah herself as the Cushite (Midrash Tehillim 7:18). DeMille was not alone among mid-century directors in de-emphasizing race relations; as Harry Benshoff notes, the American film industry generally supported and contributed to the status quo.[73] On the one hand "black" films, which were primarily musicals with Christian themes, could be used by the big studios to "advertise their commitment to art and liberal ideals."[74] On the other hand, most mainstream films showed white America as normative, and in so doing helped to perpetuate the "dominant cultural attitudes towards African Americans (and issues of race in general)."[75]

The only film in the first half of the twentieth century that directly portrays the African American experience is *The Green Pastures* (1936), directed by Marc Connelly.[76] The film briefly retells the biblical narrative, beginning with Creation and ending with the resurrection, but focuses primarily on Old Testament stories. The history is framed as stories told by a pastor in the Depression South to his Sunday school charges, and as seen from heaven, where "Da Lawd" – a highly anthropomorphized Supreme Being – relaxes with the angels when he is not making miracles or otherwise interfering in human affairs. The film is engaging and humorous, even as it reinforces a rather strict moral code, forbidding smoking and music on Sundays. Nevertheless, it illustrates the dangers of allowing African Americans, their culture, and their modes of religion and spirituality, to be represented by others. Although the white director, Marc Connelly, acknowledged the differences among the various black churches that he visited prior to making the film, he erased this diversity by choosing to focus on the most conservative ones because he felt that "their songs and movements in worship were much more energetic and affecting."[77] In addition, the film reflects a condescending attitude to African Americans, beginning with its opening scrolling text, which declares: "God appears in many forms to those who believe in Him. Thousands of Negroes in the Deep South visualize God and Heaven in terms of people and things they know in their everyday life. *The Green Pastures* is an attempt to portray that humble, reverent conception." While the intention was not racist – the director emphasized that "As an agnostic, I recognized that I must at all times respect the faith of the black fundamentalists" – the effect is to homogenize, stereotype, and misrepresent African American religiosity.[78]

Religion

Epic monotheism

While the Old Testament epics obviously express the concerns and ethos of their time, it is important to remember that their explicit subject matter – the Bible – concerns the covenantal relationship between God and Israel. But how does one represent a divine figure who is meant to be devoid of visual appearance and material substance? One answer is readily apparent: through the voice. God's voice is heard in a number of Old Testament films, most notably in the "burning bush" scenes of the Exodus movies. In DeMille's 1956 film, as in the more recent *The Prince of Egypt*, God is voiced by the actor playing Moses, whose voice is echoed and amplified to sound divinely powerful and portentous.[79]

Less directly, epic films also use big orchestral and/or choral music and big blue skies with fluffy white clouds to evoke the divine. These elements in fact predate the birth of cinema, as the music often came from familiar hymns and the great works of the European composers such as Bach and Handel, while the visual elements stem from Renaissance art. These conventions are used to playful effect in *The Green Pastures*, in which the retelling of the biblical stories of Adam, Eve, Cain, Noah, and others, is framed within a narrative about the angelic choir in heaven, which resides with "Da Lawd" in the fluffy clouds of the stereotypical divine realm.

But the presence of God is also evoked thematically and narratively, through the conflict between monotheism and idolatry that is central to the plot and characterization of many Old Testament epic movies. In *Solomon and Sheba*, as in 1 Kings 3:9–10, God grants Solomon wisdom. The cinematic Solomon, however, like his father David, sacrifices wisdom, or at least common sense and political savvy, for the love of a woman. Smitten by Sheba, Solomon is ready to abandon God, to the point of witnessing, if not quite participating in, the orgiastic pagan rituals required by Sheba's god. In this regard, the film is faithful to the biblical text, which roundly criticizes Solomon's tendency to idol worship: "Then the LORD was angry with Solomon, because his heart had turned away from the LORD, the God of Israel, who had appeared to him twice, and had commanded him concerning this matter, that he should not follow other gods; but he did not observe what the LORD commanded" (1 Kgs 11:9–10). In the movies, however, all is made right by the end, when God answers the repentant and now monotheistic Sheba's prayers for Solomon's safety in the face of his ruthless and power-hungry brother Adonijah. The same conflict between idolatry and monotheism is at work in the relationships between Moses and Ramses (*The Ten Commandments*), Ruth and Mahlon (*The Story of Ruth*), and Samson and Delilah. In *David and Bathsheba*, it is not so much idolatry but the loss of faith – atheism, perhaps, or at least a rigid rationalism – that stands between the king and the God of Israel.

Given that the conflict between idolatry and monotheism is central to the Hebrew Bible, it is not surprising that it appears in Old Testament films as well. But why is this conflict so prominent in films made in America, where idolatry, at least in its narrow sense of worshipping idols or multiple gods, is no longer a threat?[80] The answer is to be found not so much in the pagan practices associated with the ancient Egyptians, Moabites, and Shebans, but in the statements made by those who represent those pagan religions (the old Pharaoh Seti), those that are attracted to them (Solomon), or those that are estranged from the God of Israel (David). These statements do not proclaim that faith in many gods is superior to faith in the one God of Israel, but rather cast doubt on the existence of any God at all. Idolatry stands in for atheism, rationalism, and other forces that might be seen as a threat to a dominant Christian culture, especially in the atheism associated with communism.[81] Ramses II explains the plague of blood as a natural phenomenon: water cataracts that spew red mud. David refuses to believe that the ark of the covenant has the power to instantly kill a man who touched it, preferring to see the man's death as the result of a medical condition such as heatstroke or dehydration.

In all of these films it is the God of Israel who wins the "battle of the Gods"[82] and thereby exposes the falseness of idolatry and affirms the supremacy and truth of Israel's faith. By linking rationalism with paganism, Hollywood in effect links rationalism to atheism, and asserts that faith is superior to reason. Given the association of atheism and communism, it is clear that in these films the conflict between idolatry and monotheism stands in for the conflict between communism and American democracy. Herzog comments that "even in 1947, before the most widespread attempts at Cold War sacralization commenced, 70 percent of Americans believed Communists would destroy Christianity if given the chance. Two years later, only one in ten believed that a person could be both a Communist and a Christian."[83] It would seem, however, that the end of the Cold War has not put an end to the cultural controversy between atheism and monotheism; in that sense, these Old Testament epics mount a subtle critique of a secular and rationalist worldview that is not only familiar but also appealing to many in post-war America and today as well.

Prayer

The positive value accorded to monotheism goes hand in hand with the positive, indeed, transformative, role of prayer in these Old Testament movies. Prayer nearly always leads to a substantial improvement in fortunes. In *The Story of Ruth* Naomi prays that Ruth's death sentence for idolatry be averted, and sure enough, it is. Ditto for David, who prays for the life of Bathsheba, and in doing so signals the restoration of his own faith, and of the rains that will ensure his land's fertility.

Prayer takes place either in the Temple or facing some familiar ritual object such as the menorah. Sheba goes to the Temple to pray that God may "forgive my sin against thee and thy people"; she asks that God preserve Solomon against his enemies and she promises to return to the land of Sheba and cast down false gods. Echoing the words of the Ten Commandments, she vows that "there shall be no other gods before thee." The glorious and large orchestral music of the soundtrack implies that her prayer has been answered as the camera cuts to Solomon looking out over the same sky. Sheba fulfills the vow at the end and returns to Sheba, Solomon's baby – the future and very first king of Sheba – in her womb.

Ethnicity – or non-ethnicity

In the Old Testament epics, allegiance to the God of Israel does not constitute an affirmation of Judaism. To be sure, the Israelites, often called the Hebrews, are God's people and the theological winners over their idolatrous enemies. Furthermore, as we have seen, some films contain Hebrew letters, words, prayers, and other elements of Jewish practice. For the most part, however, Jewish particularity is absent. Even Moses, whose Hebrew identity is crucial to the story line of Exodus and the Exodus movies, ends up as an ethnically undifferentiated, individual. In DeMille's 1956 rendition, this ambiguity paradoxically comes to the fore most clearly in the scene in which he discovers his Hebrew identity. Bithia, Moses' Egyptian mother, has come to Goshen to offer freedom to Moses' birth mother, Yochabel, and her other children. Just as Aaron and Miriam are packing their things, Moses bursts into the room and demands to know if Yochabel is really his mother. She hesitates, but finally admits that she is indeed the one who gave birth to him. Bithia wonders why he is not ashamed to be a Hebrew, but, echoing the Jewish moneylender Shylock in *The Merchant of Venice*, he replies that he is the same person, whether Egyptian or Hebrew: "What change is there in me? Egyptian or Hebrew, I am still Moses. These are the same hands, the same arms, same face that were mine a moment ago."[84]

The negation of ethnic particularity is evident also in the epics' treatment of biblical law. The films often address legal issues that are integral to plot lines that revolve around adultery, idolatry, and murder. *The Story of Ruth*, like its biblical source, refers to levirate law, according to which the childless widow is bound to marry her husband's closest relative; without this law, the romantic triangle of Tob, Boaz, and Ruth would neither make sense nor be resolved.[85] Ruth also mentions other laws, notably, the requirement to extend hospitality to the stranger in one's midst.[86] But overshadowing these laws is the Decalogue – The Ten Commandments – which takes center stage not only in Exodus films such as DeMille's 1956 *The Ten Commandments* but in many of the Old Testament epics. In *The Story of Ruth*, the Moabite protagonist carries with her an amulet made by her beloved Mahlon, on which the Decalogue is inscribed; it foreshadows and also symbolizes her conversion and her commitment to Naomi and Naomi's people. Sheba's solemn prayer to God in the Temple includes her commitment to keeping the Ten Commandments.

This focus on the Ten Commandments is easily explained. The Decalogue has a prominent role in American culture and therefore would be familiar to movie-going audiences in North America and other western countries. Most of them are generic enough to be seen as universal. Perhaps most important, they represent a heritage common to both Judaism and to Christianity, and provide a bridge between the ancient Israelite stories and the context of these films and American society in the mid-twentieth century.[87] In the Old Testament movies, however, other aspects of biblical law are portrayed as overly harsh and negative. As Babington and Evans note,

> certain aspects of Judaism have to vanish. Though it represents the Law, this Law must be purged of ethnic particularity and tend at all times to the universal. Thus in both of DeMille's *The Ten Commandments* all that Moses imposes on the Israelites are the ten strictures taken over by Christianity… [These] are de-ethnicized literally in the replacement of Hebrew script on the tablets by an invented writing. The rest of the body of the Law, the food taboos, the regulations on sacrifice and sexuality… are expunged.[88]

While the Ten Commandments are upheld – even if infringements are sometimes implicitly justified – characters who uphold the law, such as the prophet Nathan in *David and Bathsheba*, are portrayed as legalistic and insensitive functionaries.[89]

The triumph of Christianity

In fact, the epics of the 1950s and 1960s convey a subtle supersessionism even as they tell the foundational stories of the people of Israel. This supersessionism is evident not only in their omission or critique of much of biblical law but also in the insertion of Jesus or Christological interpretation into almost all of these Old Testament narratives. The films imply that Christianity is the true heir of and the primary vehicle for the ideas that are valorized in these films. This is not to say that Jews were discouraged from viewing these stories as their own. Indeed, for Jewish audiences, these films brought admirable and positive views of Israelite history.[90] Yet the ultimate message is an affirmation of Christian faith.

The Christian perspective is apparent even in DeMille's iconic film. In *The Ten Commandments* Moses, claimed by Jews as their great leader and prophet, is recast as a Christ-like divinely sent redeemer figure whose coming is announced by Joshua. Like Jesus, Moses fulfills the words of the prophet Isaiah, and is glorified by his mother Yochabel who recites the Magnificat from Luke 1:46–55.[91]

Other biblical characters also cite Christian scripture. When Solomon is saved from death, Sheba piously paraphrases the Lord's Prayer, declaring that "his is the power and the glory forever." She also experiences something akin to a resurrection; after being stoned, apparently to death, she recovers completely and instantaneously as soon as Solomon carries her to the altar of the Temple. In *The Story of Ruth*, Naomi is visited by a mysterious prophet who tells her: "Trouble your heart no more. Be strong through this time. For of the widow of your son will issue children and children's children numbering among them a great king and a royal house and a prophet whom many will worship as the messiah." Such quotations remind us that these films are "Old Testament" epics rather than "Hebrew Bible" or "Jewish Scripture" epics.

Finally, and perhaps most subtly, the epic Old Testament movies turn the biblical stories about the covenant between God and the people of Israel into narratives about larger-than-life personalities whose actions change the course of history forever. To be sure, these personalities have their sources in Old Testament narrative, but the movies provide a much more intense focus on the individual, and, by implication, attribute primary and often more redemptive agency to them than do the biblical stories as such.

The Protestant Christian subtext of these films coheres with their articulation of American identity. As Davis notes,

> The special relationship with the lands of the Bible that Americans constructed for themselves was premised on a single metaphor, remarkably potent and synoptic, which explained the United States as a new Israel, a New World promised land reserved for members of a favored nation.... [Jerusalem] stood variously for the historical Israelite capital and its people, the thriving, righteous nation envisioned by American colonists, and the true Protestant church rooted in and predicted by scripture.[92]

Yet the Cold War context may have been a factor here as well. As Benshoff notes, Hollywood directors and producers worked under the shadow of the House Un-American Activities Committee; in some cases, allegations of

communist affiliation went hand in hand with antisemitism. By sympathetically representing Jews as oppressed minorities in films such as *The Ten Commandments* (1956), Hollywood could distance itself from antisemitism while
aligning it securely with mainstream Protestant Christianity.[93]

Use of epic conventions in later films

The ongoing popularity of the Old Testament epics ensured that their conventions and even specific details lived on in cultural memory. The best evidence of their durability is their use as a target for spoof or parody.[94] The most
famous example is Mel Brooks' *History of the World Part I* (1981) which has a
brief biblical segment in which Moses hears God's majestic voice and goes off
to Sinai to pick up the three tablets to give to the Israelites. Being a clumsy
individual, Moses accidentally drops one of the tablets, and therefore delivers
only ten of the fifteen commandments that God had given him. This Moses is
the Lower East Side Jewish wise guy version of Charlton Heston, complete
with white hair, long white beard, staff, and Moses' Levite robe of red with
black stripes. A more recent Israeli spoof, *This is Sodom* (2010), is a no-holds-
barred slapstick comedy that uses the biblical story of Lot and Sodom, and the
conventions of the epic genre to send up all aspects of Israeli society.

One Night with the King *(2006)*

Since the 1960s, however, serious Old Testament feature films have been few
and far between. One recent example is the 2006 movie *One Night with the
King*. Like the epics of the 1950s, this film is filled with spectacle and extravagance of scale. It begins and ends with a voice-over narration, apparently by
Mordecai, and it is set in the Persian city of Susa, and its massive royal palace
complex. There is the requisite cast of thousands, and abundance of horses,
weaponry, and spectacle. Like *David and Bathsheba* and *Solomon and Sheba*, the
plot revolves around the twin themes of love and war.

One Night with the King revises the mood and themes of the biblical book by
turning it from a comedy into a drama, and from a harem tale into a love
story.[95] The young Hadassah is raised by her elderly uncle Mordecai and is set to
leave on a caravan to Jerusalem the night of the king's banquet. When the king's
wife Vashti refuses to appear before the assembled courtiers, the king must find a
new wife before he goes off to war against the Greeks (nowhere mentioned in
the biblical book). His men round up young Jewish girls as potential wives, and
at the same time capture young Jewish boys as eunuchs. The teenage Hadassah
and her boyfriend Jesse are both captured; Jesse is "cut" and Hadassah – now
calling herself by the pagan name Esther to hide her Jewish identity – is prepared
by the chief eunuch for her "audition" before the king.

The chief eunuch, however, takes a liking to Esther. When he discovers
her ability to read in several languages, he arranges for her to go to the king –
not to sleep with him, but to read to him. She begins to read from the royal

chronicles but soon departs from that script to tell the biblical love story of Jacob and Rachel. In this way she signals her love for the king; he falls in love with her and they marry; only then do they make love for the first time. Meanwhile, his minister Haman plays out his grand plan to avenge the death of his ancestor, the Amalekite King Agag, at the hands of the Israelites some five centuries earlier. Haman incites anti-Jewish hatred in the streets, and authorizes a plan to have all the Jews massacred some six weeks hence. Esther intercedes, finally reveals her own Jewish identity, and saves the day. The transformation of a delightful, almost farcical biblical comedy into a high-minded drama is ultimately unsuccessful; the young earnest and naïve but certainly attractive King Xerxes is far less interesting than his buffoonish literary counterpart. It is hard to see what the young Esther sees in him aside from his buff body. By portraying Xerxes as a sympathetic character, the film makes a subtle argument for intermarriage, a major issue for American Jewry; by showing Mordecai as an elderly and fussy man, the film misses out on the delicious erotic subtext in the Hebrew and Greek versions of the story, in which there are subtle hints, never played out, of the possibility that Mordecai himself hoped to marry Esther.[96]

In contrast to the earlier epics, this film would seem at least initially to be a "Hebrew Bible" movie rather than an "Old Testament" film in that it directly situates the film within Jewish history, and refers frequently both to Jewish beliefs and to Jewish history. The film is hardly subtle in its association of Haman with the Nazis; the villain wears a family heirloom in the shape of a swastika, made five centuries earlier by the wife of the Amalekite King Agag who is slain by the Israelite King Saul at God's command (1 Samuel 15). The amulet keeps alive the spirit of revenge, which Haman is determined to exact. Like Hitler, Haman is a demagog who incites the crowds against the Jewish people, whom he blames for all the ills of the land. Ultimately, however, this movie, like earlier epics in which the Hebrew language and Jewish liturgy and customs are portrayed, is Christianized, by repeated references to the coming of a messiah, a message which, though certainly present in traditional Jewish thought and liturgy, nevertheless can easily be heard as a reference to Jesus.

The Prince of Egypt *(1988)*

Much more successful, aesthetically and financially, was the 1998 Dream-Works animated film *The Prince of Egypt* (dir. Steven Spielberg). Here too there is a (computer-generated) cast of thousands, rousing music, and a spectacular chariot race between Moses and his brother Ramses II that recalls the famous chariot scene in *Ben-Hur*. This film has numerous explicitly "Jewish" elements: the characters have dark skins and Semitic features; some of the key songs are in Hebrew and are sung by Ofra Haza, a very well-known Israeli singer (1957–2000).

The film also reconfigures romance and gender roles in ways that are more acceptable in a late-twentieth-century context. Spielberg's film expands the role of Moses' wife Zipporah, providing her with a cameo appearance as a feisty slave whom Ramses purchases for Moses' pleasure. Moses is initially as interested in the enjoyment of this beautiful young Midianite woman as his brother believes he will be, but is then embarrassed by his mother, who glances at him sternly when he speaks disrespectfully to Zipporah. Moses then spots the young woman trying to escape, and creates a diversion that makes it possible for her to do so. She remains feisty when he finds her again in Midian, but they fall in love and marry. In the film it is she, and not Aaron (as it is in DeMille's film), who accompanies Moses on his first interview with the Pharaoh Ramses to beg for the freedom of his people.[97]

Also prominent is Moses' sister Miriam, who is a prophet and leader. The film draws upon some of the legends about Miriam that have circulated throughout the history of Jewish biblical interpretation. Most famous are the legends of Miriam's well, which was said to have accompanied the Israelites throughout their 40 years of desert wanderings, until Miriam's death.[98] Not only does Miriam follow the baby Moses in the bulrushes, but she is also the one who recognizes him as an adult, and confronts him with the message that he is destined to be Israel's deliverer.[99] This point is based on the Jewish tradition that Miriam knew that her brother Moses would deliver the Israelites from Egyptian bondage.[100] Nevertheless, it is also at this point that the film conveys a Christian-sounding message. Most viewers, whether Jewish or not, are unlikely to be aware of the Jewish sources for this aspect of Miriam's prophecy, and therefore will hear in Miriam's declaration an echo of Christian theology in which Moses the Deliverer becomes a prototype of Jesus the Savior.[101]

Implications regarding the Bible

The very act of making a Bible film implies a conviction on the part of filmmakers concerning the ongoing role of the Bible in American culture, consciousness, and value system. This conviction includes the hope that even those viewers who do not know much about the Bible, do not personally believe in its divine origins or do not belong to a community that views the Bible as a repository of absolute and ultimate truths, will recognize its ongoing cultural relevance and its formative role in (American) history and identity. Old Testament epics employ a variety of techniques or conventions to signal that the Bible is their source and point of reference. In addition to deriving some of their narrative, characters, and dialog from the Bible, films employ special fonts, occasional Hebrew letters, words, phrases or songs, and costumes as well as imitations of art or photography that bear prior biblical associations in American culture and society. They also convey a particular understanding of the Bible, its purpose and meaning, and its special role in American life. While the Old Testament films, like all Hollywood movies, are primarily entertainment vehicles, there is no doubt that their audiences absorb information and viewpoints about the Bible from watching them, particularly,

DeMille's *The Ten Commandments*. Indeed, DeMille considered himself to be a preacher of sorts, boasting that *his* movie-ministry did more for biblical literacy than anyone else has ever done.[102]

So what would a person learn from the Old Testament films made by DeMille and others at the height of the golden era of the epics in the mid-twentieth century? The first lesson is that there is a special relationship between the story of the establishment of ancient Israel and the founding of America: both involved the righteous struggle of an oppressed people against an immoral authoritarian regime. Even after America was well-established, it retained an obligation to do whatever was necessary to fight against new threats to its democracy, an ongoing struggle for which ancient Israel continues to be an inspiration. Biblical Israel is presented as the precursor of America. The films describe the origins of democracy, represented by the Israelites in battle against authoritarianism and empire, represented by Egypt, Moab, and the other nations against which Israel fought. The victory of democracy, that is, America, is inevitable, because both Israel and America have God on their side.

Second, the Bible, as a divinely inspired book, is both a religious and a moral beacon. The faith in the one God of Israel overrides all other systems of knowledge and values, such as science and reason. The true faith is concretized in Judaism, to be sure, but even more perfectly in Christian faith. Indeed, these movies uphold a Christian view of the Old Testament as a narrative that builds inevitably to the coming of Jesus as the messiah, and reads a longing for a messianic figure back into all of biblical narrative. The Bible belongs first and foremost to Christian America, although its origins in Israelite religion and connections to and sympathies for Judaism (to some degree) are acknowledged. It is important to believe in the historicity of the Old Testament; its usefulness as confirmation of the supremacy and rightness of the American way depends upon it being a historical account of God's relationship with the chosen people.

Third, the ideal society is primarily white, male, and American-born. Non-whites and foreign-born men and women are accepted as long as they adapt to American society and culture and adopt American values, which, according to these films, include individual freedom and the struggle against oppression, the power of the individual to make a difference, and the primacy of faith over reason. In American social life, women are protected by men but they can speak their mind and contradict their spouses, often serving as the moral compass and voice of restraint against the passions that occasionally override the good sense and clear thinking of their men. Sexual intimacy outside of marriage is not to be condoned, but is looked on with sympathy when the two partners are driven together by love and passion (it helps if they are also A-list movie stars).

Fundamentally, the theology and ideals that these movies express is consonant with a Protestant worldview that can be traced back to the Puritans. As George McKenna has noted, there are five principal elements that continued to influence American politics and culture long after the Puritans themselves were no longer a political force: the view that America is a special people whose historical role is parallel to that of biblical Israel; the belief that Christianity is not a purely contemplative faith but requires action in the world; a covenant theology according to which America will prosper as long as it remains faithful to God's word; a need to carry on a fight against the Antichrist, and the importance of "anxious introspection" due to the belief that our private sins can have an adverse impact on society at large.[103] All of these elements are present, to various degrees, in the Old Testament movies. While the epic genre is not conducive to the portrayal of introspection, the sins of David and Solomon are seen as causing a drought that can only be alleviated once they have returned to the one true God; while the term Antichrist is obviously not used in these films, certain characters – often Egyptian Pharaohs, are portrayed as archenemies of the divine; and prosperity is connected directly to faith, and to divinely sanctioned activity in the world. Most important, and most prominent, however, is the belief in the parallels between America and biblical Israel, with regard to their relationship to God, and their special role in the world and in the cosmos as a whole.

It must be stressed that this image of American society, culture, and religion was created in the immediate post-war era, before the full bloom of the Civil Rights movement, and large-scale immigration of non-Europeans and non-Christians, and before the tremendous social changes that occurred in the wake of the traumatic events of 11 September 2001. Yet the fact that these movies, especially DeMille's magnum opus, continue to be viewed, also means that these views continue to be perpetuated, even as they may correspond less and less to the realities outside the big or small screen. It is not too much to imagine that they also continue to play into our notions of romantic love, the ideal society, and the role of America on the world stage.

Notes

1 The emphases and exclamation marks are in the original.
2 Pearson, "Biblical Movies," 69.
3 Babington and Evans, *Biblical Epics*, 7–8.
4 For a history and discussion of the films in the silent and golden eras, see Foster Hirsch, *The Hollywood Epic* (South Brunswick, NJ: Barnes, 1978), 11–28.
5 David L. Petersen, "The Bible in Public View," in *Foster Biblical Scholarship: Essays in Honor of Kent Harold Richards*, ed. Frank Ritchel Ames and Charles William Miller (Atlanta, GA: Society of Biblical Literature, 2010), 122. On the popularity of this film on television, see http://tvbythenumbers.zap2it.com/2011/04/04/charlton-heston-portrays-moses-in-the-dramatic-biblical-epic-the-ten-commandments-saturday-april-23-on-abc/88166, Saturday, 23 April, ABC 2011 (accessed 9 May 2013); on the internet, see: Dandelion Salad website, http://vodpod.com/watch/6512847-the-ten-commandments-1956-1?u=dandelionsalad&c=dandelionsalad (accessed 20 May 2011). See also Evan Samuel Heimlich, "Divination by 'The Ten Commandments': Its Rhetorics and their Genealogies," Dissertation, Lawrence, University of Kansas, 2007.

6 The attribution of historical and biblical accuracy to DeMille's film is acknowledged in numerous, and diverse, sources. See, for example, Vivien Goldman, *The
Book of Exodus: The Making and Meaning of Bob Marley and the Wailers' Album of the
Century* (New York: Three Rivers Press, 2006), 154. As Niv Elis commented,
"*The Ten Commandments* continues to influence American culture more than 50
years after the director's death. Broadcast on television most Easters, it has become
one of the main sources of American knowledge about the Exodus story. By
now, the image of Heston as Moses and the film's presentation of a thundering
God, voiced by Heston himself, are seared into American minds." Niv Elis, "The
Film That Launched a Thousand Court Cases," *Moment Magazine*, 2010, http://
oldsite.momentmag.net/datetalk/ten_commandments.html (accessed 9 May
2013).

7 For discussion, see Hillary Warren, *There's Never Been a Show Like Veggie Tales:
Sacred Messages in a Secular Market* (Lanham, MD: AltaMira Press, 2005). Another
recent but little-known Old Testament film is *The Kingdom of Solomon*, 2010, an
Iranian film directed by Shahriar Bahrani, based on Qur'anic as well as Jewish
texts. Shahriar Bahrani, *The Kingdom of Solomon*, Drama, History, 2010, www.
imdb.com/title/tt1706450 (accessed 9 May 2013). See also www.storykeepers.
com and www.friendsandheroes.com (accessed 9 May 2013).

8 See Ellen Schrecker, *The Age of McCarthyism: A Brief History with Documents*
(Boston, MA: Bedford Books of St. Martin's Press, 1994); Jack D. Meeks, "From
the Belly of the HUAC: The Red Probes of Hollywood, 1947–52," 2009,
http://hdl.handle.net/1903/9140 (accessed 9 May 2013).

9 Jonathan P. Herzog, *The Spiritual-Industrial Complex: America's Religious Battle
Against Communism in the Early Cold War* (New York: Oxford University Press,
2011), 158.

10 Babington and Evans, *Biblical Epics*, 34.

11 Ibid.

12 On the role of Jews in Hollywood, see Neal Gabler, *An Empire of Their Own:
How the Jews Invented Hollywood* (New York: Crown Publishers, 1988).

13 See Wood, *America in the Movies*, 168.

14 Babington and Evans, *Biblical Epics*, 9–10.

15 Ibid., 8.

16 Ibid.

17 Sobchack, "'Surge and Splendor,'" 40.

18 Barry Keith Grant, *Film Genre: From Iconography to Ideology*, Short Cuts 33
(London; New York: Wallflower, 2007), 20.

19 "Judeo-Christian" has been used to describe the ethics, values, and heritage that are
often thought to be common to Christians and Jews. For a critique of this term, see
Arthur A. Cohen, *The Myth of the Judeo-Christian Tradition* (New York: Harper &
Row, 1969).

20 Joan DelFattore, *The Fourth R: Conflicts over Religion in America's Public Schools*
(New Haven, CT: Yale University Press, 2004); David L. Johnson, "The Case for
Empirical Assessment of Biblical Literacy in America," in *The Bible and the University*, ed. C. Stephen Evans and David L. Jeffrey, The Scripture and Hermeneutics Series v. 8 (Grand Rapids, MI: Zondervan, 2007), 240–52; Mark
Chancey, *The Bible and Public Schools*, http://faculty.smu.edu/mchancey/public_
schools.htm (accessed 25 January 2012). See also the work of the First Amendment Center, "The Bible & Public Schools: A First Amendment Guide" (First
Amendment Center, n.d.), www.firstamendmentcenter.org/madison/wp-con-
tent/uploads/2011/03/bible_guide_graphics.pdf (accessed 9 May 2013). For a
study of ethnic/racial preferences in film, see Stuart Fischoff, Joe Antonio, and
Diane Lewis, "Favorite Films and Film Genres as a Function of Race, Age, and

Gender," *Journal of Media Psychology* 3, no. 1 (1998), www.calstatela.edu/faculty/sfischo/media3.html (accessed 9 May 2013).

21 Arbitron, *The Arbitron Cinema Advertising Study: Appointment Viewing by Young, Affluent, Captive Audiences*, n.d., www.adbay.com/downloads/Arbitron_Cinema_Study.pdf (accessed 9 May 2013).

22 The turn of the third millennium saw the phoenix-like return of the epic genre. Massive blockbusters such as *Gladiator* (2000), *The Lord of the Rings* (2001–3), and *Avatar* (2009), like the epics of the immediate post-war era, boast a cast of thousands, grand settings, and spectacular effects, this time through the wonders of technology, which provided all the epic thrills – and box office success – at a fraction of the cost. But aside from Mel Gibson's *The Passion of the Christ* there is nary a Bible film among them. See Hall, *Epics, Spectacles, and Blockbusters*, 255. According to some, *Gladiator* singlehandedly "revived the epic movie genre after hiatus of 30 years." Technology allowed for a spectacular recreation of the Coliseum in Rome as it may have been in the early centuries of the common era, and for thrilling battle scenes, without the recruitment of thousands of extras, to say nothing of thousands of horses. Philip C. DiMare, *Movies in American History: An Encyclopedia* (Santa Barbara, CA: ABC-CLIO, 2011), 199–200.

23 According to the Internet Movie Database, *David and Bathsheba* (1951) was filmed in Arizona, on the Mexican border, *Solomon and Sheba* (1959) in Spain, and the 1956 version of *The Ten Commandments* in California and Egypt. On the importance of these films in shaping attitudes about the Middle East, see Melani McAlister, *Epic Encounters: Culture, Media, and US Interests in the Middle East since 1945* (Berkeley, CA: University of California Press, 2005), 55.

24 See Richard Slotkin, *Gunfighter Nation: The Myth of the Frontier in Twentieth-Century America*, Oklahoma paperbacks ed. (Norman, OK: University of Oklahoma Press, 1998).

25 Sobchack, "'Surge and Splendor,'" 35.

26 For example, the priestly and high priestly outfits are described at length in Exodus 28 and 39.

27 On the popularity of James Tissot, and his influence on DeMille's movies, see Stephen R. Prothero, *American Jesus: How the Son of God became a National Icon* (New York: Farrar, Straus, and Giroux, 2003), 87–89. On the popularity of Gustave Doré and his influence on DeMille, see Sumiko Higashi, *Cecil B. DeMille and American Culture: The Silent Era* (Berkeley, CA: University of California Press, 1994), 185–92.

28 See Babington and Evans, *Biblical Epics*, 101. For DeMille's own comments about his use of illustrated bibles and many other works of art, see the original trailer for *The Ten Commandments* at www.youtube.com/watch?v=sRGhOcnmChI (accessed 9 May 2013).

29 On art, see John Davis, *The Landscape of Belief: Encountering the Holy Land in Nineteenth-Century American Art and Culture* (Princeton, NJ: Princeton University Press, 1996); Debra N. Mancoff and David Roberts, *David Roberts: Travels in Egypt and the Holy Land* (San Francisco, CA: Pomegranate, 1999).

30 For discussion of "allusionism" as a cinematic technique, see Noël Carroll, "The Future of Allusion: Hollywood in the Seventies (and Beyond)," *October* 20, Spring (1982): 51–81.

31 This repetition works not only because of the dialog itself but because of its association with a particular actor. This association in itself constitutes another form of allusionism: the casting of a well-known actor in a key role will inevitably evoke the roles that he or she has played in other films. See Noël Carroll, "The Problem with Movie Stars," in *Photography and Philosophy: Essays on the Pencil of Nature*, ed. Scott Walden (Malden, MA: Blackwell Pub., 2008), 248–64; Babington and Evans, *Biblical Epics*, 53.

32 Carroll, "The Future of Allusion." See also Noël Carroll, *Interpreting the Moving Image* (Cambridge; New York, NY: Cambridge University Press, 1998), 240–64.

33 See Paul C. Gutjahr, "The Letter(s) of the Law: Four Centuries of Typography in the King James Bible," in *Illuminating Letters: Typography and Literary Interpretation*, ed. Paul C. Gutjahr and Megan Benton (Amherst, MA: University of Massachusetts Press, 2001), 19–44. Hannibal Hamlin and Norman W. Jones, *The King James Bible after 400 Years: Literary, Linguistic, and Cultural Iinfluences* (Cambridge; New York: Cambridge University Press, 2010).

34 On historical expectations, see George Frederick Custen, *Bio/pics: How Hollywood Constructed Public History* (New Brunswick, NJ: Rutgers University Press, 1992), 7. Audience expectations concerning historicity in biographical or historical movies was amply evident in the media discussions of three 2012 Oscar nominees: *Lincoln*, *Argo*, and *Zero Dark Thirty*. See Manohla Dargis and A. O. Scott, "The History in 'Lincoln,' 'Argo' and 'Zero Dark Thirty'," *The New York Times*, 22 February 2013, sec. Movies/Awards Season, www.nytimes.com/2013/02/23/movies/awardsseason/the-history-in-lincoln-argo-and-zero-dark-thirty.html (accessed 9 May 2013).

35 For a detailed discussion of the role of voice-over narration, see Sarah Kozloff, *Invisible Storytellers: Voice-Over Narration in American Fiction Film* (Berkeley, CA: University of California Press, 1988).

36 Harold F. Schiffman, *Linguistic Culture and Language Policy* (London; New York: Routledge, 2002), 61. Jan Gorak, *Canon vs. Culture: Reflections on the Current Debate* (New York: Garland, 2001), 108.

37 The film includes at least two Hebrew prayer melodies that would have been familiar to the Jewish members of the filmgoing audience in the mid-twentieth century. One is the prayer for healing called "*el na r'fa na la*" ("Please God please heal her") (see Num. 12:13); the other, the prayer for the soul of the dead, "*'el male raamim*"("God, full of compassion") chanted after Abigail's death. The latter originated in Europe in the period of the Crusades. Ronald L. Eisenberg, *The JPS Guide to Jewish Traditions* (Philadelphia, PA: Jewish Publication Society, 2004), 87. According to Jack Gottlieb, the melody is attributed to the Russian cantor Osias Abrass (1820–84). Gottlieb notes that "Such incongruities [the anachronistic use of cantorial melodies] can be explained by the prevalence of cantor-performers on the Jewish vaudeville circuit in the early 1900s, where *Kol nidrei*, *El malei rachamim*, *Eli Eli*, and other Ashkenazic chants were staple tear-jerkers." Jack Gottlieb, *Funny, It Doesn't Sound Jewish: How Yiddish Songs and Synagogue Melodies Influenced Tin Pan Alley, Broadway, and Hollywood* (Albany, NY: State University of New York Press in association with the Library of Congress, 2004), 102. See also Macy Nulman, *The Encyclopedia of Jewish Prayer: Ashkenazic and Sephardic Rites* (Northvale, NJ: Jason Aronson, 1993), 64; Adele Berlin and Maxine Grossman, *The Oxford Dictionary of the Jewish Religion* (New York: Oxford University Press, 2011), 241. On prayer in the Hebrew Bible, see Samuel E. Balentine, *Prayer in the Hebrew Bible: The Drama of Divine-human Dialogue*, Overtures to Biblical Theology (Minneapolis, MN: Augsburg Fortress Press, 1993). On the origins of "hazzanut" (Jewish cantorial singing) see Marsha Bryana Edelman, *Discovering Jewish Music* (Philadelphia, PA: Jewish Publication Society, 2003).

38 Amnon Shiloah, *Jewish Musical Traditions* (Detroit, MI: Wayne State University Press, 1992), 41.

39 A good introduction to the role of music in film is Kathryn Marie Kalinak, *Film Music: A Very Short Introduction*, Very Short Introductions (New York: Oxford University Press, 2010).

40 Lev, *Transforming the Screen*, 163.

41 Ibid.

42 The classic treatment of style in biblical narrative style, and its contrast to Homeric style, is found in the first chapter of Auerbach's work on mimesis,

dealing with "Odysseus' Scar." Erich Auerbach, *Mimesis: The Representation of Reality in Western Literature* (Princeton, NJ: Princeton University Press, 1953), 1–20.

43 See Philo, *On the Life of Moses (De Vita Mosis)*, vol. 6, *Philo: In Ten Volumes (and Two Supplementary Volumes)*, trans. F. H Colson, G. H Whitaker, and Ralph Marcus (Cambridge, MA; London: Harvard University Press: W. Heinemann, 1966).

44 For detailed discussion of both Philo's and Josephus' portraits of Moses, see Louis H. Feldman, *Philo's Portrayal of Moses in the Context of Ancient Judaism* (Notre Dame, IN: University of Notre Dame Press, 2007); Louis H. Feldman, "Josephus' Portrait of Moses," *The Jewish Quarterly Review* 82, no. 3/4 (1992): 285–328; Louis H. Feldman, "Josephus' Portrait of Moses: Part Two," *The Jewish Quarterly Review* 83, no. 1/2 (1992): 7–50; Louis H. Feldman, "Josephus' Portrait of Moses: Part Three," *The Jewish Quarterly Review* 83, no. 3/4 (1993): 301–30.

45 Although DeMille does not state that Philo and Josephus had access to the Scrolls (probably they did not) themselves, his statement could easily be taken that way. This is unlikely to have been the case with regard to Philo, who lived in Alexandria and whose knowledge of Hebrew was likely not very good. See Ellen Birnbaum, *The Place of Judaism in Philo's Thought: Israel, Jews, and Proselytes*, Brown Judaic Studies, no. 290 (Atlanta, GA: Scholars Press, 1996); Samuel Sandmel, "Philo's Knowledge of Hebrew: The present state of the problem," *Studia Philonica* 5 (1978): 107–12; Alan Mendelson, *Philo's Jewish Identity*, Brown Judaic Studies, no. 161 (Atlanta, GA: Scholars Press, 1988). Daniel Schwartz comments that Josephus may have known or not known of the scrolls, although he does not quote them or cite them directly (Daniel R. Schwartz, personal communication, 7 August 2011). Any discussion of whether Josephus knew the scrolls would need to demonstrate that a) the Essenes to whom Josephus refers are the same as the Qumran group to which the Dead Sea Scrolls pertain, and b) that Josephus had access to the scrolls when he lived among the Essenes. Both of these are conjectural and disputed, but cannot be ruled out completely.

46 Biblical law does not explicitly exclude women from the role of witnesses in cases of capital crime. See Deuteronomy 19:15–20, Exodus 20:16, 23:1–2, and women apparently did serve as witnesses in the Qumran community. Cecilia Wassen, *Women in the Damascus Document* (Atlanta, GA: Society of Biblical Literature, 2005), 88. Other texts from the first century and beyond, however, limit women's roles as witnesses. See Josephus, Ant 17.64–65 War 1.584–90, as well as rabbinic legislation (Mishnah Rosh Hashanah 1:8, Sifre Deuteronomy 190). See Janice Elster, *Women's Public Legal Roles as Judges and Witnesses in the Bible and Early Rabbinic Literature* (Cincinnati, OH: Hebrew Union College-Jewish Institute of Religion, 2007); Ross Shepard Kraemer, *Unreliable Witnesses: Religion, Gender, and History in the Greco-Roman Mediterranean* (New York: Oxford University Press, 2011).

47 Leger Grindon, *Shadows on the Past: Studies in the Historical Fiction Film* (Philadelphia, PA: Temple University Press, 1994), 1.

48 Whether the attempt to construct the "then" as "now" is conscious and deliberate, or unconscious and inadvertent, varies. DeMille's introduction to his 1956 film confirms the deliberate attempt to draw an analogy between past and present at least with regard to the main theme of liberation from an authoritarian regime. Other analogies, however, are far more subtle, and, as Babington and Evans suggest, the close parallels may well be "the unconscious product of a certain view of history and the forms and conventions of a particular kind of film." Babington and Evans, *Biblical Epics*, 53.

49 On women in postwar America, see Nancy Woloch, *Women and the American Experience*, 4th ed. (Boston, MA: McGraw-Hill, 2006), 493–554.

50 Catherine Gourley, *Gidgets and Women Warriors: Perceptions of Women in the 1950s and 1960s*, Images and Issues of Women in the Twentieth Century (Minneapolis, MN: Twenty-First Century Books, 2008), 16–41.

51 Meir Sternberg, *The Poetics of Biblical Narrative: Ideological Literature and the Drama of Reading* (Bloomington, IN: Indiana University Press, 1985), 186–229.

52 Laura Mulvey, "Visual Pleasure and Narrative Cinema," *Screen* 16, no. 3 (1975): 6.

53 Howard Eilberg-Schwartz, *God's Phallus and Other Problems for Men and Monotheism* (Boston, MA: Beacon Press, 1994), 96–97.

54 In her analysis of the biblical passage, Cheryl Exum asks whether Bathsheba's encounter with David can be considered as rape. While the text does not indicate that force was used, in Exum's view the point is not what Bathsheba might have done or felt; the point is we are not allowed access to her point of view. There is no attempted seduction recounted, which would give the woman a role, even if one in which she is manipulated. Exum notes that the denial of subjectivity is an important factor in rape, where the victim is objectified and, indeed, the aim is to destroy her subjectivity. The issue of force versus consent is crucial for constructing the woman's point of view, and it is never raised. By denying her subjectivity, the narrator symbolically rapes Bathsheba, and by withholding her point of view, he presents an ambiguous portrayal that leaves her vulnerable to the charge of seduction. See J. Cheryl Exum, *Fragmented Women: Feminist (Sub)Versions of Biblical Narratives* (Valley Forge, PA: Trinity Press International, 1993), 173–74.

55 David M. Gunn, "Bathsheba Goes Bathing in Hollywood: Words, Images, and Social Locations," *Semeia* 74 (1996): 75–101.

56 Woloch, *Women and the American Experience*, 493–534.

57 Miriam is traditionally regarded as a prophetess (Ex. 15:20–21) and in Micah 6:4, is mentioned alongside Moses and Aaron as one of the three leaders of the Jewish people during the Exodus. In Numbers 12:1–16 she is also mentioned as an opponent to Moses' marriage. When stricken with a skin condition as penance for her actions, the entire camp refused to move until Miriam had been reintegrated into society following her illness and seclusion. For sources, see Louis Ginzberg, *Legends of the Jews* (Philadelphia: Jewish Publication Society, 1909–38), 5–22.

58 This corresponds to an Ethiopian Christian text, the Kebra Nagast (The Glory of Kings) that expands on the Queen of Sheba's visit to Solomon. A digitized version of the translation by E. A. Budge (*The Queen of Sheba and Her Only Son Menyelek (I) Being the Book of the Glory of Kings, Kebra Nagast*) is available at www.yorku.ca/inpar/kebra_budge.pdf (accessed 9 May 2013). The legend itself can be found at www.sacred-texts.com/chr/kn (accessed 9 May 2013). On the Ethiopian legends about the Queen of Sheba, see Glen W. Bowersock, "Helena's Bridle and the Chariot of Ethiopia," in *Antiquity in Antiquity: Jewish and Christian Pasts in the Greco-Roman World*, ed. Gregg Gardner and Kevin Lee Osterloh (Tübingen: Mohr Siebeck, 2008), 383–93.

   Some Jewish legends suggest that Solomon and Sheba were lovers, or, at least, that they had a one-night stand. Pseudo Ben-Sira says that she gave birth to Solomon's son, who was Nebuchadnezzar, the future Babylonian conqueror and the one responsible for the destruction of Solomon's temple. Reference to this tradition can also be found as an interpolation in the commentary of Rashi. Jacob Lassner, *Demonizing the Queen of Sheba: Boundaries of Gender and Culture in Postbiblical Judaism and Medieval Islam*, Chicago Studies in the History of Judaism (Chicago, IL: University of Chicago Press, 1993), 22–23.

59 Gary Smith, *Epic Films: Casts, Credits and Commentary on over 350 Historical Spectacle Movies*, 2. ed. (Jefferson, KY: McFarland, 2004), 296.

60 Ibid.

61 For an example, see the famous novel by Leon M. Uris, *Exodus* (Garden City, NY: Doubleday, 1958). The novel was made into a film in 1960.

62 Kozloff, *Invisible Storytellers*, 76.

63 Babington and Evans, *Biblical Epics*, 34, suggest that the pro-Israel sentiment evident in the Old Testament epics of the 1950s reflects Jewish ethnic pride and the disproportionate role played by Jews at all levels of Hollywood's activities, as well as gentile American pro-Israeli feeling and reparative guilt over the Holocaust. See also Gabler, *An Empire of Their Own*.

64 See David Harris, "America and Israel are Inseparable," *Der Tagesspiegel*, 26 May 2011, www.ajc.org/site/apps/nlnet/content3.aspx?c=7oJILSPwFfJSG&b=8566 343&ct=12476627 (accessed 9 May 2013). On DeMille's *Ten Commandments* and Israel, see Wright, *Moses in America*, 89–127; Michael Paley, "The Hollywood Midrash," *Jewish Folklore and Ethnology Review* 16, no. 1 (1994): 34–37.

65 For the Puritans, the Exodus "became the mirror of the whole history of human salvation and redemption [...] For Puritan emigrants to America, the flight from England to New England symbolized in vivid and concrete terms their exodus from bondage in Egypt." Avihu Zakai, *Exile and Kingdom: History and Apocalypse in the Puritan Migration to America* (Cambridge; New York: Cambridge University Press, 1992), 65. Jim Sleeper, "AMERICAN BRETHREN: Hebrews and Puritans," *World Affairs* 172, no. 2 (31 December 2009): 52.

66 See Albert J. Raboteau, "African Americans, Exodus, and the American Israel," in *African-American Christianity: Essays in History*, ed. Paul E. Johnson (Berkeley, CA: University of California Press, 1994), 1–17. Eddie S. Glaude, *Exodus! Religion, Race, and Nation in Early Nineteenth-Century Black America* (Chicago, IL: University of Chicago Press, 2000).

67 Babington and Evans, *Biblical Epics*, 55.

68 Wood, *America in the Movies*, 187.

69 Caroline T. Schroeder, "Ancient Egyptian Religion on the Silver Screen: Modern Anxieties about Race, Ethnicity, and Religion," *Journal of Religion and Film* 7, no. 2 (2003). www.unomaha.edu/jrf/Vol7No2/ancienteqypt.htm (accessed 9 May 2013).
Schroeder comments that in this film, "religion is the vehicle for spreading the values of truth and democracy. The social backdrop to the film is the United States' war against communism and the burgeoning civil rights struggle. The solution to both of these problems, for DeMille, is 'Judeo-Christian' monotheism, the foundation for a free society.... Freedom against tyranny is the mantra of the film, and throughout Moses is the agent of liberation of his people." See also Alan Nadel, "God's Law and the Wide Screen: *The Ten Commandments* as Cold War 'Epic'," *PMLA* 108, no. 3 (1 May 1993): 415–30.

70 Herzog, *The Spiritual-Industrial Complex*, 160.

71 On the pre-war civil rights movement, see Stephen Tuck, "Black Protest During the 1940s: The NAACP in Georgia," in *The Civil Rights Movement Revisited: Critical Perspectives on the Struggle for Racial Equality in the United States*, ed. Patrick B. Miller, Therese Frey Steffen, and Elisabeth Schäfer-Wünsche (Lit; Distributed in North America by Transaction Publishers, 2001), 61–81, 39–60. See also ibid., 83–86.

72 Wright, *Moses in America*, 49.

73 Harry M. Benshoff, *America on Film: Representing Race, Class, Gender, and Sexuality at the Movies* (Malden, MA: Blackwell Pub., 2004), 75.

74 Ibid., 81.

75 Ibid., 75.

76 Roark Bradford, *Ol' Man Adam An' His Chillun Being The Tales They Tell About The Time When The Lord Walked The Earth Like A Natural Man* (New York: Harper, 1928). For discussion of the stage production, see Marc Connelly, *Voices Offstage: A Book of Memoirs* (Chicago, IL: Holt, Rinehart & Winston, 1968), 144–202.

77 Judith Weisenfeld, *Hollywood Be Thy Name: African American Religion in American Film, 1929–1949* (Berkeley, CA: University of California Press, 2007), 58.

78 Connelly, *Voices Offstage*, 148. Other "black" films of this era included *Hallelujah* (1929), *Hearts in Dixie* (1929), *Cabin in the Sky* (1943), *Stormy Weather* (1943), *Carmen Jones* (1954), and *Porgy and Bess* (1959). Benshoff notes that "Despite the fact that these films were allegedly about black culture and (some of them) feature black musical idioms, all of these films were produced, written, and directed by white men. Because of this, the films present a romanticized and somewhat paternalistic vision of black culture, and they are also filled with stereotypes now commonly viewed as derogatory. Interestingly, Christianity was invoked in many of these films in order to make a plea for social tolerance, much as the civil rights movement of the 1950s would be galvanized by Christianity. Yet it should also not be forgotten that many white supremacist groups invoked (and continue to invoke) Christianity to uphold their beliefs regarding the superiority of white people." Benshoff, *America on Film*, 81.

79 Heston claimed to provide the voice of God, in the 2004 DVD release, but DeMille's publicist and biographer Donald Hayne claims that he himself provided the voice of God in the scene of the giving of the Decalogue at Mount Sinai. For details of the controversy, see www.imdb.com/title/tt0049833/trivia (accessed 18 May 2011).

80 Contemporary paganism may arouse the ire of fundamentalist Christian groups, it was likely not yet an issue in the 1950s when most of the epics were made, nor does the group constitute a major threat to the overt monotheistic ethos of the United States today.

81 Americans were very conscious of Communism's atheistic stance. See Herzog, *The Spiritual-Industrial Complex*, 171.

82 Babington and Evans, *Biblical Epics*, 57.

83 Herzog, *The Spiritual-Industrial Complex*, 171.

84 See *The Merchant of Venice,* Act 3, scene 1, lines 50–58. William Shakespeare, *The Merchant of Venice: The "New Shakespeare" Text with Notes*, ed. E. F. C Ludowyk, (Cambridge: Cambridge University Press, 1964). On the role of ambiguity in the Moses films, see Brian M. Britt, *Rewriting Moses: The Narrative Eclipse of the Text*, Journal for the Study of the Old Testament Supplement series 402 (London; New York: T & T Clark International, 2004), 40–58.

85 Levirate marriage is mandated by Deuteronomy 25:5–6, which states: "When brothers reside together, and one of them dies and has no son, the wife of the deceased shall not be married outside the family to a stranger. Her husband's brother shall go in to her, taking her in marriage, and performing the duty of a husband's brother to her, and the firstborn whom she bears shall succeed to the name of the deceased brother, so that his name may not be blotted out of Israel." See also Dvora E. Weisberg, "The Widow of Our Discontent: Levirate Marriage in the Bible and Ancient Israel," *Journal for the study of the Old Testament* 28, no. 4 (2004): 403. Dvora E. Weisberg, *Levirate marriage and the Family in Ancient Judaism* (Waltham, MA: Brandeis University Press; Hanover, NH: University Press of New England, 2009).

86 Hospitality is viewed as a legal obligation by observant Jews. See Leviticus 19:34 and Exodus 12:49. Abraham famously extended hospitality to three disguised angels (Genesis 18:2–5), to the point that Abraham is the "paradigm for hospitality in Jewish thinking." Steven A. Hunt, "And the Word Became Flesh – Again? Jesus and Abraham in John 8:31–59," in *Perspectives on our Father Abraham: Essays in honor of Marvin R. Wilson*, ed. Steven A. Hunt (Grand Rapids, MI: W. B. Eerdmans Pub. Co., 2010), 88. Hospitality is mentioned as an obligation in Mishnah Avot 1:5 and in the Talmud, notably Shabbat 127a, which discusses hospitality as being greater and more important than other duties. See also A. E. Arterbury, "Abraham's Hospitality among Jewish and Early Christian Writers: A Tradition History of Gen 18:1–16 and Its Relevance for the Study of the New Testament," *Perspectives in Religious Studies* 30, no. 3 (2003): 359–76.

87 On the controversial role of the Ten Commandments inscribed on public build-ings and in public space, see Eugene Garver, "The Ten Commandments: Pow-erful Symbols and Symbols of Power," *Law, Culture and the Humanities* 3, no. 2 (2007): 205–24 and Herzog, *The Spiritual-Industrial Complex*, 169.

88 Babington and Evans, *Biblical Epics*, 35.

89 This attitude may betray the depiction of Jewish law as rigid legalism in some Protestant strands of interpretation of the Pauline letters. See E. P. Sanders, *Paul and Palestinian Judaism: A Comparison of Patterns of Religion* (Philadelphia, PA: Fortress Press, 1977), 33–59; George Foot Moore, "Christian Writers on Juda-ism," *The Harvard Theological Review* 14, no. 3 (1 July 1921): 197–254.

90 Babington and Evans, *Biblical Epics*, 35.

91 Anton Karl Kozlovic, "The Construction of a Christ-figure within the 1956 and 1923 Versions of Cecil B. DeMille's *The Ten Commandments*," *Journal of Religion and Film* 10, no. 1 (2006): 10. The name Yochabel comes from Josephus, *Jewish Antiquities* 2.217.

92 Davis, *The Landscape of Belief*, 3, 15.

93 Benshoff, *America on Film*, 70.

94 Wes D. Gehring, *Parody as Film Genre: "Never Give a Saga an Even Break"* (Westport, CO: Greenwood Press, 1999); Dan Harries, *Film Parody* (London: BFI Pub., 2000).

95 For discussion of Esther as comedy, see Kathleen O'Connor, "Humour, Turn-abouts and Survival in the Book of Esther," in *Are we Amused? Humour about Women in the Biblical Worlds*, ed. Athalya Brenner (London; New York: T & T Clark International, 2003), 52–64.

96 The film does nod toward this theme in a brief scene in which the king returns unexpectedly from the battlefield and spies Esther and Mordecai in each other's arms; although they are doing no more than discussing the dire situation of the Jews, he believes that his wife has betrayed him. Yet we viewers have no reason to believe that they are anything other than uncle and niece.

97 www.imdb.com/title/tt0120794/parentalguide (accessed 9 May 2013). In this film Miriam eclipses Aaron, who is portrayed primarily as the skeptical brother who is suspicious of Moses and argues with Miriam about whether Moses is the deliverer or not. The film portrays the flirtation and gentle love between Moses and Zipporah in a subtle, charming but much less smouldering way than is nor-mally done in epic romances. This subdued depiction is likely due both to the changing norms of film romance and also to the juvenile audience that this ani-mated feature intended to attract (though it still had a PG rating, due to the "intense depiction of thematic elements").

98 See Mishnah Avot, 5:6 and http://jwa.org/encyclopedia/article/miriam-midrash-and-aggadah (accessed 9 May 2013).

99 For the legend that Miriam persuaded her parents to have sex so that Moses could be born, see Ginzberg, *Legends of the Jews* 5:396, note 38.

100 See Mechilta Shemot 15:20, Megillah 14a, and Sotah 12b. Exodus Rabbah 1.22 p. 28. H. Freedman and Maurice Simon, trans. *The Midrash Rabbah* (London: Soncino Press, 1977), vol. 2; Ginzberg, *Legends of the Jews*, 2:264.

101 On Christian typological understanding of Moses, see John Lierman, *The New Testament Moses: Christian Perceptions of Moses and Israel in the Setting of Jewish Reli-gion* (Tübingen: Mohr Siebeck, 2004).

102 Kozlovic, "The Construction of a Christ-figure," para. 2.

103 George McKenna, *The Puritan Origins of American Patriotism* (New Haven, CT: Yale University Press, 2007), 49.

3 "I have seen the Lord"

Jesus on the silver screen

On 25 February 2004, thousands of people across North America, New Zealand, and Australia, flocked to their local movie theaters to see a man being systematically and brutally tortured, hauled off to the authorities, condemned to death, tortured some more, and executed. Within a few weeks, Mel Gibson's *The Passion of the Christ* had spread like a virus around the globe and, by the time of its re-release in March 2005, had grossed $370,782,930 in the US alone.[1]

Gibson's film cashed in on one of the most popular film subjects of all time: the life and death of Jesus. It was by no means the first to do so. From the very earliest days of cinema to the present, there have been hundreds of Jesus-movies made, in North America and throughout the world, some for wide release, others more local, still others only on DVD or television. While some were barely noticed, others made a major splash when they appeared, and some continue to be viewed by many thousands of people annually.

The Jesus-movie challenge

The sources

The importance of the Jesus story for western history, society, and culture can hardly be overestimated. One might think that the Gospels' stories of Jesus would be much easier to render on film than the Old Testament sagas of David or Moses. The primary sources – the Gospels – are potentially easier to work with than many other biblical and indeed non-biblical sources. They are relatively short and very focused on their hero, with few subplots or competing characters. The stories are often lively, and the action – healings, exorcisms – dramatic. The Passion stories in particular are so vividly told that they would seem to have been custom-made for the stage or screen.[2] And there are four of them. With the notable exception of Pasolini's *The Gospel According to Saint Matthew* (1964) and Philip Saville's *The Gospel of John* (2003), which draw their dialog from a single Gospel, filmmakers freely pick and choose from all four, often adopting John's longer time frame (two or three years compared to the single year in Matthew, Mark, and Luke) and then inserting scenes from all four to create maximum impact. Many, for example, will include some combination of Matthew and Luke's infancy narratives, as well as the Beatitudes from the Sermon on the Mount (Matthew 5–7), the wedding at Cana (John 2:1–12), parables (Mark 4 and parallels), and the raising of Lazarus (John 11). Other extracanonical sources, such as the Infancy Gospels, provide raw materials from which to fill in the gaps in Jesus' early life, while the writings of Josephus are a good source from which to reconstruct the social and political context of the Jesus story. Two thousand years of reflection, as expressed in commentary, art, music, drama, scholarship and, most recently, film, are also helpful for gap-filling purposes. Most important, perhaps, are the expectations that many viewers bring to their viewing of a Jesus-movie. Cinema, perhaps more than any other medium, offers everyone the opportunity to see, even to encounter, Jesus for themselves.[3]

The hero

And yet, many Jesus-movies, while long on piety, fall short in the one basic measure of good cinema: entertainment. Responsibility for this rests with the subject himself, or, to be more precise, his two-dimensional nature of the hero. Whereas the heroes of the Old Testament are "round" figures, capable of both good and evil, of change and transformation, Jesus lacks the deficiencies in character or behavior that make human beings so interesting. Though the evangelists claim that David is his ancestor, Jesus has none of David's flair, his romanticism, or his willingness to transgress the Ten Commandments in order to satisfy his desires. And though he is seen as a "prophet-like-Moses"[4] he does nothing as impulsive as hit a rock with a staff, or smash the tablets of the Law in anger. If the Jesus of scripture might nevertheless be imagined as a human being, the Jesus of popular Christianity is locked into a straitjacket of celibacy and sinless perfection.

  Woe betide the filmmaker who strays from this two-dimensional representation. As Jon Solomon has commented,

> Directors and actors who attempt to portray the life of Christ or the era of early Christianity inevitably tread on perhaps the thinnest ice in filmdom – a border between the sublime and the ridiculous, between reverence and boredom.... Too much bland reverence yields a dramatic void.[5]

Solomon concludes that "It is almost easier for a camel to pass through a needle's eye than for an actor to portray Christ with both reverence and dramatic conviction."[6] Filmmakers flesh out (so to speak) this flat Jesus-persona at their peril, as the protests surrounding the portrayal of Jesus as imagining sex and marriage in Scorsese's 1988 film, *The Last Temptation of Christ*, showed.[7]

Survey of the Jesus–movie genre

While all Jesus-movies depend, to greater or lesser extent, on the same few sources, the ways in which they tell Jesus' story vary over time, in tandem with cinema technologies, audience tastes, and changing circumstances. As we have seen, Passion Play movies, such as the *Horitz Passion Play* (1897) and *The Passion Play of Oberammergau* (1898), were among the very earliest films to be made. These Passion Play films, as well as lengthier and more comprehensive cinematic treatments, such as *From the Manger to the Cross* (1912) and *Christus* (1916), present a series of slow-moving tableaux, often staged to imitate popular devotional paintings or famous paintings by Leonardo Da Vinci, Donatello, and Rembrandt.[8] Some silent Jesus-movies move beyond such formulaic presentations to emphasize specific aspects of Jesus' life. The 1923 film *INRI*, reissued as a "talkie" in 1934 as *The Crown of Thorns*, fills out the character of Jesus' mother, transforming her from a virginal maiden to a resourceful, adventurous, and assertive woman who will go to any lengths to be with her son in his moment of need.

The most famous Jesus film of the silent period, and still immensely entertaining today, is Cecil B. DeMille's *The King of Kings* (1927). In contrast to earlier Jesus films, DeMille's movie paid attention to character development and also created a coherent plot and subplots that incorporated cause-and-effect. Its intertitles not only quote from scripture and provide background information, but also convey witty dialog as well as the narrator's commentary on the characters and story. DeMille's work had a major influence on the Jesus-movie genre and there are frequent direct allusions to his film in later films.[9]

With the exception of DeMille's film, the silent Jesus is often not much more than an animated version of the illustrated Jesuses found in Bible storybooks and devotional literature. No doubt the limitations of the silent genre itself, which was superseded soon after DeMille's film was released, contributed to this cardboard treatment. But reluctance to offend public mores also played a part. Filmmakers met the challenge of portraying the son of God by stripping him of all human affect and robbing him of the ability to engage in normal human relationships and behavior.

The Jesus-movie mill went into a 30-year hiatus after DeMille's epic. While one reason may have been the tremendous success of *The King of Kings*, the strictures on the portrayal of religious figures and subjects that were built into the Hays censorship code that was in effect from 1930 to approximately 1960 may also have been a factor. In 1930, the Motion Picture Producers and Distributors of America adopted a Production Code, which, in 1934, was endorsed and promoted by the powerful Catholic Legion of Decency. From 1930 to 1966, no film could appear in American movie theaters unless it was certified by the Production Code Administration (PCA). Films which did not conform to the Code were subject to censorship.[10] It was not until the 1960s that Jesus returned to star in his own films: *King of*

Kings, directed by Nicholas Ray (1961), and *The Greatest Story Ever Told*, directed by George Stevens (1965). The return was short-lived, however. Like the Old Testament subgenre, the Jesus epics were affected by the overall economic, social, and political conditions that led to the demise of the epic genre as such.

Yet, in contrast to Old Testament films, Jesus-movies continued to be made, turning profits, and occasionally garnering critical acclaim. Some, to be sure, adopted many of the features of the epic genre; Zeffirelli's 6.5-hour extravaganza, originally made for television, as well as Heyman's *Jesus* (1979), and Robert Young's 1999 television mini series, also called *Jesus*, offered the scale and scope associated with the classic Bible epic. Others, however, consciously rejected, subverted, or played with these conventions, and struck out in original directions.

Perhaps the most highly acclaimed of the non-epic Jesus films is Pier Paolo Pasolini's sparse and powerful black-and-white film, *The Gospel According to Saint Matthew* (1964). Although the film has a large cast – primarily local villagers and other non-professional actors – it stands out from the epic crowd for its skilful deployment of the handheld camera, its brilliant use of music, its powerful political and social allegory, and its dialog's strict adherence to the text of Matthew.[11]

Other Jesus-movies that did not fit into the epic mold were two rock musicals, *Jesus Christ Superstar* and *Godspell*, both of which appeared in 1973. The most delightful spoof of the epic genre is the 1979 comedy, *Monty Python's Life of Brian*. Though it is a "Brian"-movie and not a "Jesus"-movie, *Life of Brian* both uses and mocks the clichés of the genre.[12] The fictional Brian is an unintentional and reluctant messiah whose life parallels Jesus' biography in its public nature and tragic death, without the reverence, sanctity, and perfection of the hero or the virginity of his mother. Despite the fictional premise of the spoof, *Life of Brian* is meticulously researched and satisfyingly intelligent. Aside from Jesus himself, the film spares no one. Its hilarious darts are aimed at the conventions of Jesus' portrayal in film and popular culture, as well as at targets such as the British school system.

Perhaps the most serious challenge to the stereotypical Jesus of cinema is Martin Scorsese's iconoclastic film, *The Last Temptation of Christ* (1988). In contrast to other Jesus-movies, Scorsese's film does not claim authenticity, historicity, or fidelity to scripture. Rather, as its opening scrolling text declares, it claims only to be a film adaptation of a fictional work, a novel by the Greek author Nikos Kazantzakis. This claim is somewhat disingenuous, in that the film involves the same cast of characters and narrative line as other Jesus-movies. By disclaiming historicity, however, Scorsese is free to explore areas that conventional Jesus-movies leave untouched, especially Jesus' subjectivity, his sexuality, and his urge toward domesticity. For most of the film, Jesus is unsure as to whether he is being driven by God, the devil, or his own demons. In the final section of the film, Jesus, while still alive, is led down from the cross by a young, red-haired girl claiming to be his guardian angel.

He marries, has children, and lives to a ripe old age. Only at the end do we learn that this sequence is a dream or hallucination; Jesus dies on the cross in this film as in every other Jesus biopic. But the mere suggestion that Jesus may have desired sexual intimacy and the domesticity was enough to trigger protests, angry letters, and editorials even before the film was released.[13]

The iconoclastic moment did not last long, however. After another, shorter hiatus in the making of Jesus feature films in the 1990s, the early years of the new millennium saw three new films. The first, in 2000, was the British made-for-TV "claymation" movie *The Miracle Maker*. This film, though novel with regard to its medium, remained quite conventional in its narrative. Its major innovation was to tell the story from the point of view of Jairus' daughter, a young girl whom Jesus raises from the dead or near dead, according to Mark 5:22–43. This film borrowed significantly from Zeffirelli's magnum opus, but attempted to tell the story in a way that was more accessible to children and more acceptable to their parents. The second was Philip Saville's *The Gospel of John* (2003), which reproduced the entire Good News Bible translation of the Fourth Gospel. This in itself posed a unique cinematic challenge: how to overcome an overabundance of words? Thanks to the skill of the camera operators and the actor, this Jesus manages – if barely – to keep our attention throughout the nearly five chapters of farewell discourses that John inserts between the final supper and the betrayal in the garden (John 13–17).

The best-known recent addition to the Jesus film genre is Mel Gibson's *The Passion of the Christ* (2004, released in slightly altered form in 2005). Gibson's film is an account of Jesus' final hours. Its heavy-handed violence and its negative representations of the Jewish authorities touched off a major controversy that may well have contributed to its box-office success. Like the early silent Jesus films, Gibson's film is opaque to viewers who do not already know the story. On its own, the film does not provide enough information for viewers to know what Jesus has done to raise the ire of Jews and Romans alike or why he is subjected to such violence culminating in death on the cross. From this point of view, we have come full circle, from the faked *Passion Play* at Oberammergau to the overwrought *Passion of the Christ*.

Other films of the early twenty-first century were less successful. The 2006 film *The Nativity* avoided the story's usual tragic ending by focusing solely on the story of Jesus' conception and birth. *The Color of the Cross* (2006), directed by Jean Claude Lamarre, was a Passion Play film with an unusual premise: that the death of Jesus – here portrayed as a black man – was racially motivated. The premise is ultimately unconvincing historically, since there is no evidence that there were "white" Jews and "black" Jews in first-century Judea; no doubt most were similar to other Semitic peoples in appearance.

Jesus-movies as epics

The Jesus-movies of the epic era, and beyond, employ many of the same conventions as the Old Testament epics. The American West and Hollywood studios stand in for the Galilean hills and the cities of Nazareth, Bethlehem, and Jerusalem.[14] The influence of the Western film genre is palpable in films such as George Stevens' *The Greatest Story Ever Told*, whose landscape resembles the settings of *Shane* (1953) and other Westerns made by the same director.[15] In these films, as in the Old Testament movies, class and power are indicated by the level and expense of decoration on the robes. Furthermore, the Romans are often soldiers, roles which require armor and helmets or hats, and the other accoutrements of the military legions. The Jewish leadership, on the other hand, is often dressed in high priestly garb, loosely reconstructed from the descriptions in Exodus 28 and 39 but also modelled after the biblical drawings of Tissot and Doré, who also influenced the mise-en-scène of particular events, such as the Sermon on the Mount and the Passion story.[16]

The influence of visual art and music is even more palpable in the Jesus-movies than in the Old Testament films. The Last Supper scene is frequently set up to imitate, or pay homage to, Leonardo's famous fresco (1495–98) that graces the refectory of the church of Santa Maria delle Grazie in Milan; that this image itself had become conventional is demonstrated by Mel Brooks' 1981 spoof, *History of the World Part I*, in which Jesus and his disciples commission Leonardo to come and paint a group portrait, thereby inconveniencing the waiter serving up the soup at the Last Supper. Leonardo, like a good wedding photographer, has everyone shift around one side of the table, so that he can get everyone into one picture. Michelangelo's famous sculpture of the *Pietà* (1498–99, in St. Peter's Basilica in Vatican City) is mirrored in numerous Jesus-movies, which make the most of the emotional moment that Jesus' mother receives her dead son into her arms. The Jesus-movie soundtracks feature large orchestral as well as choral works, some of them composed especially for the film, others taken from famous works. Perhaps the most popular is the Hallelujah chorus from Handel's *Messiah*, which accompanies the intertitle quoting John 6:15 in *The King of Kings* (1927) and the raising of Lazarus in *The Greatest Story Ever Told* (1965).

Whereas casting an Old Testament hero was simply a matter of finding a handsome celebrity, choosing an actor to play Jesus was a somewhat trickier affair. Although the historical Jesus was patently a Jew, none of his cinematic personas look at all Semitic.[17] Instead, most of them closely resemble the well-known and iconic 1940 image by Warner Sallman, in which Jesus has northern European or British facial features, wavy, shoulder-length brown hair, and blue eyes.[18]

And then there is spectacle. This is most evident in Cecil B. DeMille's magnificent film, *The King of Kings* (1927), which has scenes featuring near-nudity and circus animals. The scene of Herod's banquet, at which Herodias demands the head of John the Baptist (Matt. 14:3–11; Mark 6:17–28) provides the most obvious opportunity for spectacle in these films. Finally, these films, like Old Testament epics, allude to other movies, including other Jesus-movies. Gibson's Pilate in *The Passion of the Christ* strongly resembles Steven's Roman governor in *The Greatest Story Ever Told*; in Young's *Jesus*, Joseph takes Jesus and John the Baptist to see Jerusalem, and exclaims, "Jesus, we're not in Nazareth anymore," a close paraphrase of Dorothy's famous line in The Wizard of Oz: "I don't think we're in Kansas anymore, Toto."

Although it is customary to speak about the "Jesus film genre," Jesus-movies, like many other films, often belong to two or more genres and therefore adhere to multiple sets of conventions. David Greene's *Godspell* (1973) and Norman Jewison's *Jesus Christ Superstar* (1973) are rock operas that share many features with other famous productions such as Milos Forman's *Hair* (1979) and Ken Russell's *Tommy* (1975). Mel Gibson's 2004 film *The Passion of the Christ* owes much to the spiritual memoirs of Anne Catherine Emmerich (1833) but even more to the contemporary action movie genre to which Gibson himself has contributed.[19]

But Jesus-movies also belong to another category of film: the biographical movie, or "biopic" for short. Biopics are feature films set in a specific historical time and place whose subjects are historical figures. Biopics tend to feature a common narrative template that initially situates its subject within a family and circle of friends, and subsequently places him or her in an antagonistic relationship with an individual or group. Conflict ensues, inflicting physical and mental pain upon the hero. The conflict is resolved in a judicial trial that provides the occasion for an impassioned summation of the hero's primary message for the benefit of the viewing audience.[20]

Jesus-movies easily package Jesus' story into the same overall plot structure, which also corresponds well with the general outline of the Gospel narratives. Jesus is born into a family, grows up, interacts with his social and religious milieu, gathers a circle of disciples, performs miracles and other acts that draw the attention of both the people and the authorities; these activities lead to an antagonistic relationship with the Jewish leadership which ultimately leads to his trial(s) and crucifixion, in the course of which he suffers great physical pain and mental anguish. Throughout he takes every opportunity to expound his message. This basic structure is present in all of the Jesus-movies.

The claim to historicity

Biopic and epic conventions overlap to a considerable extent. Both types of films claim to be authentic, though what it means to be authentic may vary. And both create coherent narratives from partial sources by filling in the gaps and fleshing out the characters. Jesus-movies, like Old Testament movies, use various techniques, such as voice-over narration and scrolling texts, to create an aura of authenticity. Some also make an explicit claim to historicity. For example, the silent movie *From the Manger to the Cross* (1912) introduces itself as "a review of the savior's life according to the gospel-narrative." DeMille's 1927 *The King of Kings* states categorically that: "The events portrayed by this picture occurred in Palestine nineteen centuries ago, when the Jews were under the complete subjection of Rome – even their own High Priest being appointed by the Roman procurator." The 1961 film *King of Kings* begins with a sonorous voice-over narration by Orson Welles:

> And it is written, that in the year 63 BC the Roman Legions like a scourge of locusts poured through the east laying waste to the land of Canaan and the kingdom of Judea. Rome's imperial armies went unto the hills and struck Jerusalem's walls in a three-month siege. Reaching the gates, these legions laid the dust of battle in a shower of blood.

Despite these claims, and the undisputed historical status of their protagonists, biopics are fundamentally fictional narratives, a fact which in turn creates an unresolved tension with the historicity of the subject or hero, and the broader claims to historicity that these films make or imply. For these reasons, biopics invite comparison between their fictionalizing narrative and the "facts" presented in biographies or other sources. This paradoxical position creates ambiguity for the viewer and invites a contradictory response in the viewers. Viewers may acknowledge the fictionalizing activities of biopic filmmakers, but they also perceive these films as "real" or historical and expect them to cohere with the "facts" as they know them.[21]

The tension between historicity and fiction is inherent in the Old Testament films already examined, as well as in most other biographical films. But two factors differentiate Jesus-movies from other films within the Bible and biopic genres. One is the nature of the hero. While viewers may have strong feelings about figures such as Abraham Lincoln, Johnny Cash, Moses, or Solomon, the connection of Christian viewers to Jesus is on a different plane altogether. Even non-Christian viewers will acknowledge that Jesus' importance to society and history far exceeds that of either Lincoln or Cash. The second factor is the role of faith. As we have seen, Old Testament films promote monotheism, the value of prayer, and, less explicitly, the superiority of Christianity. The Jesus-movies, however, claim not only to tell an authentic story of Jesus but also explicitly to inculcate or reinforce Christian faith in their viewers. DeMille's *The King of Kings,* for example, reminds viewers that Jesus "Himself, commanded that His message be carried to the uttermost parts of the earth. May this portrayal play a reverent part in the spirit of that great command." The 1979 evangelical film *Jesus* has, at last count, been released in 1,178 different languages,[22] it has been seen by more than six billion viewers (in all versions) and there have been more than 200 million "indicated decisions for Christ following a film showing."[23] The film explicitly encourages such decisions with a lengthy evangelical epilog that addresses viewers directly and urges them to pledge faith to Jesus, then and there, by repeating a faith formula that the narrator proceeds to recite.

The majority of films do not go as far as Heyman's *Jesus* in promoting Christian faith, or, more accurately, a particular brand thereof. Nevertheless, many Jesus-movies implicitly affirm the belief that Jesus' life and teachings have an ongoing prescriptive importance in the life of the Christian. The Old

Testament epics also took care to present positive moral and religious choices, for example, by emphasizing the value of prayer and the punishment that attends the violation of the Ten Commandments, at least in part because these elements were prescribed by the production code that was in force during the golden era of the epics. But the moral and religious scrutiny is intensified with regard to the Jesus-movies due to the illusion of personal encounter that the movies foster, that reinforces a theology in which the individual's relationship with Jesus is central.

Gap-filling: narrative and characterization

Like the Old Testament films, the Jesus-movies must fill in the gaps in their sources, with respect to both plot and characterization. Some films make use of apocryphal sources such as the Infancy Gospel of James to fill out the events of Jesus' youth. Young's made-for-TV miniseries *Jesus*, for example, depicts Jesus as a young boy who finds himself capable of bringing a dead bird back to life. This echoes two stories in the Infancy Gospel of Thomas, one in which Jesus, like God in Genesis, creates living beings – in this case a group of birds – from clay[24] and the other in which Jesus resurrects a dead child.[25] Other filmmakers simply create scenes to show that Jesus had a typical, happy, childhood. Pasolini's 1964 film adds a vignette that one might call "the happy holy family at the beach" as a pastoral interlude in the journey of the family home from Egypt to Nazareth. The scene portrays Mary spreading out a blanket and exchanging a warm smile with her husband. The toddler Jesus runs gleefully into Joseph's outstretched arms.[26]

The Jesus-movies exhibit a plot structure similar to that of the Old Testament epics, in which a small and oppressed nation, led by a special prophet or king, stands up against a vile imperial regime, and the biographical film genre, in which a lone hero with strong convictions makes some important enemies who try to do him in. In the Old Testament movies, the nation is Israel, the hero is Moses or David, and the vile regime is Egypt, the Philistines, or another pagan stand-in. In the Jesus-movies, the oppressed are the ordinary Jews in Judea and Galilee, the oppressive regime is Rome – aided and abetted by the Jewish religious leadership – and the leader of the resistance is Jesus, who is physically defeated but spiritually triumphant.

The context of Roman imperial power and colonization is often set up in the very first frames of the film. *The Gospel of John* (2003) opens with a scrolled text that states that the Fourth Gospel, and hence the film too, are "set in a time when the Roman Empire controlled Jerusalem." *The Gospel of John* is a model of understatement compared to many of the films that came before it. The silent films and epics elaborate vividly, and often melodramatically, upon the hardships caused by Roman occupation. The opening title of the silent film *INRI* identifies its story's setting as Jerusalem, "across whose shoulders the yoke of Rome had lain heavy for almost a hundred years." The silent film *Golgotha* implies the same by beginning its treatment with a reference to "Tiberius Caesar of Palestine," a map of Judea under Roman rule, and a reference to Israel's strong desire to be free. DeMille's *The King of Kings* describes Judea as "groaning under the iron heel of Rome."

The emphasis on Roman power usually continues throughout. These films are filled with images of legions of Romans galloping through the streets of Nazareth wreaking havoc among the frightened residents (even interrupting Jesus' bar mitzvah in *Jesus of Nazareth*) and include scenes in which Roman soldiers or Jewish tax collectors working for Rome extract exorbitant tax payments from poor Galilean residents.[27]

In portraying the suffering of the Jews under Rome, the Jesus-movies prepare the way for three key points that emerge in almost all of these films: God sends his son to save the Jews from their suffering under Rome; the ordinary people are receptive to Jesus and his message; the Roman and Jewish authorities are alarmed by Jesus, whom they perceive as a threat to their power. This cinematic Jesus is not all that different from his predecessor, Moses, who, though not God's son, was commissioned by God to liberate his people, was accepted by his people but feared and pursued by his enemies.

Unlike Moses, however, Jesus cannot in the end consummate his act of liberation. The unfortunate fact is that Roman rule continued; some decades after Jesus' death, the Jewish revolt against Rome ended in defeat and the destruction of the Temple. Even the most imaginative filmmaker cannot seriously rewrite this part of the story. Another impediment is that the portrayal of Jesus as the leader of a rebel force clashes with the more popular view of Jesus as the champion not of war but of love. How else to make sense of Gospel sayings such as "love your enemies" (Matt. 5:43–44), "turn the other cheek" (Matt. 5:39), and "love your neighbor as yourself" (Mark 12:31), and Jesus' assertion that his kingdom is not of this world (John 18:36)?

If Jesus cannot bring the revolution, in what sense is he a hero, a savior, a redeemer? For both narrative and theological reasons, the only answer can be: in the spiritual sense. But this is hardly the most satisfying answer from a dramatic point of view.

Then as now

Like the Old Testament films, the Jesus-movies construct the past in analogy with the present; in doing so, they anachronistically project the concerns and norms of the present upon the past, and thereby also imply that the Bible remains relevant to the problems and concerns of the filmmakers' own time and place.

Gender

Despite its overall male perspective, the New Testament portrays women as leaders in the early Jesus community.[28] The woman who, aside from Jesus' mother, receives the most attention in the Gospels is Mary Magdalene.

Christian tradition turned Mary Magdalene into a promiscuous woman, but the Gospels themselves do not portray her as such.[29] Indeed, the Gospel of John portrays her as "apostle to the apostles" (John 20:1–18). Movies, however, prefer the traditional view, because it allows them to portray her transformation from prostitute and adulteress into a pious, chaste, follower of Jesus and companion to Jesus' mother Mary. The notion that Mary Magdalene may have been an authoritative apostolic figure is absent from many of these films, in which her testimony "I have seen the Lord" is ignored or disbelieved by the other disciples. There are exceptions, however. In Young's *Jesus* Mary's post-crucifixion testimony is taken seriously by everyone, although the disciples initially require some convincing. In *The Gospel of John*, she is a full-fledged disciple, present during many key scenes including the Last Supper.

Jesus' mother herself is sometimes given a role in the leadership of the Jesus movement. The most detailed portrayal of Mary as leader is found in Rossellini's *The Messiah*. In this film, Mary becomes Jesus' partner in his mission; just as she taught the young boy Jesus about his Jewish heritage before his coming of age, so does she teach children and adults as they mend their nets and cook their dinners by the shores of the Sea of Galilee. This film goes even further, however. Rossellini's Mary does not age.[30] By the time Jesus embarks on his mission, mother and son look the same age. The effect is heightened in the Passion sequence. The camera dwells on her suffering face as she watches him die on the cross, and then again when she cradles the dead Jesus in her arms, an image that has been described as the "most stunning iconographic aspect" of this film.[31] Some view this shot as blatantly sexual. This effect is heightened by the slow zoom of the camera through the icon onto the men watching behind the cross, thereby drawing attention not only to the mother–son couple but also to the prurient gaze of the nearby men.[32]

None of the Jesus-movies, including relatively recent entries such as Scorsese's *Last Temptation*, disrupt traditional gender hierarchies in any fundamental way. The gender roles in the holy family correspond closely to those presented as the ideal in the nuclear family of the 1950s: Mary keeps house and cares for the child, and Joseph supports the family materially. Whether intentionally or not, these films are amenable to a "family values" agenda that often separates conservative from liberal Christian social agendas in the United States.[33]

America, the champion of democracy

The Jesus-movies resemble the Old Testament epics not only with regard to their hierarchical portrayal of gender relations, but also in their overall narrative structure – an oppressed people seeks and gains freedom – which in turn makes them equally expressive of an underlying analogy to America's self-image as the enemy of communism and the champion of freedom and democracy.[34] The Cold War analogy is most apparent in the two major epics of the 1960s, Ray's *King of Kings*, and Stevens' *The Greatest Story Ever Told*. Both of these films conflate all evil empires, including Nazism and communism, and represent them by Rome, much as DeMille did with Pharaoh's Egypt.

Only one film acknowledges that there may have been at least some positive consequences of the Roman presence in Judea. Monty Python's *Life of Brian* (1979) portrays a meeting of one of the many protest movements in Judea that is planning a guerrilla attack on Pilate's palace. To maintain the appropriate anger and sense of outrage, their leader, Reg, proclaims: "They've bled us white, the bastards. They've taken everything we had, and not just from us, from our fathers, and from our fathers' fathers." Others pipe up: "And from our fathers' fathers' fathers… And from our fathers' fathers' fathers' fathers." Yet when Reg asks, rhetorically, "And what have they ever given us in return?!" a rather long list emerges in response, including: the aqueduct, sanitation, roads, irrigation, medicine, education, wine, public baths, and public safety. Finally Reg, disgusted, shouts: "All right, but apart from the sanitation, the medicine, education, wine, public order, irrigation, roads, a fresh water system, and public health, what have the Romans ever done for us?" "Brought peace," says one. Reg gives up: "Oh. Peace? Shut up!"[35]

The civil rights movement

The epic Jesus-movies of the 1960s show some awareness of the civil rights movement. In the *Greatest Story Ever Told*, the camera pans slowly over the crowd watching Pilate interrogate Jesus from behind the barricades, and lingers on the face of an African American woman, implying that Jesus came to free her too.

The issue of civil rights comes to the fore most directly in *The Color of the Cross*, in which, as noted earlier, Jesus is portrayed as a black man and his enemies, Jewish and Roman, are depicted as white racists who seek his death. Though the premise, while historically improbable, does have dramatic potential as well as social importance, the film itself is problematic for many reasons, among them the portrayal of Jesus' enemies, the Jewish chief priests. These elderly men look and sound like nothing other than (the stereotype of) Eastern European Jewish immigrants on the lower east side of New York in the early decades of the twentieth century. These men punctuate their conversations with a heart-felt "oy." Caiaphas the high priest tries to keep control of his council by shouting "Sha! Sha! Sha!" (meaning "Quiet!" and uttered with a hiss that I remember well from my teachers at the afternoon Yiddish school in the late 1950s and early 1960s). Jesus' Jewish background is acknowledged; he recites the blessings in Hebrew and his Passover table is graced with the requisite ritual objects as well as matzah (unleavened bread). But while not all Jews are portrayed as racists, the fact that some are against Jesus on racial grounds contradicts the focus on his Jewish background and returns us to the same "us-and-them" polarity that is at play in the Jesus films from the epic era.

Antisemitism

The depiction of the Jewish priests in *The Color of the Cross* raises the most difficult social issue percolating through these films: antisemitism. The New Testament itself expresses conflicted views about Jews and Judaism, and throughout the history of Christianity some statements in the canon – the description of Pharisees as hypocrites, the association of the Jews with the devil, and, above all, the deicide charge – were used to promote and justify hatred and violence against Jews.[36] Early films vary in their focus on the deicide charge when it comes to portraying Jesus' Passion, but the epics of the post-war era, which were being produced at the time when the true scope and tragedy of the Holocaust were penetrating Americans' consciousness, more or less explicitly identify Nazi Germany with Roman oppression, and reflect a sincere attempt to avoid antisemitism.

Ray's *King of Kings* begins with a lengthy voice-over narration delivered by Orson Welles. Ray's narration is based heavily on Josephus' account. Both the text and the visuals draw an analogy between the horrors of the first century and those of the twentieth:

> Under the eye of General Pompey the holy city trembled; the people were strewn like wheat in harvest time of Rome.... for more than fifty years after Pompey's invasion, the history of Judea would be read by the light of burning towns. If gold was not the harvest, there was a richness of people to be gathered. The battalions of Caesar Augustus brought in the crop. Like sheep, from their own green fields, the Jews went to the slaughter.

The images of Jews going like sheep to the slaughter, and the relentless, greedy, and bloodthirsty Pompey suggest that the "facts" taken from Josephus' writings have been presented so as to recall Jewish experience under the Nazi regime, as much or more than Judean realities under Roman occupation. The introduction therefore implies that Roman imperialism, Jewish suffering, and Jesus' arrival were analogous to Nazi imperialism, the Holocaust, and the founding of the state of Israel (or perhaps vice versa). At the same time, the Jews' dream of a messiah in the first decades of the first century CE paralleled the Jews' dream of a homeland in the first half of the twentieth century. Thus the film posits the creation of Israel as the world's response to the Holocaust just as it posits the appearance of Jesus as God's response to Roman oppression.

At the same time, the Jesus films can perpetuate antisemitic attitudes and images due to the role that the Gospels themselves assign to the Jewish leaders and the Jewish crowds in the process leading to Jesus' death. The Gospels of Mark and Matthew depict the high priest and council as convicting Jesus on the charges of blasphemy – a capital crime – and of delivering him to Pilate and urging the governor to condemn him to death (Mark 14:55–64;

Matt. 27:59–68). Some films omit the most egregious New Testament passages, such as Matthew 23, Jesus' lengthy diatribe against the scribes and Pharisees in which he refers to them repeatedly as hypocrites; Matthew 27:25, in which Pilate washes his hands of the moral responsibility for Jesus' death and the Jewish crowds take his blood upon themselves and their children; and John 8:44, in which the Johannine Jesus claims that the Jews with whom he is speaking have the devil as their father.

Pasolini's *The Gospel According to Saint Matthew* is one of the few films that presents Matthew 23 in its entirety. The film is allegorical; its use of non-professional actors drawn from the local population and the visual emphasis on the oppressive role of the Roman state draw an analogy between the Romans' oppression of Jesus and his followers and the Italian state's oppression of the poor in the post-war period. The allegorical level of meaning is made explicit by the visuals that accompany Jesus' impassioned recitation of Matthew 23. As Jesus passionately denounces the scribes and Pharisees as hypocrites, the camera lingers not on the Jewish leaders but on the Roman soldiers who treat the crowds of common people with contempt. For an Italian viewer, therefore, the scene is surely a powerful indictment of the Italian state; for a Jewish viewer, however, the words sound threatening and hostile.

Matthew 27:25, in which the Jews take the blood of Jesus upon themselves and upon their children, is an even more difficult passage. It is highly dramatic, and therefore perfect for the silver screen but as one of the main sources for the deicide ("Christ-killer") charge, it is also highly anti-Jewish. In *Der Galiläer*, the high priest Caiaphas incites the crowd to call for Jesus' death. The crowd rushes to Pilate's palace screaming for Jesus' death. Pilate, filled with compassion, offers to release him, but the crowd demands Barabbas alive and Jesus dead. Pilate does not wash his hands, but puts the blood curse on the Jews: "On you comes his blood" [auf euch komme sein Blut]. The huge crowd takes Jesus' blood upon themselves and their children, not once, as in Matthew, but twice: "On us and on our children comes his blood. We take it upon ourselves" [auf uns und unsere Kinder komm' sein Blut. Wir nehmen es auf uns]. In repeating the blood curse three times, the film magnifies the scriptural elements upon which the deicide charge is based. Also noteworthy is the visual appearance of Caiaphas and the other Jewish leaders, who wear headgear that looks suspiciously like horns, another prevalent antisemitic image.[37]

Even in the pre-Holocaust era, some filmmakers attempted to downplay the antisemitic potential of the Gospel account. In doing so, they adopted a number of strategies. One of these was to draw attention away from the entire Jewish people and focus it on one particular character, most often, the high priest Caiaphas. In the Gospel of John, Caiaphas is portrayed as the one who articulated the need and rationale for Jesus' death (John 11:49–52). On the basis of this passage, many works of scholarship, fiction and film portray Caiaphas as the mastermind of the plot against Jesus and the one who bears primary moral responsibility for Jesus' death. This approach is taken in DeMille's *The King of Kings*, which blames Jesus' death directly and exclusively on Caiaphas. DeMille's high priest is portrayed with typical anti-Jewish imagery, much of it taken directly from medieval art. He is physically grotesque, almost comical, and he wears a remarkable head covering. Elsewhere in DeMille's film he is described as being extraordinarily fond of money, and fearful that Jesus will take control of the Temple and therefore also the Temple treasury. When Pilate asks: "Shall I crucify your king?" it is Caiaphas, not the crowd (as it is in John 19:15), who declares "We have no King but Caesar." After Pilate washes his hands of the affair, it is the High Priest and not the crowd who proclaims a version of Matthew 27:25: "If thou, imperial Pilate, wouldst wash thy hands of this Man's death, let it be upon me and me alone!"

The contrast between the Roman governor and the Jewish high priest is nowhere more apparent than in the aftermath of this exchange. Pilate pronounces the death sentence but declares himself "innocent of the blood of this just Man"; he then stalks off to sob alone in his throne room. Caiaphas, self-satisfied, smirks, and, arms folded, savors his victory. Babington and Evans describe DeMille's Caiaphas as "the Romans' Jew," an "anti-Semite's dream caricature of wickedness: obese, cynical, rubbing his plump fingers together in gleeful anticipation of his plots, appearing like a well-fed devil at Pilate's side to whisper 'Crucify him!' The scapegoat ... is the living epitome of ethnic guilt."[38] DeMille's portrait is at home in 1920s America, in which antisemitism was an almost respectable response to waves of Eastern European immigration, Jewish connections to labour unrest, all fed by well-established antisemitic caricatures.[39] At the same time, DeMille's deflection of responsibility from the Jewish people as a whole to only one man, the Jewish high priest, can be seen as a way to diminish the antisemitism inherent in the deicide charge itself.[40]

In most post-Holocaust films, the so-called blood curse is omitted altogether. Interestingly, however, Matthew 27 was at the centre of a controversy in the most recent major Jesus film, Mel Gibson's *The Passion of the Christ* (2004). In an attempt to make his film sound "authentic," Gibson had his characters speak only in Latin and Aramaic. In his version of the trial scene, Pilate washes his hands, and the Jews cry out "Let his blood be on us and on our children" in Aramaic. The inclusion of the blood curse prompted strong protests, and demands that Gibson remove the scene from the final version. Gibson refused to do so but as a compromise, the English subtitles are omitted at this point. Nevertheless, the high priest and the entire Jewish crowd were portrayed as extremely hostile to Jesus.

Gibson's film also provides the most graphic illustration of Jesus' accusation in John 8:44. The direct quotation of this verse is omitted in most films, with the exception of Saville's *The Gospel of John*, which, by contractual arrangement between the production company and the American Bible Society, was bound to reproduce the entire text of the Good News translation of the

Gospel of John.[41] Gibson, however, illustrates it very clearly without quoting it. After Jesus' arrest, Judas experiences a remorse so powerful that he can only sit down in the middle of the city in despair. Two children approach him, curious about a man who is just sitting there not doing much of anything. As they interact with Judas, the camera shows them turning into demon children with bloody teeth, crazed eyes and wizened faces, thereby enacting John 8:44 in which Jesus describes the Jews as the children of the devil. Even though we are meant to see the boys' metamorphosis as the product of Judas' guilty and fevered brain, the image of these Jewish demon-children is now a permanent entry in Hollywood's visual lexicon.

Romance

Romance is one of the fixed conventions of the epic film genre, and it is also an important feature of biopics, as well as in Hollywood cinema as a whole.[42] Unlike his forerunner King David and other biblical kings and prophets, Jesus is an unpromising romantic lead. If filmmakers are comfortable with Jesus' human suffering and compassion, they almost always avoid any hint of romance and sexuality. Nevertheless, there are films that gesture in this direction, and one – Scorsese's *Last Temptation of Christ* – that, as noted, aroused serious protests even before its release due to its portrayal of a Jesus who imagines marriage, sex, procreation, and family life as a positive and significant alternate path.

Films move only tentatively in the direction of providing Jesus with a romantic partner. In the 1999 made-for-TV movie called *Jesus*, the adolescent savior is interested in Mary of Bethany, and must make a difficult decision to follow his heart or his God-given mission. He reluctantly breaks up with her. This decision upsets her initially but she comes to accept it as time goes on. Jesus' innocence remains intact. (The same cannot be said for his less perfect, and more amusing, counterpart, Brian of Nazareth, who did have a real lover, at least, according to his biographer Monty Python [*Monty Python's Life of Brian*].)

The main candidate for Jesus' affections – and then only in films that allow themselves any speculation – is Mary Magdalene. According to Luke 8:2, Mary Magdalene, along with other women, provided material support for Jesus and the disciples, perhaps as a consequence of the exorcism of her seven demons. Her presence at the foot of the cross along with Jesus' mother Mary implies a long-standing and close association with the family. According to John 20:1–18, Mary goes to Jesus' tomb alone early on Sunday morning, finds it empty, and then encounters the Risen Lord. Most important, however, is her post-canonical representation as a "fallen woman," a prostitute who gave up her life of sin when she met Jesus. In this tradition, she is often conflated with the woman who anoints Jesus and wipes his feet with her hair (Luke 7:38; John 12:3) and the adulterous woman whom Jesus saves from stoning (John 7:53–58:11).[43]

In early silent movies, such as *INRI*, Mary is a wealthy courtesan who holds court in her salon. Although she accepts gifts from her many suitors, she holds herself aloof from them. When she sees Jesus, however, she cannot tear her eyes away from him. Jesus prevents the crowd from stoning her; she collapses on her bed from emotion. In any other context, this scene would be the beginning of a great love story. As a story about Jesus, however, the hints of romance remain unfulfilled.

This theme reaches both its height and its depth in DeMille's *The King of Kings*. Here too Mary is "a beautiful courtesan"; fearless, sensual, irreverent, and scantily clad. She is surrounded by suitors but is preoccupied by the absence of her lover, Judas. Another woman, she fears, but no! One of her suitors reveals, "Nay, 'twas no woman I saw him with – but a band of beggars, led by a carpenter from Nazareth." The hitherto indolent courtesan is stirred into action. Anointed with her richest perfumes, she orders her servants to "Harness my zebras – gift of the Nubian King!" she sets off for Nazareth to take Judas back, and teach "this carpenter … that He cannot hold a man from Mary Magdalene!" But the moment she fixes her sultry gaze upon Jesus her confidence evaporates. Captivated by Jesus' intense gaze, Mary loses her resolve. One by one, he exorcises her seven demons: the seven deadly sins of Lust, Greed, Pride, Gluttony, Indolence, Envy, and Anger. Suddenly she notices her own state of semi-nudity, and wraps her gauzy shawl around her body. From this point she is the dutiful, obedient and silent disciple, having gained her salvation but lost her flair. In this way DeMille fulfills the genre requirements of the epic film – splendidly and with great humor – and then domesticates his wild Mary so that she is no longer a threat to the chastity of Jesus or the morality of the audience.

DeMille's Jesus is impervious to Mary's charms. The same is true in the epics of the 1960s in which Mary is no longer the defiant courtesan of the silent Jesus films but a troubled woman, whose spirit is healed when she meets Jesus and becomes friends with his mother. In these films too, her love for him is apparent, as is his lack of sexual interest in her. Indeed, only Scorsese has the audacity to explore the relationship between Jesus and Mary, and then only after disavowing any claim to historicity.

Sexuality and eroticism in The Last Temptation of Christ

In Scorsese's film, Mary is Jesus' childhood friend who became a prostitute when Jesus rejected her love. Before he goes off on his soul-searching sojourn in the desert, Jesus comes to her home, and waits the entire day and evening until the long line of men waiting for her services have been satisfied. Again she offers her love to him; he is sad but steadfast: he must go into the desert and he must not get involved with her. He meets up with her again after his ministry has begun. She has been caught in adultery; just as the crowd prepares to stone her, Jesus arrives. A confrontation ensues between Jesus and the crowd's leader, Zebedee, the father of James and John of Zebedee. Zebedee drops the stone, caught in his own hypocrisy. Jesus lifts up the terrified Mary Magdalene, who has been silent throughout. They cling to each other and walk away. Disciples follow behind, subdued. To himself, Jesus mutters: "God does so many miracles. What if I say the wrong thing? What if I say the right thing?" Jesus sits Mary down beside him, and asks the disciples to come closer.

Scorsese's scene amplifies and illustrates the main point of the biblical story. We are each fallible and hence unworthy to pass judgment on another's sins. Only God, who is all-forgiving, can be the judge. The scene also marks a turning point in the narrative of the relationship between Jesus and Mary. Whereas earlier Jesus had refused her company, from this point on she travels with him, not as his wife or lover but as a follower or disciple. In a final fantasy scene, the dynamic changes completely. Jesus steps down from the cross and walks across a bright meadow to wed Mary Magdalene. Mary is wearing virginal white; their sexual union is joyful and uncomplicated by guilt. She becomes pregnant, but dies before the child is born. Jesus then cohabits with both Mary and Martha of Bethany, with whom he has a number of children.

Many found the idea, and the images, of Jesus making love with Mary, Mary, and Martha very disturbing. Yet what has generally gone unnoticed is yet another film that many might find even more problematic: the homo-erotic undertones to Jesus' relationship with Judas. In the backstory to this film, Jesus and Judas are friends from their youth. As an adult, Judas has become involved with the anti-Roman revolutionary group, the Zealots, whereas Jesus, a carpenter, earns his living making and setting up crosses for Roman crucifixions. Early in the film, his bosses send Judas to kill Jesus, but he finds that he cannot. Instead, he joins Jesus' group to see for himself whether Jesus is "the one" who will save Israel from Rome or whether he is collaborating with the evil empire. Throughout their wanderings, the two men argue over how best to attain freedom. One evening, they move away from the rest of the group. Their voices rise with the passion of their discussion, Andrew comes over to find out what is going on. Jesus puts him off: "It's alright, Judas and I are talking." At the end of their conversation, Jesus says to Judas: "I'm afraid. Stay with me." Jesus sleeps in the shelter of his doubting friend's arms. The camera zooms in on their faces. Jesus rises, takes an apple out of his pocket and begins to eat. He opens the apple, removes the seeds and scatters them. An apple tree grows immediately, miraculously, in the place where the seeds had fallen. Whatever his own doubts, Jesus has powers that can only come from the Creator God. The apple also evokes the forbidden fruit of Genesis, hinting at forbidden sexual desires. In the background can be heard the tinkle of bracelets and the exotic theme music associated with Mary Magdalene, further accentuating the erotic subtext.

Judas finally comes to believe in Jesus when his friend turns from the way of love to the way of the axe. Judas runs to Jesus, falls to his knees, looks up at Jesus' face, exclaims "Adonai!" (meaning, "my God!"), and kisses his feet. Judas

is here uttering a confession of profound faith. He denounces violence, however, after Jesus raises Lazarus from the dead. For Judas, Lazarus is proof of Jesus'
greatest miracle. It is Jesus whom he follows, no one else. It is now time for
Jesus to reveal his "terrible secret from God": that he must die on the cross.
Judas is incredulous: "Die? You mean you're not the Messiah?" "I am,"
responds Jesus, "I have to die on the cross and I have to die willingly." They
return to the Temple area, but Jesus feels faint. Blood flows from the holes that
the nails will soon make in his hands and feet. He turns to Judas: "Stay with
me. Don't leave me." Judas supports Jesus until they can sit down and rest in a
deserted passageway. Judas walks away to center frame and looks around him,
then back at Jesus. He walks back to Jesus and sits down beside him. He checks
Jesus' forehead, with concern, to see if he has a fever. Jesus tries to reassure
Judas: "I wish there was another way, I'm sorry, but there isn't. I have to die on
the cross." Judas is vehement: "I won't let you die." But Jesus explains that they
have no choice; this is the only way to bring "God and man together." Jesus
must be sacrificed, but unless Judas agrees to betray him, there will be no
redemption. Judas refuses: "Get somebody stronger."

Has Judas lost his nerve or has he been overcome by love? The fateful
moment arrives during the Last Supper. Jesus distributes the wine, which
looks like blood, to each of the disciples. The last one to drink is Judas. He
looks carefully into the cup and drinks with great reverence, then takes a
blood clot out of his mouth, the blood running down his hand. Judas gets up
to leave. A disciple shouts: "We're not finished." Jesus says: "Let him go. I
want to tell you something." The camera cuts to Judas walking through the
deserted woods.

At the moment of betrayal, Jesus sees Judas at the head of the soldiers. Judas
says, "Welcome, Rabbi," and kisses him intensely on the lips. Judas watches as
Peter cuts off a man's ear, and Jesus heals it. Jesus turns to look at him. "Take
me with you. I'm ready." Judas doesn't respond. The camera moves in to an
extreme close-up of Judas as Jesus walks away. Judas betrays Jesus out of love
and devotion to his master, his rabbi, his God, the one whom he loves. Yet
the dream or hallucination that Jesus experiences while he is hanging on the
cross, turns this relationship around to declare, in an ironic twist, that it is
Jesus who betrays Judas. In this dream, Jesus lives a long, satisfying, and
entirely ordinary life. As he lies on his deathbed, in the year 70, the Temple is
burning and the Jewish people are in distress. Among the friends who come
to visit him is Judas. Judas is still furious with Jesus for having stepped off the
cross at the behest of his young "guardian angel." As Judas continues to shout,
the guardian angel bursts into flames, and is revealed to be Satan. The dream-
spell is broken. Jesus slithers across the floor like the snake of Genesis and
returns to the cross.

The story has now come full circle. Judas has been the instrument of Jesus'
death, as Jesus, and God, had intended. He becomes the voice of faith, the
one through whom God speaks to Jesus and urges him to do what he was
supposed to do. He is indeed the strong one; Jesus has been unable to stay

focused and carry out God's plan. Jesus has succumbed to Satan's Last Temptation: the ordinary life of domesticity and day to day pleasures. Judas, in his love for Jesus, has fully comprehended the necessity of Jesus' death, even as he now fights in the armed revolution that he had so long anticipated.

The homoerotic undertones are evident in Jesus' and Judas' body language, their proximity, their tenderness toward one another, the intensity of their relationship, and the fact that they are bound together in the service of God and Israel. Whereas the protests that attended the release of the film focused on the dream sequence in which Jesus is seen making love with Mary Magdalene, the more "scandalous" aspect is in fact this relationship with Judas, which, though it does not come to sexual fruition, remains the driving force behind the plot and the development of Jesus' character.

Scorsese is not the first and he is not the only filmmaker to include such hints in his Jesus-movie. In Pasolini's version of the betrayal scene, Judas approaches Jesus, followed by the chief priests together in a group. Judas then pulls free and runs to Jesus. The two embrace passionately. Judas then watches with concern as Jesus moves toward his death on the cross. Given Pasolini's own homosexuality, his allusion to the homoerotic potential in this intense relationship is not surprising. Other films, however, intimacy also portray this. And it is to be found even in a silent film such as *INRI*, made long before audiences developed a tolerance for viewing homoeroticism in the movies. The image is fleeting but evident nonetheless, as Jesus approaches Judas, he touches his shoulders, looks down slightly, and draws Judas closer to him. It is Judas' kiss (Matt. 26:49; Mark 14:45; Luke 22:47), that provides an opening for this subtext.

The Milky Way

An even more scandalous romantic liaison is suggested in Luis Bunuel's *The Milky Way* (1969). Bunuel's film implies that there was something vaguely unhealthy, if not downright unholy, in the relationship between Mary and Jesus, or, more precisely, in Mary's feelings about her son. In one scene, Bunuel's Mary is a young, frivolous woman who admires her son the carpenter because of his handsome beard, just as a young bride might admire her manly husband. In another scene, we see Jesus running energetically down a path in the forest. One of his disciples stops him and reports: "Master, the guests have arrived. Your mother and brothers await you." Jesus answers, "Here is my mother and brother …" This leads us to expect that, as in the Synoptic Gospels, he will now redefine his notion of family. But no, after a brief interlude, we return to the scene of an outdoor wedding feast set up in a clearing. Jesus is seated at the table, eating, drinking, talking, and laughing. At a neighboring table, his mother regales those around her with stories of Jesus' birth. When the angel announced that she was pregnant by the Holy Spirit, she reveals, "At first I didn't believe, then I was very happy." This Mary never ages either physically or emotionally; she remains an adolescent mother enamored of and awestruck by the famous son to whom she gave birth. Bunuel's targets here are not Mary and Jesus as such, but the clichés and conventions of the art and film tradition as well as Catholic Mariology.

Ethnicity

Another challenge posed by Jesus' humanity is his ethnicity. The Jesus films' attempt to portray him as a universal savior who remains relevant for and central to twentieth- or twenty-first-century western culture, overrides any acknowledgment that Jesus was a Jew who likely engaged in the same level of observance of Jewish law and customs as other Galilean Jews.[44]

Jesus' Jewishness is not in any doubt, yet one would hardly know it from watching the Jesus-movies from the epic era. The reticence to show a fully Jewish Jesus may reflect the age-old tendency to define Jesus over against Judaism just as Christianity defines itself as "other" than Judaism. Theologically, Jesus' Jewish identity stands in tension with his role as the universal savior and messiah who transcends any notions of religion or ethnicity. The epics often portray the wedding at Cana, the Jewish festival of Passover, and occasionally make reference to the Sabbath, and they also show Jesus visiting the synagogue, because these occasions are mentioned in the Gospels, but they tend to minimize the Jewish context of these events. Some more recent films do introduce some Jewish elements. Zeffirelli's *Jesus of Nazareth* lavishly portrays the Jewish rituals and celebrations, particularly in the segments dealing with the courtship of Joseph and Mary, and with Jesus' own young life. In Scorsese's rendition of the wedding scene, the groom recites the traditional formula: "You are sacred to me through this ring according to the laws of Moses and Israel." *Godspell*'s clown-faced Jesus celebrates the Passover *seder* while sitting on the ground surrounded by his disciples, and recites the traditional Hebrew blessings over the bread and wine.

It is striking that the film that pokes the most fun at the Jesus-movie genre is also the one that is the most direct about Jesus' Jewish context. *Monty Python's Life of Brian* (1979), while not strictly speaking a Jesus-movie, emphasizes the Jewishness of its protagonist, an unwitting Messiah figure. If Jesus' ethnicity is murky, Brian is adamantly Jewish, proudly embracing every twentieth-century antisemitic epithet. When his mother tells him that his father was a Roman soldier, Brian protests: "I'm not a Roman, and I never will be! I'm a kike, a yid, a hebie, a hook-nose, I'm kosher, Mum, I'm a Red Sea pedestrian and proud of it!" This scene draws upon the ancient satirical Jewish legend that Jesus was the illegitimate child of Mary and a Roman soldier.

Christology

The Romans, like the Egyptians, Moabites, and Shebaites of the Old Testament epics, do not represent idolatry so much as the rejection of Christian monotheism and, within the symbolic system of the Hollywood epic, American democracy. Much as the films might decry the rationalism of their pagan characters, they themselves struggle with how to portray the "irrational" aspects of Jesus' activities. While Old Testament films revel in miracles such as the Burning Bush and the splitting of the Red Sea, Jesus-movies often convey a sense of discomfort with the miraculous dimension of the Gospel accounts.[45] Some films avoid showing miracle scenes and describe them verbally instead. In the opening scene of DeMille's *The King of Kings*, Mary Magdalene's suitors tell her that the Carpenter who wooed Judas away has been said to heal the sick and raise the dead. In *The Greatest Story Ever Told*, Jesus' miracles are reported to Pilate by an official reading a written report. To be sure, the most spectacular events, such as the raising of Lazarus, are still portrayed, but overall the miracles are much less prominent in the Jesus-movies than in the Gospels themselves. In general, it is Jesus the teacher, not Jesus the miracle-worker, who dominates the Jesus-movies.

The cinematic emphasis on Jesus' human dimensions also emerges in other aspects of his depiction. In *The Gospel According to Saint Matthew* (1964), Pasolini's Jesus is a young man whose anger is directed not so much at the spiritual ills of his society but at the Roman state machine. As in the First Gospel, Jesus cuts his ties with his biological family but he quietly sheds a tear when he walks past his mother's home. Both his anger and his tears draw attention to his human aspects far more than to his divine nature.

The most incoherent and conflicted presentation of Christology is to be found in Mel Gibson's 2004 *The Passion of the Christ*. The film opens with a scrolled text quoting from Isaiah 53: "He was wounded for our transgressions, crushed by our iniquities; by His wounds we are healed" (cf. Isa. 53:5). By introducing the film in this way, Gibson implies that Jesus fulfills the prophecy of the suffering servant messiah to which many Christians believe this passage is alluding, and attaches a salvific significance to the terrible crushing of Jesus' body that is the major theme of the film. The film emphasizes Jesus' suffering and the forbearance with which he endured it. To some, and perhaps to Gibson himself, this portrayal may underscore Jesus' divine nature, as the suffering exceeds what a mere human being could endure. Yet visually, Gibson's Jesus seems to be reduced not to his humanity but to his physicality; he does not resemble a god or even a man, but a hunk of raw flesh. This portrayal erases not only Jesus' divine identity but his human one as well.[46]

Much more appealing is the conflicted, tormented, insecure Jesus of Scorsese's film, perhaps the only Cinematic Savior who truly models not only the despair of his unavoidable fate but also the exaltation of his spiritual triumph over evil. As we have noted, Scorsese's film explicitly denies any claim to historical authenticity or even fidelity to scripture. The film begins with a scrolling text, quoting from the novel by Nikos Kazantzakis, *Christ Recrucified*, and declaring that "This film is not based upon the Gospels but upon [the] fictional exploration of the eternal spiritual conflict" between spirit and flesh. This introduction was no doubt intended to defend Scorsese's decision to draw a three rather than two-dimensional portrait of Jesus. Scorsese's Jesus is tortured by insecurity and self-doubt. He is ashamed of his behavior – for as a carpenter, he specializes in making the crosses for Roman crucifixions – and driven by fits and voices to engage in behaviors whose source – the devil? God? – he cannot identify. Jesus eventually comes to understand that he is indeed God's son, but this knowledge does not strengthen him or allow him to defeat the forces of evil in the world. Indeed, he struggles against this knowledge and the destiny that it dictates until his final breath. At the moment of his death, however, he is truly transformed into the Son of God, in a scene that is perhaps the most exultant of any in the Jesus-movie genre. Jesus' doubt about his relationship with God has been resolved. The eternal conflict between spirit and flesh has now finally been won.

Implications regarding the Bible

Like the Old Testament epics, the Jesus-movies presuppose the ongoing relevance of the Bible as well as an abiding interest on the part of the audience. Despite their different subject matter, these films have very similar narrative structures and employ similar conventions as do the Old Testament films, including the tendency to address present issues by retelling an ancient story. Nevertheless, the nature of the subject matter, and particularly the limitations imposed by the perceived attempt to safeguard (a particular Christian view of) Jesus' unchanging and eternally pure nature, as well as the bare historical facts, precludes the successful deployment of the full conventional narrative (in which the underdog bests the superpower) as well as the requisite romantic subplot. Furthermore, if the hero is a Galilean peasant rather than an Israelite king, it is difficult to provide the glitter and glamor that provides so much entertainment value in the epic film. Here too, even more obviously than in the Old Testament films, the Bible is the province of Christianity, specifically, Protestantism, as can be seen in the tendency to downplay the miraculous elements present in the Gospel sources themselves.

As entertainment, most of these films fall short. Their characters, especially Jesus himself, talk too much and do too little. Their story lines, dictated by the exigencies of the biopic template and the requirements of popular piety, are unfailingly predictable. Their pace is often agonizingly slow, based apparently on the (dubious) assumption that reverence is best conveyed in slow motion.

If Jesus' coming did not bring an end to Roman oppression, what did it signify? According to these films, it meant the coming of a new, interiorized, spiritual order that was in itself transformative even if the external, political order remained the same. It also meant a new cast of characters, and a powerful new story, that could be mobilized to convey messages about American identity to domestic and international audiences. But first, and foremost, it meant the beginning of Christianity, a major new player that, from Hollywood's perspective, led in a straight line to America itself. The fact that Jesus – despite the narrative expectations set up in the Jesus epic films – did not liberate Judea from Rome is eclipsed by the importance of Christianity in the long view of western history, and in American self-understanding. The Jesus-movies themselves can only adumbrate this importance. The theme is more fully fleshed out in the "sword-and-sandal" films to which we now turn.

Notes

1 These figures are taken from the Internet Movie Database, www.imdb.com/title/tt0335345/business (accessed 19 January 2012). The television show *South Park* parodied the film in its episode "The Passion of the Jew," originally aired on 31 March 2004. www.southparkstudios.com/full-episodes/s08e04-the-passion-of-the-jew (accessed 9 May 2013).

2 Jo-Ann A. Brant, *Dialogue and Drama: Elements of Greek Tragedy in the Fourth Gospel* (Peabody, MA: Hendrickson Publishers, 2004), 4–7.

3 Roger E. Olson, *The SCM Press A-Z of Evangelical Theology* (London: SCM, 2005), 153.

4 The expectation of a future "prophet-like-Moses" is based on Deuteronomy 18:15, in which Moses tells the people: "The LORD your God will raise up for you a prophet like me from among your own people." For the theme of the Prophet like Moses in the Gospel of John, see A. Reinhartz, "Jesus as Prophet: Predictive Prolepses in the Fourth Gospel," *Journal for the Study of the New Testament* 11, no. 36 (1989): 3–16.

5 Solomon, *The Ancient World in the Cinema*, 179.

6 Ibid.

7 Tatum, *Jesus at the Movies*, 191–92, 199–200.

8 Roy Kinnard and Tim Davis, *Divine Images: A History of Jesus on the Screen* (New York: Carol Pub. Group, 1992), 32.

9 Johnny Meyer, Howard Hughes' sidekick in *The Aviator* (2004), tells Hughes about DeMille's *The King of Kings*: "You ought to hear about what's going on with DeMille. He's shooting his Bible picture. He's gotta do a crucifixion in Fresno."

10 Solomon, *The Ancient World in the Cinema*, 3; Stern *et al.*, *Savior on the Silver Screen*, 62.

11 Although the dialog in Pasolini's film is drawn exclusively from Matthew's Gospel, other elements of the film – principally the mise-en-scène and the musical soundtrack – amplify and expand upon the story in ways that evoke the other canonical Gospels as well as a broad range of artistic reflections on Jesus.

12 See Tatum's acknowledgments in the second edition of his book, in which he explains how he changed his mind and therefore added a chapter on this film in the second edition of his book. W. Barnes Tatum, *Jesus at the Movies: A Guide to the First Hundred Years*, Rev. and expanded (Santa Rosa, CA: Polebridge Press, 2004).

13 Cf., Michael Medved, *Hollywood vs. America: Popular Culture and the War on Traditional Values* (New York, NY; Grand Rapids, MI: HarperCollins; Zondervan, 1992), 37–49; Babington and Evans, *Biblical Epics*, 106.

14 *The King of Kings* (1927) was shot in the Hollywood studio; *The Greatest Story Ever Told* was shot in Arches National Park, Moab, Utah.

15 On the impact of the Western genre on the Jesus movies, see Richard G. Walsh, *Reading the Gospels in the Dark: Portrayals of Jesus in Film* (Harrisburg, PA: Trinity Press International, 2003), 74; Baugh, *Imaging the Divine*, 27.

16 Prothero, *American Jesus*, 88.

17 The main exceptions to this overall portrayal are the African American Jesus in *The Color of the Cross* and the claymation Semitic Jesus in *The Miracle Maker*. For an image of a Middle Eastern Jew from the early first century, see the BBC Worldwide/Reuters 2001 computer-generated reconstruction of the face of a first-century Judean male, based on the skull of a man buried in Jerusalem 2,000 years ago. www.lightplanet.com/mormons/basic/christ/physical_appearance.htm (accessed 9 May 2013).

18 www.godweb.org/sallman.htm (accessed 9 May 2013). For more detailed discussion of the Sallman image, see Prothero, *American Jesus*, 116–23, and David Morgan, *The Sacred Gaze: Religious Visual Culture in Theory and Practice* (Berkeley, CA: University of California Press, 2005), 155–57. The most accurate recreation of Sallman's image was achieved by Robert Powell, who played Jesus in Zeffirelli's *Jesus of Nazareth*.

19 On the indebtedness of this film to other genres, including Gibson's own previous films, see Susan Thistlethwaite, "Mel Makes a War Movie," in *Perspectives on The Passion of the Christ: Religious Thinkers and Writers Explore the Issues Raised by the Controversial Movie* (New York: Miramax Books, 2004), 127–45. On the influence of the horror film genre, see Richard G. Walsh, "The Passion as Horror Film: St. Mel of the Cross," *Journal of Religion and Popular Culture* 20 (Fall 2008), http://utpjournals.metapress.com/content/yl64p102j8875102/?p=02f4200e0e744212954 5957c1f03e03a&pi=1 (accessed 9 May 2013).

20 Due to the centrality of the trial scenes in the Gospels, it is not surprising that trials are present in all of the Jesus films. The Synoptics present a trial before the high priest and a second one before Pilate (cf. Matt. 26:59–66 and 27:11–14 and parallels). John has an interrogation by Annas, the high priest's father-in-law (18:19–24) – but no trial – a visit to the high priest Caiaphas (18:24), and a trial before Pilate (18:28–38). But this feature also signals these movies' excellent fit with the biopic genre as a whole. Custen, *Bio/pics*, 181.

21 For discussion of Gibson's use of history, see the essays in Kathleen E. Corley and Robert L. Webb, ed., *Jesus and Mel Gibson's The Passion of the Christ: The Film, the Gospels and the Claims of History* (London; New York: Continuum, 2004).

22 As of 20 February 2013, according to The Jesus Film website www.jesusfilm.org/progress/translations.html.

23 As of 1 January 2013, see www.jesusfilm.org/film-and-media/statistics/quarterly-statistics.

24 The Infancy Story of Thomas, 2.2. Oscar Cullmann, "The Infancy Gospels," in *New Testament Apocrypha. Volume I: Gospels and Related Writings*, ed. Wilhelm Schneemelcher and Robert MacLachan Wilson (Cambridge; Louisville, KY: J. Clarke & Cogon; Westminster John Knox Press, 1991), 444.

25 The Infancy Gospel of Thomas, 9.3. It is not surprising to note, however, that films overlook the less admirable stories, such as Jesus' killing of a child who bumped against him (4.1). Ibid., 446.

26 Adele Reinhartz, "The Happy Holy Family in the Jesus Film Genre," in *On the Cutting Edge: The Study of Women in Biblical Worlds: Essays in Honor of Elisabeth Schüssler Fiorenza*, ed. Jane Schaberg, Alice Bach, and Esther Fuchs (New York: Continuum, 2004), 123–42.

27 These portrayals are very similar to the Westerns, such as *Pale Rider* (1985), in which poor villagers are victimized by a powerful family that owns the mining rights in the area. For analysis of *Pale Rider* see Adele Reinhartz, *Scripture on the Silver Screen*, (Louisville, KY: Westminster John Knox Press, 2003), 177–84.

28 See, for example, Kevin Madigan and Carolyn Osiek, *Ordained Women in the Early Church: A Documentary History* (Baltimore, MD: Johns Hopkins University Press, 2005); Ute E. Eisen, *Women Officeholders in Early Christianity: Epigraphical and Literary Studies* (Collegeville, MN: Liturgical Press, 2000); William R. Telford, "Jesus and Women in Fiction and Film," in *Transformative Encounters: Jesus and Women Re-Viewed*, ed. Ingrid R. Kitzberger (Leiden; Boston, MA: Brill, 2000), 353–91.

29 For a brief history of Mary Magdalene's depiction as a prostitute, see Joyce E. Salisbury, *Encyclopedia of Women in the Ancient World* (Santa Barbara, CA: ABC-CLIO, 2001), 216–18.

30 The most striking example is Michelangelo's *Pietà*, in which a beautiful and very young Mary cradles her full-grown son on her lap after he is taken down from the cross. Michelangelo himself explained Mary's youth as a reflection of her perpetual virginity. See Timothy Verdon and Filippo Rossi, *Mary in Western Art* (New York: In Association with Hudson Mills Press, 2005), 158.

31 Peter Brunette, *Roberto Rossellini* (New York: Oxford University Press, 1987), 346–47.

32 This representation echoes central elements of Catholic Mariology, in which Mary is seen as having a vital role as an instrument in redemption, as "Advocate, Auxiliatrix, Adjutrix, and Mediatrix." This Mary is the disciple par excellence, elevated above all other disciples. Elizabeth A. Johnson, *Truly Our Sister: A Theology of Mary in the Communion of Saints* (New York: Continuum, 2003), 130.

33 See George Lakoff, *Moral Politics: How Liberals and Conservatives Think* (Chicago, IL: University of Chicago Press, 2002).

34 Stern et al., *Savior on the Silver Screen*, 85.

35 The positive Roman contribution to the quality of life in Judea is mentioned also in the Babylonian Talmud, Shabbat 33b. For discussion, see Adele Reinhartz, *Jesus of Hollywood* (Oxford; New York: Oxford University Press, 2007), 61.

36 See, for example, Rosemary Radford Ruether, *Faith and Fratricide: The Theological Roots of Anti-Semitism* (New York: Seabury Press, 1974); Joshua Trachtenberg, *The Devil and the Jews: The Medieval Conception of the Jew and Its Relation to Modern Antisemitism* (New Haven, CT; London: Yale University Press, 1943); and Adele Reinhartz, *Befriending the Beloved Disciple: A Jewish Reading of the Gospel of John* (New York: Continuum, 2001).

37 Adele Reinhartz, *Caiaphas the High Priest* (Columbia, SC: University of South Carolina Press, 2011), 180–92.

38 Babington and Evans, *Biblical Epics*, 122.

39 Ibid.

40 On the different portrayals of Caiaphas in art, drama, literature, and film, see Reinhartz, *Caiaphas the High Priest*.

41 This was much discussed within the academic advisory group, of which I was a part. Only very minor omissions ("he said," "she said") were permitted.

42 For the centrality of romance in Hollywood films, including biopics, see, for example, Custen, *Bio/pics*, 159.

43 On the textual history of this passage, see Raymond E. Brown, *The Gospel According to John* (Garden City, NY: Doubleday, 1966), 1.332–34. On the afterlife of this story, see Jennifer Wright Knust, "Too Hot to Handle? A Story of an Adulteress and the Gospel of John," in *Women of the New Testament and their Afterlives*, ed. Christine E. Joynes (Sheffield: Sheffield Phoenix Press, 2009), 143–63.

44 For a thorough discussion of Jesus' Jewish practice, see John P. Meier, *A Marginal Jew: Rethinking the Historical Jesus*, 4 vols. (New Haven, CT: Doubleday, 1991–2009).

45 Many early filmmakers such as Georges Méliès in fact exploited the new possibilities that cinema afforded to depict miracles and other unusual experiences. Michael Richardson, *Surrealism and Cinema* (Oxford; New York: Berg, 2006), 21. Some filmmakers, such as DeMille, who freely depicted Old Testament miracles, were much more inhibited with the healings and exorcisms that the Gospel attributes to Jesus.

46 Mark D. Jordan and Kent L. Brintnall, "Mel Gibson, Bride of Christ," in *Mel Gibson's Bible: Religion, Popular Culture, and the Passion of the Christ*, ed. Timothy K. Beal and Tod Linafelt (Chicago, IL: University of Chicago Press, 2006), 81–87. Kent L. Brintnall, *Ecce Homo: The Male-Body-in-Pain as Redemptive Figure* (Chicago, IL: University of Chicago Press, 2011).

4 "Make disciples of all nations"

Swords, sandals, and Christianity

The 1953 epic *The Robe* ends on a note both tragic and triumphant, as the handsome heroes, Marcellus (Richard Burton) and Diana (Jean Simmons) face the camera and the viewer, and walk calmly yet joyfully down the long central aisle of Emperor Caligula's vast throne room toward the camera, their certain death, and their happy afterlife together in their Christian heaven.

The Robe is a classic example of the so-called "sword-and-sandal" or "peplum" film genre that, like the Old Testament and Jesus epics, flourished in the silent era and then again during the two decades immediately after the Second World War.[1] The label comes from the costume design, which uniformly features pepla (plural of peplum, from the Latin for tunic, toga, or robe of state), swords, and, of course, sandals. Although Old Testament and Jesus-movies also clothed their actors this way, the label initially designed specifically Italian historical films set in the ancient past, and then was broadened to include epic films set in ancient Greece and Rome.[2]

The sword-and-sandal movies relevant to this study embed events from the Gospels into fictional narratives that are set in the same era as these same Gospel events. Unlike the Jesus-movies, sword-and-sandal movies are explicit, rather than disguised, fictions, often based on novels, and therefore only loosely tied to canonical sources. Without exception, these films are epics and therefore marked by the conventions of scale and extravagance that are typical of the epic genre; they also have much in common with the gladiator films, such as *Spartacus* (1960), particularly in their use of the gladiator motif itself, which is a major plot feature in many peplum films. Like the Jesus-movies, sword-and-sandal movies build on the film medium's ability to foster the illusion of immediacy and personal connection with Christ. A viewer could find Jesus – if not always see him face to face – through the eyes of the handsome and compelling protagonists whose lives were transformed through Christian faith.

Brief history

Like other Bible movies, peplum films date back to the silent era, which saw the production of such classics as *Ben-Hur* (1907, 1925), *Quo Vadis?* (1901,

1910, 1912, 1924), and *The Sign of the Cross* (1914, 1932). Production abated in the early sound era, the notable exception being *The Last Days of Pompeii* (1935), which on the basis of no evidence whatsoever links Jesus to the eruption of Mount Vesuvius in 79 CE.[3] Sword-and-sandal films re-emerged alongside other Bible-related epics with yet another remake of *Quo Vadis?* in 1951 and, more prominently, *The Robe* in 1953.

The Robe was heralded with much fanfare, due to its pioneering use of CinemaScope, the earliest widescreen technology.[4] CinemaScope allowed for a much wider frame and larger scenes, with broader perspectives than had been possible with earlier technologies.[5] The wide frame also allowed for two or more characters to be on the screen at once in medium or close up range.[6] One reporter quipped that CinemaScope was the "Moses" that would lead Hollywood "out of a film wilderness."[7]

The Robe was followed by a sequel, *Demetrius and the Gladiators* (1954), and other films, such as *The Silver Chalice* (1954), *The Big Fisherman* (1959), *Barabbas* (1961), and, most famously, *Ben-Hur* (1959). For the most part, these films were adaptations of pious nineteenth- and twentieth-century novels such as *Ben-Hur: A Tale of the Christ*, by Lew Wallace (1880); *Quo Vadis: A Narrative of the Time of Nero*, by Henryk Sienkiewicz (1895); *The Robe*, by Lloyd C. Douglas (1942); *The Big Fisherman*, also by Lloyd C. Douglas (1948); and *The Silver Chalice*, by Thomas B. Costain (1952). Like other Bible epics, peplum films fell out of favor after the end of the golden era, for both financial and social reasons. Like other epics, peplum movies were far too expensive to produce. Moving to widescreen revived movie audiences for a short time but the technology was abandoned within a decade; the slide in attendance was due to fundamental problems that could not be solved by technology alone.[8] Social changes in America, such as secularization and the influx of immigrants from diverse religious and ethnic backgrounds likely contributed to a growing distaste for films that conveyed a blatantly evangelizing Christian message.

Plot summaries

This chapter will focus on four of the best-known and best-loved peplum films: *Ben-Hur* (1959), *Barabbas* (1961), *The Robe* (1953), and *Quo Vadis?* (1951), each of which tells a unique (and often convoluted) story. *Ben-Hur*, set at the time of Jesus, centers on the relationship between the wealthy Jewish merchant (and prince) Judah Ben-Hur and the Roman military tribune, Messala. Ben-Hur and Messala had been childhood friends. When Messala arrives in Jerusalem in 26 CE as the commanding officer of the Roman garrison, both attempt to rekindle their friendship. Their happy reunion is short-lived, however; their opposing political allegiances surface. At this time, Ben-Hur and his family welcome back Zaimonides, their loyal slave and assistant, and his lovely daughter Esther, from a voyage. Ben-Hur and Esther confess their love, and Ben-Hur gives Esther her freedom. The timing is unfortunate, however, as Esther is already promised to a man whom she barely knows. An unfortunate accident complicates matters further. As Valerius Gratus (the Roman governor of Judea prior to Pontius Pilate) arrives in Jerusalem, Ben-Hur's sister accidentally loosens a roof tile, which clatters to the ground, and startles Gratus' horse. Gratus is thrown to the ground. Although he survives this fall, Messala decides to prosecute. To protect his sister, Ben-Hur takes responsibility for the accident; he is sentenced to slavery in the Roman galley ships and his mother and sister are imprisoned. After numerous adventures at sea, Ben-Hur saves the life of the Consul Quintus Arrius, who adopts him as his son and arranges for his exoneration. On his way back to Judea, Ben-Hur encounters Balthasar and his host, Arab sheik Ilderim. Once home, he learns that Esther did not after all marry. He unsuccessfully attempts to secure the release of his mother and sister, who have disappeared. Enraged by Messala's actions, Ben-Hur enters the chariot race against him, driving Ilderim's chariot. Ben-Hur wins the race; Messala is trampled. Before he dies, he reveals to Ben-Hur that his mother and sister are in the Valley of the Lepers. At this point, Esther, who heard the Sermon on the Mount, begins to believe in Jesus. Ben-Hur witnesses the Crucifixion, and his mother and sister are healed miraculously.

Whereas the action in *Ben-Hur* takes place during the same period covered by the Jesus story, most other films in this category take place in the years after the crucifixion. *Barabbas* is about the criminal whom Pilate released instead of Jesus (Matt. 27:16–26; Mark 15:7–15; Luke 23:18; John 18:40). Immediately after his release, Barabbas, a real lout, returns to his friends and his lover, Rachel. During Barabbas' imprisonment, Rachel had become a follower of Christ; she is later captured and stoned to death by the priests responsible for Jesus' death. Barabbas attempts to rescue her, but fails and is tried and condemned to a Sicilian sulfur mine. After 20 hellish years, he is chained to a Christian, Sahek, who slowly brings him around to Christian faith. The two survive an earthquake and come to the attention of the local prefect's wife, Julia, who brings them back to Rome, where they train as gladiators. Sahek is executed for his Christian beliefs but Barabbas becomes the top gladiator after winning an epic battle in the arena against their trainer. Freed by Nero, Barabbas arranges for Sahek's body to be buried in the catacombs, where the local Christians worship. He emerges from the catacombs to discover that Rome is on fire; believing that this fire heralds the end of the world, he begins to set more buildings on fire. He is imprisoned and then crucified by Roman soldiers for his Christian beliefs.

The Robe also takes Jesus' crucifixion as its narrative starting point. In approximately 32 CE, the Roman tribune, Marcellus Gallio, buys the Greek slave Demetrius in an auction, outbidding Caligula, the Emperor Tiberius' great-nephew and heir. Marcellus falls in love with Tiberius' ward, Diana, whom he had known as a child. Diana, however, is promised to Caligula. Angry and embarrassed by Marcellus, Caligula arranges for him to be transferred to Jerusalem. Marcellus and Demetrius arrive in Jerusalem at the same time as Jesus makes his triumphal entry. Demetrius is impressed by Jesus; Marcellus, however, is put in charge of the detail of soldiers assigned to Jesus' crucifixion. Marcellus wins Jesus' robe in a game of dice; in the post-crucifixion downpour, Marcellus has Demetrius throw the robe on him. But far from protecting him, the robe makes Marcellus seriously ill, both physically and mentally. Demetrius grabs the robe from his suffering master and disappears. Tiberius commissions the ill Marcellus to find and destroy the robe and to gather a list of Jesus' followers, but he also frees Diana to marry Marcellus despite his fall into insanity. Marcellus arrives in Cana. There he poses as a cloth merchant, and encounters the Christian leaders Justus and Miriam, who have a powerful influence on him. He later finds Demetrius, who has also come to Cana, and demands the robe. He finds, however, that he is no longer afraid of the robe, and donning it no longer makes him ill. Marcellus believes that his cure has occurred through the power of the robe, and therefore through Christ, and he becomes a believer. He is arrested and condemned by Caligula. Diana joins him, in faith, in death, and in glorious marriage in the afterlife.

Quo Vadis? is set some decades later, in 64 CE. Marcus Vinicius, a Roman military commander, has returned from the wars and has fallen in love with a Christian former hostage, Lygia. Lygia was raised as a daughter in the household of retired general Aulus Plautius; she is intrigued by Marcus, but put off by his apparently callous nature. Nero concocts and carries out his mad scheme to burn Rome, blaming the Christians, who are not only trapped in the fire but also persecuted for their presumed role in the tragedy. Marcus attempts to save Lygia and her adoptive family, but they are captured and condemned to death in the arena. Nero's wife Poppaea, angry with Marcus for spurning her advances, forces Marcus to watch as Lygia is tied to a stake in the middle of an arena in the path of an angry wild bull. Lygia is saved by her bodyguard, the giant Ursus, who kills the bull with his bare hands. Nero reluctantly spares them all, at the urging of the crowd and the senators of Rome, and the mad emperor dies just before having the empire wrested from him by General Galba. Marcus, Lygia, and Ursus leave Rome and live happily ever after.[9]

Peplum films as epics

Like the Bible movies of the same era, peplum films are epic in length and in scope, featuring big skies, big music, big settings, and big casts. They star top Hollywood actors such as Charlton Heston (Judah Ben-Hur), Anthony Quinn (Barabbas), Richard Burton (Marcellus), Jean Simmons (Diana), and Deborah Kerr (Lygia). They also draw on famous works of art, such as Michelangelo's *The Creation of Adam* – a prominent visual and theological theme in *Ben-Hur* – his *Pietà*, which provides the model for mourning scenes in *Quo Vadis?* and the Bible illustrations of James Tissot and Gustave Doré, upon which *Ben-Hur*'s Sermon on the Mount scene is modelled.

Despite their overtly Christian content, peplum films include the requisite feasting and orgiastic dancing scenes that are a hallmark of the epic genre. As in the Old Testament films, these scenes are usually associated with pagan practices; for the sword-and-sandal films, these are entertainments hosted by the Roman emperor or other dignitaries. At the same time as these films linger on the spectacle scene, for the enjoyment of the viewing audience and the attendant box office rewards, they also convey their disapproval of such pagan frivolity. The male hero is usually an honored guest at the festivities. If he is a pagan, like Marcus (*Quo Vadis?*) the filmmakers permit him to enjoy himself while disapproval is voiced by a Christian character, such as Lygia, who is the moral center of the film. A Jew like Judah Ben-Hur is visibly uncomfortable in these pagan surroundings, as are other peplum heroes who are en route to Christian conversion. Yet the camera lingers, and thereby maximizes the entertainment value for the viewer, who may identify with the Christian critique of pagan revelry but is likely able to cope with the discomfort in order to enjoy the party.

War scenes provide another occasion for spectacle. Exhilarating scenes featuring hundreds of soldiers riding horses or driving chariots to face their enemies, accompanied by stirring military music, are a staple of this genre, as of war movies more generally.[10] Another standard feature is the gladiatorial contest, a stock scene in epic films about the Roman Empire.[11] In *Quo Vadis?* dozens of Christians are sent into the arena to fight wild animals. In *Barabbas*, the eponymous hero and his buddy are trained in a gladiatorial school and then proceed to win numerous contests against other gladiators. In *The Robe*, Marcellus buys his slave Demetrius from a market that specializes in gladiator-slaves.

Like the orgiastic and feasting scenes, the gladiatorial spectacles arouse both pleasure and disgust. This is particularly true in the long conclusion to *Quo Vadis?* The camera lingers at length on the huge Roman crowd that is practically salivating over the Christians' slaughter. While we as viewers might be repelled by their pleasure, we may nevertheless be riveted (or so the filmmakers hope) by both the gladiatorial spectacle and the crowd's enjoyment thereof. The climax comes with the torture that Poppaea has devised for Marcus, in which "the gaze" – multiple gazes – is all important. Poppaea's sadistic desire is to see the man who has spurned her witness his beloved Lygia being gored by a wild bull, a sight that will make him experience extraordinary, indeed, unbearable, distress. Because the Christians must win out in the end, however, the tables are turned. Poppaea is forced to watch as Ursus, Lygia's bodyguard, vanquishes the bull. Although the explicit message of the film concerns the power of the Christian message against the domination of a totalitarian and evil empire, and the growth of the church through conversion, the visuals provide many minutes of decidedly un-Christian entertainment.

These and other conventions of the Christian epic are marvellously spoofed in the 1981 Mel Brooks film, *History of the World Part I*. The Roman section of this film hits all the buttons: Roman excess and lasciviousness, the lavish architecture – suspiciously similar to Caesar's Palace in Las Vegas, the hilarious portrayal of the Roman emperor as pompous, effete, and despised by his wife. There is even the requisite chariot race, and the insertion of scenes from the Gospels, including, as we have seen, a Last Supper scene painted for posterity. While the segment is simply funny in the slapstick manner of 1980s comedy, it also plays upon audience familiarity with the conventions of the Christian epic genre.

Peplum films as Bible movies

Historicity and authenticity

Like the Old Testament and Jesus-movies, sword-and-sandal films use techniques such as scrolling text and voice-overs to situate their stories in time and space. *Ben-Hur* opens with a stylized map of Judea and an on-screen text dating the events to "Anno Domini" (the year of our Lord), that is, the year of Jesus' birth.[12] A "voice-of-God" narrator solemnly refers to the imperial decree requiring all to return to their places of birth for a census and taxation, and to Jerusalem as "the troubled heart of their land, the old city of Jerusalem dominated by fortress of Antonia, seat of Roman power and the temple, the outward sign of inward and unperishable faith." The story then quickly moves forward from Jesus' birth to his Passion, dated "Anno Domini 26." *Quo Vadis?* begins in Rome, in 64 AD.; a voice-over solemnly describes the setting (imperial Rome) and the era (some 30 years after the crucifixion). For this narrator, imperial Rome is the center of a corrupt empire in which "there is no escape from the whip and the sword" … except by faith in the man, who 30 years earlier, had died on a Roman cross in order "to make men free" and to "spread the gospel of love and redemption." By labelling Rome as the villains and the Christians as the heroes, the voice-over cues viewers with regard to the appropriate interpretation of and perspective on the story and its players.

The visual vocabulary of these films also emphasizes their biblical – or more specifically, the Christian – contexts and content. One element of this vocabulary is the repetitive use of Christian tokens or symbols. In *Quo Vadis?*, the token is the image of the fish, which Lygia draws in the sand during her first intense conversation with Marcellus. In *The Robe*, it is the "peplum" that Jesus wore just prior to his crucifixion, a token that Demetrius guards with love, that causes such distress for Marcellus until he comes to Christian faith himself, and that Diana has delivered to Peter. In the other films, it is a cross. In *Ben-Hur* the cross is evident in the crossbeams of the room in which Ben-Hur has his most emotional encounters with Messala, in the cruciform position that he takes when lying exhausted in the sand, and in numerous other visual moments. In *Barabbas*, the cross is etched onto a disk that initially belonged to his friend in the mines, and that he then guards after his friend dies.

Allusions to other films

The peplum films reproduce conventional scenes from other epics, principally in the Jesus-scenes that they insert into their main narratives, such as the Sermon on the Mount or the crucifixion. These movies themselves, however, also became a source of iconic scenes and images that are repeated in other films. The most famous example is the chariot race in *Ben-Hur*. Within the film's narrative, the chariot race resolves, with great tension and suspense, the ongoing conflict between Messala and Ben-Hur. Ben-Hur wins, as expected, despite the unfair, and illegal, advantage that Messala has given himself by putting spikes on the wheels of his own chariot. The race continues for some time, and is tremendously exciting (especially when viewed on a big screen and with surround sound).[13]

Romance

The sword-and-sandal films have a major advantage over the Jesus films with regard to another convention of the epic genre: romance. By foregrounding Christians rather than Christ, these films can satisfy the romantic imperative as easily as the Old Testament epics do.

In *Ben-Hur* the love between Judah and Esther is only a minor motif. But love takes center stage in the Roman films. *Quo Vadis?* features no less than three romances, and one full-blown romantic triangle. The main romance involves the Roman soldier Marcus, who falls in love at first sight with the hostage Lygia, a secret Christian. By contrasting the Romans' treatment of Lygia as a commodity that can be bought, sold or given away, with the Christians' treatment of her as a beloved daughter who has her own voice and the authority to accept or reject the advances of a potential suitor, the film establishes the superiority of Christian ethics and values as the champion of women and the liberator from slavery. In doing so, it also implies the congruence between these Christian values and America's self-presentation as a land of liberty and justice for all.

The other two romances in *Quo Vadis?* are less developed but nevertheless play an important role in establishing a perspective on romance and gender relations. The film briefly portrays the love of the Spanish slave Eunice for Marcus' uncle, the Roman senator Petronius. Petronius is initially oblivious to Eunice's feelings for him until he attempts to give her away to Marcus. Like the typical ancient Roman male (as portrayed in the peplum films), he cares only for beauty; when he orders her to be lashed for her refusal to go to Marcus, he stipulates that the punishment not damage her skin. Eunice is not deterred by her master's callousness and disregard. Instead, she summons the courage to declare her love for him. He responds, and over the course of the film, without too much fanfare, one glimpses both the love and the growing equality between them. At the end, they preside as a couple over a "last supper" with friends before their joint suicide. Petronius' change of heart does not extend to his faith; he remains an atheist pagan to the end. But he is essentially a good man, whose latent moral sensibility is revealed by the love of a good woman.

Somewhat more sinister, and even less developed, is the unrequited love of a harem woman, Acti, for the emperor Nero. Acti appears only twice, first, when she welcomes the unhappy Lygia into Nero's house, and again at the end of the film. When Nero, defeated and disgraced by his burning of Rome, is left whining in his quarters, until Acti appears and, out of love, forces him to commit suicide, the only honorable resolution to his dire situation.

Like the Old Testament movies, peplum films turn up the heat by adding a love triangle to the standard romance between a pagan and a Christian. In *Ben-Hur*, the triangle – involving Esther's off-screen fiancé – is a minor element in the story. In other films, however, the love triangle is crucial to the plot and to the film's overall emotional tenor. In *The Robe*, Caligula, the unattractive, manipulative, and vengeful nephew of the emperor Tiberius, has two desires: the empire and Diana. He acquires the first, but is denied the second when Diana falls for the handsome Marcellus. Diana tends to Marcellus throughout his long illness, and remains with him even after he becomes a Christian. In the end, both she and Marcellus become martyrs, but not before she defiantly testifies to her newfound faith before the vengeful and truly insane Caligula.

In *Quo Vadis?* the romance between Marcus and Lygia infuriates Poppaea, Nero's cunning and beautiful wife, who has her own designs on Marcus. As Lygia's erstwhile rival, Poppaea is the negative image of Lygia's Christian virtue: she is sharp-edged, exploitative, and voracious – in Marcus' words, a "spider who eats her mate." Poppaea holds no particular attraction for Marcus, who is consumed with love for Lygia, but she has the power to summon him at her whim, and, in the climactic gladiator scene, to torture him to her heart's content.

These films illustrate a common pattern. The third person in the love triangle is invariably a non-Christian, most often a pagan; he or she inevitably suffers from unrequited love as the featured couple cements their love along with their Christian faith. In most cases (*Ben-Hur* being the exception) the spurned lover does not slink away to lick her or his wounds in private; rather, the rejection becomes the impetus for public cruelty and vengeance. This representation was in keeping with the strictures of the Production Code, which stipulated that "The sanctity of the institution of marriage and the home shall be upheld." By extension, those who threatened to disturb that sanctity – or the integrity of "Christian" marriage – were to be reviled, even as the titillation that their personalities, emotions, and behaviors created could be enjoyed.[14]

The peplum Jesus

Although Jesus is not front and center in the sword-and-sandal movies, it is his life, his message, and, especially, his death, that constitute the backstory and provide the motivation for much of the action. To remind the viewer of this backstory, the films include one or more Jesus-scenes. In these scenes, the focus is not so much on Jesus as a historical figure as on his significance for those around him, and therefore, by implication, on the viewing audience. The films invite viewers to see Jesus through the eyes of their characters, and thereby to make a choice: to identify with those who reject him or those who accept him. Ironically, Jesus' face as such is rarely seen in these films. This avoidance may be due in part to satisfy the censorship requirements in the different countries in which the studios sought to distribute these films,[15] but it also allows for the gaze of the fictional characters to mediate the encounter between Jesus and the film viewer.

Ben-Hur *(1959)*

Peplum films portray Gospel events in two different ways: through dramatizations that are either woven directly into the fictional story line or are presented as flashbacks, and through the testimony of Christian characters such as Peter. *Ben-Hur* relies on both modes. The film integrates dramatizations of the Nativity, the Sermon on the Mount, and the Passion into the fictional frame by portraying the fictional characters such as Esther, Ben-Hur, and Balthasar, as witnesses to the events. Also dramatized is a fictional scene from Jesus' youth that recalls the gap-filling efforts as well as the narrative arc of the Jesus epics. As Joseph is busy at work in his Nazareth carpentry shop, the Romans are making their presence felt in the town. A customer wonders at the absence of Joseph's son: is Jesus not neglecting his work? Joseph responds: "He said to me, I must be about my father's business." The customer presses him: "So why isn't he here, working?" Joseph replies that he is indeed working. The camera cuts to a young man with flowing brown hair, seen from behind as he walks the Galilean hills, then cuts away quickly to the Romans. The camera, in combination with the dialog, implies that Jesus' work is in some, as yet unspecified, way a response to the Romans' oppression of the Galilean Jewish peasants.

The core spiritual message of the film, however, is conveyed in two dramatic scenes in which Ben-Hur meets Jesus face to face. The first occurs when Ben-Hur, now a prisoner, is on a forced march with many other prisoners, through a hot and barren desert. Exhausted and parched, the prisoners eagerly approach a well, only to be chased away by their Roman captors. A woman tries to give them water, but a Roman guard spills it before they can drink. Watching from the window of his workshop, however, is a young carpenter. As Ben-Hur prays for relief, the music suddenly changes as a hand pours water on the prisoner's face and hands. This hand touches Ben-Hur's own hand gently, then gives him water to drink, helps him sit up, and smoothes his hair. Ben-Hur gazes up at the man gratefully and drinks again. The soundtrack is completely silent. The Roman soldier attempts to intervene, but the man persists until Ben-Hur is refreshed and restored. The man then departs, exchanging a meaningful glance with Ben-Hur but alas not with the audience; his face is hidden from view, as it has been throughout the scene.

The meaning of the scene is obvious. The carpenter is Jesus, easily identified – for viewers familiar with western art and the Jesus-movies – by his long hair and flowing robe; his elevated spirituality is signalled by the changes in lighting and music that accompany his appearance. The water symbolizes the satisfaction not merely of Ben-Hur's urgent physical needs, but also of his spiritual needs (as in Jesus' encounter with the Samaritan woman by the well, in John 4; see also Mark 9:41). In splashing water on Ben-Hur's face and hands, Jesus not only cools the suffering prisoner, but also anticipates, or foreshadows, Judah's future baptism. The quiet showdown between Jesus and the Roman signifies the struggle for liberation that the young carpenter will inspire. Most potent, perhaps, is the image of the two hands touching, which replicates Michelangelo's image of the hands of God and Adam touching.

This same scene is inverted toward the end of the film. Ben-Hur watches the procession of a condemned man and recognizes him as Jesus. When Jesus collapses under the weight of the cross, Ben-Hur rushes to give him some water. Again we see their hands touching as they look into each other's eyes. Jesus bends down to drink but a Roman soldier kicks the water out of the way. Whereas Jesus could overcome Roman opposition to soothe Judah's suffering, Ben-Hur could not do the same for Jesus. This contrast that highlights Jesus' power to resist Roman opposition in order to accomplish what mere mortals, even well-meaning ones, cannot.

Jesus is present – if not fully visible – not only on camera but also through testimony from eyewitnesses about Jesus and his impact on their lives. The two most prominent witnesses are the wise man Balthasar, and the new convert, Esther. Balthasar recounts how he and the two other wise men found the child in a manger.[16] He has returned to Jerusalem in the hope that he will see the child, now a young man, again. After hearing Jesus preach of peace during his Sermon on the Mount, Esther tells Ben-Hur of her conviction that Jesus is more than a man. Ben-Hur is unconvinced by either of these witnesses. Only blood will wash this land clean, he declares. Ben-Hur is referring to the blood of warfare, but of course the words are ironic, for as the film concludes it is the blood – the death – of Jesus that will wash through the land. The magnificent rainstorm that occurs during the crucifixion scene mixes water with Jesus' blood and spreads it throughout the city. The land is cleansed, and Judah's mother and sister are healed, and, symbolically, the cleansing of the land from Roman oppression. The latter of course does not occur in a military sense; here, as in the Jesus-movies, historical constraints prevent the fulfilment of the theme of political freedom. But the spiritual impact of Jesus' blood is evident in the life of Ben-Hur, who becomes a believer. Setting aside his rationalism and skepticism, he embraces Jesus as the fulfilment of his Jewish convictions.

Similar techniques for integrating the Jesus segments into the fictional frame are evident in the other peplum films of the epic era. The movie *Barabbas*, as the name implies, responds to a gap in the Passion narrative: what happened to the bandit Barabbas after he was released by Pilate? The movie begins with the trial before Pilate, during which the crowd chooses Barabbas over Jesus. The scene affords a brief view of Jesus, dressed in a white robe, with dark hair but, as in *Ben-Hur*, his face is not visible. Other Gospel scenes include the scourging of Jesus, the release of Barabbas, the Via Dolorosa, the crucifixion, the deposition, and the discovery of the empty tomb. These scenes are often presented through the point of view of Barabbas and/or his love-interest, Rachel. As they observe the events of Jesus' Passion, we viewers, in turn, observe them observing the events even as we ourselves view them on the screen.

Jesus in other peplum films

Like *Ben-Hur*, *The Robe* weaves fictional characters into its Jesus segments. Marcellus, accompanied by Demetrius, takes up his new post in Jerusalem just at the moment of Jesus' triumphal entry. Marcellus is preoccupied, but Demetrius pays very close attention and even exchanges a lengthy and intent gaze with Jesus himself. Both master and slave are also present on the Via Dolorosa. Marcellus observes Jesus' slow and labored progress toward Golgotha with some indifference, while Demetrius enters boldly into the fray: when a Roman soldier beats Jesus for collapsing under the weight of the cross, Demetrius attacks the soldier but is beaten himself, foreshadowing the theme of Christian suffering and martyrdom that runs throughout the Christian sword-and-sandal films. The indifference of the master and the passionate engagement of the slave are most dramatic in the crucifixion scene. Demetrius watches Jesus die, at the same time as Marcellus is among the Roman soldiers squatting at the foot of the cross rolling dice for Jesus' clothing. Jesus' last words – "Father, forgive them for they know not what they do" – are heard in voice-over, for here, as in *Ben-Hur*, Jesus' face is never clearly seen. Marcellus wins the robe, which, as we have seen, causes him to fall gravely ill, until he is cured by Diana's love and his own conversion to Christian faith.

Like Ben–Hur, Marcellus not only sees Jesus but also hears about him from eyewitnesses to the carpenter's words and deeds. Marcellus travels to Cana, where, the emperor hopes, he will both recover from his illness and spy on the Christian group that is active there. One evening he stumbles upon a group of people listening as a paralyzed and blind woman, Miriam, sings about the empty tomb and the resurrection. Later Marcellus meets Miriam again. She tells him what happened to her on the evening of the wedding in Cana. Everyone in the village was invited, but she stayed home, too depressed about her own disabilities to step out of the house. When her parents returned home after the wedding, however, they found her content and smiling; Jesus had stopped in on the way to the wedding and lifted her spirits. She and the entire village, she tells Marcellus, know that he has come to spy on the Christians, but they love him and will care for him during his stay.

Marcellus' experiences in Cana mark the turning point in his journey to Christian faith and his eventual martyrdom.

Dramatization and narration are also interwoven in *Quo Vadis?* In this film, the main vehicle for the Jesus story is Peter, the "big fisherman." Peter narrates the Gospel story, the scenes, which include the call of the disciples, Peter's denial, the Passion, the resurrection appearances, and the Beatitudes, are dramatized as flashbacks. Especially moving is the denial, as it highlights the failings of Peter himself, and thereby implicitly asserts that all others, including the movie viewers, can also be forgiven.

Through these devices, the Christian sword-and-sandal epics themselves become a vehicle for the spreading of the Christian message. They do so not only by portraying familiar Gospel scenes in a familiar way but also, even more powerfully, by dramatically, at times histrionically, demonstrating the transformative effect of Christian faith on both pagans (Marcus) and Jews (Judah Ben-Hur).

Then as now

Gender

As in the Old Testament films, the portrayal of gender roles corresponds to the stereotypes (and not necessarily the reality) of the mid-twentieth century. The men are strong, upper-class, but sometimes coarse in speech and behavior; they occupy themselves with war and trade. Aside from the vengeful wives of Roman emperors, the women are refined, devoted, and steadfast; they are caretakers and healers, exercising common sense and good judgment.

Though they may be demure, peplum women are by no means easy to ignore. As in the Old Testament films, the women who are or who become believers over the course of the film constitute the moral center of the film; they bear the Christian message of love of others and often function as spokespeople for the Christian message. *The Robe*'s Diana is perhaps the most defiant, and remains so even in the face of certain death. It makes no difference, she tells the mad and vengeful Caligula, whether he believes the stories about Jesus or not. At the very least, there is no story that Jesus ever blinded or crippled anyone, as Caligula and others before him have done. "I have no wish to live another hour in an empire ruled by you," she declares. "You corrupt Rome with your spite and malice. As for me I have found another king, I want to go with my husband into his kingdom." Other women have formal leadership roles. Miriam (*The Robe*) and Rachel (*Barabbas*) are portrayed as Christian preachers and leaders. This depiction may have rung true to Protestant viewers who were aware of the role of women preachers in American Protestant churches from the eighteenth century onwards.[17]

The early conversations between the pagan hero Marcus and the demure Christian hostage Lygia in *Quo Vadis?* highlight the contrast between crass

Roman men and refined Christian women. At the same time, they stress the woman's simultaneous attraction to and yet disapproval of the tall, dark, handsome, and stereotypically sexist male. Lygia calls Marcus on his condescending line that "Lovely women should not have the time to think that deeply"; she lets Marcus know that while she is all too conscious of his physical attributes, she looks beyond the surface: "I'd be lying if I'd say I wasn't attracted by what I see; it is what I hear I don't like … Ugly stories of conquest and bloodshed." With trenchant sarcasm, she points out Marcus' own sexism. When he wishes she were a slave so that he could simply take her away, she mocks him: "What a way for a conqueror to win a woman! To buy her like an unresisting beast."

Yet like the cinematic versions of Old Testament women, Lydia is fully domesticated – brought under her husband's control – by the time the final credits roll. When the love-smitten Marcus proposes marriage by asking: "Will you give me the greatest triumph a man ever had?" she swoons: "Oh yes, Marcus." The feisty woman has been vanquished by her handsome Roman warrior.

The "other" women – like Poppaea – by contrast are associated with paganism, lasciviousness, and sadism, making them far more interesting, if also morally reprehensible from the film's Christian perspective. They are unpredictable, seductive, enticing, simultaneously repulsive and fascinating. Just as the peplum epics linger lovingly on the very spectacle scenes of which they disapprove, so too do they apparently delight in portraying the true, and delicious, depths of unbridled female passion, which, it would seem, goes hand in hand with viciousness, jealousy, and vengefulness.

In sickness and in health

Another plot motif that may reflect the mindset of the 1950s concerns psychology and mental illness. In *Quo Vadis?* Lygia analyzes Marcus' blatantly sexist and offensive language as follows: "What false security you must have in your heart and soul, in your manhood, Marcus Vinicius. What hidden scorn you must have for yourself!" In *The Robe*, Marcellus' mental and physical illness is brought on by a seizure that he experienced when he was touched by Jesus' robe. The emperor Tiberius, skeptical about the physician and soothsayer – those "men of science" who heal by the entrails of an owl – embraces the insights of "modern" medicine. Instead he suggests that finding the robe and confronting his fears will help heal Marcellus, who is haunted by the crucifixion and his own role in bringing it about. In the end, however, it is Demetrius who provides the correct diagnosis and treatment. "You think it's his robe that made you ill," he tells Marcellus, "but it's your own conscience, your own decent shame." Marcellus clutches the robe to his face, and sees that it does him no harm. The music changes abruptly, Marcellus looks up to the heavens and declares that he is not afraid. He is now a believer! His faith has made him well! Faith's healing power later saves Demetrius too. After Caligula has Demetrius tortured within an inch of his life, the doctor throws up his hands in defeat: "There are limits to what science will achieve. I can't put shattered flesh together again or restore the blood he's lost." But Marcellus prays, paraphrasing Ps. 22:1 (and thereby also Jesus, who quotes this verse in his final words according to Matt. 27:46): "Why hast thou abandoned him?" Demetrius lives. But how did Marcellus, who is not even a doctor, succeed where medicine failed? The physician accuses Marcellus of sorcery and Marcellus' own father declares him to be an enemy of Rome. But Demetrius, Diana, and we viewers know the truth: through his faith in Christ Marcellus has acquired the gift to heal as Christ did. The motif of illness and recovery thus exhibits a tension between the insights of 1950s medicine, and the belief that faith is superior to science.[18]

American identity

These films, like other Bible films, reflect the conventional discourses around race, gender, faith, and science; they also act as a vehicle for (a particular brand of) American identity. The peplum films depict Rome as the evil empire that oppresses the simple and sincere Jewish and Christian residents of Judea and Galilee as well as the small Christian enclave in Rome. Messala, the fictional Roman tribune of *Ben-Hur*, complains that the Jews refuse to pay their taxes, and that they harbour an "irrational resentment of Rome," are "drunk with religion," and despise idolatry. In his view, the Jews are an unruly people who smash the statues of the Roman gods, even those of the emperor himself. Messala knows that rebellion is in the wind, but he has faith that Rome will crush it. Ostensibly out of friendship, Messala offers to spare Ben-Hur and his family when that time comes. In exchange, however, he demands that Ben-Hur, a man of power and influence, persuade his countrymen not to revolt against Rome lest the entire people be destroyed. Ben-Hur refuses to collaborate. He will do anything for his old friend Messala except betray his own people. Rome is strangling his country, his people, and, indeed, the whole earth. But his pleas that Messala withdraw his legions and give the Jews their freedom fall on deaf ears. Ben-Hur here represents the values of loyalty and patriotism, strongly associated with American national identity.[19]

This scenario takes place near the beginning of the movie, during the first encounter between Ben-Hur and Messala, newly arrived in Judea. The scene sets the stage by filling the backstory of their childhood friendship and mutual devotion, and by setting up the political conflict that will be played out in the film, most spectacularly in the iconic chariot-race scene. To those familiar with Jewish history of the first century, the setup sounds familiar. The writings of Josephus, the first-century Jewish historian who is the major historical source for events on the era of Jesus, describe the unrest in Judea and throughout Palestine against Roman oppression and the winds of rebellion that gather strength throughout the first century, culminating in the Jewish revolt against Rome in 66–74. The revolt was crushed, the temple was destroyed, and many Jews were killed or sent into exile from Judea.

The Christian films, like the Jesus-movies, ascribe the Jews' restlessness to their longing for a messiah who will lead them, in the words of Messala's second in command, Sextus, "into some sort of anti-Roman paradise." As the emperor Tiberius comments in *The Robe*: "When it comes, this is how it will start. Some obscure martyr in some forgotten province, then madness, infecting the legions, rotting the empire. Then the finish of Rome." The greatest madness of all is humanity's desire to be free.

Whereas the Jesus-movies develop the contrast between the false expectations of Jesus as a political leader and the true knowledge of his spiritual significance, *Ben-Hur* and the other "sword-and-sandal" movies focus on the spiritual side. Their main concern – Judah Ben-Hur's Jewishness aside – is the conflict between Rome and Christianity. Even *Ben-Hur* makes this move. Although its hero eventually becomes a Christian, his conversion is seen as a triumph over Rome on the political plane, and as an affirmation rather than a rejection of his Jewish identity on the personal level. In other peplum films, the conflict is resolved not in battle or in a chariot race but in the arena. Whereas the Romans have the power to kill these Christian "rebels," their ostensible victory means eternal life and therefore ultimate victory for the Christians, who, in dying for their faith, show that they, unlike the Romans, live for something beyond their own mundane pleasures.

Like other Bible movies, the sword-and-sandal films create a transparent analogy between their ancient stories and the major political conflicts of the mid-twentieth century. These films were made during the decades immediately following the Second World War. The use of the eagle to represent Rome, while historical, also called to mind Mussolini's Italy, in which the dream of Imperial Rome was revived, as well as the Nazi regime with which Mussolini aligned himself. Americans could resonate with a message of the importance – national, political, and spiritual – of dying for a cause greater than oneself, to sacrifice oneself for the cause of freedom and democracy. The scenes in which Roman tribunes, such as Marcellus, go off to war and must part sorrowfully from their loved ones, would have been familiar to many families. This was also, as we have noted, the era of the Cold War, when the possibility of nuclear war with the Soviet Union hung in the air. The idea of fighting for liberation from a godless, imperialistic, and totalitarian regime, as represented by Rome, would have appealed both in terms of the war that had just been won and the struggle that many feared would come very soon. At the same time, American society in the 1950s was still publically Christian. It was possible to identify American values as Christian values. The superiority of democracy over both atheism and communism would have been axiomatic, and the willingness of Christians to die for their faith both admirable and motivating.[20]

Anti-communism, atheism, and idolatry

These movies explicitly pit Christianity, Christian beliefs, and Christian values against the idolatry and atheism of the pagan Roman empire. The polytheism of the Roman state is stressed in the gladiator scenes in *Quo Vadis?* which open with a prayer intoned by the priestess: "Gods of Rome, mighty, eternal, beneath whose auspices Rome rules the world. Hear us, we worship you ... Venus, Goddess of Love, Mars, God of War, Juno, goddess of heaven; Jupiter father of the gods, and Nero, his divine son." The idea that Nero was the divine son of Jupiter is ridiculed throughout the film. His portrayal as a ridiculous, self-centered madman and fop, despised and pitied by his entire entourage makes the point effectively enough: this man surely can be no god.

Nero and Caligula are portrayed as buffoons; they may be "bad guys" but they provide much-needed comic relief in these overly earnest spectacles. Also important are the less flamboyant, more moderate, and rather sympathetic Roman characters, who, like the old Pharaoh in DeMille's 1956 version of *The Ten Commandments*, articulate a rationalistic worldview that would have been quite at home in twentieth-century America. In *The Robe*, for example, Marcellus' father articulates a set of individualistic values – Roman values – that he hopes his son will remember when he is in Jerusalem: "Take nothing on faith. Bind yourself to no man; above all, be a Roman, my son, and be a man of honour." These men are misguided but well-meaning.

Other figures take a stand against faith itself, by expressing skepticism about the God of Israel, and Jesus, but also about the Roman gods. During a naval battle in which he and others are shipwrecked, Ben-Hur – now known only by his slave number, 41 – believes that he "will be saved by the God of my fathers." The commander contradicts him: "Your god has forsaken you, he has no more power than the images I pray to. My gods will not help me, your god will not help you. But I might ... Does that interest you, 41?" This expresses succinctly the contrast between the secular Roman viewpoint and the faithful "Jewish" response to disaster.

In *The Robe* the still-pagan Diana is similarly skeptical. She gets angry and upset when Marcellus goes off to try to save Demetrius. Her love should mean more to him than his faith! "Marcellus, what you've told me is a beautiful story, but it isn't true. Justice and charity, men will never accept such a philosophy. The world isn't like that, it never has been and it never will be." On this basis she also questions his altruism: "Why must you throw your life away for a slave?" Though she is presented sympathetically, as a Roman she is oblivious to the values of freedom and equality that motivate Marcellus after his conversion. Diana is so in love with Marcellus that she is willing to tolerate his devotion to his God even if she does not (yet) see Christian faith as a reasonable option: "I want to be your wife whatever you believe. I'd marry you if I had to share you with a thousand gods." Of course, Marcellus is asking her to share him with just one, but that one is probably more demanding than the many gods of the Roman pantheon, at least from the point of view of these atheistic upper-class Hollywood Romans. Similarly, Marcus, in *Quo Vadis?*, is nearly ready to tolerate Lygia's faith in order to be with her, but his inability to take Christianity seriously scuttles his chances as he begins to mock her faith. He calls Peter "a childish old man speaking in riddles" but declares to Lygia: "I'm willing to accept your God if it makes you happier." In offering to put up a special pedestal for her Christ, he mocks her faith in an unseen God: "There is such an army of gods these days we can always find room for another." For her part, Lygia does not ask for his conversion as a condition of marriage, but she hopes for it.

These statements express the rationalism, individualism, and independence of mind often associated with America and Americans, but they echo ironically in these films, which urge their viewers to take everything on faith, and to bind themselves to Christ and to other Christians. At the same time, in their mid-twentieth-century context, these films, like DeMille's 1956 *The Ten Commandments*, are a weapon, if an indirect one, in America's fight against communism and its supposed supporters in America and within the Hollywood studio system itself.

Judaism, anti-Judaism, Holocaust, state of Israel

For the most part, peplum heroes are either Roman or unidentified – even Barabbas, who logically must have been Jewish, is not directly presented as such. The notable exception is Judah Ben-Hur; his Jewish identity as well as that of his family and his beloved Esther is central to the plot. Indeed, it is his Jewish religious and political perspective that provides the context for his conflict with his former best friend, the Roman Messala. Ben-Hur presents Jews as obeying the will of Caesar but clinging proudly to their ancient heritage, including the hope of a redeemer who would bring them to salvation. Messala acknowledges that the country belonged to the Jews before it belonged to Rome – a statement that would affirm the Jewish right to a homeland in Israel in the years immediately after the creation of the state of Israel in 1948 – but insists on the Jews' capitulation to Roman authority.

Ben-Hur is an observant Jew: he and his family engage in familiar Jewish rituals such as washing their hands and then blessing the bread before commencing a meal, and touching the mezuzah on the doorpost when entering or leaving the house. The Star of David on the door of the house, although anachronistic, also signals Jewish identity, particularly to a mid-twentieth-century audience familiar with the symbol as used in American synagogue architecture.[21] In the chariot race, Ben-Hur wears blue and white, the colours of the Israeli flag.

Ben-Hur implicitly acknowledges not only the creation of the state of Israel but also the Holocaust. The invisible narrator opens with an account of

Judean suffering under Roman rule, including the decree requiring Judeans to register and be taxed in their birthplace. He continues:

> The converging ways of many of them led to the gates of their capital city Jerusalem, the troubled heart of their land. The whole city was dominated by the fortress of Antonia, the seat of Roman power, and by the great golden Temple, the outward sign of an inward and imperishable faith. Even while they obeyed the will of Caesar, the people clung proudly to their ancient heritage, always remembering the promise of their prophets that one day there would be born among them a redeemer to bring them salvation and perfect freedom.

As these words are being intoned, we see Jews obediently lining up to register in Bethlehem under the watchful eyes of Roman soldiers. While not quite as sinister as the film footage of Jews being herded into the ghettoes during the Nazi regime, the sense of powerlessness and oppression is unmistakable. At the same time, the film conveys a subtle supersessionism, by suggesting that Jesus is the answer to the Jews' longing for a redeemer and that Judah was not happy or complete until he became a believer in Christ.

Most peplum films, however, focus very little on Judaism as such. Perhaps for this reason, they exhibit little outright antisemitism. Unlike the Jesus-movies, the sword-and-sandal movies do not have to engage with the tricky historical and theological questions concerning the role of the Jewish authorities or the Jewish crowds, in the events leading up to Jesus' crucifixion. Although they do depict the Passion and crucifixion, these films sidestep the Jewish question by presenting the Romans as the main villains of the piece, both with respect to Jesus' death and also the persecution of his followers. None dramatizes the trial before the high priest, which is so prominent in many of the Jesus-movies. Of the movies we are focusing on, only Barabbas refers to the Jewish priests as bearing some responsibility for Jesus' death; in this film, these same priests also order the stoning death of Rachel. Barabbas fights them, and as punishment is sent to the mines by Romans. Indeed, in these films it is Christians who are persecuted, hounded, and sent to the lions. For this reason they must celebrate secretly instead of out in the open. The need for secrecy is portrayed most explicitly in *Quo Vadis?* in which Marcellus, while in Cana, comes across a secret enclave of Christians praying and singing a version of the Mass, as the apostle Paul baptizes new believers "in the name of the Father, the Son, and the Holy Ghost."[22]

Secrecy to avoid persecution is also implied in *The Robe*, which features a similar scene of Christian worship, this time involving a large group of Christians who are listening to the beautiful and pious Miriam sing the Passion story, primarily based on Matthew, while accompanying herself on a harp. Nevertheless, this film does contain one disturbing note. While in Cana, pretending to be a fabric merchant, Marcellus is assisted by a man who

describes himself as a "poor Syrian guide." He looks the part, with an elaborate outfit and turban typical of the ancient Arabs, Hollywood-style. Yet he
has a vaguely Eastern European accent and the way he handles the fabric calls
to mind the stereotypical Eastern European Jewish immigrant in the
"shmatte" (rag) business in the Lower East Side of New York in the early
twentieth century. The figure is somewhat sleazy, dishonest, and self-serving;
the combination of his "Syrian" appearance and his "Jewish" accent carries
just a whiff of both anti-Arab and antisemitic sentiment.

On the other hand, *Ben-Hur* presents not only Jews but also Arabs in a
positive way. The main exemplar is the sheikh whose horses Ben-Hur drives
in the chariot race against Messala. The sheikh is a warm, open-minded, and
intelligent man who extends unconditional friendship to this Jew and takes
offence at slurs against either Arabs or Jews. This attitude emerges when he
enters an upper-class bathhouse to seek bets on the upcoming chariot race.
The men are stunned to hear that Ben-Hur will drive the sheikh's chariot. He
cajoles them, "Would no one back the noble tribune against a Jew, a galley
slave?" One man finally gives him odds of four to one in favour of Messala:
"four to one: the difference between a Roman and a Jew, or an Arab." The
sheikh and his men recognize the racism, but feign amusement: "Bravely
spoken," comments the sheikh. When Ben-Hur enters the race, the sheikh
pins a large Star of David to his robe: "The Star of David will shine out for
your people and my people together and blind the eyes of Rome." In
focusing on the friendship and trust between them, the film portrays Arabs
and Jews as capable of friendship with each other, and allies against the
evil Roman empire and all totalitarian governments since that time. This
portrait expresses optimism for Arab-Jewish co-existence in the modern
Middle East.

Christian faith

Like the Old Testament movies, the peplum films do not address matters of
biblical law to any great extent, with the exception of the Ten Commandments. Given the central role that conflict and violence play in this genre, it is
not surprising that the principal legal precept addressed in this subgenre is
"Thou shalt not kill." Restraint is illustrated in both *Barabbas* and *The Robe*, in
which the protagonist wins a contest against a Roman and therefore has the
possibility of killing him but elects not to do so.

The core Christian belief, however, is the message that in dying, Jesus took
the sins of the world upon himself (John 1:29). As Ben-Hur watches the
crucifixion, he says to Balthasar: "He gave me water and a heart to live; what
has he done to merit this?" Balthasar responds: "He has taken the world of
our sins onto himself; to this end he said he was born, in that stable where I
first saw him. For this cause he came into the world." Belief in the afterlife is
also expressed by Esther, who tells Ben-Hur that if his mother and sister could
meet Jesus, they would know that death is nothing to fear for one who has

faith. *Barabbas'* Rachel, the preacher, describes a new world in which pain and sorrow will be buried, when the Son of God has risen from the God and the world has become his kingdom. Ben-Hur uses Christian resurrection language when he promises Messala that while his people are now subjugated by Rome, "we will rise again." While Ben-Hur may be talking politics, the conversion motif in the film suggests a second level of meaning, as an allusion to bodily resurrection.

In *Quo Vadis?* Peter also articulates the Christian belief in the afterlife and the importance of martyrdom when he prays before the Roman crowds with and for the Christian martyrs before their death in the arena:

> Peace to the martyrs ... Take thy children, Lord, numb their wounds ... Blessed are you my children who die in the name of Jesus, I say to you that this day you shall be with him in paradise. Here where Nero rules today Christ shall rule forever.

These movies are also in the end constrained by history; as they are set in the early centuries of the common era, they cannot posit an end to empire which did not happen for many centuries, or for the full acceptance of Christians, which did not happen until the early fourth century with the Christianization of the Roman empire under Constantine. Nevertheless, they perpetuate the belief that in one way or another, Christian faith is a prelude to the salvation of the individual and liberation for all.

Christian morality

The Christian characters in these films model Christian ethics and morality. One important principle, it seems, is ethical business practice. In *The Robe*, the Christian leader Justus requires the good Christian denizens of Cana to return the excess money they received from Marcellus for the purchase of their cloth. Charity is evident when the young Christian boy Jonathan gives his donkey away to a less fortunate boy. In the same film, the apostle Paul speaks out against slavery – "you can't buy human beings", Paul tells Lygia, a stand that he does not take in his canonical letters.[23]

But perhaps the most prominent Christian principle in the peplum films is the love commandment. In *Ben-Hur*, Esther worries about Judah's desire for revenge against Messala for the pain that he has caused his family. She tells him that she has seen what hatred can do close up, for her father is burned up with it. But, she tells Judah, "I have heard of a young rabbi who says that forgiveness is great and love more powerful than hatred." Later Esther marvels that Jesus' voice "travelled with such a still purpose" as he gave his great Sermon on the Mount. Surely he is more than a mere mortal man.

The love theme is echoed by Rachel in *Barabbas*. Rachel describes to Barabbas what she saw at the empty tomb. Barabbas mocks her; his eyes see only real things. But Rachel persists: "He said: love one another." Barabbas laughs with derision: "And they crucified him for that?" In *The Robe*, Miriam expands upon this theme:

> He was no sorcerer, Marcellus. He cast no spells; he only asked two things of us: love God, he said, and love you one another. And he meant not only the Jews, but the Romans, the Greeks, the slaves and soldiers, the strong and the weak, everyone, he asked us to build our lives on this love, this charity, to build a new world.

The disbelief of the Roman characters serves only to underscore the love commandment. Marcus calls Demetrius "a whining beggar for God" and wonders: "What sort of love is it that acknowledges a force greater than itself?" Poppaea in *Quo Vadis?* accuses Petronius of being a Christian; he denies it on these grounds: "I have heard that the Christians teach you to love your neighbour, and as I see what men are, I cannot for the life of me love my fellow man."

Along with love comes forgiveness. The most dramatic expression of this value appears in *The Robe*, in which Peter and Marcellus compete for the dubious "honor" of being the one who has committed the most egregious sin against Jesus. Which is worse, denying Jesus, as Peter did, or crucifying him, as Marcellus did? In either case, however, God's forgiveness is assured. As Peter told Marcellus, when the latter asked him for forgiveness, "He forgave you from the cross. Can I do less?" Peter's forgiveness allows Marcellus to take the final step toward conversion; he offers Jesus his sword, his fortune, and his life, pledging on his honor as a Roman. The message: contrary to the views of Caligula, Christian identity is fully compatible with loyalty to the Empire.

As these examples show, the peplum films focus on a number of central moral precepts that are widely thought to have originated with Jesus himself. In doing so, they also claim that their heroes represent a Christianity that is in direct continuity with Christ's own teachings. Insofar as these heroes also represent contemporary America, the implicit but quite perceptible message is that America too, as a Christian country, is built on the values and principles articulated by Jesus himself.[24]

Conversion

Conversion is the central theme that runs through both the political and the romantic plot lines of these films. In each case, the protagonist, whether Jewish, as in *Ben-Hur* and *Barabbas*, or Roman, as in *The Robe* and *Quo Vadis?* becomes a Christian. Ben-Hur converts after witnessing the healing power of Jesus for himself and his family, experiences that are reinforced by the testimony of his beloved Esther. In *The Robe*, Marcellus converts after his encounters with Miriam, and by the end is joined by his true love Diana. Barabbas, the bandit saved from crucifixion by the crowds who want Jesus' blood, is influenced both by his lover Rachel and his prison friend. In *Quo Vadis?* Marcus converts out of love for Lygia and growing contempt for the Roman emperor Nero. This theme seems specific to these Christian films, but in fact is quite similar to the Old Testament epics, in which the good-hearted pagan woman (Ruth the Moabite; the Queen of Sheba) takes on the religious beliefs of her lover and rejects the cynicism and idolatry of the nation into which she was born.

In the peplum films, of course, none of the characters, with the exception of young children, such as Jonathan of Cana who is a minor character in *The Robe*, is born Christian. This is not surprising, as the films are all set in the first century CE. The narratives therefore illustrate Paul's directives on mixed marriages between Gentile believers and Gentile non-believers:

> If any believer has a wife who is an unbeliever, and she consents to live with him, he should not divorce her. And if any woman has a husband who is an unbeliever, and he consents to live with her, she should not divorce him. For the unbelieving husband is made holy through his wife, and the unbelieving wife is made holy through her husband. Otherwise, your children would be unclean, but as it is, they are holy.
>
> (1 Cor. 7:12–17)

In the movies, at least, Christian lovers always manage to save their beloved, from idolatry if not from death in the arena.

Conversion is not a peripheral but an essential ingredient of the narratives in these peplum films. This much is clear from the sequel to *The Robe*, a 1954 film called *Demetrius and the Gladiators*. In *The Robe*, Demetrius, Marcellus' slave, becomes a believer the moment he locks eyes with Jesus during the triumphal entry, and the film derives much of its power and drama from the contrast between the pagan tribune and the Christian slave. In the sequel, however, Demetrius loses his faith when his lover Lucia apparently dies, and he finds it again when she awakes from her coma. In order for the sequel to "work," the Christian hero must unconvert, so that he may convert again.

In most films of this genre, the resolution of the romantic, the religious and the political plot lines occurs with the martyrdom of the Christian protagonists. *Ben-Hur* is the exception to this pattern, due, perhaps to the fact that it concludes around the time of the crucifixion, some decades before the first organized Roman persecutions of Christians. Whether by firing squad (bow and arrow; *The Robe*), crucifixion (*Barabbas*), or in the arena (*Quo Vadis?*), the films provide the opportunity for Christian heroes to make speeches about their faith to one another and to their persecutors.

The Robe is the most dramatic in this regard. Caligula, incensed at Diana's rejection of his love, orders her to sit at his side as if she were his wife, and summons Marcellus. He commands Marcellus to bow down and pledge allegiance to him, which Marcellus is prepared to do, until Caligula specifies that this pledge also entails an act of public devotion to the gods of Rome. This

Marcellus cannot do. Caligula urges the assembly to judge the tribune accordingly, as someone who has committed treason. At this point Diana speaks up: the only man she cares to sit beside is Marcellus. Her ensuing speech summarizes the film's critique of secularism and authoritarianism and declares that killing Jesus was the greatest mistake Rome ever made. As she and Marcellus walk slowly away from Caligula, the music turns from ominous and ponderous to joyful, transforming the finality of death to the glory of eternal life in the everlasting kingdom of God. As martyrs, Diana and Marcellus are also bride and groom, as Diana's white garments and festive hairdo confirm.

Christianity as a global power

These films prophecy the eventual triumph of Christianity. Although Christianity is a persecuted sect during the Roman period, it will soon enough become a world power, and remain that way. The Romans in these films dismiss Christianity as a small, secretive, and marginal group. In *Barabbas*, the preacher Rachel is warned not to speak too openly about the Christian message. "You better mind what you say. Don't you know what can happen to you if they hear you? Anybody now caught spreading such stories, the Son of God, the messiah and such, is to be judged an enemy of the state and stoned until he's dead." In this reference to the curtailment of freedom of speech, the Cold War context may also be discerned.

Secrecy is also a major theme in *Quo Vadis?* Upon learning that the beautiful Lygia is a Christian, Marcus comments: "Christians. Are they the ones who worship some dead carpenter? ... a rebel against the state, a Jew called ..." His uncle Petronius finishes: "Christ. Crucified in Palestine, as I remember. The sect's a secret one, it consists of Jews, Greeks, and many others, who meet in secret and spread their superstitions among the Romans."

After Nero has burned the city and contrived to blame the Christians for this disaster, Petronius asks him to consider carefully whether this is the right move. Petronius represents the moderate and respectable side of the Roman Empire that expresses the values of moderation, compassion, and secularity:

> Pause, Nero, before you sign this decree. Rome has given the world justice and order. Sign that and Roman justice will receive a blow from which it may never recover. Condemn these Christians and you make martyrs of them and ensure their immortality. Condemn them and in the eyes of history you condemn yourself.

Petronius' prophecy comes to pass. Nero, however, does not understand the true significance of the events at hand, nor does he comprehend the wisdom of Petronius' counsel. He predicts that "when I have finished with these Christians, Petronius, history will not be sure that they ever existed."

The irony is obvious; as all viewers would know, Christianity did anything but disappear. Indeed, the spectacular success of Christianity is proven by the very existence of this movie in the mid-twentieth century and of audiences interested in watching it.

Notes

1 For a brief account of both terms, see Michael G. Cornelius, "Introduction," in *Of Muscles and Men: Essays on the Sword and Sandal Film*, ed. M. G. Cornelius (Jefferson, NC: McFarland & Company, Inc., Publishers, 2011), 2–4.
2 For a history of this Italian genre, see Peter E. Bondanella, *A History of Italian Cinema* (New York: Continuum International Pub. Group, 2009), 159–79.
3 For discussion, see Hirsch, *The Hollywood Epic*, 21.
4 Wyke, *Projecting the Past*, 29–31.
5 Keith M. Johnston, *Coming Soon: Film Trailers and the Selling of Hollywood Technology* (Jefferson, NC: McFarland, 2009), 49–58.
6 Lev, *Transforming the Screen*, 107–26.
7 Ibid., 118.
8 Hall, *Epics, Spectacles, and Blockbusters*, 158.
9 Peter plays a major role in the film. Indeed, the title comes from the Latin for "Where are you going?" The phrase appears in John 13:36, as the question that Peter asks Jesus at the Last Supper, but the film, and the book from which it is adapted, refers more directly to the tradition based on the apocryphal Acts of Peter (Vercelli Acts XXXV), in which Peter meets the crucified Lord as Peter is escaping Rome. Peter asks Jesus "Quo Vadis?" to which Jesus replies, "I am going to Rome to be crucified again." Peter then returns to Rome, continues his ministry, and meets his fate, much as portrayed in the film. www.earlychristianwritings.com/text/actspeter.html (accessed 10 May 2013).
10 On war movies as spectacle, see Hall, *Epics, Spectacles, and Blockbusters*, 58–61.
11 Solomon, *The Ancient World in the Cinema*, 34–72. This convention is shared with other gladiator movies, however, from *Spartacus* (1960) to *Gladiator* (2000) that are not directly connected with the Bible but which do portray the punishment of anti-Roman rebels in the arena.
12 This is a notional, rather than historical, birthday. Most scholars believe that Jesus was actually born between 6 and 4 BCE, based on an assumption that the Gospels of Matthew and Luke are correct in stating that Herod the Great was still alive at the time of Jesus' birth. Herod died in 4 BCE. Craig Blomberg, *Jesus and the Gospels: An Introduction and Survey* (Nashville, TN: Broadman & Holman, 1997), 222.
13 The rumor that a stunt man died in the making of the chariot race is apparently false. www.snopes.com/movies/films/benhur.asp (accessed 10 May 2013).
14 http://productioncode.dhwritings.com/multipleframes_productioncode.php (accessed 10 May 2013). On the censoring of sexuality in the Production Code, see Marybeth Hamilton, "Goodness Had Nothing To Do With It: Censoring Mae West," in *Movie Censorship and American Culture*, ed. Francis G. Couvares (Washington, WA: Smithsonian Institution Press, 1996), 187–211.
15 The full text of the Code is available in the appendix to Leonard J. Leff and Jerold Simmons, *The Dame in the Kimono: Hollywood, Censorship, and the Production Code from the 1920s to the 1960s* (New York: Grove Weidenfeld, 1990), 283–92, and at http://productioncode.dhwritings.com/multipleframes_productioncode.php (accessed 10 May 2013).
16 Usually Balthasar is portrayed as African but this is not the case in *Ben-Hur*. See Mario Valdes, "The Black Wiseman in European Symbolism," *Journal of African Civilizations* 3, no. 1 (1981): 67–85.

17 For a comprehensive history of women in Protestant movements in North America, see Rosemary Skinner Keller, Rosemary Radford Ruether, and Marie Cantlon, *Encyclopedia of Women and Religion in North America*, vol. 1 (Bloomington, IN: Indiana University Press, 2006), 221–505.

18 See John C. Burnham, "American Medicine's Golden Age: What Happened to it?," in *Sickness and Health in America: Readings in the History of Medicine and Public Health*, ed. Judith Walzer Leavitt and Ronald L. Numbers (Madison, WI: University of Wisconsin Press, 1978), 284–94. Burnham identifies the early to mid-1950s as the period when it became more acceptable to criticize medicine, which until the early 1950s had been in a "golden age" of prestige and status. For a general consideration of the cinematic portrayal of the medical profession, see Brian Glasser, *Medicinema: Doctors in Films* (Oxford; New York: Radcliffe Pub., 2010).

19 On the role of loyalty and patriotism in American identity, see Cecilia Elizabeth O'Leary, *To Die For: The Paradox of American Patriotism* (Princeton, NJ: Princeton University Press, 1999); McKenna, *The Puritan Origins of American Patriotism*.

20 On the role of religion and movies in the American struggle against communism, see Herzog, *The Spiritual-Industrial Complex*.

21 Although the Star of David appears in other eras, it became a ubiquitous symbol of Judaism in the nineteenth century and was used for the first time in Baltimore, in the stained glass window above the Torah ark in the Baltimore Hebrew Congregation's Lloyd Street synagogue (1845). See Henry Stolzman, Tami Hausman, and Daniel Stolzman, *Synagogue Architecture in America: Faith, Spirit and Identity* (Mulgrave, Vic.; Woodbridge, VA: Images; ACC Distribution, 2004), 28, 41.

22 As in the Old Testament films, such as *David and Bathsheba*, anachronistic rituals and prayers are included to create an aura of sanctity and authenticity. The origins of the Catholic Mass, while ancient, are likely no earlier than the fifth or sixth century CE, some four centuries later than the historical setting of this fictional film. Michael Kunzler, *The Church's Liturgy* (London; New York: Continuum, 2001), 182.

23 Paul's attitude to slavery remains a controversial question. For a variety of views, see John Byron, *Recent Research on Paul and Slavery*, Recent Research in Biblical Studies (Sheffield: Sheffield Phoenix Press, 2008). Richard A. Horsley, "Paul and Slavery: A Critical Alternative to Recent Readings," *Semeia* 83–84 (1998): 153–200.

24 On the historicity of the love commandment, see Meier, *A Marginal Jew*, 478–321. On America as a Christian country, see John Fea, *Was America Founded as a Christian Nation? A Historical Introduction* (Louisville, KY: Westminster John Knox Press, 2011).

5 "What would Jesus do?"

Epic and allegory

In 1922, after the critics panned his latest film, *Adam's Rib*, Cecil B. DeMille made an unusual decision: to ask his audiences to come up with an idea for his next film. Prizes were sponsored by *The Los Angeles Times*; first prize was $1,000. DeMille commented:

> The letters came from men and women of every station, creed, and trade. They ranged in subject matter from the most sacred to the most profane, and in value from the most ridiculous to the sublime. I was struck by the number that suggested a religious theme; and there was one that, for both subject matter and power of expression, kept surviving every winnowing process devised by the editors and kept coming back again and again to my mind. It was not from a professional writer. It was from a manufacturer of lubricating oil in Lansing, Michigan. His name was F. C. Nelson, and this is the beginning of the one page he wrote: "You cannot break the Ten Commandments – they will break you."[1]

Bible movie conventions revisited

Mr. Nelson unwittingly had put his finger on the most salient convention of the epic Bible movie: the analogy between then and now. Hence they tend to reinforce the status quo when it comes to gender, race, and class, but they also confront the perceived threat of the day – communism. Bible movies, like all films set in the past (and perhaps also in the future) express the norms as well as the anxieties of the time in which they are made, even as they often also speak to the concerns of the filmmakers themselves.

Bible movies, as we have seen, share other recognizable conventions. Some of these conventions – the grand settings, music, casts, and spectacles – are common to the epic genre as such. The scope and scale of these films befit their grand subject matter, and their grandiose box office expectations. The conventions that tie these movies to their biblical sources, however, are specific to the Bible movie genre.

These latter conventions fall into four broad categories. The first is comprised of visual depictions of the Bible or aspects thereof, including scrolls, fonts, and the use of Hebrew on the screen. These visual references may evoke the language and appearance of what we take to be ancient Bibles (Hebrew scrolls) but more often they recall the language of the iconic King James Version and the fonts associated with large, venerable family Bibles. In some films the two are mixed, so that an English font is given a Hebraic flourish. The second category includes all manner of quotation and allusion, from the titles of the films, which refer to biblical characters (*David and Bathsheba*), narratives (*The Story of Ruth*) or concepts (*The Ten Commandments*), to the dialog, some of it taken directly or indirectly from the Bible. Third, and perhaps most decisive, is the fact that Bible movies take their main plot and characters from their biblical sources; in doing so, they continue a genre of storytelling – the rewritten Bible – that is almost as ancient as the Bible itself.[2] Although the Old Testament movies are based on a range of stories chosen for their centrality to Christianity and/or Judaism (the Jesus story, or the Exodus) or their amenability to the Hollywood penchant for romance and war, their overall plot structure shows considerable uniformity: a small God-fearing nation is threatened or oppressed by a large godless power and succeeds, with God's help and against all odds. Finally, the movies' use of the Bible is filtered through the long history of biblical representation in other art forms (literature, music, painting, sculpture), and through Christian theology. Even films about the Old Testament are fundamentally Christian in nature.

In all of these films, the Bible is central to the messages that are being conveyed, whether overtly or covertly. First, the films assert that the social and political views they espouse are grounded in the Bible and therefore in accordance with God's own will and worldview. In this genre, the Bible, and therefore also God, are on the side of America, and of romantic love; and these movies come down forcefully in favor of monotheism and faith, capitalism and democracy, and in opposition to atheism, rationalism, communism, and autocracy. Second, the films promote a particular set of values and theological beliefs, the most important of which is theodicy. As in the biblical book of Deuteronomy, God punishes rebellion and disobedience and rewards the faithful and obedient. God is merciful, however, and restores good fortune to those who repent sincerely. So, for example, in *David and Bathsheba* the land of Israel is parched as punishment for David's sins and his mocking of miracles. As he finally turns to God in sincere prayer, the rains fall and the fortunes of his land and his kingship are restored. In *Solomon and Sheba*, the seductive idolatress sheds her bad reputation when she turns to God, casts away her false gods, and prays for Solomon's deliverance. God answers her prayers, and even restores her to life after she is stoned nearly to death.

The point that unifies these conventions, and the Bible film genre as a whole, is the use of the Bible to impart thematic depth to the film, that is, to assert that the meaning of the film goes beyond entertainment, the simple telling of a compelling story, or the titillation created by sexual innuendo and the semi-nudity of the orgiastic spectacle scenes. No, these movies are about the central narratives of Christianity and Judaism (but especially Christianity), the relationship between the individual and God, the nation and the cosmos, God's working in the world, and the promise of salvation.

This thematic depth, in most cases, is deeply entwined with the "then as now" element that is evident in just about every Bible epic. In the epics, the "now" part of the equation is evident in the characters' accents and appearance, in the language, and even in the plot structure, as in, for example, the Jewish Ben-Hur's friendship with the sheikh. Other films, however, make the analogy directly by juxtaposing the ancient story with a modern one, thereby demonstrating that Mr. Nelson's view about the ongoing relevance of the Ten Commandments holds true for filmmakers, and many moviegoers.

Side-by-side juxtaposition

The Ten Commandments *(1923)*

Plot summary

Cecil B. DeMille's 1923 film, *The Ten Commandments*, made as a result of Mr. Nelson's suggestion, represents a simple juxtaposition technique: he tells the biblical story, then tells a modern one that picks up on the themes, language, and character types of the scriptural tale.

In telling his double tale, DeMille followed in the footsteps of another silent movie giant, D. W. Griffith, whose 1916 film *Intolerance: Love's Struggle through the Ages* was the first film of truly monumental proportions.

Both of these movies dramatize a biblical story – the Gospel story in the case of *Intolerance*, and the Exodus story in the case of DeMille's silent *The Ten Commandments*. And in both films, the biblical stories are dramatized in the typical silent manner: with the use of tableaux that recall the biblical illustrations of Tissot and Doré, and intertitles of direct quotations from the biblical story or explanations of plot and character. These intertitles create continuity and allow the viewer to follow the narrative. Finally, both feature a modern story (in the case of DeMille's film), or a modern story plus two historical narratives (in the case of Griffith's film) that are placed alongside the biblical story and dramatized so as to highlight the parallels between then and now.

Then: the biblical prolog

In contrast to Griffith, DeMille does not intercut his two narratives, but places them side-by-side. The biblical story is dramatized in a lengthy prolog that opens with a scrolling text that relates the Exodus story to the contemporary situation in the aftermath of the First World War and expresses the theme of the film.

> Our modern world defined God as a "religious complex" and laughed at the Ten Commandments as OLD FASHIONED. Then, through the

laughter, came the shattering thunder of the World War. And now a blood-drenched, bitter world – no longer laughing – cries for a way out.

There is but one way out. It existed before it was engraven on Tablets of Stone. It will exist when stone has crumbled. The Ten Commandments are not rules to obey as a personal favor to God. They are the fundamental principles without which mankind cannot live together.

They are not laws, they are the LAW.

The statement portrays the early twentieth century as a secular era in which humankind mocked both God and religion. Now in the aftermath of war, DeMille proposes the Ten Commandments, or rather, the fundamental religious principles which predated them, as the "way out" of this Godless state of affairs.

The next intertitle moves the viewer into the Exodus story by quoting Exodus 1:13–14: "And the Egyptians made the children of Israel serve with rigour. And they made their lives bitter with hard bondage, in mortar and in brick, and in all manner of service in the field." The opening scenes show the Israelite slaves toiling under their burden, then introduce Moses' sister Miriam as she prays to God for help, after which Moses appears on the screen and pleads with the Pharaoh for the Israelites' release. The juxtaposition of these scenes implies that Moses is God's answer to Miriam's prayer. Omitted are Moses' birth, his trip down the Nile in a waterproof basket, and his childhood, indeed, all the gaps that DeMille's 1956 movie focused on in such detail. Also omitted are his escape from Egypt to Midian, his marriage to Zipporah, and the Burning Bush in which God revealed his identity and his purpose for Moses.

Indeed, this silent version has only a few similarities to the 1956 version. Early in the film, an overbearing Egyptian slave driver refreshes himself with the water intended for the slaves, brought to them by the young and beautiful Israelite woman Miriam. This scene is similar to a segment in the 1956 film in which the Hebrew slave driver Dathan harasses and then kidnaps Joshua's love interest, Lilia, as she is bringing water for the thirsty slaves. For the most part, the 1923 film resembles other biblical movies of the early silent era, such as *From the Manger to the Cross*, presenting a series of living tableaux drawn from familiar biblical images such as the illustrations by Tissot and Doré.

The characterization of the main figures is minimal, but nevertheless differs from the 1956 version. Here Moses and Aaron enter the scene as elderly men. With his full white beard and intense expression, Moses looks like he has just stepped off the pedestal from Michelangelo's famous sculpture (1513–15). Aaron is by his side initially, but by the end of the film, both Aaron and Miriam have strayed: they become the priest and priestess of the idolatrous people.

Now: the modern story

The prolog ends with Moses's decent from the mountain and a violent thunderstorm punishes the Israelites for having turned from the worship of God to the worship of idols. There is widespread panic and death. A domestic scene of early twentieth-century America gradually fades in: Danny and Johnny McTavish, two adult brothers, are sitting at the dining table with their elderly mother, who is reading from the Bible. The characters transparently represent different stances toward God and humankind. The mother lives out a rigorous legalism ever so slightly tempered by love for her children. She represents the unyielding God of the Old Testament. Danny is the lawless, amoral, rebellious son. Johnny is the dutiful, moral, upright, and God-fearing son who, unlike his mother, does not reduce God's will to the law, especially the Ten Commandments, but balances law with Christ-like love and patience for the foibles of his fellow human beings. Johnny represents the Christian life.

The conflict in this portion of the film revolves around Danny. DeMille is careful to show that he breaks every single one of the Ten Commandments: he mocks God by pretending to worship a statue of his own making (made out of a cigarette and a spoon, supported by the Holy Book), he blasphemes, he mocks his mother, breaks the Sabbath by dancing, covets the property of others, and commits adultery. In the end, of course, he receives his comeuppance. Danny becomes a building contractor, and is commissioned to build a church, employing his brother as the carpenter for the project. Johnny discovers that Danny has been cheating – in effect, stealing – by using inferior cement and confronts him, but at that very moment, the church collapses, trapping their mother inside. Thus Danny breaks the most important commandment: murder. Even an amoral man like Danny cannot live with this sin; rather than repent, however, he takes to the bottle, and eventually dies while attempting to escape by sea.

Danny's affinity with the Israelites who worshipped the Golden Calf is obvious, but, for any who missed it, DeMille makes the connection explicit through the intertitles.[3] When his mother upbraids him for his violation of God's law, Danny declares: "All that's the bunk, Mother. The Ten Commandments were all right for a lot of dead ones – but that sort of stuff was buried with Queen Victoria!" When Johnny expresses concerns, he quips, "I'd like your Ten Commandments better if they could mend *this* sole – instead of the one Mom's worried about." At this point his mother comments: "If you're setting a pair of shoes above your God, Dan McTavish – you'll get just what the Children of Israel got when they worshipped the Golden Calf." His brother later warns: "Laugh at the Ten Commandments all you want, Danny – but they pack an awful wallop." Danny is not persuaded: "Oh forget it! How do I know there is a God? And as for the Ten Commandments, they never got me anything, and they can go plumb to – !" thereby blaspheming.

Despite its relentless focus on the Decalogue, the film emphasizes that law is not enough. Law must be tempered with love and compassion. Johnny deplores his mother's harsh response to her recalcitrant son, whom she boots out of the house for blaspheming: "You're holding a cross in your hand, Mom – but you're using it like a whip." When Johnny discovers that Danny has been cutting corners, he admonishes: "Danny, you've got to make this concrete right. You can't break every law of God and Man and get away with it." Danny is unrepentant: "I told you I'd break the Ten Commandments – and look what I've got for it, SUCCESS! That's all that counts! I'm sorry if your God doesn't like it – but this is *my* party, not His!" Yet all this changes when the church collapses, crushing the Ten Commandments inscribed on the tablets hanging on the wall of the church, as well as their mother who has come to visit. A crane shot from above establishes that from God's point of view this church is corrupt, because it has been built from inferior materials by a man who mocks God and his fellow humans alike.

Johnny holds his dying mother in his arms, in a direct inversion of Michelangelo's *Pietà* image of Mary cradling her dead son. His mother repents for teaching fear rather than love, and Danny, sitting nearby, regrets his disobedience and wishes he could start again. Redemption comes, not for Danny, but for Mary, Danny's flapper wife. Mary, like Mary Magdalene in Christian tradition, repents of her sins. And like Miriam in the film's biblical prolog (and Numbers 12), she contracts leprosy. In DeMille's version, Moses does not forgive Miriam, but Johnny forgives Mary, just as Jesus does Mary Magdalene in DeMille's later film *The King of Kings* (1927). Whereas the prolog here ends on a note of divine vengeance, the film itself ends on a note of divine redemption. Johnny reads to Mary from the Gospel story of Jesus healing the lepers as she rests her head on his knees. The camera cuts to a flashback from the life of Jesus, seen from behind, as he heals a leprous woman who is kneeling before him with reverence, as the disciples look on and marvel. The scene dissolves back into the "present" as Mary leans towards Johnny and exclaims: "Why, John – in the light, it's gone!" Johnny puts his hand on her hand, and the movie ends. There are crosses on the windowpane; Mary is healed, the rain has stopped, light has come.

Epic conventions

EXTRAVAGANCE AND SPECTACLE

This films shares many of the conventions that later become staples in the later golden era of the epic film. What they did have were big budgets, casts of thousands, and spectacle, especially large crowd scenes. DeMille's film also included that epic feature, the chariot chase, in which the Egyptians chase the Israelites on their way to the sea, as well as a long orgiastic scene at the foot of the Golden Calf.

Like the spectacles in later epics such as *Solomon and Sheba*, the latter scene both exploits and deplores the decadence of idolatrous Israelites. The true depth of their depravity is emphasized by the lengthy focus on Miriam, as she fashions the calf, polishes it lovingly with her long hair, and then dances erotically on and around it. As the frenzy increases, she tears off her clothing and dances provocatively in a skimpy burlesque outfit. A man embraces her from behind and caresses her breast, but then suddenly pulls away: she has become leprous! When Moses comes down from the mountain, she beseeches him to heal her. This sequence is based loosely on Numbers 12:10, in which Miriam is struck with leprosy when she criticizes Moses for marrying a Cushite woman. The image of Miriam as an idolatrous woman is completely at odds with the biblical and later Jewish portrait of Miriam as a prophet and leader in her own right. In the film it serves a narrative and moralistic purpose by suggesting that the corruption, weakness, and idolatry of the Israelites reached the highest levels such that even Moses' own siblings were involved. In drawing on imagery more frequently associated with Mary Magdalene (whose name in Hebrew would also have been Miriam), the film implies the susceptibility of women to corruption. More obviously, however, the scene is intended to draw the male gaze, and satisfy the appetite for nudity and spectacle that these sorts of scenes were intended to engage.

MUSIC

One element that functioned differently in the silent epics, of course, was music. Whereas later films had music composed for them, or made use of familiar works, such as Handel's *Messiah*, silent movies were not recorded with music. Music was played live during the screenings, and many DVD releases of silent movies include a musical soundtrack. A melody used in the recorded soundtrack of both *Intolerance* and *The Ten Commandments* is the one traditionally used for *Kol Nidre*, the famous prayer associated with the Jewish holy day of Yom Kippur (Day of Atonement). In Griffith's film, *Kol Nidre* is the background music to the Judean scenes.[4] The use of a melody associated so strongly with the Jewish Day of Atonement plays ironically in this film, by implicitly underscoring Jesus' role as the one who brings forgiveness of sins, and also implicating the Pharisees – and their modern-day successors, the "Uplifters" – as needing forgiveness for their intolerance. Most striking is the speeded-up carnivalesque version of the tune that is used in the market scenes. As Gottlieb notes, "Such incongruities can be explained by the prevalence of cantor-performers on the Jewish vaudeville circuit in the early 1900s, where *Kol nidrei*, *El malei rachamim*, *Eli Eli*, and other Askenazic chants were staple tear-jerkers."[5]

The same melody appears in *The Ten Commandments*. In the prolog's final scene, the camera cuts back and forth between Moses receiving the Ten Commandments alone on the mountain and inscribing them with great effort onto the stone, and the multitudes, led by Aaron and Miriam, who fashion the Golden Calf and then worship it, and dance around it. The switching back and forth contrasts the Israelites' idolatry with Moses' purity, and draws attention to the lone struggle of the religious man. The cuts to Moses always include the solemn sounds of *Kol Nidre* and the cuts to the Israelites include lively, frivolous music. The association of *Kol Nidre* with Moses implies the need for the Israelites to atone for their egregious violation of their covenantal relationship with God. Just as the hedonism of the Egyptians is contrasted early in the prolog with the pure piety of Moses and Aaron, so here are the hedonism and theological corruption of the Israelites contrasted with the single-minded and pure devotion of Moses to the God of Israel.

BIBLICAL AUTHENTICITY

The film does not claim historicity in any overt way – perhaps because the focus is not on accuracy. Nevertheless, elements such as the natural and constructed settings, the direct quotation from scripture, the fonts, and the explanations of certain customs and personalities imply biblical authenticity. The main focus, however, is on the "then as now – the ongoing significance of the biblical message – and in developing this analogy, the film touches on many of the same themes as do other Bible movies.

Then as now

JUDAISM AND SUPERSESSIONISM

DeMille's film gives a decidedly mixed message as far as Jews and Judaism are concerned. DeMille himself, as we have seen, expressed positive appreciation of Orthodox Jews, especially those whom he drafted to be extras in the crowd scenes of the prolog. And of course the film emphasizes the importance of the Decalogue. Nevertheless, the film itself is thoroughly Christian and even supersessionist. The Christian elements come to the fore explicitly at the conclusion, but they are also present throughout, for example, in some of the intertitles, which feature a small Star of David with a cross etched in the middle. On the Exodus from Egypt, one woman carries a white lamb in the foreground, foreshadowing the association of the lamb and Jesus that was conventional in the silent Jesus-movies, and that appears prominently in DeMille's own Jesus-movie, *The King of Kings*. Both films use the image of a young child carrying a doll as a symbol of innocence and hope. Moses is portrayed with outstretched arms in cruciform position, as he signals the seas to part and the intertitle reads: "And Moses stretched his hand over the sea, and the Lord caused the sea to go back, and made the sea dry land, and the waters were divided" (Exod. 14:21). These elements associate the Exodus with the redemption and liberation that, this film asserts, can only come about fully through Christ.

The film that is ostensibly celebrating and exploring the importance of an "Old Testament" event concludes with a decidedly Christian message. In a sense, the film as a whole undercuts the opening title. In the aftermath of the First World War, it suggests, it is not really Law that is the answer but love and Christian faith. True, for DeMille faith includes morality, which, broadly speaking, means adherence to the Ten Commandments, but rigid adherence to the Decalogue must be tempered with Christian faith, love, and compassion. As Babington and Evans note,

> At the end, the mother's too masculine upholding of a puritanical law is transcended by Christ healing both the leprous woman who appears before him and Mary (contrasting with Moses' refusal to forgive the repentant female orgiast who begs him for mercy), a replacement of the phallic mother by a feminising Christ who moves the film at its close out of the Old Testament orbit.[6]

THEN AS NOW FOR REAL

Spectacles cost money, and DeMille's film went well over budget. DeMille's film caused his backers considerable grief, as the film exceeded its million dollar budget by 50 percent. Although the film grossed well over $4 million, it strained DeMille's relationship with his backers.[7] The film boasted 2,500 people and 3,000 animals for the Exodus and Crossing of the Red Sea scenes alone. The scenes were shot on the sand dunes at Guadalupe, near Santa Maria, California, and several hundred Orthodox Jews were brought from Los Angeles to fill out the scene because, as DeMille says, "we believed rightly that, both in appearance and in their deep feeling of the significance of the Exodus, they would give the best possible performance as the Children of Israel." Apparently the extras took a first-day mix-up – when they were served a ham dinner – well in stride. DeMille noted

> these Orthodox Jews were an example to all the rest of us, not only in their fidelity to their laws but in the way they played their parts. They *were* the Children of Israel. This was their Exodus, their liberation.[8]

The Passion in present tense

But juxtaposition is not the only way to make overt the "then as now" dimension of the Bible movie. There exists also a small, and somewhat idiosyncratic, subset of films that rather than tell the biblical and modern stories as two separate narratives, embed one within the other, so that the biblical elements constitute a story within a larger fictional frame. Most striking are Passion Play films. These movies portray a village, or perhaps just a small group of actors as they prepare and perform a Passion Play. These movies take their cue from the real-life Passion Plays that were prevalent in Europe throughout the middle ages, and that still take place today in some locations around the world. The most famous such play has been performed in the Bavarian Catholic village of Oberammergau since 1634. The legend is that in 1633, in the midst of the Thirty Years War and a terrible outbreak of the bubonic plague, the residents of Ober-ammergau swore an oath that they would perform the "Play of the Suf-fering, Death and Resurrection of Our Lord Jesus Christ" every ten years, in the hope that God would recognize their piety and put an end to their suffering. The first performance took place at Pentecost 1634, on a stage erected in the cemetery above the fresh graves of the plague victims. Miraculously, the plague stopped. To this very day, Oberammergau con-tinues to stage its Passion Play in every decade as well as on the 50th and 100th anniversaries of the original play. Auditions, rehearsals, and the performances themselves occupy the better part of a year. Those who have landed the major roles arrange to take time off work; those men who play Jewish peasants grow their beards and their hair; the proprietors of bed-and-breakfasts, restaurants, and bars, prepare for the welcome onslaught of tourists, and church groups from all over the world plan their trips. The village gives itself over entirely to the production. The play is so central to the activity, economy, and identity of Oberammergau that villagers will often introduce themselves – or their deceased relatives – with a resumé of the parts that they played over their lifetimes.[9] Indeed, it can be difficult, for actors and villagers alike, to separate the play from their real lives. This confusion is to some extent encouraged by the village itself; until recently, for example, only unmarried woman under the age of 35 were eligible to play the Virgin Mary.[10] The actor who played Judas had to come to terms with his own perfidy, and could even expect verbal or even physical abuse by devout playgoers who happened to run into him around the village on his day off.[11]

Perhaps the tendency to endow the actor with the attributes of the char-acter he or she plays, was, and is, a common experience in the numerous town and villages that have staged Passion Plays from the middle ages down to the present time.[12] At least, that is what one might guess from the Passion Play movies that are based on the European tradition.

A classic example is Denys Arcand's *Jesus of Montreal* (1989), in which both the frame narrative and the embedded Passion Play are developed in some detail. *Jesus of Montreal* portrays a group of actors that have been commis-sioned by the priest of St. Joseph's Oratory in Montreal to refresh the Pas-sion Play that has been performed on the church grounds for decades. Daniel Coulombe, the "Jesus" of Montreal, conducts research in the local libraries, consults eminent theologians, and then works hard with his friends to write, rehearse, and perform the Passion Play. The result is an unusual, and riveting account of Jesus' Passion that not only dramatizes the Gospel Passion narrative but also makes use of documentary style to support its revisionist version over against the traditional story as told in the Catholic churches. Audiences come and critics applaud. But instead of relishing the success of his initiative, the priest, and the ecclesiastical establishment, shut the play down: how can the church support a play in which Mary is an unwed mother, and Jesus is just another miracle-worker? The cast attempts to stage the play one last time. The authorities stop it, the audience protests, and the mêlée causes the cross on which the actor is suspended to topple, pinning his head to the ground. Daniel dies, and his organs are donated for transplantation.

Virtually every detail of the Gospel stories, and many aspects of New Testament and historical Jesus scholarship, are present, or, more accurately, concealed, for the knowledgeable viewer to discern.[13] Yet the film systematically and thoroughly sets out to deconstruct the historicity of the Gospels and Catholic tradition: "Disciples lie; they embellish." The "then" of the film – the Passion Play – is a revisionist and yet very powerful account that contextualizes Jesus as a Jewish magician living in the era of Roman domination of Judea. The "now" is a pointed critique of the Catholic Church in Quebec, the commercialization of art and culture, and the degradation of women.

By contrast, *Jesus Christ Superstar* (1973), a Passion Musical, includes almost no frame narrative at all; that these are actors putting on a play is evident only from the brief introduction and conclusion, and from a range of anachronistic details throughout. *Superstar* was originally a record album, and then became a very successful Broadway show. The live musical is periodically revived, most recently at Canada's Stratford Festival (2011; Stratford, Ontario), a production that played to great acclaim on Broadway in 2012.[14] The film version, by comparison, was not a smash hit, but nevertheless over the years has become part of the canon of the most important American Jesus-movies, and therefore has received its fair share of discussion.[15]

The film is perhaps the most minimalist of the Passion Play subgenre. In contrast to *Jesus of Montreal*, which gives us both the frame and the embedded Passion Play, *Jesus Christ Superstar* merely hints at a fictional frame narrative taking place in the present – the late 1960s or early 1970s – but neither dramatizes nor narrates that frame. In a brief opening scene actors arrive at an isolated location in the Negev Desert in Israel, pour out of their bus, and prepare the set, the costumes and the props for their re-enactment of the last week of Jesus' life. In the evening, at the end of the film, they pack up the bus and leave, but one person is missing: the actor who played Jesus. The others look back wistfully at the landscape. A change has occurred but exactly what it is we do not know.

The "then" aspect of the film is evident in its characters and narrative, which closely mirror the Passion Narratives as harmonized from the four canonical gospels. But it is the "now" that predominates. Although the present-day context is not narrated, the interpenetration of the present into their narrative of the past is overt and intentionally intrusive. Except for Jesus, the cast does not dress in the typical bathrobes and sandals costume of the Bible film genre, but in the "hippie" garb that was widespread in the 1960s and 1970s. The rock music genre itself is a constant reminder of the contemporary context of the film. Occasional shots of tanks and airplanes over the desert are reminders of the 1967 war, and inadvertently foreshadowing the 1973 war that took place the same year that the film was released. The temple is violated not by the merchants selling animals and birds for the ritual sacrifices, but by booths that sell postcards, souvenirs, and women to gullible tourists who wander around in modern dress. The movie is also self-referential: men with movie cameras wander around the temple marketplace; Judas assures Jesus: "You'll escape in the final reel."

Finally, the casting of Judas as an African American ensures that his role and his lyrics will be understood better against the background of the civil rights movement, rather than of the Jews' opposition to their Roman oppressors. It is Judas who provides the thematic perspective of the film as a whole; the point is not so much to recount and celebrate Jesus' Passion as to criticize the cult of celebrity. Even Herod gets the message, claiming that he is asking Jesus only what he would ask of any superstar: "What is it that you have got that puts you where you are?" The staging of the 2011 Stratford and 2012 Broadway productions made this point even clearer, by incorporating a theater marquee into the set of the musical itself.

No-Passion Play films

At the opposite end of the spectrum are two, lesser known films, the 1957 French/Italian film, *Celui qui doit mourir* (*He Who Must Die*) and Pasolini's *La ricotta* (1962). Both of these films focus so intently on the frame narrative that the actual Passion Play is never performed. The events in the modern frame often mirror the gospels' Passion accounts, just as the modern actors in the frame play out the parts of their Gospel counterparts. These two films adopt, play upon, critique, mock, and subvert the conventions established by the Bible epic, and they also posit a complex, often ironic, relationship between the biblical stories and contemporary life as depicted in the fictional frame.

These films are a subset of the Jesus-movie genre as such themselves, and as such they depend upon the Passion Play tradition. The Passion Play films do not require viewers to know anything at all about this medieval tradition, or even to know such a tradition existed. What counts most of all is the modern day Jesus and how he affects both the world he lives in and the viewers who watch him.

Celui qui doit mourir (He Who Must Die) *(1957)*

Plot summary

This film, directed by Jules Dassin, is an adaptation of the 1948 novel *Christ Recrucified* by Nikos Kazantzakis.[16] Though it was highly praised at the time of its release, the film is rarely seen today.[17] Set in 1921, the movie explores the tense relationship between the Greeks and the Turks, Christians, and Muslims, in the post–First World War period. The opening scene portrays a massacre perpetrated by their Turks in a small Christian village in Crete; many people die, and the village itself is burned to the ground. The remaining villagers, led by their priest Fotis, embark on a three-month trek to find a new home. Meanwhile, in another Christian village, this one prosperous and peaceful, plans are underway for the Passion Play, staged every seven years. With great ceremony, the local priest, Pope Grigoris, calls the village to the church, announces the names of the actors who will play the principal roles – Jesus, Peter, John, James, Judas, and Mary Magdalene (but not, interestingly enough, Caiaphas and Pilate) – and charges them to be worthy of their roles in the sacred drama. The peaceful atmosphere in the village is disrupted by the arrival of Fotis and his starving and exhausted flock. The refugees ask for food and, more important, for permission to take over the uncultivated lands on the hillside opposite the village, known as the Sarakina. This development alarms both the political leader of the prosperous village, the Patriarcheas, who owns most of the land in the village, and the religious leader, Pope Grigoris. Fearing the refugees may threaten their prosperity, the Patriarcheas and the priest accuse the newcomers of harboring cholera, and banish them from the village. Grigoris does not recognize the stark contrast between the pious sermon he has just delivered and his own behavior, but his hypocrisy is evident to the audience, as well as to his counterpart Fotis. The refugees despair, but they prepare to continue their journey. Fotis, however, digs in his heels; despite the harsh welcome, he rules that the refugees will settle on the uninhabited Sarakina. Some of the villagers – those chosen to play Jesus, his disciples, and Mary Magdalene, decide to help them, and soon many in the village are persuaded to do so. Among the commoners, only Judas refuses. A dramatic and violent confrontation ensues. The powers that be judge Manolios, the villager who plays Jesus, to be the ringleader; he is tortured, then dies of his wounds, but not before his friends mobilize on the side of the refugees.

Now as then

This film is entirely, and explicitly, allegorical, as indicated by the overt identification of villagers with particular characters in the story. Those chosen to be Judas, Peter, John, and Mary Magdalene act out their parts in obvious ways, as does Manolios/Jesus. Pilate and Caiaphas are easily recognizable in the figures of the Agha (Pilate) and the priest Grigoris (Caiaphas). The Patriarcheas may be identified with Herod, who is the local agent of the Agha and at the same time, ethnically and historically associated with the villagers themselves, just as Herod Antipas is subservient to Pilate but not a Roman himself.[18] Although the film frames these events within the broad political and religious tensions in Greece in the 1920s, it focuses primarily on the tensions within the Christian Greek communities. The main message concerns the ways in which oppression can lead people to turn against their own compatriots, as well as the different approaches that the villages and the refugees take to the Muslim authorities: collusion, represented by the Patriarcheas and Grigoris, or opposition, represented by Fotis.[19]

Like the sword-and-sandal movies, *He Who Must Die* portrays the impact of Christ or Christ-like behavior in a specific time and place. "Jesus" is a simple shepherd, uneducated and politically naïve but goodhearted. Like Moses, he has a stammer that disappears after he uncovers his divinely given mission, in this case, after he is chosen by Father Fotis to present the refugees' case to the villagers. "Mary Magdalene" is the widow Katerina, who provides sexual favors for the Patriarcheas and many of the other men in town, including both "Jesus" and "Judas." When Katerina sees Manolios stand up to the authorities, and later speak with passion and eloquence to the villagers, she drops the other men and stays with him. Had Manolios survived, they would have married and had children. The other disciples follow Manolios' lead in caring for the refugees. Even Michelis, the son and heir of the Patriarcheas, who defies his father in order to help the refugees. He becomes Manolios' close associate, symbolizing the Beloved Disciple, John the Evangelist.

The Agha, like Pilate, is very reluctant to get involved; he tries to persuade Manolios to withdraw his demands on behalf of the refugees. When Manolios refuses, the Agha hands him over to Grigoris, thereby reversing the Gospel story in which it is the ecclesiastical authority – the high priest – who hands Jesus over to the political and administrative authority, Pilate. "Judas," who had aspired to play Jesus in the Passion, has it in for Manolios from the outset, and betrays him in the end; he sees Manolios as his rival not only for the choice role of Jesus but also for the attention of Katerina. His behavior shows that, as the name of Kazantzakis' novel suggests, were Christ to return, he would be recrucified.

The moral and spiritual center of the film belongs to Fotis. As an outsider to the village, he is also outside the allegorical circle, but one may suggest that he represents God. He commissions Manolios to speak to the people and removes his stutter. Fotis takes up arms against the forces of oppression. In this film, God is on the side of those who engage in armed struggle against imperialism, and the forces of complacency and collusion.

Conventions

The Passion Play film subgenre – including its "No-Passion" variants – has one major convention: the fictional frame narrative imitates the Passion and the lives and personalities of the actors mirror those of the Passion. This convention turns the fictional frame itself into a Passion narrative. *He Who Must Die* takes this convention to its logical extreme, as the fictional

frame itself is the entire film; though a Passion Play is mentioned and preparations begun, it is never enacted. Therefore the entire film is the Passion.
The only trace of the Passion Play was the assignment of the villagers to
their parts. The play itself has disappeared; there are no rehearsals, only a
brief conversation among Jesus and two drunk disciples about having a
rehearsal, and there is certainly no performance of the play. Instead, the
Passion is played out, for real, in the lives of the villagers themselves in their
conflict not with the "Roman" authorities (the Agha) but their displaced
Greek compatriots.

In this Passion, as in all others, Jesus must die, an outcome anticipated by
the very title of the film. This inevitability is accentuated by the camera work,
especially in the climactic scene of Manolios' death. As Clifton notes, the
camera angle determines the effect. Whereas in the Passion story it is the chief
priests who bring Jesus to Pilate, here it is the Agha who orders Manolios
brought to the Pope Grigoris. Manolios is bound by a rope which is dragged
into a wide hall by a Turkish soldier on a horse, whose hoofs clatter omi-
nously on the tiled floor.

> The soldier rides around the pillar and away, leaving Manolios on the
> floor, his hands tied behind his back, his tether dropped beside him.... In
> a long down shot, the wealthy village magnates, who stay on the
> right side of their Turkish overlords, form a circle around Manolios.
> Panayotaris – Judas in the Passion Play – draws his knife and completes
> the ring. The time of Manolios was accomplished; there was no escape.[20]

The story's contemporary context allows for a direct rather than allusive
presentation of key themes and issues. In contrast to the Jesus-movies, the
films in this category do not have to tiptoe around the question of whether Jesus had a love life; Jesus can remain pure while the actor who plays
Jesus can freely enter into a romantic and sexual relationship like any
mortal can. Accordingly, there is a love triangle between the villagers who
play Judas, Mary Magdalene, and Jesus. Katerina, who is to play Mary
Magdalene in the Passion Play, is a merry widow who bestows her affections freely but she saves her true love for Manolios, the shepherd who
plays Jesus. Yet, initially at least, she does not see Manolios for who he is,
but attributes to him the courage and principles she associates with Jesus
himself, such as the ability to stand up to authority. Her first declaration of
love comes when she believes him to have defied the Patriarcheas and
Grigoris with regard to supporting the villagers. When he tells her that he
backed down at the last moment, she throws him out of her house. This
rejection jolts Manolios to the core. Later he does measure up to the hero
of the Passion Play: he takes a public stand for the need to help the
refugees, and at the climax of the film he makes an impassioned speech at
the Feast of Elijah, thereby becoming, in death, the man that Katerina
thought and hoped him to be.

The main theme of the film, however, is political. The movie portrays the conflict between the Turks and the Greeks as parallel to that between the Jews and the Romans in the Gospel story. In both cases, the good shepherd who tries to mediate on behalf of the poor is killed for his troubles. The film, like the Gospels, compares two different approaches to the fact of imperial occupation and oppression: confrontation, as exemplified by the refugees who attempt to resist the occupation and as a result must suffer and die for their cause, and the way of appeasement, exemplified by the leaders of the prosperous village. The Pope and the Patriarcheas, who collaborate and remain on good terms with the Muslim Agha, and make small gains, such as permission to stage the Passion Play. But also then refuse to assist the refugees for fear of incurring the wrath of the Agha upon whom their own welfare and, in their view, the well-being of their village, depends. The film itself supports a liberation theology that emphasizes the need for Christians to care for the poor and needy and take responsibility for others.[21]

La ricotta *(1962)*

Plot summary

The short (35 minute) film *La ricotta* ("Curd Cheese"), Pasolini's contribution to the composite film *RoGoPaG* (a film whose four segments are directed by Rossellini, Godard, Pasolini, and Gregoretti) concerns the making of a Passion film. *La ricotta* opens with a scrolling text that is also narrated aloud. The text proclaims the purity of its director's intentions: "It's not difficult to predict – for this story of mine – biased, ambiguous and scandalized judgments. In any case, I want to state here and now that however *La ricotta* is taken, the story of the Passion, which *La ricotta* indirectly recalls, is for me the greatest event that ever happened and the books that recount it the most sublime ever written." This devotion is little in evidence in the film itself, however, and Pasolini was right to predict a scandalized response. The film was considered blasphemous and the director was charged and convicted of contempt for the state religion. The legal proceedings prevented him from proceeding with his next film, *Il Padre Selvaggio*. He was in prison for four months, after which the conviction was thrown out by an appeals court.[22]

The director of the film within the film is played by Orson Welles, who overtly stands in for Pasolini himself. Indeed, at one point Welles reads a poem written by Pasolini that appears in the preface of the published script of *Mamma Roma*, which had just been released at the time *La ricotta* was being made (1962). In casting Welles as the director, Pasolini is mocking himself as the potential maker of a Jesus-movie (*The Gospel According to Saint Matthew*, 1964), as well as drawing upon Welles' previous screen role as the invisible voice-of-God in Nicholas Ray's *King of Kings*, 1961.[23] These associations suggest that film directors are not unlike God in that they create worlds and populate them with people who possess and exercise their free will to play or not play their assigned roles in a manner that would please their creators.

Like the Jesus-movies, including Pasolini's own 1964 film, *La ricotta* uses art – *The Deposition from the Cross* (c. 1528) by Pontormo (Jacopo Carruci) – as the basis for its mise-en-scène of Jesus' Passion. Much of the film is devoted to unsuccessful attempts to set up this scene; the actors keep tumbling down, to the general amusement of all concerned. The plot, such as it is, focuses on Giovanni Stracci, a local down-and-out man chosen to play the role of the "good thief" who is crucified alongside Jesus. In the Gospel accounts, Jesus is crucified between two other men, traditionally described as thieves. According to Luke, one of these men – the "good thief" – asked Jesus to remember him when he came into the Kingdom. Jesus replied, "Truly I tell you, today you will be with me in Paradise" (Luke 23:42–43). The name Stracci, meaning "rags," points to his extreme poverty, as a result of which he is literally starving all the time. The entire plot of the film revolves around his efforts to find lunch for himself. At long last he finds a large amount of ricotta cheese, on which he gorges himself with an animal-like frenzy. When the lunch break is over, Stracci climbs onto his cross, where he expires from indigestion. His own life, and especially his frantic search for what turned out to be his last meal, was itself a Passion, though whether he indeed enters the Kingdom is uncertain. The Passion film itself is not completed.

Themes

The film is fascinating, grotesque, and trenchant in its critique of Italy as a society that worships beauty and pays lip service to piety and faith, yet fails to meet the basic needs of the poor. In producing a Passion film that is intended to glorify Christ, the film draws attention to the poor man who is crucified by the indifference of the very society for whom the Passion film is produced. The superficiality of that society is symbolized by the twist music to which the cast dances lightheartedly during the lunch break, and by the callous treatment of Stracci by the regular actors. Particularly striking are the shots of the elaborate luncheon – a shot of color in this primarily black-and-white film – that is laid out for the film's sponsors, who barely touch it. The film therefore inverts the usual convention of the Passion Play film. In Pasolini's contribution to this genre, the actors do not absorb the saintly elements of the characters they play, but rather their saintly parts are tainted by the vulgarity of the actors themselves. The ultimate collapse of the human pyramid required by Pontormo's scenario may in itself reflect the inability of the Catholic Church to sustain the elaborate institution that it has created and a failure of its mandate to care for the needy.

Conclusion

Films that place biblical and fictional narratives side-by-side, or that embed a Passion story within a fictional frame narrative (or at least explicitly evoke that embedding) straddle the categories of Bible on film and Bible in film. The biblical narratives which these films portray or evoke, direct viewers to see biblical elements in their fictional frame narratives, and to reflect on the resonances of the biblical past in the cinematic present. But filmmakers reinforce this connection by including numerous biblical quotations, allusions, and references in the fictional frames as such, thereby ensuring that the biblical analog is not forgotten by viewers as they become involved in the non-biblical story.

It may simply be a coincidence that aside from *Jesus Christ Superstar* the Passion Play movies are "foreign language" films (French, Italian) that come from outside of Hollywood – from Canada (*Jesus of Montreal*) or Europe (*He Who must Die*; *La ricotta*). The sample is not large enough to determine whether there is significance to this coincidence. At the same time, one may speculate that these filmmakers did not perceive the epic film genre and its conventions to be the best vehicles for developing the analogies between the Christ's Passion and the contemporary themes that they wished to address. This may reflect a conscious or subconscious decision to distance their films from the ways in which the American epics addressed the themes of gender, politics, race, and other forms of oppression. Or it may reflect a sense that the epic conventions were simply inappropriate, or uninteresting, for addressing the motifs of celebrity, the degradation of art, religious hypocrisy, and class and political struggle.

It could be that in addition to the economic, cultural, and historical reasons for the decline of the epic film genre, American filmmakers also began to find other, more nuanced, genres and cinematic forms for using the Bible to address a broader range of issues and anxieties. The fact is that the majority of Bible-related films since the golden era of the epics forego the explicit rendering of a biblical narrative and instead employ quotations, allusion, and reference, as well as the visual presence of the Bible on the screen, to emphasize the ongoing relevance of the Bible, its characters, and its stories, to the dilemmas of the modern world. It is to these films that we now turn our attention.

Notes

1 Cecil B. DeMille, *The Autobiography of Cecil B. DeMille* (Englewood Cliffs, NJ: Prentice-Hall, 1959), 249.
2 On "rewritten Bible" as a genre of postbiblical literature, see, for example, Daniel J. Harrington, "Palestinian Adaptations of Biblical Narratives and Prophecies: The Bible Rewritten," in *Early Judaism and Its Modern Interpreters*, ed. Robert A. Kraft and George W. E. Nickelsburg (Philadelphia, PA: Fortress Press, 1986), 239–47; George W. E. Nickelsburg, "The Bible Rewritten and Expanded," in *Jewish Writings of the Second Temple Period*, ed. Michael E. Stone (Assen, Netherlands: Van Gorcum, 1984), 89–156; Anders Klostergaard Petersen, "Rewritten Bible as a

Borderline Phenomenon – Genre, Textual Strategy, or Canonical Anachronism?" in *Flores Florentino: Dead Sea Scrolls and Other Early Jewish Studies in Honour of Florentino Garcia Martinez*, ed. A. Hilhorst, Eibert J. C. Tigchelaar, and Emile Puech (Leiden: Brill, 2007), 285–306; Adele Reinhartz, "'Rewritten Gospel': The Case of Caiaphas the High Priest," *New Testament Studies* 55 no. 2 (2009): 160–78.

3 For a list of analogies between the two parts of the film, such as the parallel between the drowning at the Red Sea and the collapse of the church, see Babington and Evans, *Biblical Epics*, 44–47.

4 On the history of the *Kol Nidre* melody, see A. Z. Idelsohn, "The Kol Nidre Tune," *Hebrew Union College Annual* 8 (1931): 493–509. See also Gottlieb, *Funny, It Doesn't Sound Jewish*, 102. On the use of music in *Intolerance*, see Rick Altman, *Silent Film Sound* (New York: Columbia University Press, 2004), 296–300. Altman's detailed discussion, however, does not address the music in the "Judean Story" segment of the film, and the use of the *Kol Nidre* melody is not mentioned. DeMille's 1923 *Ten Commandments* also includes *Kol Nidre*, at least on the DVD version. Other films that make use of this melody include *The Jazz Singer* (1927) and the Danish movie *Häxan* (1922). For the use of this melody in *The Jazz Singer*, see Joel Rosenberg, "What You Ain't Heard Yet: The Languages of *The Jazz Singer*," *Prooftexts* 22, no. 1/2 (2002): 11–54. See also Alison Tara Walker, "The Sounds of Silents: Aurality and Medievalism in Benjamin Christensen's Häxan," in *Mass Market Medieval: Essays on the Middle Ages in Popular Culture*, ed. David W. Marshall (Jefferson, NC: McFarland & Co., 2007), 42–56. Walker's article is particularly interesting in its discussion of the way in which the film uses this melody in service of an antisemitic message.

5 Gottlieb, *Funny, It Doesn't Sound Jewish*, 102.

6 Babington and Evans, *Biblical Epics*, 46.

7 DeMille, *The Autobiography of Cecil B. DeMille*, 258.

8 Ibid., 252–53.

9 This was my personal experience on a visit to Oberammergau in May 2010, for the premiere of the Passion Play of that year. During that visit I participated in a tour of the small church cemetery, led by the assistant director, Otto Huber, who took us from stone to stone and listed the parts played by each eminent villager buried there. On that trip I also met the proprietor of a large inn, who introduced herself to me as "Jesus' mother," that is, the mother of one of the two young men who performed Jesus on alternate days.

10 James S. Shapiro, *Oberammergau: The Troubling Story of the World's Most Famous Passion Play* (New York: Pantheon Books, 2000), 4.

11 Ibid., 5.

12 In the medieval era, Passion Plays were commonly performed throughout Europe in the period immediately preceding Good Friday, sometimes over a period of several days. Ibid., 19–22.

13 For detailed analysis, see Adele Reinhartz, "History and Pseudo-History in the Jesus Film Genre," in *The Bible in Film – and The Bible and Film*, ed. J. Cheryl Exum (Leiden: Brill, 2006), 1–17.

14 See reviews in *The Toronto Star*, 4 June, www.toronto.com/article/687848 – review-stratford-s-superstar-is-an-absolute-knockout (accessed 14 June 2011) and the *National Post*, 6 June, http://arts.nationalpost.com/2011/06/06/theatre-review-jesus-christ-superstar-the-grapes-of-wrath (accessed 14 June 2011).

15 This may have not been the case when Goodacre commented on the tendency to overlook this film. See Mark Goodacre, "Do You Think You're What They Say You Are? Reflections on Jesus Christ Superstar," *Journal of Religion and Film* 3, no. 1 (1999): 1–13. For studies of this film, see Tatum, *Jesus at the Movies: A Guide to the First Hundred Years and Beyond*, 109–41; Reinhartz, *Jesus of Hollywood*, passim; Jeffrey Lloyd Staley and Richard G. Walsh, *Jesus, the Gospels, and Cinematic*

Imagination: A Handbook to Jesus on DVD (Louisville, KY: Westminster John Knox Press, 2007), 63–68.

16 As with most book adaptations, the film is not entirely faithful to the novel. See Peter Bien, "Nikos Kazantzakis's Novels on Film," *Journal of Modern Greek Studies* 18, no. 1 (2000): 164.

17 Kinnard and Davis, *Divine Images*, 102.

18 For detailed discussion of Herod Antipas, see Morten Hørning Jensen, *Herod Antipas in Galilee: The Literary and Archaeological Sources on the Reign of Herod Antipas and its Socio-Economic Impact on Galilee* (Tübingen: Mohr Siebeck, 2006).

19 See Vamik D. Volkan and Norman Itzkowitz, *Turks and Greeks: Neighbours in Conflict* (Huntingdon: Eothen Press, 1994).

20 N. Roy Clifton, *The Figure in Film* (Newark, DE; London: University of Delaware Press; Associated University Presses, 1983), 91.

21 At the time this film was released, its message was identified as a Marxist vision. Indeed, Dassin himself was blacklisted by the HUAC. See Rebecca Prime, "Cloaked in Compromise: Jules Dassin's Naked City," in *Tender Comrades: A Backstory of the Hollywood Blacklist*, ed. Patrick McGilligan and Paul Buhle (New York: St. Martin's Press, 1997), 142–51. Brian Neve, *Film and Politics in America: A Social Tradition* (London; New York: Routledge, 1992), 115–19.

22 Ibid., 100.

23 Sam Rohdie and Pier Paolo Pasolini, *The Passion of Pier Paolo Pasolini* (Bloomington, IL; London: Indiana University Press; British Film Institute, 1995), 10, 25.

Part II
The Bible *in* film

6 "Make them known to your children"

The Old Testament in modern guise

The Philadelphians who went to the first performance of the *Horitz Passion Play*, the crowds who flocked to DeMille's epic renditions of *The Ten Commandments* and *The King of Kings,* the hordes who thronged to the opening night of Mel Gibson's *The Passion of the Christ:* these moviegoers expected to see the Bible on film, and the Bible is what they saw. No matter that the Bible they saw on the silver screen was not exactly what they read in church or at home, that it was filtered through centuries of visual and other media, and that it said more about modern America than about ancient Israel. It was, nevertheless, the Holy Scriptures, the Word of God.

Since the birth of cinema, however, countless moviegoers have walked into a theater and seen or heard the Bible without expecting it in the least. Throughout the period of the epic Bible movies, from the early twentieth century until the mid-1960s, other films were being made that quoted the Bible or otherwise made use of biblical passages, motifs, stories, and characters. Even after the decline of the epic genre, the Bible continued to be evoked in countless films of all sorts, and was therefore encountered by an incalculable number of viewers, the majority of whom did not expect it in the least. Only those moviegoers who were knowledgeable in matters biblical would have realized that in "consuming" these films they were "consuming" the Bible at the same time.

The Bible *in* film

In their use of the Bible, and their overall, over-the-top, storytelling style, Bible movies – "the Bible *on* film" – are readily recognized as a distinct genre, with strong ties to the epic film genre more generally. By contrast, films that use the Bible to tell other sorts of stories – "the Bible *in* film" – belong to just about every genre imaginable, from the Western to the romantic comedy, and their visual, aural, editing styles and other cinematic conventions reflect the Hollywood genre or genres to which they most obviously belong. Boxing movies set their action in dark interiors and include scenes of boxing matches and betting; prison break movies feature flawed protagonists who succeed in escaping incarceration. Trailers and reviews can conceal the use of the Bible (and other cultural sources, allusions, and influences) until the viewers are in their seats. Some films may then be quite explicit in their use of the Bible, but in some cases the biblical elements may only be evident to those whose familiarity with the Bible is quite extensive.

Although instances of "the Bible *in* film" are for the most part easily distinguished from "the Bible *on* film," the former often use similar techniques to establish their scriptural connections. They may show the Bible or parts thereof on the screen; they may quote or allude explicitly to the Bible and/or to specific biblical verses, passages, or stories; and they may use biblical narratives as the paradigms for their own plots and characters. And, like the Bible movies, they often filter their use of the Bible through other media such as art, literature, and music; they use the Bible as a vehicle for expressing the views of the filmmakers and examining issues of importance to contemporary (usually American) society. Perhaps most important, they add depth by implying that the meaning of their stories exceeds or overflows the specific events being portrayed on the screen.

Films vary greatly in terms not only of how but also how much they draw on the Bible. *Babel* (2006), for example, is biblical only in its title; there are no other biblical quotations or allusions. *Evan Almighty* (2007) has countless biblical references and allusions, and indeed replicates, in an anachronistic, oversimplified, and highly humorous mode, the plot of the flood story of Genesis 6–7. Films that make heavy use of the Bible frequently draw on all three major conventions; they portray Bibles or biblical passages on the screen; they quote from the Bible and they use biblical paradigms of plot and character.

In other cases, the biblical quotation or reference summarizes a plot which otherwise does not derive from or allude to a biblical narrative at all. *True Grit* (2010), for example, opens with a scrolling text of Proverbs 28:1: "The wicked flee when none pursueth." The second part of the verse, not mentioned in the film at all, reads: "but the righteous are bold as a lion" (KJV). Taken in its entirely, the verse sums up the plot of the film as well as the personality of two of the main characters: a wicked man has killed another, and fled with impunity, with no one except the dead man's teenage daughter – a young woman both righteous and bold – who cares enough to pursue him. In this case, the biblical epigraph provides a brief commentary on the plot, but the film itself does not rely on the Bible for its story, characters, or dialog.

Bibles as "props"

Bibles often appear on screen as elements within the plot, characterization, and themes of the movie as a whole. Characters read Bibles (*Bigger Than Life*, 1956), buy and sell them (*O Brother, Where Art Thou?*, 2000), and carry them around (*Sling Blade,* 1996). Bibles appear in hotel rooms (*Coneheads,* 1993), bedrooms (*Evan Almighty,* 2007), backpacks (*The Book of Eli,* 2010), synagogues (*A Serious Man* [2009]), and churches (*Gran Torino* [2008]). These on-screen Bibles serve numerous roles. In *Nell* (1994), for example, a large old family Bible found in the home of a young "wild woman" telegraphs a backstory in which her family once lived within society, had the means to own such a Bible, and a home in which to display it. The Bible also contributes to the depth of this young woman's character: although she lived alone in a cabin in the woods, she was raised to value the Bible, to quote from it, and to live by it.[1] In *The Apostle* (1997) the Bible is the site of the protagonist's struggle over who he is and how he should live. As an apostle of the Lord, the Bible is his livelihood, but also his source of faith and inspiration. As a sinful person, however, the Bible is also his accuser, and, in the end, his source of succor and salvation.[2]

Not only Bibles but also pages of printed biblical texts appear on the screen for the viewer to read. In *Fried Green Tomatoes* (1991), for example, Ruth Jamison sends a page of the biblical book of Ruth to her friend Idgie Threadgoode, thereby implying that she plans to leave her abusive husband and come live with Idgie, just as the biblical Ruth left Moab to make a new life with her mother-in-law Naomi.[3] In *Barton Fink* (1991), the printed page from the King James Version of Genesis 1 slowly morphs into the text of Barton's drama, dramatizing the failed playwright's fantasy that he is about to write a drama as grand and timeless as the biblical story of creation.

The Bible as a source of dialog, reference, and allusion

Direct quotations from the Bible abound in American feature films. Many characters read from the Bible (Ed Avery in *Bigger Than Life*), or quote it from memory (sometimes falsely, as in *Pulp Fiction*, 1994[4]). The lawyer-protagonist in the comedy *Liar Liar* (1997) quotes John 8:32, in which Jesus declares that "the truth shall set you free." Pi, the hero of the 2012 film *The Life of Pi* (2012), falls in love with Christ in an Indian church in which the priest quotes John 3:16: "For God so loved the world that he gave his only son." Freddie Quell in *The Master* (2012) hears Ella Fitzgerald's rendition of the 1936 Irving Berlin song "Get Thee Behind Me Satan" (cf. Matthew 16:23) played over the sound system at the department store in which he works; the song gives voice to the uncertainty about Freddie's moral state that overshadows the entire film.

Quotations also occur in movie titles, such as *In the Valley of Elah* (2007) or *The Good Shepherd* (2006), and in epigraphs to films, as in the *Tree of Life* (2011), which begins with a quotation from Job 38:4, 6–7: "Where were you when I laid the foundations of the earth? … What supports its foundations, and who laid its cornerstone as the morning stars sang together and all the angels shouted for joy?" Some films use visual references. A spectacular example is the plague of frogs in *Magnolia* (1999), which also refers repeatedly and in many different ways to Exodus 8:2 just to reinforce the point.[5]

The Bible as a source of plot and character

Finally, there are numerous films that pattern all or part of a plot or subplot on a biblical story and, in doing so, also model one or more of their characters on a biblical prototype. One entertaining example is *Evan Almighty*, which employs every means possible to ensure that viewers notice its biblical prototype: the flood story of Genesis. Evan, a local television news reporter turned congressman, is very obviously Noah. Shortly after moving to a Washington suburb, he is mysteriously contacted by God and ordered to build an ark; he is to follow the specifications and instructions found in Genesis 6:14 to the letter. From this moment on, viewers know that against all odds he will build this ark, that the animals will come on board two by two, and that a flood will happen. Being a comedy, the film departs from the biblical story in its ending, for while the flood is catastrophic, not only Noah and his family but even the less-than-righteous survive. The story has a modern, ecological message – the exploitation of the natural environment for personal and political gain is wrong – but viewers may more easily remember how well Morgan Freeman suits the role of the benevolent and good-natured deity, and how funny it is to watch the animals march on Washington.

Like Evan in *Evan Almighty*, the protagonist of *Bigger than Life*, Ed Avery, explicitly takes a biblical figure as his role model. In Avery's case it is the patriarch Abraham, and the consequences are far from comedic, for he believes that, like Abraham, he is commanded to kill his only son. Thankfully he fails, and viewers understand that Avery's behavior is a perversion of the patriarch's actions, as, unlike Abraham, Avery was compelled not by divine command but by psychosis.

In most films, however, the connections to biblical characters and plot lines are extra-diegetic, apparent to the audience but not to the characters within the film. *East of Eden* (1955) models its main characters – the rancher Adam and his two sons Cal and Aron – on the biblical Adam, Cain, and Abel. *The Lion King* (1994) offers the Moses-like story of a young lion who flees his homeland, settles comfortably in a desert land that sounds and looks like California, to return, reluctantly, only after hearing a prophetic voice summoning him to his duty. In none of these cases however, does the biblical paradigm constitute the main plot of the film. The dramatic act at the climax of *Bigger Than Life* is part of a larger plot line that traces the descent of a decent husband and father into drug-induced madness and his eventual recovery. *East of Eden* uses the Cain and Abel narrative to tell a story of estrangement and reconciliation, against the background of the Depression, changing values, and popular psychology that condemns parental favoritism and blames a son's failure to mature on his father's neglect. *The Lion King* is also about father–son relationships; it follows the life journey of a young son who feels himself responsible for the death of his father as he matures and takes his rightful place in the world. The Coen Brothers' *A Serious Man* is a modern-day Job story, whose hero is tested and tried in every way possible. None of these films are *about* the Bible, yet by recognizing the underlying paradigm viewers may more easily grasp the themes of the films themselves.

Why the Bible?

Now, most of these points can easily be made in other ways. So the question is: why is the Bible used in films that are not really or not primarily about the Bible at all? On one level, the answer is straightforward. Cinema is a medium that necessarily makes extensive use of the stories, sources, events, symbols, and ideas, as well as objects, places, events, customs, and other elements of the "real world" that would be familiar to their audiences. The Bible is only one of many texts used by filmmakers to connect to their audiences, and to provide entertainment and meaning; others include the works of Shakespeare and of Jane Austen, popular novels such as Dan Brown's *The Da Vinci Code*,[6] and foundational documents such as the American Bill of Right, as well as popular psychology.

In some cases, a film's biblical connections may be crucial but nevertheless secondary, coming about through that film's use of another source that itself makes use of the Bible. A delightful example is *Moonrise Kingdom* (2012), which tells a magical story of Sam and Suzy, "troubled" 12-year olds who run away together to an excluded cape of the (fictional) island of New Penzance. The story, set in 1965, plays out over a three-day period before "the Black Beacon Storm," a "ferocious and well-documented storm" that "was considered by the US Department of Inclement Weather to be the region's most destructive meteorological event of the second half of the twentieth century."[7]

The rain and flooding caused by the hurricane are of epic proportions, warranting comparison with Noah's flood, both in its devastation, and in the abundant regeneration that followed, in which, as the film's narrator explained, "harvest yields the following autumn far exceeded any previously recorded, and the quality of the crops was said to be extraordinary." The Bible is not mentioned once, however; there are no quotations from Genesis 6–8, nor is a Bible present at any point on the screen. Instead, the film uses Benjamin Britten's 1958 sacred opera, *Noye's Fludde*, as an important touchstone throughout. The music is used both diegetically, that is, as an element within the story of the film as such, and extradiegetically, as part of the background soundtrack that helps create mood and theme, but is not at those moments heard by the characters within the story. Britten's *Noye's Fludde* was intended for performance in churches with audience participation, and features many children who play key roles.[8]

It is backstage, during a performance of *Noye's Fludde* at St. Jack's Church, on the island of New Penzance, that Sam and Suzy first meet. Suzy plays the "raven," an important role within the opera, as it is the raven that is sent out by Noye to determine whether there is dry land after the flood. The climax of the film takes place in the same church, the following year, when a performance of the opera is cancelled at the last moment due to the Black Beacon Storm. The church becomes a refuge for the community, as Noah's ark was for the animals during the biblical flood, and the connection is explicit both through a shot of a stained glass picture of Noah's Ark and by the animal costumes worn by the children. Sam and Suzy hope to escape attention as they evade the well-meaning adults who are trying to keep them apart. In addition to *Noye's Fludde*, the soundtrack features music by Hank Williams and Françoise Hard. The film begins and ends with the intradiegetic use of Britten's *Young Person's Guide to the Orchestra*, along with other music by Britten, Hank Williams, and others, which in a similar fashion functions both diagetically and extradiagetically. Although the Bible is not mentioned or used directly, the story of Noah's flood structures the action, provides the theme, and, I would suggest, is in the mind of many as they watch this fantasy unfold.[9]

Finally, film is a highly self-referential medium.[10] The fact that the Bible has been a source for films since the beginning of cinema supports its ongoing use as a resource today, as films often reproduce the ways in which other films have used the Bible. Most important, however, are the associations that the Bible carries in contemporary western, especially American, society, as a moral compass, as a repository of foundational history, and as testimony to and blueprint for the relationship between humankind and the divine.

Like Bible movies, fictional feature films use the Bible to convey certain ideas, values, opinions, and perspectives, on fundamental issues including the social, the political, and the theological, and to support as well as critique developments in American life and society. These points are well-illustrated by three films: *Babel*, *Inglourious Basterds*, and *In the Valley of Elah*.

Babel *(2006)*

Plot summary

Babel (2006), directed by Alejandro González Iñárritu, is the third part of his Death Trilogy, which began with *Amores Perros* (2000) and continued with *21 Grams* (2003).[11] The plot concerns the accidental shooting of a female tourist, Susan Jones, who is on vacation with her husband in Morocco. Through rapid intercutting and editing, the film gradually brings us deeply into four sets of stories, occurring simultaneously, but set in Morocco, the United States, Mexico, and Japan. Initially it appears that these stories are independent of one another, but it becomes clear that they intersect to produce the shooting and its aftermath.

The film begins in Morocco, with a family of goatherds. The father buys a hunting rifle from a neighbor, and gives it to his two young sons so that they can hunt down the jackals that are plaguing the herd. As the boys argue over who is the better marksman, one of them shoots at a faraway tourist bus. The bullet shatters a window, seriously wounding an American tourist named Susan Jones. The rest of the Moroccan plot moves between the efforts of police to find the shooter, initially assumed to be a terrorist, and the efforts of the injured woman's husband, Richard Jones, to save her from bleeding to death in a village with no ambulance and no doctor. Meanwhile, the couple's two young children are being cared for by a loving Mexican nanny working illegally in the United States. She receives permission from Richard to go to Mexico for her son's wedding, but as she cannot make alternate childcare arrangements, she takes the children with her. After a series of mishaps in which the children nearly die, she is caught by border police when trying to return, and deported back to Mexico. At the same time, in Japan, a hearing-impaired teenage girl explores her sexuality and identity. Since the suicide of her mother, she has lived alone with her father, who loves her but is at a loss as to how to deal with his daughter. She attempts a relationship with the policeman who has come to interview her father; it is the father's rifle, which he had given to his guide while on a hunting trip to Morocco, that had been used in the shooting of Susan Jones.

Babel in the Bible

The film's plot has no biblical foundation whatsoever; the Bible does not appear as a prop, and no character quotes from the Bible. The only biblical connection is the title. The absence of the Bible from the rest of the film raises the question as to the connection between the title and the film itself.

Iñárritu often invokes the Bible in his films. His previous film, *21 Grams* (2003) – part two of the Death Trilogy – revolves around a heart transplant. The movie's numerous biblical references and allusions include Exodus 33:10 and Romans 9:15 ("I will have mercy on whom I will have mercy, and I will have compassion on whom I will have compassion," KJV), Revelation 21:8 ("But the fearful, and unbelieving, and the abominable, and murderers, and whoremongers, and sorcerers, and idolaters, and all liars, shall have their part in the lake which burneth with fire and brimstone: which is the second death", KJV), and Revelation 3:19 ("As many as I love, I rebuke and chasten", KJV). Iñárritu's thoughtful use of scripture in *21 Grams* to explore the complex relationship between the protagonist and the widow of the man whose heart saved him from certain death suggests that the title *Babel* was carefully chosen to allude to the biblical story in Genesis 11.

The biblical story tells of humankind, which "had one language and the same words" (Gen. 11:1). In the course of their migration, the people settled on a plain in the land of Shinar, and said to each other: "Come, let us build ourselves a city, and a tower with its top in the heavens, and let us make a name for ourselves; otherwise we shall be scattered abroad upon the face of the whole earth" (Gen. 11:4). The ambitious plan alarmed God, who decided to nip it in the bud: "Look, they are one people, and they have all one language; and this is only the beginning of what they will do; nothing that they propose to do will now be impossible for them. Come, let us go down, and confuse their language there, so that they will not understand one another's speech" (Gen. 11:6–7). And the Lord "scattered them abroad from there over the face of all the earth, and they left off building the city" (Gen. 11:8). The narrator sums up: "Therefore it was called Babel, because there the LORD confused the language of all the earth; and from there the LORD scattered them abroad over the face of all the earth" (Gen. 11:9).

Why God found the prospect of limitless human possibilities so alarming is unclear. In Jewish tradition, the tower was viewed in a variety of ways: as a rejection of God in favor of many gods (Sanh. 109a; Gen. R. 38:6; *et al.*); as an attempt to escape a future flood (Josephus, Ant., I, IV), or as an act of extreme hubris (Jubilees 10:18–28). These same motifs were echoed in the writings of the church fathers.[12]

In its "plain meaning," however, the story accounts for the existence of different nations and languages across the known world. Human beings strive for the unity and mutual understanding that unilingualism can foster. The widespread scattering of human beings, and their division into nations with discrete languages, on the other hand, throws up obstacles that constantly remind humans of their limitations.

Babel and Babel

The themes of dispersion and misunderstanding are integral to the film *Babel* even though the plot lines do not draw upon the Genesis passage in any way. The film's intersecting stories concern people who are scattered across three continents and four countries: America (US and Mexico), North Africa, and Asia. Among them they speak five different languages: English, Arabic, Spanish, Japanese, and Japanese Sign Language, thereby drawing most viewers – most of whom would know only one or two of these languages – into the confusion as well.

Furthermore, each story line includes specific, and crucial, confusions caused by the inability of characters to comprehend one another's language and culture. In some cases an interpreter steps in to bridge the gap; at times it is simple human kindness that overcomes obstacles. Richard's efforts to seek medical help for Sarah in the tiny and isolated Moroccan village are frustrated by the lack of facilities (an economic and cultural barrier). The American couple is helped by locals, the tour guide who interprets, and a wise old woman who does not speak at all but understands what is needed and provides it through touch and empathy. The greatest barrier in their situation is posed by the competing needs, impatience, and lack of understanding of their fellow American tourists, who finally drive away in the tour bus, leaving Richard and Sarah stranded until they are rescued by an American helicopter.

In other cases, however, the confusion remains, with serious consequences for the characters. The characters in the American and Mexican stories speak both English and Spanish, but are thwarted by legal and emotional barriers. The Mexican caregiver is separated forever from her beloved young charges by an immigration officer who lacks empathy for her situation. In the Japanese story line, all characters speak Japanese, but the teenager's hearing impairment poses a communication challenge that she herself overcomes: she reads lips, uses sign language, and writes notes. In this case she is her own mediator; though she seems to be emotionally needy, she is resourceful in finding ways both to understand others and to make herself understood.

As in the biblical story, the diversity masks an underlying interconnectedness. Although the actors in the various stories do not interact directly, they are all implicated in and affected by the random shooting in the Moroccan countryside. The movie connects to the biblical story visually as well, through the camera work which plays with the notion of height and depth to great effect. The boy with the gun is standing on a mountain top, from which he shoots at the tourist bus as it drives along the road in the valley far below. Yasujiro and Chieko Wataya, the Japanese father and daughter, live in a high-rise apartment building. The most dramatic parts of their story take place on the balcony that overlooks the city from a great height. Indeed, the balcony, like the tower of Babel, is a potentially dangerous place. Chieko tells the policeman that her mother jumped to her death, information that is either a delusion or an outright lie. Her father returns home to find his daughter standing naked on the balcony; he, and we viewers, fear that she will jump, but she does not. Instead, she turns to him for comfort. The conclusion of the film is both tragic – the shooter's innocent brother is shot by police and the caregiver is deported to Mexico for good – and happy – Sarah and her children survive their ordeals; Richard and Sarah appear to have achieved a reconciliation, as have Yasujiro and Chieko.

By evoking the biblical confusion of tongues in the title, the film provokes viewers to understand these stories, and their interconnections, in the broader context of the human condition. The scattered situation of people prompts them to seek ways to overcome distance, whether geographic, linguistic, or emotional, succeeding at least on occasion.

Inglourious Basterds *(2009)*

Plot summary

War, and its connection both to national identity and to personal trauma, is a theme that runs through the entire history of cinema. Old Testament epics focus on the notion of a just war of the democratic God-loving underdog against the autocratic, pagan, or atheistic empire. People die in battle but for a righteous cause that strengthens the chosen people. In their mid-twentieth century contexts, these films echo America's sense of its own destiny, as filtered through the lens of Puritan theology that identifies America with biblical Israel. But also at stake is the experience of America in the First World

War, and, for films made in the golden era of the epic from 1949–65, the Second World War, the Holocaust, and the Cold War. These films inevitably glorify war and America. More recent films run the gamut from glorification to vilification.[13] They also reflect upon the war in Vietnam (*Apocalypse Now* [1979]), the war on terror (post 9–11, e.g., *United 93* [2006]; *Zero Dark Thirty* [2012]) and the wars in Afghanistan and Iraq (e.g., *The Hurt Locker* [2008]). In doing so, they reflect the ambivalence of the American public about these wars, including their causes, and also the ways in which they are carried out.

Quentin Tarantino's engrossing film, *Inglourious Basterds*, traces two parallel plots to assassinate Hitler, one initiated by a young French Jewish woman, Shosanna Dreyfus (Mélanie Laurent) whose entire family had been killed by the Nazis, and the other by a team of American Jewish soldiers led by First Lieutenant Aldo Raine (Brad Pitt). The film is a glorious fable about the power of cinema to change the world; it leaves the viewer (or, at least, *this* viewer) with the wistful thought: If only Tarantino's fantasy had come true! Like many of Tarantino's films, this one combines graphic violence with humor both whimsical and dark, and, as in his 1994 masterpiece, *Pulp Fiction*, the biblical story of Cain and Abel plays a small but important part.

Cain and Abel in the Bible

According to Genesis 4, Cain and Abel were the first two children of Adam and Eve, and like most siblings, their relationship included a large dose of rivalry. Abel kept sheep, and Cain tilled the soil, and each brought offerings to God in keeping with their occupations. When God favored Abel's offering over that of Cain, Cain flew into a rage, and killed his brother. When confronted by God as to Abel's whereabouts, Cain famously, and disingenuously, replied: "Am I my brother's keeper?" (Gen. 4:9). But God was not fooled:

> What have you done? Listen; your brother's blood is crying out to me from the ground! And now you are cursed from the ground, which has opened its mouth to receive your brother's blood from your hand. When you till the ground, it will no longer yield to you its strength; you will be a fugitive and a wanderer on the earth.

Cain was distraught: "My punishment is greater than I can bear! Today you have driven me away from the soil, and I shall be hidden from your face; I shall be a fugitive and a wanderer on the earth, and anyone who meets me may kill me." But this was not God's plan: "Not so!" he tells Cain. "Whoever kills Cain will suffer a sevenfold vengeance." The narrator concludes the tale: "And the LORD put a mark on Cain, so that no one who came upon him would kill him" (Gen. 4:1–15).

The expression "mark of Cain" has entered into English idiom and into art, literature, film, and other forms of popular culture.[14] The concept includes two main components: the physical mark itself, as an external sign of evil or sinful character or behavior; and the notion of wandering. The allusions to the story also include varieties of Cain's challenge to God: "Am I my brother's keeper?"[15] In *Pulp Fiction*, the allusion is brief and occurs in the final scene, when one gangster, Jules (Samuel Jackson) explains to his buddy Vince (John Travolta), that he is leaving his life of crime behind in order to "walk the earth ... like Caine in *Kung Fu*." Vince scoffs: "So you decided to be a bum?" Jules insists that, no, "I'll just be Jules, Vincent – no more, no less." Caine is the main character in the television western series *Kung Fu* (1972–75). In each episode, Caine took on a fight for justice, and then moved on, to avoid capture and to avoid possible repercussions for those whom he helped. The scene, like many others in this clever film, has several leaves of meaning, alluding to both the biblical Cain and the pop-cultural Caine.

Cain and the "Basterds"

In Tarantino's 2009 film, the Cain narrative works in a more complicated way, bookending the major plot line involving First Lieutenant Aldo "The Apache" Raine's Jewish unit of Inglourious Basterds, and bringing closure to the film as a whole. Early in the film, Aldo introduces himself and his mission as follows:

> My name is Lt. Aldo Raine, and I'm putting together a special team. And I need me eight soldiers. Eight – Jewish – American – Soldiers ... We're gonna be dropped into France, dressed as civilians. And once we're in enemy territory, as a bushwackin' guerilla army, we're gonna be doin' one thing, and one thing only: Killin' Nazis ... Nazi ain't got no humanity. They're the foot soldiers of a Jew-hatin', mass-murderin' maniac, and they need to be destroyed. That's why any and every son-of-a-bitch we find wearin' a Nazi uniform, they're gonna die.... And all y'all will get me, one hundred Nazi scalps, taken from the heads of one hundred Nazis or you will die trying.

With gusto and in graphic detail, Aldo describes the suffering that he and his Basterds will inflict on the Nazis. But while he has insisted that "any and every" person wearing a Nazi uniform will die, he intends to spare the life of a few Nazis, so that they may be unable to conceal their Nazi identities when they shed their army uniforms. The viewer is made to watch as Aldo carves the swastika onto the forehead of one Nazi, as he explains:

> We let you live so you could spread the word through the ranks what's going to happen to every Nazi we find.... See, we like our Nazis in uniforms. That way you can spot them.... But you take off that uniform, ain't nobody going to know you's a Nazi. And that don't sit well with us.... So I'm going to give you a little something you can't take off.

At the end of the film we see Aldo do it again, as he celebrates his victory over his archenemy, Colonel Landa. After reciting the same speech he has made to many other such "Cains," Aldo carves a swastika on Landa's forehead and then admires his own handiwork: "You know something … ? This just might be my masterpiece."

The Cain motif underscores the profound conviction about the evil of Nazism that fuels the entire film. Tarantino does not waver for one moment from this theme, and, never a squeamish director, he is unflinching in his portrayal of the cruel treatment deserved by Nazis from Hitler down to the cowardly foot soldiers of the German army. The swastika with which Landa and others are branded not only marks them as Nazis but also ensures that they will carry out an important task: to bear witness to Nazi crimes against humanity. The witness motif is absent from the biblical story, but to someone like Tarantino with a strong Catholic education, it readily calls to mind Augustine's famous statement that God has preserved the Jews, their scriptures, and their customs, and made them spread throughout the world, as an eternal witness to the truth of the Christian message. In Augustine's exegesis of Cain and Abel, the Jews are identified as Cain: like Cain, they have slain their "brother," Jesus, and like Cain they are branded but preserved, so that all whom they encounter shall know of their sin, and thereby also the truth of the Christian message.[16]

The film reverses Augustine's exegesis of Genesis 4 by casting the Jewish Basterds in the role of God, as they brand the Nazi sinners with the mark of Cain so that in their wanderings they will bear witness to the evils that they have perpetrated against the Jews. This treatment taps into the larger theme of reversal that characterizes the film as a whole: Hitler is not a diabolical and methodical mastermind but a megalomaniacal fool outwitted by a young Jewish woman, the epitome of the nation that he was trying to annihilate. His death at the cinema, masterminded by the cinema's owner Shosanna, is warranted by the millions of deaths, of Jews and others, caused by his regime. The Jews are transformed from victims of genocide to warrior Apaches who avenge the death of their people, led by a commander who though not himself Jewish is singlemindedly committed to this cause. The centrality of the reversal theme is signaled by the misspellings in the title of the film itself, and, indeed, far from "inglourious," the "basterds" show themselves to be glorious in their dedication to and fulfillment of their mission. The theme of reversal returns us to the passage itself, in which God reverses Cain's own expectations: whereas the murderer expects to be punished by death, God has other plans.

In The Valley of Elah *(2007)*

Plot summary

Reversal is also a major plot motif in the film *In the Valley of Elah*, and in the biblical passage upon which it draws. While many moviegoers are likely to be familiar with the biblical event associated with Babel, few may remember exactly what took place in the Valley of Elah until they are told the names of the dramatis personae: David and Goliath. The confrontation between these two people is itself built on reversal, as the young, small Israelite shepherd boy David defeats and slays the fearful giant Philistine warrior Goliath with a mere slingshot (see 1 Samuel 17).

The film's protagonist, Hank Deerfield (Tommy Lee Jones), is a former military policeman, who has learned that his son Mike, a soldier recently returned from a tour of duty in Iraq, has gone missing from his army base. Mike's body is found in a field, burned and dismembered. With the help of a policewoman, Emily Sanders (Charlize Theron), Hank sets out to discover the identity of his son's killer. The film is based on the actual events surrounding the disappearance and death of Specialist Richard Davis, a mystery unraveled through the persistent efforts of his father, Staff Sergeant Lanny Davis, retired, a United States Army veteran. The story was told in an article entitled "Death and Dishonor," by Mark Boal, published in Playboy magazine in 2004.[17]

The film firmly establishes Hank's commitment to the army, not only through his own service but through the strong positive value that he attached to military service. This was a value that he passed along to his sons, both of whom enlisted, and died in the course of their service though not in active combat (we learn early on that Hank's older son was killed in a helicopter accident at Fort Bragg). Hank is self-disciplined and organized; in fact, he still makes his bed military style, even when staying in a motel that presumably has a daily housekeeping service.

Hank's attempts to find out what happened to his son Mike, and why, are repeatedly and vigorously blocked by the military police. He is aided only by Emily Sanders who herself has trouble getting the time of day even from her own colleagues in the police force. As he continues his investigation, Hank gradually loses his confidence in and respect for the army; as time goes on he comes to believe that they were less interested in finding out what happened than in covering it up and protecting their own. In the end, through persistence and strategic thinking, Hank and Emily succeed in learning the truth.

The film does not address the basic question of whether the war in Iraq was a necessary or justified war. Rather, its focus is on the effect of war on the behavior and the emotional and psychological health of the soldiers who participate in active combat duty. The film implies that there is something very wrong with the army when it turns a blind eye both to the needs and the illegal and antisocial behaviors of those upon whom it depends. The movie focuses on the soldiers – including Hank's son Mike – who turn to drugs and violence, and who find themselves abusing prisoners of war or running over the children in their path who simply happen to be playing or walking in the street. Hank is driven by guilt as he realizes that his son had tried to tell him that he could not live with his own actions, a plea that Hank ignored at the time.

Hank's increasingly critical attitude toward the army is signaled in several ways. The state of order and cleanliness of his room declines as his view of the army declines. He no longer makes his bed and lets the litter pile up. A second signal concerns the motif of the American flag. Near the beginning of the film, Hank enters the local high school to complain about the fact that the American flag is flying upside down. Hank seeks out Juan, the Salvadoran custodian, and helps him hang the flag correctly, explaining that an upside down flag is an international distress signal: "It means we are in a whole lot of trouble, so come save our ass, cause we haven't got a prayer in hell of saving ourselves." Hank's demeanor makes it clear that in his view America could never be in that situation; indeed, as the world's superpower, it is America's role to "save the asses" of weaker countries overseas, such as Iraq, a mission that he and his sons served with pride. At the end of the film, Hank notices that the parcel that had arrived from Mike during Hank's absence had been opened; it contained a tattered American Flag. Hank brings the flag to the high school where he runs it up the flagpole as Juan looks on. Juan comments: "Looks really old," to which Hank responds, "It's been well used." Hank instructs Juan not to take it down, even at night, then walks off. The last shot of the film is of the tattered flag, hanging upside down, flapping in the breeze. The message? America is a country in distress. But who will save her?

The title of the film signals a connection between biblical Israel and America and the biblical parallel is further accentuated by the small but symbolically significant role that a copy of the Bible plays in the action. When Hank first goes to Mike's army base, he looks through his things and finds his camera. He pockets it, and then covers this act up by asking the officer, who is supervising the visit, whether he can take the Bible. We sense that the Bible does not actually mean much to Hank. At this point the officer refuses; later on, however, one of Mike's buddies, Bonner, brings the Bible over to Hank: "I overheard you asking if you could have Mike's Bible. I thought it might bring you some comfort." We also see him sitting on the bed of his motel room, leafing through the Bible, perhaps in search of comfort, or perhaps hoping to get a better sense of his dead son.

What happened in the Valley of Elah?

Although the Valley of Elah, located southwest of Jerusalem, is not well known today, it is the site of a very famous biblical story: the victory of the young David over the giant Philistine Goliath. The story is told in 1 Samuel 17, the story of David and Goliath. Knowing that many viewers would not be familiar with the reference, the filmmakers create a scene in which Hank tells the story, in detail, to Emily Sanders' young son, appropriately named David. Hank tells David that he is named after King David and then tells him the story: "There were two armies assembled, the Israelites and the Philistines; they were both on hills, with the Valley of Elah between them.

That's a place in Palestine. You know where that is?" David shakes his head. Hank continues: "It doesn't matter. Anyway, the Philistines had a champion, a giant named Goliath.... every day for forty days, Goliath strode out into the field and challenged somebody from the other side to fight him, and nobody would. The strongest and bravest warriors that the king had were all too scared." David interjects, "Why didn't they just shoot him?" Hank responds:

> They didn't have guns. They had arrows, but there are rules to combat. You don't shoot somebody who is challenging you to fight with a sword. So, this kid, not much older than you, he comes delivering bread. And he says to the king, "I'll fight Goliath." ... So, the king dressed David in his own armor, but it was much too big and heavy. So, David takes it off. He looks around and finds five smooth stones, about yea big. He steps into the field, with his slingshot in his hand. And Goliath comes running, yelling, this horrible scream. And David lets fly the stone. And hits him in the forehead. Cracks his skull. And Goliath falls down, dead ... You know how he was able to beat him? ... First thing David had to fight was his own fear. He beat that, he beat Goliath. Cause when Goliath charged, David just planted his feet, took aim, and waited. You know how much nerve that took? A few more steps and Goliath would have crushed him. And then he threw the rock.

David, Goliath, and the American Army

The entire scene described in the preceding section is extraneous to the plot and characterization of the film. The biblical passage, and Mike's Bible itself, play no part in the plot, nor are they integrated into the development of the characters, as for example are the quotations and allusions in *Inglourious Basterds* or *Evan Almighty*. Instead, the title and the biblical story to which it refers, like the title of the film *Babel*, provide the key to the theme of the film. The film is about the ability of a small and relatively unempowered individual to use his wiles and the weapons available to him, to defeat a larger, better armed, bully. Were this an Old Testament epic film, we would know that the big bully is Egypt or some other ancient power, and the young victorious upstart is biblical Israel. We would also know that these biblical figures represent America's (moral) victory over an authoritarian ideology such as fascism or communism. *In the Valley of Elah*, however, the conflict is not between America and Iraq, but between a grieving father and the American army. The army, with its secrecy, bureaucracy, and ideology, is the bully who is unexpectedly vanquished by an old ex-army cop and a lowly female police detective. This plot line provides depth and content to the message conveyed by the upside down American flag, about America as a country whose combative tendencies are failing her own citizens. If films such as *The Ten Commandments* and *David and Bathsheba* glorify America's role as a military power that defends democracy in the face of the evil forces of fascism and communism, films such as *In the Valley of Elah* project a much more ambivalent perspective on the American army, at least in its relationship to its young soldiers.

Conclusion

Films such as *Babel*, *Inglourious Basterds*, and *In the Valley of Elah* treat the Bible as a common and well-known cultural resource that has a special, formative, and normative status in western society. This is not to say that they presume wide and deep knowledge of the Bible. On the contrary, fictional films tend to draw on a small number of stories – Noah's flood, the Tower of Babel, the Exodus. When drawing on lesser known stories, or on lesser known aspects of those stories, films employ mechanisms to teach those stories to their audiences, as illustrated by the scene in *In the Valley of Elah* in which we viewers listen in as Hank tells the story of David and Goliath to the little boy named David. Second, and more important, the use of the Bible signals to readers that the meaning of the film extends beyond the specifics of its own plot and characters to say something broader about the human experience. In this way, the Bible becomes a conventional element in the cinematic repertoire for ascribing meaning to films themselves. Indeed, films can change the world, as *Inglourious Basterds* declares, through the courageous act of Shosanna, the courageous Jewish cinema owner, who destroys Nazi leadership through a spectacular cinematic event.

Notes

1 For a detailed analysis of this film, see Adele Reinhartz, "Pale Rider, Nell, and the Misuse of Scripture," in *Scripture on the Silver Screen* (Louisville, KY: Westminster John Knox Press, 2003), 177–78.
2 Adele Reinhartz, "The Apostle and the Power of the Book (John)," in *Scripture on the Silver Screen* (Louisville, KY: Westminster John Knox Press, 2003), 114–28.
3 Adele Reinhartz, "Fried Green Tomatoes and the Power of Female Friendships (Ruth)," in *Scripture on the Silver Screen* (Louisville, KY: Westminster John Knox Press, 2003), 54–66.
4 Adele Reinhartz, "Pulp Fiction and the Power of Belief (Ezekiel)," in *Scripture on the Silver Screen* (Louisville, KY: Westminster John Knox Press, 2003), 97–113.
5 For discussion, see Adele Reinhartz, "Magnolia and the Plague of Frogs (Exodus)," in *Scripture on the Silver Screen* (Louisville, KY: Westminster John Knox Press, 2003), 24–38.
6 Dan Brown, *The Da Vinci Code: A Novel* (New York: Doubleday, 2003).
7 Of course, the storm, the island, and the US Department of Inclement Weather are all entirely fictional.
8 Eric Walter White, *Benjamin Britten: His Life and Operas*, ed. John Evans, second edition (Berkeley, CA: University of California Press, 1983), 214.
9 For an introduction to Britten's *Noye's Fludde*, and his use of the sacred opera genre, see William Anthony Sheppard, *Revealing Masks: Exotic Influences and*

Ritualized Performance in Modernist Music Theater (Berkeley, CA: University of California Press, 2001), 117–21.

10 On the different aspects of self-reference in film, see Gloria Withalm, "The Self-Reflexive Screen: Outlines of a Comprehensive Model," in *Self-Reference in the Media*, ed. Winfried Nöth and Nina Bishara (Berlin; New York: Mouton de Gruyter, 2007), 125–42.

11 Scott L. Baugh, *Latino American Cinema: An Encyclopedia of Movies, Stars, Concepts, and Trends* (Santa Barbara, CA: Greenwood, 2012), 22, 217.

12 In City of God 16.4, Augustine describes the Tower of Babel as an act of arrogance and pride, for "The safe and true way to heaven is made by humility, which lifts up the heart to the Lord, not against Him." He views Nimrod as the architect of the tower; Nimrod and his people were punished: "As the tongue is the instrument of domination, in it pride was punished; so that man, who would not understand God when He issued His commands, should be misunderstood when he himself gave orders. Thus was that conspiracy disbanded, for each man retired from those he could not understand, and associated with those whose speech was intelligible; and the nations were divided according to their languages, and scattered over the earth as seemed good to God, who accomplished this in ways hidden from and incomprehensible to us." Augustine, *The City of God*. Trans. Marcus Dods. From Nicene and Post-Nicene Fathers, First Series, vol. 2, ed. Philip Schaff (Buffalo, NY: Christian Literature Publishing Co., 1887). Revised ed. by Kevin Knight. www.newadvent.org/fathers/120116.htm (accessed 10 May 2013).

13 Peter C. Rollins and John E. O'Connor, *Why We Fought: America's Wars in Film and History*, Film & History (Lexington, KY: University Press of Kentucky, 2008).

14 On the representation of Cain in art, see Ruth Mellinkoff, *The Mark of Cain* (Berkeley, CA: University of California Press, 1981). On Cain in literature, see Ricardo J. Quinones, *The Changes of Cain: Violence and the Lost Brother in Cain and Abel Literature* (Princeton, NJ: Princeton University Press, 1991). For a lengthy list of songs, movies, novels and television shows, see http://en.wikipedia.org/wiki/Cain_and_Abel#Popular_culture (accessed 10 May 2013).

15 This line appears, for example, in the 1955 film *East of Eden*, when Adam confronts his older son Cal concerning the disappearance of the younger brother, Aron. It is also the title of a 1998 album by the group Kane and Able. www.stlyrics.com/songs/k/kaneable2119.html (accessed 10 May 2013).

16 On Augustine's use of the Cain motif, see Paula Fredriksen, *Augustine and the Jews: A Christian Defense of Jews and Judaism* (New York: Doubleday, 2008), 260–89. On Cain in Christian theology, see Lisa A. Unterseher, *The Mark of Cain and the Jews: Augustine's Theology of Jews and Judaism*, Gorgias Dissertations 39 (Piscataway, NJ: Gorgias Press, 2009).

17 For the story, see http://memoriesofrichard.tripod.com/id6.html (accessed 23 February 2012).

7 "One like a son of man"
Christ-figure films

In the dramatic climax to the 2008 film *Gran Torino*, Walt Kowalski, a grumpy old Korean War veteran, stands on a dark street, staring at a duplex. A group of young Hmong men are visible in the upper windows. They are talking, swearing, and laughing loudly. Walt continues to stare until a couple of the young men come out. "Any swamp rats in there?" he sneers. One man opens his mouth to reply but Walt cuts him off: "Shut up, gook. I've got nothing to say to you, shrimp-dick. Midget like you." Another man points a pistol at Walt, who continues: "Ya, ya, watch out for your boyfriend. Cuz it was either he or you or someone who raped someone in their own family. Your own blood, for Christ's sake! Go ahead, pull those pistols, like miniature cowboys, go ahead." Walt reaches into his pocket and slowly pulls out a cigarette. "Gotta light?" he asks, then answers softly, "No." He raises his hand: "Me, I've gotta light." He slowly reaches into his jacket, as he whispers to himself, "Hail Mary, full of grace." Six Hmong "gangbangers" machine gun him down. Walt falls to the ground in cruciform position. The camera zooms in on his hand, which slowly falls open to reveal his Zippo lighter, and the blood slowly trickling out of the palm of his hand, like Christ's stigmata.

With this act of sacrifice – undertaken to save the life and protect the future of his teenage Hmong neighbor, Tau – Walt joins other Eastwood characters, such as the Man-with-No-Name in *A Fistful of Dollars* (1964) and the equally anonymous preacher in *Pale Rider* (1995) as well as countless other cinematic Christ-figures. Among them are Andy Dufresne (*Shawshank Redemption*, 1994), Carl Childers (*Sling Blade*, 1996), the Extra-Terrestrial (*E.T. the Extra-Terrestrial*, 1982), Maggie Fitzgerald (*Million Dollar Baby*, 2004), Rocky Balboa (*Rocky*, 1976), Superman (e.g., *Superman Returns*, 2006), and Spider-man (e.g., *Spider-man*, 2002).

Christ-figures have long been popular in fictional feature films. As Lloyd Baugh has pointed out,

> From early in the development of cinema, filmmakers have told stories in which the central figures are foils for Jesus and in which the plot is parallel to the story of the life, death and, sometimes, the Resurrection of Jesus, stories in which the "presence" of Jesus is sensed and discerned in the person and struggle of the protagonist.[1]

As early as 1916, when D. W. Griffith compared the Boy in the Modern Story to Jesus in the "Judean story" (*Intolerance*) and 1923, when DeMille made his Johnny a wise, good, loving, forgiving, and pious young man (*The Ten Commandments*), fictional characters have been endowed with Christ-like characteristics and their stories with Gospel-like narratives.

Genres

Christ-figures appear in films of virtually every genre in commercial cinema, and they can take numerous guises: saints, priests, women, clowns, fools, madmen, outlaws, children, and even actors who play objects.[2] The following examples indicate the broad range of films in which Christ-figures can be found.

- *Westerns* frequently include the motif of the mysterious stranger who rides into town, saves the hardworking folk from marauders, and rides off into the sunset. He is usually excluded from the community he saves by his special status as well as his use of violence (e.g., *Shane*, 1953; *Pale Rider*, 1985; *The Good, The Bad and the Ugly*, 1966). In this context *Unforgiven* (1992) is a counterexample that deromanticizes the genre even as it adheres to some of its most salient conventions.
- *Boxing movies* portray boxing as a metaphor for the triumph over adversity. Most of the protagonists come from the lower and poorer segments of society, allowing these films to address issues pertaining to class and poverty (e.g., the *Rocky* series, 1976–2006; *Million Dollar Baby*, 2004; *Cinderella Man*, 2005).
- *"Psych" movies* often use Christ imagery to address our society's tendencies to marginalize people with psychiatric disorders or diminished mental capacity. In most of these films, the protagonist is depicted as outside the framework of mainstream society, not only psychologically but also physically: some are imprisoned (e.g., *Sling Blade*, 1996; *The Green Mile*, 1999), or in a psychiatric institution (*One Flew over the Cuckoo's Nest*, 1975) or threatened with one (*Nell*, 1994). Others get by because they are not perceived as disabled (*Being There*, 1979). Not all movies of this genre make use of Christ-imagery (e.g., *Rain Man*, 1988), but many of these protagonists do act in ways that save others, if not always themselves.
- *Science fiction and apocalyptic movies* project the future, whether they envision an alternative world (*The Matrix*, 1999), a world in which human beings have taken upon themselves the divine role of giving life and taking it away (*Frankenstein*, 1931; *Blade Runner*, 1982), or one in which humans must cope with a catastrophe on a gigantic scale (e.g., *Deep Impact*, 1998; the *Star Wars* series, 1977–2005; the *Terminator* series, 1984–2009; *The Fifth Element*, 1997; *Children of Men*, 2006).[3]
- *Spy movies* involve heroes who, with all their imperfections, nevertheless save others, often preventing massive destruction from befalling their own

countries and/or other countries and the (western) world order (e.g., *The Good Shepherd*, 2006; *The Constant Gardener*, 2005; *Walk on Water*, 2004).

• *Mob movies* often use Christian, specifically, Catholic imagery, a feature that is natural given that the most famous mafia movies, *The Godfather I, II*, and *III* focus on Italians or Italian-Americans with strong Catholic identities. More surprising is the fact that some of these mobsters take on Christ-like roles despite the illegal and often murderous nature of their activities (e.g., *The Godfather* series, 1972–90; *Goodfellas*, 1990; *The Departed*, 2006).

• *Superhero movies* feature super-people with extraordinary powers which they use to save others; their exploits nevertheless involve some risk to themselves. Like Jesus, they often have mysterious parentage, eschew romantic relationships, and fight the forces of evil (e.g., *Superman Returns*, 2006; the *Spider-Man* trilogy, 2002–7; *The Incredibles*, 2004).[4]

• *Romantic comedies*, perhaps the most unlikely Christ-figure films, portray the male or female protagonist as saving another from loneliness, low self-esteem, a life of promiscuity, or some other negative emotional state. These films offer light, and even frivolous entertainment; often one or even both protagonists are explicitly linked with Christ-imagery (*About a Boy*, 2002; *Music and Lyrics*, 2007; *Pretty Woman*, 1990).

• *Animated movies*, feature animal or toy protagonists who save other animals (*The Lion King*, 1994), humans (*The Chronicles of Narnia* series, 2005–8; *Babe: Pig in the City*, 1998; *Charlotte's Web*, 2006), or other toys (*Toy Story 3*, 2010).

Conventions

Bibles as "props"

Bibles as such have on-screen roles in countless feature films. In Robert Duvall's *The Apostle* (1997), as in Billy Bob Thornton's *Sling Blade* (1997), the Bible is both featured on the screen and discussed in the dialog. In *The Apostle* the Bible is endowed with the extraordinary power to stop a tractor in its tracks, whereas in *Sling Blade* it provides an important cue to the motivations and personality of the main character, as well as his opponents.

Biblical quotation or allusion

Biblical quotation or allusion – in film titles (e.g., *The Good Shepherd*, 2006; cf. John 10) and/or in dialog – is ubiquitous in Christ-figure films; it can be used dramatically, ironically, and in numerous other ways. Quotations also occur visually, as in Clint Eastwood's *Unforgiven* (1992), in which Ned, a cowboy (Morgan Freeman), is scourged and whipped as he faces the camera, arms outstretched, upper body naked and running with blood. He stands behind bars that not only evoke prison but the shape of the cross. Later, his dead body is displayed upright in a cruciform position within an open coffin. A sign inscribed with the words "This is what happens to assassins around here" forms the cross piece, calling to mind the titulus above Jesus' cross that identified Jesus as "Jesus of Nazareth, King of the Jews" (Matt. 27:37; Mark 15:26; Luke 23:38; John 19:19–22).

Characters and plot

Films that feature an on-screen Bible as well as biblical dialog often also model a major character after Jesus and all or part of their narrative on the Passion. In many cases, the hero is a Christ-figure who suffers or dies so that others may live, or live better. In a film such as *Unforgiven*, the paradigm is subtle and appears clearly only near the climax of the film, whereas in a film such as *The Shawshank Redemption*, the Gospel story more broadly is evident as a structuring element.

What is a Christ-figure film?

But what is a Christ-figure, and how can we recognize one in a darkened theater, or on any of the myriad screens on which we view feature films today? A first, important step is to distinguish Christ-figure films from Jesus films. Whereas Jesus films represent the story of Jesus "himself," set (usually) in an ancient context and directly depicting events from the Gospels, "Christ-figure films" are fictional feature movies in which characters behave in ways that are reminiscent of events in the Gospel accounts. *Gran Torino*, for example, presents Walt Kowalski as a figure who resembles Jesus in only one way: he acts decisively, altruistically, and at great and ultimately fatal risk to his own life, in order to save another. But Walt remains a very human being throughout, and a foul-mouthed, racist, grumpy one at that. A further distinction is proposed by Peter Malone, who distinguishes between those that are redeemer figures, that is, characters who take on human burdens and sinfulness through suffering, and those that are savior figures, enacting Jesus' saving mission with respect to humankind as a whole (e.g., *Deep Impact* [1998]) or to individuals (e.g., *Sling Blade*), though he acknowledges that these two categories are not mutually exclusive.[5]

The search for criteria

Many, quite reasonably, have sought specific criteria for identifying Christ-figures in fictional feature films. Lloyd Baugh proposes a list of eight criteria for identifying cinematic Christ-figures: he or she has (1) mysterious origins, (2) charisma (the ability to attract followers), and (3) a commitment to justice. Further, Christ-figures often (4) withdraw to a deserted place, (5) become embroiled in conflicts with authorities, (6) provide redemption for others, (7) suffer, and (8) achieve post-death recognition.[6] Anton Kozlovic lists 25 characteristics, pointing out, for example, that cinematic Christ-figures are often aged 30, have blue eyes, are outsiders in society, and experience betrayal and death.[7] Neither Baugh nor Kozlovic argues that every Christ-figure must contain all the qualities in their respective lists.

Criteria: a proposal

In my own study of these films, I have found it helpful to look not so much for individual details of characterization and plot but for the convergence of three different types of elements: Bible quotations, both aural (e.g., in dialog) and visual; plot; and character traits. First, to ensure that viewers grasp the presence of the Christ-figure genre, the savior-protagonist is portrayed through visual and aural images commonly linked with Christ. The most prevalent is the cross or the cruciform position. Many Christ-like protagonists walk on (*Being There*), in (*Walk on Water*) or beside (*The Constant Gardener*) a body of water.

Second, Christ-figure films include a plot line in which the protagonist confronts a harsh and often authoritarian antagonist, engages in an act that saves or redeems another, and experiences death and resurrection, whether figurative or literal. In dramas, that salvific act generally entails self-sacrifice such as loss of freedom or loss of life. Examples of the tragic Christ-figure plot line include *Cool Hand Luke*, *Sling Blade*, and *The Green Mile*. In comedies, the salvific act ends not with the death of the hero but rather with his or her triumph over adversity. Examples include *The Truman Show* (1998) and, as we shall see, *The Shawshank Redemption*.

Third, Christ-heroes exhibit altruism and love for others. These traits can be inferred from his or her behavior and his or her treatment by other characters. Christ-figures have human flaws and often grow into their roles by overcoming adversity and experiencing change. This capacity for change allows Christ figures to have a powerful effect on the viewer, in contrast to "Jesus of Hollywood", who is sinless and perfect from the outset.[8]

The Great Dictator *(1940)*

Plot summary

The convergence of these three points is well-illustrated by the famous Charlie Chaplin film, *The Great Dictator*, which makes both ironic and sincere use of the Christ-figure paradigm. In this film, Chaplin plays two characters: an amnesiac and anonymous Jewish barber, and the evil dictator of the fictional land of Tomainia, Adenoid Hynkel. Hynkel's Tomainia is a fascist regime transparently modeled on Hitler's Germany; its symbol is the double cross, and its language is a mangled parody of the German language. This film was the first major American feature film to satirize and condemn Nazism, Hitler, and antisemitism, at a point when the United States had not yet entered the Second World War and therefore was still officially at peace with Germany.[9]

Christ-figures: ironic and sincere

The film evokes the Jesus of the Gospels through direct quotation from the Gospels. Early in the film, the film satirizes Hitler's self-perception as Germany's savior. When one of Hynkel's underlings defects, Hynkel paraphrases Jesus' last words (cf. Mark 15:34; Matt. 27:46; cf. Psalm 22:1) in his lament: "Schultz, why have you forsaken me?"[10] At the end of the film, through a comic, complicated, and utterly implausible sequence of events, the barber replaces Hynkel as Tomainia's emperor. But the barber does not want to conquer or rule over anyone. Rather, as he tells the millions who hear his inaugural address, "I should like to help everyone if possible, Jew, gentile, black man, white." In this desire, the barber insists, he is like most people:

> We all want to help one another, human beings are like that. We all want to live by each other's happiness, not by each other's misery. We don't want to hate and despise one another. In this world there is room for everyone and the earth is rich and can provide for everyone.

He finds support for this humanistic perspective in the New Testament: "In the seventeenth chapter of Saint Luke it is written 'the kingdom of God is within man'" that is, not within one person, nor a group of people, but "in you, the people.... [who] have the power, the power to create machines, the power to create happiness." The barber calls on his compatriots to unite for democracy: "Let us fight for a new world, a decent world that will give men a chance to work, that will give you the future and old age and security." He concludes,

> Look up! Look up! The clouds are lifting – the sun is breaking through. We are coming out of the darkness into the light [cf. John 3:20]. We are coming into a new world. A kind new world where men will rise above their hate and brutality.... Look up. Look up.

In contrast to Hynkel, who fancies himself a new messiah, the barber invokes the New Testament not to describe himself but to express Chaplin's deep-seated beliefs in the goodness of humankind and hope for the future. At the same time, Hynkel's self-aggrandizing quotation of the Bible contrasts sharply with the barber's humble reference, a contrast that also points to the danger that can attend the quotation of the Bible to further one's own mega-lomaniacal ends.

The Great Dictator illustrates the three elements that, in my view, are needed to identify a Christ-figure film. Both Hynkel and the barber quote directly from the Bible, and are associated with visual allusions such as the twisted cross that aptly characterizes Hynkel's regime. Chaplin's characters present a twisted, self-appointed "savior" figure who causes death and destruction, and a humble barber who in fact, if inadvertently, saves his people. Both characters have Christ-like character traits, ironically in the case of Hynkel, sincerely in the case of the barber.

Why study Christ-figure films?

Hollywood's fascination with Christ-figures has not gone unnoticed. While all film critics agree that Christ-figures abound in popular film, there is no consensus as to the value of seeking them out, or what to make of them once found. Even Anton Kozlovic, who has viewed enough Christ-figure films to be able to discern 25 characteristics, warns of viewer fatigue and deplores the tendency to see Christ-figures everywhere.[11] Clive Marsh refers to the quest for Christ-figures as a "tired and sometimes tiresome pastime, so that any character who helps another to come to some major realization about themselves can be seen as salvific, and thus Christ-like. This borders on triteness."[12]

The identification of cinematic Christ-figures is often seen as a dubious enterprise, for three reasons. First, it is subjective. We may all agree more or less on the fact that certain features, such as speaking in parables, walking on water, crucifixion and resurrection, characterize Jesus in the Gospels and continue to be associated with Christ as portrayed in a variety of media. But we may easily disagree on whether the appearance of water, or the image of a person in a cruciform position, for example, necessarily directs the viewer to interpret the movie as a Christ-figure film. Second, although some of the many Christ-related motifs come from sources external to the movies, such as the Gospels, others, such as the combination of music and visual imagery that is often present when Jesus-like protagonists take on a cruciform position, come from the films themselves. For this reason, the identification of the Christ-figure film is an unavoidably circular process: the images and other Christ-related elements are extracted from the films themselves, and then used as a tool for interpreting those same films and others like them. The third element that raises suspicion is simply the enjoyment that many – including many serious New Testament scholars – derive in finding Christ-images in popular film. This enjoyment may suggest to some that the identification and analysis of these films may well be the sort of activity more appropriate for coffee shops than the halls and journals of academe.[13]

How to study Christ-figure films

Now, as one of these movie-loving New Testament scholars, I can attest to the fact that enjoyment and academic merit are not mutually exclusive, and that the mere identification of a Christ-figure in film is not an end in itself but merely a first step in the analysis. Baugh suggests that Christ-figure films can

be read on two levels: "the direct and the analogical, the literal and the figurative; and on the figurative or metaphorical level, they accept a reading that
is biblical and christological." In this regard, argues Baugh, Christ-figure films
are similar to Jesus' parables, which can be read literally as brief narratives of
human experience, but which "fairly explode with theological or christological significance" when they are read metaphorically. He views Christ-figures
as an example of a metaphorical usage that is deeply embedded in Christian
faith and doctrine. Specifically, he points to the incarnational nature of
Christian faith, which "insists that God reveals God's-self in and through
matter and in Christ – human matter – and not only once but in an ongoing
way."[14]

Christopher Deacy proposes to set aside the "quest for correlations" and to
engage in a two-fold conversation between theology and film. In his view,
the identification of Christ-figures is unimportant, and even illegitimate
except

> when that figure is no longer seen simply as a cipher who illuminates
> Jesus for the sole purpose of, say, making him accessible to a modern
> generation, but inspires or incites the viewer to engender a critical and
> productive theological conversation.[15]

Other scholars are concerned not so much with the theological implications
of these films but with their ideological messages. Bryan Stone argues that
films not only depict a world, they also promote a worldview.[16] Joel Martin
analyzes *Rocky* as a political and social text that employs christological imagery
for ideological ends.[17]

The cultural studies approach looks closely at the social, political, and cultural context that produced these films. According to Margaret Miles, a cultural studies approach "refocuses attention from the film as a text to the social,
political, and cultural matrix in which the film was produced and distributed".[18] In her view, filmgoers will tend to interpret and discuss movies in
relation to the social issues of the moment. For this reason,

> A spectator's impressions of a film … are simultaneously informed by her
> education and life experiences and trained by film conventions and
> viewing habits. This does not mean that the strong feeling a film may
> elicit should be discarded or overlooked. Rather, the emotion a film
> evokes should be acknowledged and understood as the starting point for
> an exploration of the filmic strategies that elicited it. The purpose of
> paying serious attention to film is twofold. On the one hand, the ability
> to analyze filmic representations develops an individual's critical sub-
> jectivity. On the other hand, films reveal how a society represents itself.[19]

Melanie Wright's approach builds on that of Miles, but she draws more
attention to the fact that these films have "specific histories of distribution and

exhibition" and advocates dialog with film theory, particularly aesthetics and reception.[20]

Whereas some of these scholars propose a dialog between film and theology, film and ideology, film and theory, or film and society, Larry Kreitzer argues for the value in a dialog between film and the biblical text. He argues that films that use the New Testament provide an opportunity to "reverse the hermeneutical flow." Studying movies can help to sensitize us to issues and features that can help us to better understand the biblical text as such.[21]

Virtually all of these approaches incorporate a narrative approach to the Christ-figure films, by considering the role that the Christ-figure plays in the film narrative. In discussing the figure of Superman, for example, Roy Anker suggests that

> *Superman* is far more than a pastiche of portentous allusions, pious claptrap, and melodrama, which are usually the results of Christians' trying to make popular films or of pop-culture, myth-making movies such as *The Matrix*. In the case of the first two Superman films, which were shot simultaneously, Superman as a Christ-figure is not a random allusion or image simply pasted over the top of displays of special effects or old-style heroism. Rather, in what is a rare accomplishment in Hollywood, the whole of the film serves to elucidate and impart the surprise, wonder, and delight of the fantastic possibility of an incarnation of divine love itself.... Most of this gleeful christomorphic "work" in *Superman* comes at pivotal moments in which the filmmakers borrow freely, and usually with great wit, from biblical usage and events to shape and deepen the history of Kal-El/Clark Kent/Superman.[22]

For Anker, then, the identification of Superman as a Christ-figure unlocks the meaning and power of the film.

Others propose variations on this approach. Bernard Brandon Scott views these films as myth, which he defines as narratives that mediate fundamental conflict in indirect and allusive ways.[23] Clive Marsh draws explicitly on reader-response criticism by emphasizing that a film's meaning is not determined solely by its creators but rather is negotiated through the interaction between viewer and movie. Meaning therefore depends heavily on the identities, knowledge, and experience both in the movie theater and in "real life," that viewers bring to their film-watching.[24] William Telford lays out a comprehensive list of what film analysis entails: attention to the elements of film style and narration, including characters, plot, setting, camera work, and editing; awareness of the historical and cultural context in which the film was produced, and knowledge of the biblical texts and characters to which reference or allusion is made.[25] My own essays on Christ-figure films follow this same general outline.[26]

The mere presence of a Christ-figure, however, does not necessarily denote a profound appropriation of theology, spirituality, Christianity, or any other Christ-related beliefs. While some films use Christ-imagery in a way that deepens the meaning and increases the emotional impact (e.g., *The Shawshank*

Redemption [1994]), others use it in a rather trivial, and trivializing manner (e.g., *Nell* [1994]). But many Christ-figure films offer an opportunity to benefit from the power of the Jesus figure – his attributes, his role in society, his association with the spiritual domain of existence, and with situations that test the limits of human life and mortality itself – without being limited by Jesus' reputation as a perfect, sinless, unchanging Son of God.

Christ-figure films allow a character who is endowed with Christ-like features to be imperfect, to grow into his or her salvific role, and to fall in love, thereby also permitting a romantic element that remains a staple of mainstream commercial feature films. The explicitly fictional nature of the films and the metaphorical or symbolic – rather than literal or historical – use of Christ-imagery affords more opportunity for character development and dramatic interest than do most Jesus-movies. In cases where the Christ-figure exercises a salvific or redemptive function on behalf of others, these films may be just as effective, if less direct, in conveying the belief that Christ is the answer after all. On the other hand, there is something slightly insidious about the use of Christ-imagery in films that are not overtly about Jesus. In telling a fictional story according to a Christian narrative template, Christ-figure films almost always encode a Christian subtext.

Like the Jesus-movies, the Christ-figure films point beyond themselves to the concerns and preoccupations of the society that produced them. And while the Christ-imagery itself has come under considerable scrutiny, little attention has been given to the broader questions raised by Christ's frequent if imperfect incarnation in the heroes and heroines of the silver screen. What does Christ's prominence in Hollywood say about our culture, about ourselves, and the increasingly diverse society in which we live? Even more important, why do commercial feature films continue to use Christ imagery in an era of global marketing and increasingly multi-cultural and multi-religious audiences at home, that is, in a context where many viewers belong to cultures in which Jesus does not play a central role, if any role at all?

Case studies: the prison break movie genre

Prison break movies are a very popular genre both because of their subject matter and also because they symbolically draw attention to the ways in which we are all confined by the circumstances of our lives.[27] We will look briefly at three prison break films, all of which present Christ-figures, in different ways.

A Man Escaped *(1956)*

Plot summary

Robert Bresson's classic black-and-white film follows Fontaine, a member of the French resistance, as he plans and executes his escape from a Nazi prison. Fontaine narrates much of the film in voice-over, and he is on screen in almost every scene. The film takes us into every minute detail of his escape, including its successful conclusion. In doing so it brings us into his consciousness; indeed, the film becomes so deeply engrossing that viewers can feel that through Fontaine they too have escaped from prison. The film's overall tone is matter-of-fact and low-key. Nevertheless, it has a pronounced spiritual dimension which is signaled in three main ways: through the character of a Protestant pastor, a fellow inmate to whom Fontaine turns for friendship and guidance; through the powerful extra-diegetic use of a single, glorious piece of music, Mozart's Mass in C minor (K427); and the use of the Bible.

Christ-figures

The Bible, in turn, is used in three different ways. The first is in the title. The opening frames inform us that the film is called *A Man Escaped, or The wind bloweth where it listeth (Le vent souffle ou il veut)*, which is a direct quotation of John 3:8, in which Jesus converses with the Pharisaic leader Nicodemus. Second, the Bible appears as a prop. When the pastor first arrives, he is in despair; because he was arrested while preaching from the pulpit of his church, he could bring nothing with him. But one day soon thereafter, as he and his fellow inmates are washing at the communal trough (a location which provided opportunity for some interaction among the men), the pastor takes a Bible out of his pocket and shows it to Fontaine. For the pastor, the Bible is a tremendous source of spiritual strength, and he urges Fontaine – with some success – to take sustenance from it as well.

The third use is the quotation of John 3:3, which comes in the aftermath of a tragic turn of events. After being approached by a desperate inmate, Orsini, Fontaine gave him the escape plan that he has developed. Orsini, however, did not have Fontaine's patience, and modified the plan so that he would not have to prepare so carefully. This "get out of jail quick" scheme failed when the equipment that he had hastily assembled could not bear his weight. The pastor tells Fontaine not to blame himself, for, in the pastor's words, Orsini had too much hope for a new life. At this point he quotes John 3:3: "How can a man be born when he is old?" The pastor then gives Fontaine a small scrap of paper, which Fontaine opens when he is in his cell, and reads aloud to his elderly neighbor (to whom he speaks through the window). This text too is a quotation of John 3:3. A shot is heard, and Fontaine knows that Orsini has been executed.

The scene is pivotal, for it plays on different meanings of freedom, the film's main theme. The pastor allows for the possibility that death has set Orsini free. If he is a Christian believer he may well be reborn in a better place, and even if not, death is preferable to imprisonment, as Orsini himself had declared. Fontaine hopes, however, that unlike Orsini he himself will escape prison and be free in the physical here and now. At the same time, he attempts to give some hope to his elderly and despondent neighbor. In this he is successful. Indeed, his plans for escape, his openness about those plans, and, one presumes, his success, all provide hope for his fellow inmates. Even if they themselves do not escape alive, they are cheered by his progress toward this goal. His freedom also expresses a hope that France too will be free from the Nazi scourge. The Mozart mass provides a consistent musical thread throughout the film and subtly alludes to the Christian notion of freedom through faith and divine grace.[28]

Were the Bible absent from this film, there would be little to signal the status of Fontaine and, to a lesser extent, the pastor, as Christ-figures. But the quotation of John 3 in the title and the dialog, and the relationship between John 3:3 and the themes of the film, points to the presence of the other two Christ-figure elements: plot and character traits. The quotation of John 3:3 identifies the main plot's prison escape motif as a rebirth, or even resurrection, in which the imprisoned self dies in order that the free person may live. Fontaine's escape is a liberation not only of body but also of soul, and with him, viewers can experience the emotional journey from confinement to liberation, just as Paul urges his readers to die and rise with Christ (Romans 6:5).

Fontaine may not seem like much of a savior figure. He saves only himself and – reluctantly – the young prisoner with whom he shares his cell.[29] Nevertheless, Fontaine brings hope to the hopeless, who experience his escape vicariously as their own liberation, as the pastor has brought hope to him.

Escape from Alcatraz *(1979)*

Plot summary

This film is based on the true story of Frank Morris (played by Clint Eastwood) who along with two other prisoners, engineered the only successful escape from Alcatraz in its history. Neither in history nor in the movie is it clear whether the three men drowned or made it safely to another island or the mainland. In contrast to Bresson's film, *Escape from Alcatraz* uses the Bible only as a prop. Several scenes depict Frank lying on his bed in his cell reading. At one point a guard comments, "Still reading that Bible?" to which Frank responds, "Oh yeah, it's opening up all kinds of new doors." The response is an ironic double entendre. The guard may hear Frank's words as a reference to the kingdom of God, the key to which is provided by the scriptures. But in fact Frank is enjoying a joke at the guard's expense, for the Bible is the place where he hides the nail clippers with which he has begun to dig himself out of captivity.

Frank as Christ-figure

Frank is a less likely Christ-figure than Fontaine, for he gives little thought to others. To be sure, he includes his buddies, but only because he needs their help. Yet he does satisfy the three intersecting criteria that have been identified. As we have seen, the Bible is central to the film's plot, even if not in the pious manner that the prison guards might have hoped for. The plot of the film has Frank escape his imprisoned self, thereby surviving the attempts of prison officials to crush his spirit (symbolized by the recurring image of the warden crushing a chrysanthemum in his hands). That Frank's escape is a rebirth is symbolized by the dummy head that he places on his bed to fool the guards into thinking that he is sleeping. The beatific expression on the dummy's face is the last image in the film. This final image prompts us viewers to reconsider the Bible-reading scenes and to reinvest Frank's double entendre with spiritual meaning in addition to its literal sense. The fact that the ultimate fate of Frank and his two friends is not known – though it corresponds with the historical record – hints at the Christ-figure, whose life and death are also a matter of historical uncertainty.

The Shawshank Redemption *(1994)*

Plot summary

This popular film, based on Stephen King's short story "Rita Hayworth and Shawshank Redemption," tells the story of Andy Dufresne, a banker who is wrongfully convicted of murdering his wife and her lover.[30] In Shawshank Prison, the warden learns of Andy's expertise with numbers and the banking system and Andy is soon running an elaborate kickback and money-laundering scheme on behalf of the warden and his henchmen. Over the course of his 19 years at Shawshank, Andy patiently chisels through his cell wall to the prison sewer system using a small and seemingly innocuous rock hammer. Emerging in the river on the other side of the prison boundaries, Andy exacts financial and legal revenge upon the warden and makes his way to a village on Mexico's Pacific coast, where he fulfills the dreams that kept his spirit alive while in prison.

Allusionism

The film has so many similarities to *Escape from Alcatraz* that one might almost view it as a remake, despite the fact that it is an adaptation of King's story. In both films there is a prisoner who takes care of a pet as a way of remaining human (a mouse in the case of Alcatraz, a bird in Shawshank). In each film the mess hall serves as the place where inmates meet, exchange information, and hatch plans. (The washing trough plays a similar role in *A Man Escaped*.) Like Frank, Andy uses the Bible to hide the utensil that he uses to engineer his escape. Both films feature a cruel warden, and violent inmates. In both films, the hero works in the prison library and befriends an African American prisoner who does not escape with him.

Christ-figure film

The films differ, however, in two important respects: whereas Frank is apparently guilty of the crime for which he was imprisoned, Andy is innocent; and *Shawshank Redemption*, in contrast to *Escape from Alcatraz*, has its characters quote the Bible directly and explicitly.

As a prison-break film, *The Shawshank Redemption*'s narrative is structured around the protagonist's legal conviction, imprisonment, and eventual escape. At the same time, however, the presentation of Andy's sojourn at Shawshank, the manner of his escape, and the aftermath correspond closely to the main outline of the Gospel accounts of Jesus' life. He not only thwarts the warden but also defies him openly, much as Jesus is portrayed as doing to the Jewish authorities (e.g., John 9:41). In a highly dramatic scene, Andy accuses the warden of being obtuse for refusing to give credence to a report that would result in Andy's exoneration. The enraged warden throws Andy in "the hole" and orders the murder of Tommy, a young prisoner who knows the truth about the crime for which Andy was wrongfully convicted.

While in prison, Andy gathers friends and followers much as Jesus gathered the 12 disciples. Like Jesus, Andy transformed and gave new meaning to the lives of his friends (cf., John 6:68). By acknowledging their individual humanity, and providing both hope and beer – surely a foretaste of freedom – Andy lifts his fellow prisoners from the profound despair and dehumanization of institutional life. After years of persistence, Andy oversees a major donation of books and music to the prison library, and a renovation of the space itself. There he helps others to study toward their high school certificates, and thereby to prepare for a productive life once they are on the outside again.

Furthermore, Andy's escape from Shawshank marks his own salvation from prison but also releases others from the tyrannical grip of the warden and his henchmen, whose downfall he engineers. His prison friend, Red, follows in his footsteps after his parole. Without Andy's help in providing both hope and funds, Red may well have ended up a suicide like another long-time inmate, who could not adjust to life on the outside.

Finally, the narrative includes Andy's own death and resurrection. The guards' surprise at finding Andy's empty prison cell echoes the women's astonished discovery of Jesus' empty tombs in the Gospel accounts (e.g., John 20:1–18). After his escape from prison, "Andy Dufresne" disappears and is reborn as a wealthy but reclusive individual, Randall Stephens, the beneficiary of the warden's laundered money.

The identification of Andy as a Christ-figure within the film's narrative is bolstered by a number of visual and aural images. Most explicit is the cruciform position that Andy assumes after his escape. Striding through the stream into which the prison's sewers flow, Andy rips off his shirt, stretches out his arms, and raises his face to the heavens, laughing deeply. The cruciform position signifies his death to his old, prison self and also his triumph, just as the crucifixion in Christian theology signifies both Jesus' death and his glory (e.g., John 12:22–24). The visual image is amplified by the soundtrack, which consists of majestic orchestral music often associated with biblical epics and marking this moment as the film's climax.

Andy's personal character traits also support his identification as a Christ-figure. He maintains his own dignity and humanity despite the dehumanization of the prison environment, and while he looks after his own interests, he also behaves altruistically, as the earlier examples suggest. Andy is a charismatic leader whose followers revere him while he is present and keep his memory alive after he is gone.

The many narrative, visual, and character elements that link Andy to the Jesus of the Gospels and the Christ of culture make it easy to describe *The Shawshank Redemption* as a Christ-figure film.

Subverting the Christ-figure paradigm

These and similar movies are Christ-figure films in the sense that the Bible figures explicitly whether as a prop, or as a source of aural and visual quotations and allusions. Furthermore, their plots and protagonists have significant elements in common with the Christ story and its hero. The Christ-elements not only signal the salvific theme of the film, but also establish depth for both the character and the plot, suggesting metaphorical dimensions to the film that may prompt viewers' reflections on their own lives.

At the same time, the Christ-elements in these films, while explicit, are not integral to the plot of the film. While they establish an analogy between the film's plot and protagonist and those of the Gospels, the story would still be complete without them. For example, while the Christ-elements add depth, interest, and meaning to *The Shawshank Redemption*, the story of Andy's wrongful conviction, imprisonment, and escape would be intact even without the Christ-elements. Second, these films present the Christ paradigm in relatively conventional ways that do not challenge expectations. Because we are not confronted with innovation, we can well remain oblivious to convention as well. It is for this reason that Bordwell and Thompson argue that both convention and innovation, are essential to the genre film. Innovation, that is, the undermining or frustration of the viewer expectations based on convention, is key. According to Bordwell and Thompson, film genres are characterized by "the interplay of convention and innovation, familiarity and novelty."[31]

To illustrate this point, we will look at two films that portray this interplay. By both fulfilling and frustrating the viewer's expectations, these films also call attention to the Christ-figure motif and its role in conveying meaning.

C.R.A.Z.Y. *(2005)*

The 2005 Quebec film *C.R.A.Z.Y.*, directed by Jean-Marc Vallée, is a coming of age story, featuring Zac Beaulieu, the fourth son in a family of five boys. Zac's mother, Laurianne, is a Catholic who believes fervently in God,

Christ, and the Church but is untroubled by Zac's early interest in doll carriages. Zac's father is a secular man who attends church when necessary but often expresses disdain for the Catholic Church, its priesthood, and even Jesus Christ himself. Despite his secular views, Gervais Beaulieu is very upset by the idea that his son may be gay. The film begins with Zac's birth on 25 December 1960 and concludes in 1981. The movie's title comes from a Patsy Cline recording much loved by Zac's father; the shattering of the original LP recording and its eventual replacement symbolize the fragmentation within the family and the fragile healing that takes place by the end of the film. Zac escapes the tensions of his life *en famille* by travelling to Israel without saying good-bye to his family. There he begins to come to terms with his sexuality, his asthma, and his father.

Films such as *The Shawshank Redemption* establish the Christ-figure motif through the explicit use of the Bible, as well as plot structure and character development, *C.R.A.Z.Y.*, by contrast, establishes the Christ-motif initially by visual images and character traits and then calls the motif into question when the protagonist and therefore the plot fail to carry the Christ paradigm through to its expected conclusion.

Zachary and Christ

Born just after midnight on the 25th of December 1960, Zac Beaulieu not only (grudgingly) shares Jesus' birthday, but he also exhibits a Christ-like power to heal the sick and soothe the sorrowful. To support Zac's identity as his mother's "little Jesus," the camera often lingers on the cross he wears around his neck. The final image in the film is a bright four-pointed star that shines in the black screen and then fades out before the final credits roll. This image is a brief and perhaps ironic allusion to the Christ-imagery that is pervasive in the Jesus-movies, from the epic film *The Greatest Story Ever Told* (1965) to the epic spoof *Monty Python's Life of Brian* (1979).

A not-Christ-figure film

The identification of Zac as a Christ-figure is established not only through biblical imagery, plot, and character traits but also by explicit comments to that effect by Zac's adoring mother. Initially the film supports this identification: Zac experiences death and resurrection, not once but three times. As a newborn, he is feared dead when he is accidentally dropped on the floor; as an adolescent he is hit by a car while riding his bike recklessly; on his pilgrimage to Israel he suffers dehydration and heat stroke in the desert. Each time he is restored to life.

Yet this Christ-figure falls short. Despite his healing abilities, which he himself views with some skepticism, he does not share the Christ-like attributes of altruism and love of the neighbor. Far from being a Christ-like figure, Zac is simply a typical, self-absorbed child and adolescent. He loves his parents and strives for their approval, but views them primarily in relationship to himself. He has an ambivalent relationship with his siblings, caring about them in a vague sort of way but also resenting and sometimes hating them, particularly Raymond, whom he views as the cool and hyper-masculine man he fears he will never be. Throughout the film, Zac's most fervent prayers are for himself, not others. He prays for relief from his asthma, and from his growing conviction that he is gay. He even makes bets with God, or rather, with fate, though he always loses, as is evident in the car accident that nearly takes his life. He takes petty revenge on his wayward brother, Raymond, by refusing to lend him cash.

Zac's non-Christ-like personality has narrative consequences. The supreme test of the Christ-figure paradigm arrives near the end of the film. Raymond is lying in a coma after a drug overdose. Zac arrives from Israel to find his tearful family gathered around Raymond's hospital bed. Zac's mother is tremendously relieved to see Zac, and urges him to take Raymond's hand; clearly she hopes and expects Zac to revive his brother. Zac fails, however. Given that earlier in the film he had in anger wished his brother dead, we are left wondering whether he truly was unable to restore his brother's life, or simply preferred not to. In either case, however, his impotence at this decisive moment removes the Christ-figure patina from his character.

At this point we, as viewers, must entertain the possibility that Zac's fortuitous birth date, his gift for healing, and his periodic resurrection from death or near-death have blinded us as to his true narrative role. If Zac plays the role of Jesus in his mother's narrative, his role in the narrative of Raymond's life is that of Judas. It is Zac's betrayal – his revelation to his family of his brother's vices – sex and drugs – that drives Raymond from the family home and into the relentless spiral that culminates in his death.

Zac may best be described, not as a Christ-figure, but as a "not-Christ" figure: a character who fails to live up to the Christ-like role that explicit cinematic cues have led us to ascribe to him. Furthermore, Zac is not the only not-Christ-figure in the film. Other characters are associated with Christ-like images and qualities that do not come to narrative fruition. One such character is Raymond himself, the brother whom Zac betrays. When Zac is close to death in the desert, he hallucinates that Raymond is pouring refreshing water on him (a visual allusion to *Ben-Hur*, in which Christ offers water to the parched protagonist Judah Ben-Hur). This fleeting dream may reflect Zac's hope that Raymond has forgiven him for his betrayal. Raymond causes hurt to his family and lovers, yet it is his death that heals the family, for it reveals the father's fierce love for his sons and leads in time to his acceptance of Zac. Nevertheless, Raymond is not a Christ-figure in that he does not deliberately sacrifice himself to save his family or anyone else, nor does he achieve resurrection, literally or figuratively.

At least two other minor characters qualify as "not-Christ" figures. Toto the Weirdo, a young man with whom Zac shares some intimate moments, falls into the cruciform position when Zac knocks him out in a school fight. Zac's first gay lover, in Israel, is illuminated by a bright light when Zac first catches sight of him on a gay beach on Israel's Mediterranean coast, and then sees him again at a nightclub. Neither he nor Toto the Weirdo play any further narrative role, except as the figures through whom Zac defines his sexuality.

The only unequivocal savior figure in Zac's story is the kindly Bedouin who rescues Zac from certain death in the desert. The film does not use any of the standard Christ imagery in depicting this man, but it nevertheless imputes to him Christ-like qualities. Early in the film, Zac's mother takes him to see Madame "Chose" ("thing"), the Tupperware lady. On her wall she has a brilliantly colored picture of Jesus' footprints in the desert sands. She tells Zac the story of a person who dreamed of two images: one that has two sets of footprints and another that has only one. The person reminded Christ of his promise to walk with him always. Why, then, during the most trying periods of life is there only one set of footprints? Christ replied: The times that you have seen only one set of footprints are the times when I have carried you on my back. Years later, when Zac wanders off into the desert, he steps into that same picture. After reviving him with water, food, rest, and his lost asthma puffer, the Bedouin carries Zac back to the edge of the desert on his motorcycle, a sign that he is the one who has played Christ's salvific role by supporting Zac during his time of greatest need.

The heavy-handed Christ-figure imagery in this film therefore leads us initially to identify Zac as Christ; as the film progresses, however, that identification unravels to the point where we must discard it altogether. But this failure to live up to expectations, far from undermining the film's classification as a Christ-figure film, in fact confirms it. Even more, the self-consciousness playfulness with which the Christ-figure imagery and plot structure are deployed support the identification of the Christ-figure film as a cinematic genre in its own right.

Zac's initial identification with Christ is imposed upon him not only by the camera and the "facts" of his birth, but by a character within the film itself: Zac's own mother. It is she who refers to him as her "little Jesus," and she who identifies and then nurtures his apparent ability to soothe infants and heal the sick. She is the one who takes him to a spiritual Tupperware lady who not only supports her belief in Zac's gifts but also apparently infuses Zac with her own abilities. In order to grow up, Zac must reject the role that his mother's powerful script dictates for him and replace it with an identity of his own creation. The film is therefore not only about Zac's coming of age and acceptance of his own identity but about his struggles with and against the Christ paradigm according to which his loving and well-meaning mother tries to arrange his life.

Stranger than Fiction *(2006)*

The deliberate use and transformation of Christ-figure images and narrative paradigms may not be surprising in a film from Quebec, which until the

1960s was dominated by Catholicism and which still reflects upon its power-ful Catholic heritage through the arts and in many other ways.[32] Yet the creative exploitation and manipulation of the Christ-figure paradigm is very much in evidence in Hollywood films as well.

Plot summary

Stranger than Fiction (2006), directed by Marc Forster, features a bland IRS agent named Harold Crick, who has no interests, no friends, and no life to speak of. One day, as he is brushing his teeth, Harold is startled to hear a female voice with a British accent narrate his every movement. Only he can hear this voice. His irritation turns to panic when he hears her say: "Little did he know that this simple, seemingly innocuous act, would ultimately result in his death." Harold seeks out a professor of English literature, Jules Hilbert, who helps him to understand that, strange as it might seem, Harold is not the autonomous human being he thought he was, but a character in a novel being written by this female author. He embarks on a quest for this author, in order to change her mind about his fate. As the shadow of imminent death hangs over Harold, however, life also begins to happen. He tentatively moves toward friendship with Dave, a colleague from work; he buys a guitar and teaches himself how to play; and he falls in love with a young anarchist baker, Ana Pascal, whose business he has been auditing.

One day, Harold is in Jules' office. Suddenly he hears the narrator's voice again, not in his head this time, but coming from the television set, on which the rerun of an interview with the famous author Karen Eiffel, is playing. Harold storms Eiffel's office and confronts her with her own creation. Eiffel quickly overcomes her astonishment at finding the actual protagonist of the novel she has been struggling to write for ten years standing before her in the flesh. The meeting forces her to recognize the humanity of her fictional char-acters, and the strange fact that her writing has direct consequences for their lives. Harold, for his part, starts to understand that the narrative framework into which he has been thrust not only mandates his death but is completed and made beautiful and meaningful thereby.

Christ-figure film?

Whereas *C.R.A.Z.Y.* piles on the Christ-images from the opening credits to the final frames, *Stranger than Fiction* does not overtly signal its Christ-figure motif until the plot is well advanced (though as the dark-suited Harold runs for the bus with a green apple in his mouth he looks astonishingly like the subject of René Magritte's iconic 1964 painting, *The Son of Man*). Indeed, there is virtually no plot to speak of at the outset. Each day, Harold wakes up, brushes his teeth, runs for the bus, audits IRS tax files all day, then goes home, only to repeat the same dull sequence the next day. His apartment, his appearance, and his character, are as bland and colorless as his days. Indeed, far from being a Christ-character like Andy Dufresnes, or even a non-Christ character like Zac Beaulieu, Harold Crick is barely a character at all. The sudden intrusion of the narrator's disembodied but authoritative voice into Harold's consciousness, however, changes everything. Her decision to kill Harold, and Harold's awareness of her decision, his attempts to avoid his fate and then his calm acceptance, shape the rest of the film and allow Harold to emerge as a Christ-figure after all.

If *C.R.A.Z.Y.* contains echoes of Jesus' full life from birth to resurrection, *Stranger Than Fiction* is more like a Passion Play that focuses inexorably on the events leading to the hero's death. The Christ-imagery begins to emerge when Eiffel gives Harold her manuscript, including the hand-written draft of the novel's ending – Harold's ending. Harold, too fearful to read it himself, asks Jules to read it first.

Jules then informs Harold, sheepishly, "Harold, I'm sorry. (pause). You have to die." Harold cannot believe his ears. Jules explains, "I'm sorry, but it's brilliant, Harold. It's … It's her masterpiece." And this masterpiece is "absolutely no good unless you die at the end."

Harold's response to Jules is his Gethsemane, recalling the night that Judas betrays Jesus to the authorities and sets in motion the events that lead to Golgotha. Like Jesus, Harold knows that he is destined to die, and he has been told that this death will serve a higher purpose. And like Jesus, he pleads with a "higher authority" to spare his life. Harold pleads to Jules: "Why can't…. Can't we just … ask her to … erase it … ?" echoing Jesus' plaintive prayer: "My Father, if it is possible, let this cup pass from me" (Matthew 26:39). Jules does not relent. "Your life, no one's life, is worth more than this book … It's the nature of all tragedy, Harold. The hero dies, but the story lives on forever." One could of course say the same about Jesus. Jesus dies, but remains real to many Christian believers through the Gospel stories themselves.

After Harold reads the book for himself, however, he finds himself in full agreement with Jules. He tells Eiffel: "I read it and I loved it. There's only one way it can end. It ends with me dying. I mean, I don't have much background in literary … anything, but this seems simple enough." In his calm acceptance of his fate, he again echoes the words of Jesus, who finally says to God: "My Father, if this cannot pass unless I drink it, your will be done" (Matthew 26:42).

In preparation for death, Harold, like the Jesus of the Gospels, calmly takes care of the living. Just as Jesus passes along his last words to the disciples, so does Harold convey an important message to Ana; just as Jesus promised a better future for his disciples, so does Harold fulfill his friend Dave's lifelong dream of a sojourn at Space Camp.

What turns this particular hero into a Christ-figure is not his death, which would finally identify the story as a tragedy, but rather his resurrection. This Christ-figure characteristic is reinforced through a powerful visual image, namely, the cruciform position into which Harold falls at the moment he is fatally struck by a city bus. The bright, almost blinding light that envelopes this scene emphasizes the Christ-like connections, creating a visual effect like those often used to portray Jesus' resurrection, as in, for example, Scorsese's *The Last Temptation of Christ*.

The visual Christ imagery is supported by Harold's personal character traits: the willingness with which he goes to his death and his sense of himself as the only one who can save the life of the young boy who had ridden his bike in the bus' path. As he tells Ana when she arrives, alarmed, at his hospital bed: "I had to keep this boy from being hit." Ana marvels: "You stepped in front of a bus to save a little boy … ?" Harold responds: "I didn't have a choice. (pause) I had to." In these ways, the film exhibits, albeit economically, the three major areas – plot, visual imagery, and character traits – that we have suggested as essential to the Christ-figure motif.

The idea that Harold dies and is then brought back to life is established through the interplay between the novel's typescript and the events of the film. The film has already introduced viewers to the idea that Harold's life unfolds as Karen Eiffel types. Her long period of writer's block has left him free to his own devices; perhaps it is Karen's incapacity that has determined the essentially non-eventful character of Harold's adult life. Thus it is the case that the handwritten manuscript in which Karen drafts the ending of the book, an ending over which she has struggled for so long, does not cause Harold's death. Both he and Jules read it, not only as the ending of a great novel, but as a prophecy of Harold's own fate. The tension mounts and becomes nearly intolerable, for Eiffel and for us, as she transcribes her hand-written draft onto the typescript. Karen smokes nonstop and weeps. We, the viewers, see the typewriter keys bang out the following: "realized that the man was dead. Harold Crick was de" and there it stops. We readily correlate this with the "real life" scene, in which Harold lies motionless in front of the bus, and onlookers wonder whether he is alive or dead.

The screenwriter's notes in the shooting script suggest that Harold has indeed died:

> His body lies lifeless on the asphalt. As the crowd begins to gather around him, blood can be seen pouring from his head. Despite the chaos that surrounds him, his body rests in perfect stillness.
>
> Harold's body rests, lifeless, in the middle of the street. From above, we see his legs are buckled underneath him and blood has formed a halo around his head, his arm snapped like a twig. But his face is peaceful.
>
> Harold Crick lies dead in the street.[33]

Yet, as we soon learn, Harold does not remain dead. Although his body is broken, doctors say he will make a complete recovery, with one modification: he will forever carry a shard of his watch within him. As the incredulous physician explains to Harold when he regains consciousness:

> Looks like you cracked your head, broke three bones in your leg and foot, suffered four broken ribs, fractured your right arm … and you

severed an artery in your left arm which could've been really bad, but *amazingly* a shard of metal from your watch became lodged in the artery, causing your heart rate to slow, keeping your loss of blood down enough to keep you alive … which is pretty cool … with some physical therapy and a few months of rest you should be fine. Well … sort of. We couldn't remove the shard of watch without risking major muscular damage. It'll be okay. You'll just have a watch piece embedded in your arm for the rest of your life.

Eiffel has not in fact refrained from killing this hero. Rather, she has killed him and then resurrected him to new life.

As in *C.R.A.Z.Y.*, however, Christ imagery is not linked exclusively with the protagonist but also appears with reference to other characters. The literature professor, Jules Hilbert, is quite literally a "lifeguard" who does not walk on water – though his T-shirt has a cross on it – but does oversee swimmers as he sits high above the pool. Most important, Harold looks to Jules as the one who is capable of guarding *his* life by averting the death sentence that Eiffel has pronounced. Jules does not save Harold directly and intentionally, but he is the one who set Harold on track for perceiving that his only hope lay in convincing "his" author to change her mind.

More bizarre, and more direct, is the salvific role of Harold's watch, which is described to Harold by the attending physician. From the very first scene in this film, Harold's watch has been a character, a figure with presence, aspirations, goals, and, one might almost say, personality. It is Karen Eiffel, the author/ narrator, who endows Harold's watch with character and intentionality:

> This is a story about a man named Harold Crick … and his wrist-watch … Harold Crick was a man of infinite numbers, endless calculations and remarkably few words. (pause). And his wristwatch said even less…. Every weekday, for nine years, Harold would brush each of his 32 teeth 76 times…. His wristwatch would simply look on from the nightstand, quietly wishing Harold would use a more colorful toothbrush…. Every weekday, for nine years, Harold would tie his tie in a single Windsor knot … His wristwatch thought the single Windsor made his neck look fat … but said nothing.

Like Tinker Bell in the Peter Pan story, the watch lights up with love for Harold, and tries to point him toward opportunity: it beeps and flashes madly every time Ana Pascal walks by. It also undergoes a death and resurrection, as it stops and then must be reset by Harold who, in doing so, inadvertently sets off the chain of events in which both Harold and his wristwatch will play their greatest roles. The wristwatch is the one that watches over Harold, and it is his true savior. Not Jules, not even Karen Eiffel, but the wristwatch becomes "singlehandedly" responsible for his resurrection when it lodges in Harold's arm thereby preventing his lifeblood from gushing out of his severed artery.

If Harold is Christ, Jules his "lifeguard," and the watch his savior, then Eiffel is God. She is the solemn voice-of-God narrator, evoking Orson Welles in *King of Kings* (1961) or Christopher Plummer in *The Gospel of John* (2003) and other Bible movies. Her authority stems not only from her clear enunciation and posh British accent, but from the accuracy of her narration. It is this accuracy that so unnerves Harold, and frightens him to death when he hears the fateful words: "Little did he know ..." Like God, she scripts the lives of her characters in ways that they do not know or understand but that they are powerless to escape. And she creates by the Word. Just as God speaks the world into being (Gen. 1:3 "Then God said, 'Let there be light'; and there was light"), so does Karen write, or more precisely, type Harold's life and death, into existence.

In the end, Karen is able to walk away not only from her own paradigms, but also from one of the most powerful narrative paradigms in western culture, prompting the crucial question: was it necessary for Christ to die in order for him to have a positive effect on the world?

This film explicitly plays upon the idea that story genres set up their audience's expectations in particular ways. Jules is the spokesperson for this idea. Initially Jules sees no fewer than 23 different story types as possible paradigms for Harold's story. But soon the choices are narrowed down to two: comedy or tragedy. Hilbert quotes from Italo Calvino: "The ultimate meaning to which all stories refer has two faces: the continuity of life, the inevitability of death."[34] Hilbert paraphrases for Harold: "Tragedy you die, comedy you get hitched." As Joseph Campbell noted in his classic study, *The Hero with a Thousand Faces*, there is a common pattern to heroic stories across the centuries and across cultures, the final step of which is the hero's departure, often through death.[35]

Harold's story, originally conceived by its author as a tragedy in which the hero dies, is rewritten as a comedy. The film lays bare the structure implicit in all fiction: a narrator/implied author creates and manipulates the lives of her characters in order to lead audiences through a particular experience. What is unusual about the film is not that Harold is a character in a fiction (all film protagonists are that) but that the narrator, normally an invisible even if sometimes audible figure, becomes a character herself. This allows Jules, and the viewer, to consider the question of which has priority, life or literature? For Jules, the answer is "literature." Harold is persuaded too; his willingness to die is not only for the sake of the boy, but also for the sake of the story. But it is the narrator/author herself who ultimately backs away from a worldview in which literature, though immortal, is valued more highly than life itself. She will settle for good instead of great, if it means that Harold, a good man, does not have to die after all.

In *Stranger than Fiction*, the narrative paradigm is set not by a parent, as it is in *C.R.A.Z.Y.*, but by the author-narrator whose voice only Harold Crick can hear. In the final analysis, however, it is Eiffel, and not the character, Harold, whom she has shaped, that dismantles the tragic story structure upon which she has built her entire career. In doing so, she saves Harold Crick, and allows him to live his life. She also gets on with hers. In the relationship that begins to blossom, both Karen and Jules break out of the self-imposed narratives that have confined them till now. The reclusive and eccentric author meets face-to-face with the professor who admires her, and he, in turn, can finally jump into the pool instead of only life-guarding others' watery adventures. In the end, the film fulfills the genre expectations of the Christ-figure film but also of the romantic comedy. We know that Harold and Ana will get hitched, and live happily ever after. The manipulation of genre here happens explicitly and playfully, by exposing and embodying the narrative and forcing an interaction between the creator and her creation.

Conclusion

C.R.A.Z.Y. and *Stranger than Fiction* differ from *The Shawshank Redemption* and other conventional Christ-figure films in two ways. First, their Christ-related images and plot elements, while not more abundant than those found in *The Shawshank Redemption*, are woven more deeply into their narrative and overall themes. While there is no doubt that *Shawshank*'s prison break story is enhanced and deepened by the use of Christ-figure conventions, removing those conventions would still leave a coherent and absorbing narrative. In *C. R.A.Z.Y.* and *Stranger than Fiction*, however, the Christ-figure elements could not be removed without damaging the story itself. The narrative thread that tells of Zac's relationship to his mother, and his estrangement from Catholicism, could not have been told without recourse to the Christ-elements, for the process of his maturation requires that he break free of the Christ paradigm that she has imposed on his life. Without Harold's struggle to come to terms with his impending death, and his growing ability to see himself in the noble role of the one who must sacrifice his life to save another, Karen Eiffel has no novel worth writing, and Marc Forster has no movie worth directing.

Second, at the same time as they use the Christ-paradigm as an integral part of their narrative, both films call that same paradigm into question by deviating in significant ways from its conventions. Thus Zac, whose mother has endowed him with Christ-like attributes, cannot or will not act to save his mother from the searing pain of losing a son. Neither Harold nor Karen Eiffel perceives Harold's Christ-like role until Karen has an epiphany of how to kill Harold and save her novel. Until then, who would have dreamed that a character-less IRS agent would have it in him to throw himself in front of a bus to save a little boy's life?

These films lull the viewers into expecting a conventional presentation of Christ-figure motifs, only to force us into questioning these expectations when events do not unfold as expected. In challenging the audience's expectations, these films also force an explicit consideration of the impact of the Christ-story on the way we tell our own narratives. Quebecois women and fictional authors of fiction are not the only ones who organize their narratives in parallel to the Christ story. The explicit treatment of this motif in these two films allows us to return to films such as *The Shawshank Redemption* that use but do not overtly reflect on the Christ-figure motifs and to understand that, whether explicit or not, these films too demonstrate the paradigmatic role of the Christ story in shaping the way our society tells its stories. It is in this sense that the films that exhibit the interplay of convention and innovation, and therefore challenge our expectations, thereby establish the existence of a Christ-figure film genre as a category in which we may also place films like *The Shawshank Redemption*, *Escape from Alcatraz*, *A Man Escaped*, and dozens, perhaps even hundreds, of other movies.

The establishment of the Christ-figure film as a film genre is significant because it opens up a broad range of questions that touch not only on cinema, but also on the ongoing normative role of the foundational narrative of Christianity in the context of North America's religious and cultural diversity in the twenty-first century. As Bordwell and Thompson point out, "Genres are based on a tacit agreement between filmmakers and audiences."[36] A genre cannot exist unless there is an audience that recognizes and responds to its conventions. As we have seen, the Christ-figure genre has been a fixture of North American cinema since the earliest years of the film industry. Each year sees dozens of additions to this corpus, many of them so-called mixed genre films that make use of Christ-figure conventions alongside the conventional elements of other films, be they prison break movies, boxing movies, or coming of age stories.[37] These Christ-figure films not only depend upon our understanding of and response to their conventions, but they also have a major role in perpetuating our awareness of and sensitivity to the Christ-story and Christ-figure imagery, even if we never read the Gospels or reflect on Jesus in any meaningful way.

Notes

1 Baugh, *Imaging the Divine*, viii–ix.
2 Ibid., 210.
3 Chapter 9 will examine the apocalyptic movies in more detail.
4 For analysis of the Jesus and other religious motifs in these films, see John Shelton Lawrence and Robert Jewett, *The Myth of the American Superhero* (Grand Rapids, MI: W. B. Eerdmans, 2002) and Greg Garrett, *Holy Superheroes!: Exploring the Sacred in Comics, Graphic Novels, and Film*, Rev. and expanded (Louisville, KY: Westminster John Knox Press, 2008).
5 Peter Malone, *Movie Christs and Antichrists* (New York: Crossroad, 1990), 17–18.
6 Baugh, *Imaging the Divine*, 205–10.
7 For his full discussion, see Anton Kozlovic, "The Structural Characteristics of the Cinematic Christ-figure," *Journal of Religion and Popular Culture* 8, no. 1 (2004): Para. 38.
8 For discussion of the difficulties of portraying Jesus on the screen, see chapter 3.
9 For discussions of this film, see K. R. M. Short, "Chaplin's 'The Great Dictator' and British Censorship, 1939," *Historical Journal of Film, Radio and Television* 5,

no. 1 (1 March 1985): 85–108; Astrid Klocke, "Subverting Satire: Edgar Hilsen-rath's Novel *Der Nazi und der Friseur* and Charlie Chaplin's Film *The Great Dicta-tor*," *Holocaust and Genocide Studies* 22, no. 3 (1 December 2008): 497–513.

10 That Hitler did in fact see himself as a savior figure of sorts is evident in a propa-ganda poster that portrays him as lecturing to his rapt followers, with the caption "In the beginning was the word." See the image at www.nobeliefs.com/mementoes/ HoyerHitler.jpg (accessed 10 May 2013); for discussion of Hitler's messianic self-identification, see David Redles, *Hitler's Millennial Reich: Apocalyptic Belief and the Search for Salvation* (New York: New York University Press, 2005), 108–34.

11 Kozlovic, "The Structural Characteristics of the Cinematic Christ-figure."

12 Marsh, *Cinema and Sentiment*, 48–49. Ostwalt, "Apocalyptic," 368–83.

13 For critiques of the enterprise, see Kozlovic, "The Structural Characteristics of the Cinematic Christ-figure," Para. 12–14. Marsh, *Cinema and Sentiment*, 48–49. Deacy, "Reflections on the Uncritical Appropriation of Cinematic Christ-Figures," Para. 13. Conrad Ostwalt, "Armageddon at the Millennial Dawn," *The Journal of Religion and Film* 4, no. 1 (2000). www.unomaha.edu/jrf/armagedd.htm (accessed 10 May 2013).

14 Baugh, *Imaging the Divine*, 109.

15 Deacy, "Reflections on the Uncritical Appropriation of Cinematic Christ-Figures," Para. 13.

16 Bryan P. Stone, *Faith and Film: Theological Themes at the Cinema* (St. Louis, MO: Chalice Press, 2000), 6.

17 Martin and Ostwalt, *Screening the Sacred*, 125–33.

18 Miles, *Seeing and Believing*, xiii.

19 Ibid., 10.

20 Melanie Jane Wright, *Religion and Film: An Introduction* (London; New York, NY: I. B. Tauris; Distributed in the US by Palgrave Macmillan, 2007), 29.

21 Kreitzer, *The New Testament in Fiction and Film*, 12.

22 Roy M. Anker, *Catching Light: Looking for God in the Movies* (Grand Rapids, MI: W. B. Eerdmans, 2004), 251.

23 Bernard Brandon Scott, *Hollywood Dreams and Biblical Stories* (Minneapolis, MN: Fortress Press, 1994), 11.

24 Marsh, *Cinema and Sentiment*, 37.

25 William R. Telford, "Through a Lens Darkly: Critical Approaches to Theology and Film," in *Cinéma Divinité: Religion, Theology and the Bible in Film*, ed. Eric S. Christianson, Peter Francis, and William R. Telford (London: SCM, 2005), 15–43.

26 Reinhartz, *Scripture on the Silver Screen*.

27 On prison break movies, see David Gonthier, *American Prison Film since 1930: From The Big House to The Shawshank Redemption* (Lewiston, NY: Edwin Mellen Press, 2006).

28 Peter Hogue, "A Man Escaped," *Film Comment* 35, no. 3 (June 1999): 44–48.

29 For discussion of this film, see Tony Pipolo, *Robert Bresson: A Passion for Film* (Oxford; New York: Oxford University Press, 2010), 102–23.

30 See Stephen King, "Rita Hayworth and the Shawshank Redemption," in *Different Seasons* (New York: Viking Press, 1982).

31 David Bordwell and Kristin Thompson, *Film Art: An Introduction* (New York: The McGraw-Hill Companies, 1997), 54.

32 On the Quiet Revolution, see Michael Gauvreau, *The Catholic Origins of Quebec's Quiet Revolution, 1931–1970* (Montreal: McGill-Queen's University Press, 2005); John Alexander Dickinson and Brian J. Young, *A Short History of Quebec* (Mon-treal; Ithaca, NY: McGill-Queen's University Press, 2003).

33 Zach Helm, *Stranger Than Fiction: The Shooting Script* (New York: Newmarket Press, 2006), 109.

34 Italo Calvino, *If on a Winter's Night a Traveler*, vol. 1 (New York: Harcourt, Brace, Jovanovich, 1981), 259.
35 Joseph Campbell, *The Hero with a Thousand Faces*, edited by Northrop Frye. Bollingen Series, 17 (New York: Pantheon Books, 1949), 356–64.
36 Bordwell and Thompson, *Film Art*, 53.
37 Ibid., 52.

8 "Justice, justice you shall pursue"

Films and morality

In 1882, the British theologian Stanley Leathes declared confidently: "We find the Ten Commandments accepted as the basis of moral and social life, in the most civilized nations of the world."[1] For Leathe, the moral force of the Ten Commandments, and the Bible as a whole, is rooted in divine authority: "Thus morality and religion are seen to be coordinate, and religion is not dependent upon morality but morality upon religion. Destroy the foundations of morality, and you do indeed destroy religion."[2] Leathe's views were no doubt shared by many, including Cecil B. DeMille, whose 1923 *The Ten Commandments* has the pious Johnny use Bible stories to convert the wayward Mary.

But from the outset, film was an ethically ambiguous medium. Even as Passion films and other Bible movies promoted both religion and morality to the satisfaction of Christian clergy,[3] movies as such were often seen as morally corrupting, particularly with the advent of the "talkies" in 1930. At a 1929 meeting of the Women's Christian Temperance Union in Philadelphia, the president Maude Aldrich complained "that the movies glorified 'the Jazz age baby type' of girl, thus causing 'good men and bad men alike' to ignore the 'well-mannered, old-fashioned girl.'"[4] Well-mannered, old-fashioned girls just did not draw mass audiences the same way that "sex, glamor, and entertainment" could. No doubt DeMille would have agreed, for even as he was making *The Ten Commandments* (1923) and *The King of Kings* (1927), he was also directing such steamy films as *Madame Satan* (1930) and *Cleopatra* (1934).

Motion Picture Production Code

In 1934, the Catholic Church's Legion of Decency was finally able to assert its moral influence upon the movie industry by imposing a Production Code, thus bringing the "'muck merchants' of Hollywood, that 'fortress of filth' that had been destroying the moral fiber of the American people," to its knees.[5] The Motion Picture Production Code (also known as the Hays Code, after the chief censor, Will H. Hays) was in place for over two decades in the mid-twentieth century as a de facto censorship code. Joseph Breen, the head of the Production Code Administration from 1934 to 1954, along with his staff, meticulously examined every script in order to protect audiences from sexual improprieties and "eliminate controversial subjects from the screen to maximize the worldwide appeal of Hollywood films."[6]

The Production Code was governed by three general principles:

1   "No picture shall be produced that will lower the moral standards of those who see it. Hence, the sympathy of the audience should never be thrown to the side of crime, wrongdoing, evil, or sin."

2   "Correct standards of life, subject only to the requirements of drama and entertainment, shall be presented."

3   "Law, natural or human, shall not be ridiculed, nor shall sympathy be created for its violation."[7]

Although the Code did not explicitly refer to any biblical passages, these principles were grounded in a particular Christian perspective. The specific measures that the Code spelled out were intended to bring films in line with the basic ethical precepts often traced back to the Bible, as it paid attention to cinematic treatments of murder, theft, and sexual impropriety, especially adultery. For example, with respect to sex, the Code stipulated that:

1   "Impure love must not be presented as attractive and beautiful.

2   It must not be the subject of comedy or farce, or treated as material for laughter.

3   It must not be presented in such a way as to arouse passion or morbid curiosity on the part of the audience.

4   It must not be made to seem right and permissible.

5   In general, it must not be detailed in method and manner."[8]

In addition, ministers, priests, rabbis, and other representatives of religion were to be presented with respect, so that their authority in the "real world" would not be undermined. The Code, then, upheld and reinforced the strong and positive connections among the Bible, the clergy, and morality.[9]

The Code began to crumble in the 1950s. Its 1966 revision did away with the lengthy list of rules about content, and replaced it with ten broad and vaguely worded principles, such as "Evil, sin, crime and wrong doing shall not be justified" and "Detailed and protracted acts of brutality, cruelty, physical violence, torture and abuse, shall not be presented."[10] An important new feature was the possibility of classifying particular movies as "SMA" (Suitable for Mature Audiences). This revision was intended to reflect the changing social norms of the 1960s, but even it proved too restrictive. In 1968 the Code was replaced by a new Code and Rating Administration (CARA), administered by the Motion Picture Association of America (MPAA). This classification system allowed targeted marketing to certain age groups, and satisfied the demands of concerned groups that some restrictions be placed on movies deemed to have inappropriate sexual or violent content.[11] This system is still in place today, though the categories and criteria have been revised.[12] Throughout this period of change, film-makers increasingly exercised freedom in the portrayal not only of adultery, pre-marital sex, and graphic violence, but also of the Bible and religious clergy.

The ambivalent relationship between film, morality, and the Bible that was evident in the early decades of cinema, went underground during the Production era, and resurfaced in full force in the 1960s, persists to the present day.

This chapter will examine three aspects of this ambivalent relationship: the use of the Bible to support both sides of a given legal and/or ethical position; ambivalence toward ethical precepts associated with the Bible; the use of the Bible to justify unethical behavior.

Both sides against the middle

Dead Man Walking *(1995)*

Many films involving legal themes include the citation of scripture by the supporters of each side of a debate. One striking example is found in the 1995 film *Dead Man Walking*. This film is based on the true story of Sister Helen Prejean, a Louisiana nun. Sister Helen became the spiritual adviser to death row inmates in Angola State Prison, and a vocal activist against the death penalty. The film fictionalizes the specific details – the prisoner's name, the details of his crime – but remains true to the main message: "What's the sense in killing people to say that killing people is wrong?"

This rhetorical question sounds like simple common sense. But it evokes a complex set of ethical issues in which the Bible is deeply implicated. These come to the fore in the memorable Bible-quoting test between Sister Helen and a prison guard. Both are waiting outside the room where Matt Poncelet, the death row prisoner, is taking a final lie detector test. By now Helen's strong stance against capital punishment is well known. The guard asks Sister Helen: "What is a nun doing in a place like this? Shouldn't you be teaching children? And you know what this man has done? How he killed them kids?" Sister Helen acknowledges that what Matt did was evil. But, she adds, "I just don't see the sense of killing people to say killing people's wrong." The guard counters: "You know how the Bible says, 'an eye for an eye'?" Sister Helen goes him one better: "Know what else it asks for? Death as a punishment for adultery, prostitution, homosexuality, trespass upon sacred ground, profaning the Sabbath, and contempt of parents." The guard acknowledges defeat: "I ain't gonna get in no Bible quoting with no nun 'cuz I'm gonna lose."

This exchange highlights two points. One is the use of biblical passages such as *lex talionis* (Exodus 21:22–25; Leviticus 24:19–21; Deuteronomy 19:16–21) to justify capital punishment.[13] The second is the incontrovertible fact that numerous biblical stipulations are no longer accepted – by anyone – as a basis for law, policy, or behavior. To Sister Helen's list one might add slavery, which was accepted in the Bible but is no longer acceptable today, as well as other restrictions and injunctions that do not find a place in our society today. This second point complicates and perhaps even undermines the first: if so many biblical laws are ignored today, what is an acceptable criterion for determining which ones should be normative?

The scene plays upon two common assumptions. The first, as the good doctor Leathes knew so well, is that the Bible is a repository of ethical instruction.[14] Even those who are not regulars at church or synagogue may well view the Decalogue as a statement of the fundamental ethical principles needed for human society to function,[15] or point to other well-known biblical principles, such as the "Golden Rule" – you shall love your neighbor as yourself (Lev. 19:18; see also Lev. 19:34; Luke 10:27) and "do unto others as you would have them do unto you."[16] The film warns us, however, that not every word in the Bible is to be used to inform law, policy, and ethics. The second assumption is that the knowledge of scripture and the ability to quote it from memory convey moral authority. *Dead Man Walking* reinforces this point by presenting a nun as the scriptural authority. Her religious status, in turn, confers authority on her nuanced understanding of the relationship among scripture, ethics, and law.

Inherit the Wind *(1960)*

These same assumptions are at play in an older classic, *Inherit the Wind*, a fictional treatment of the famous 1925 Scopes Monkey trial. Like the mid-twentieth-century Bible epics, this film uses an older historical event to express American anxieties about communism and the Cold War. But the explicit conflict at stake in the film is evolution versus creationism. In a small Tennessee town, a high school teacher, Bert Cates, is put on trial for teaching the theories of Darwin, in violation of state law. The main plot concerns the face-off between two famous lawyers: Matthew Harrison Brady, for the prosecution, and Henry Drummond, for the defense. What is really on trial, however, is the relationship between the Bible and science. Cates is ultimately found guilty but the judge sentences him to a small fine. This light sentence acknowledges the main point of Drummond's case: that every person has the right to think for him or herself. The trial should have provided ample opportunity for both lawyers to call on their witnesses and develop their cases, except that Drummond's efforts to call scientists as expert witnesses are quashed by the judge. Finally, Drummond calls on the only witness available to him: Brady himself. Brady is pleased to be called but loses his composure under cross-examination and discredits his own position.

As it turns out, Drummond too knows his Bible, but, unlike Brady, he does not consider it to be the sole and supreme authority in all areas of human knowledge and endeavor. In court, Drummond places the Bible and Darwin's *On the Origin of Species* side by side, and at the end of the trial he walks out of the courtroom holding both in his hands. When asked, he cites, from memory, the verse from which the film's title is taken, Proverbs 11:29: "He that troubles his own house shall inherit the wind: and the fool shall be servant to the wise of heart."

Although commentators view the film as a reflection on communism, the explicit concern about evolution and creationism sounds contemporary to our ears. Indeed, in the present cultural moment, the debate between Brady and Drummond seems to refer more to the question of biblical authority. Is the Bible a literal account of the story of creation? Is every word of it "true" and if so, in what sense, and how do we know? Most striking is the venom spewed by the townspeople who hold Brady up as a figure who will save them from the wrath of God that is sure to come down on Bert Cates for teaching heresy, and engage in mass vilification of the beleaguered school-teacher.

Footloose (1984)[17]

The idea that the Bible is open to different interpretations is a major theme in *Footloose*. This film is set in a small town in Illinois. The local minister has forbidden dancing and loud music after several teens, including the minister's son, were killed in a car crash after a dance. An early scene takes place inside the church, in which Reverend Shaw is preaching against corruption. Reverend Shaw, like the preacher, the townspeople, and the lawyer Brady in *Inherit the Wind*, has a rigid understanding of what the Bible teaches about moral behavior.

> Every, every day, our Lord is testing us.... If our Lord wasn't testing us, how would you account ... for the proliferation these days ... of this obscene rock and roll music ... with its gospel of easy sexuality ... and relaxed morality? If our Lord wasn't testing us, why, he could take all ... these pornographic books and albums ... and turn them into one big fiery cinder like that! But how would that make us stronger for him? One of these days, my Lord is going to come to me ... and ask me for an explanation ... for the lives of each and every one of you. What am I going to tell him on that day? That I was busy? That I was tired? That I was bored? No! I can never let up! I welcome his test. I welcome this challenge from my Lord ... so that one day I can deliver all of you unto his hands. And when that day dawns ... I don't want to have to do any explaining!

This sermon contains numerous biblical allusions: the notion of God testing believers (Gen. 22:1; 1 Thess. 2:4), the judgment that will take place "on that day" (Mal. 4:1), "pestilence" on the "face of the earth" (Exod. 9:15), and, finally, "Praise the Lord in singing" (Ps. 149:1). This is an austere film with little room for teenage fun.

Then a big-city boy, Ren McCormack arrives in town. Ren chafes at the restrictive policies of his new home, and confronts the city council in the hope of reversing the decree against dancing. In his speech to the council, Ren shows that far from forbidding dancing, the Bible actively promotes it as a means of serving God.

> From the oldest of times, people danced for a number of reasons. They danced in prayer ... or so that their crops would be plentiful ... or so their hunt would be good. And they danced to stay physically fit ... and show their community spirit. And they danced to celebrate. And that is the dancing we're talking about. Aren't we told [in Ps. 149:3] "Praise ye the Lord. Sing unto the Lord a new song. Let them praise his name in the dance,".... And it was King David – King David, who we read about in Samuel. And what did David do?.... David danced before the Lord with all his might ... leaping and dancing before the Lord. Leaping and dancing [2 Sam. 6:5]. Ecclesiastes assures us that there is a time for every purpose under heaven. A time to laugh and a time to weep. A time to mourn ... and there is a time to dance. And there was a time for this law, but not anymore. See, this is our time to dance. It is our way of celebrating life. It's the way it was in the beginning. It's the way it's always been. It's the way it should be now.

Ren does not persuade the council, but he wins over the Reverend, who helps the teens organize a dance outside the town boundaries, and dances with his own wife there as well.

Footloose, like *Inherit the Wind* and *Dead Man Walking*, steers viewers away from a simplistic, literal, interpretation of the Bible, and from a complacent certainty about the Bible's relationship to ethics and morality in the here and now.

"Thou shall – or shalt not – lie"

As we have just seen, the Bible can support both dancing and the prohibition of dancing, capital punishment and the abolition of capital punishment, creationism and less literal ways of understanding God's creative role. Some movies, however, address more mundane ethical matters, among them, lying. The prohibition of lying is a general principle that is often derived from the ninth commandment of the Decalogue, "You shall not bear false witness against your neighbor" (Exod. 20:16).[18] Proverbs 6:16–19 includes "a lying tongue" and "a lying witness who testifies falsely" among the seven things that are an abomination to the Lord. The point is repeated in Proverbs 12:22, which declares that "Lying lips are an abomination to the LORD, but those who act faithfully are his delight." Colossians 3:9–10 warns its audience not to lie to one another, as they used to do before coming to faith in Christ, while the Gospel of John has Jesus declare that "the truth shall set you free." The Evangelist likely has theological truth in mind, but the verse is often used, in films and elsewhere in popular culture, as a statement about the enslaving power of lies.[19]

Lying is a theme in spy movies and thrillers, romantic comedies, and numerous other films in which trust, hypocrisy, or other variations on the truth/lying dichotomy are central to characterization and plot development. Two humorous films that present very different ethical assessments of lying are *Liar Liar* (1997) and *The Invention of Lying* (2009).

Liar Liar *(1997)*

Fletcher Reede, a career-obsessed, divorced defense lawyer in Los Angeles, is a habitual liar. Much as he loves his young son Max, he chronically misses important events such as birthdays and then lies about the reasons why. He also lies habitually in his work life, a trait that has helped him build a stellar professional reputation. For his birthday, Max makes a wish: that his father will become incapable of telling a lie for 24 hours. The wish immediately becomes true, leading to Fletcher's triumphant announcement in court that "the truth shall set you free" (John 8:12). In keeping with the comedy genre, Fletcher is eventually reunited with his wife and son and while he still lies once in a while, his behavior is much improved.[20]

The ethical point here is obvious: tell the truth! Fletcher wins his case, wins the respect of his son, and wins back the love of his wife. Although his inability to lie was limited to one 24-hour period, it would seem that he has learned a life lesson that the film graciously passes along to its viewers.

Invention of Lying *(2009)*

Plot summary

But lying can be a good thing, even essential to good will and happiness. So argues the romantic comedy *The Invention of Lying*. The film is set in a fictional society in which people do not – and apparently cannot – lie. The film's protagonist, Mark Bellison, is a failed lecture/film writer, whose current assignment is to write about the 1300s, a "very boring" era. His life is miserable: he gets fired from his job, evicted from his apartment, and rejected by his date, the beautiful, charming, and wealthy Anna McDoogles. When he goes to the bank to close his account, the clerk tells him that the computers are down. He asks Mark approximately how much money he had in his account – a question possible only in a society where lying is unthinkable. Mark has a brainwave: he doesn't have to tell the truth! He soon tries lying in a variety of other circumstances, and learns that it can be a very effective way of achieving a variety of goals: he has sex with a beautiful woman, helps a friend avoid arrest, and keeps a neighbor from committing suicide. He then earns a fortune by creating an imaginative screenplay about aliens who land in the fourteenth century. He has learned that the ability to lie frees up the imagination to be truly creative. Now that he is financially secure, Anna is willing to date him. Indeed, she enjoys his company and thinks that he would be a great husband and father, but she refuses to marry him because he is not very handsome. If they procreated, he would be contributing half the genetic code and, as she explains earnestly: "I don't want little fat kids with snub noses." In keeping with the romantic comedy genre, Mark and Anna eventually marry, and do indeed give birth to "little fat kids with snub noses," but by that point Anna's priorities, and her ideas of beauty, have changed.

Lying and the Bible

Mark's life is improved by his newfound capacity to lie, which encompasses a range of activities including bending the truth, and exercising the imagination. But Mark's flexible attitude toward strict veracity also transforms the lives of the people around him because he can imagine a world beyond the here and now.

Life after death

One night, while at dinner with Anna, Mark receives a phone call and rushes to the hospital to find his mother on her deathbed. She has suffered one heart attack, and, as the doctor cheerfully tells Mark, in his mother's presence, she will in a matter of hours suffer another, massive attack that will kill her. The doctor recites her symptoms and prognosis without any emotion. After explaining that there is no hope for the elderly woman, he tells Mark, "Side note, it's fajita night downstairs in the cafeteria, so you might want to grab yourself a little bite down there after mom dies." This hilarious scene implies that callousness is the end result of absolute truthfulness. The scene is also a dig at the medical profession, which, it is implied, is inured to death and blind to the feelings of sorrow and loss that the families experience during an end of life crisis. Not so Mark. When his mother confesses how frightened she is of "an eternity of nothingness" he takes a leap of imagination and, one might say, faith that goes against the grain of his entire culture and upbringing: "Mum," he says with conviction,

> Mum, you're wrong about what happens after you die ... you're going to your favorite place in the whole world, and everyone you've ever loved and who's ever loved you will be there. You will be young again ... there's no pain, there's love, happiness, everyone gets a mansion, and it lasts for an eternity, an eternity, Mum. Say hello to Dad for me, tell him I love him.

But Mum is not the only one listening to these words as if her life depended on it. That same doctor who had cheerfully reported on her imminent death is transfixed by his message of life after death. He and the nurses urge Mark to go on. The doctor asks, "What else happens?" One nurse is overjoyed: "I'm going to see my mother again when I die." The doctor repeats, "Can you tell us more, please?"

The promise of life after death, while absent from the Hebrew Bible, became a standard Christian – and Jewish and Muslim – belief.[21] The world after death that Mark imagines for the sake of his mother alludes explicitly to John 14:2, in which Jesus proclaims that "In my Father's house are many mansions" (KJV).

The ten rules

The hospital medical staff are not the only ones hungry for information about life after death. The promise of an eternal mansion becomes the cornerstone of an entire belief system that captures the imaginations of the entire community (imaginations that had seemed to be absent from their psychological makeup to this point). Initially, Mark himself was unable to see that this new "knowledge" (which he perceives as his – well-motivated – lies) would be comforting not only to his dying mother but to the world. He is unprepared for the crowds anxious multitudes or the interest of the global media. Suddenly he is afraid of what he has begun: "This is bad." His home is soon surrounded by clamoring hordes. Anna and his best buddy Greg push their way through the crowds and come into the house. Anna convinces him that he must speak out. Sharing this wonderful information will not only help others, she argues, but also make him feel as wonderful as when he was able to comfort his mother in the face of her death. Mark spends all night writing draft after draft of a speech to the people. As day breaks, he is ready. He has ten rules; he looks around for "something better to put these on, like tablets," finally settling on an empty pizza box.

When he finally emerges, he reads out the Ten Rules, which, he says, were given to him by a "Man in the Sky" who controls the world. The key message: anyone who does no more than three "bad things" during their lifetime will be rewarded after death. Initially he stutters and hesitates, recalling Moses' speech impediment,[22] but he gains momentum and strength as he goes along. Throughout, the people interrupt him, grumble, complain, but finally are satisfied, much like their biblical counterparts, to whom Moses periodically reports the will of the "Man in the Sky."[23]

The first rule is that "There is a man in the sky who controls everything." When pressed for details, he describes the man as a mixture of all ethnicities, and tall, with big hands (perhaps because "he's got the whole world" in them?[24]), and lots of hair. The next four rules describe the mansion awaiting everyone, in a place with all the people you love, and free ice cream, all day and all night, in every imaginable flavor (a point that prompts the crowds to shout out the most disgusting flavors they can imagine). The last five explain that if you do bad things you won't go to this great place when you die, and that ultimately it will be the Man in the Sky who decides who will go there and who will not, and, perhaps more to the point, who will die and who will live. In other words, these last rules address the topics of ethics, theodicy, and grace. The people push back on every point: what counts as a bad thing? Forgetting to feed the dog and the dog dies? No, answers Mark, but deciding to stop feeding the dog so that the dog dies, yes. And, someone asks, if the Man in the Sky controls everything, was it he who gave a loved one cancer? And he who cured her? Yes, to both. But in the end, Mark assures them with Rule Number Ten: "Even if the Man in the Sky does bad stuff to you he makes up for it by giving you an eternity of good stuff when you die." How does he know all this? The Man in the Sky told him. As the scene closes out, we hear a weather reporter say, "Today's forecast calls for blue sky." The newspapers and magazines blast the headlines around the world: "Finally a reason to be good" but also blame the Man in the Sky for giving AIDS to children and causing a tsunami that killed 40,000 people.

The truth about lying

This revelation scene is played for laughs, spoofing both DeMille's 1956 *The Ten Commandments* and also the rendition of the Sermon on the Mount in the Jesus epics. It also however touches on some fundamental issues regarding the Bible, religion, and ethics. Are happiness, goodness, and compassion truly motivated only, or most forcefully, by the promise of a blessed afterlife existence in a big mansion in the sky? Does it matter if these promises are truth or lies as long as they make people happy, good, and compassionate in the present? The infantile language of the ten rules, and the patient, condescending manner in which Mark delivers them, implies that the belief system that he has made up out of love for his dying mother and does not himself believe in is a sop to the childish and unimaginative people. Although the rules are attributed to the "Man in the Sky," it was Mark himself who made them up. The implication is that lying is not only acceptable, but a necessary part of the civilized life, a point that is a brutally honest observation of the blunt sort that the film itself mocks.

In the end, however, the movie steps back from an all-out endorsement of lying. This retreat emerges in the romantic subplot. Mark has a rival for Anna's affections: his very handsome former co-worker, Brad Kessler. Brad is blunt, even rude, but Anna agrees to marry him for the sake of the gene pool. Mark is dejected, but, emboldened by his best friend Greg, he attends the wedding and publicly objects to the marriage. Both Brad and Anna implore Mark to consult with the "Man in the Sky" but this time he refuses; he wants Anna to decide. At this point he also confesses to his invention of lying.

When Anna asks why he did not just lie to convince her to choose him over Brad, Mark says that "it wouldn't count." In other words, there are situations when lying is the wrong thing to do. In this case, his truth-telling gets him the girl.

More important is the definition of "lying" itself. Certainly Mark lies, for example about the amount of money in his bank account. But most of his "lies" are not in this category. Rather, they posit an unverifiable realm of human experience and imagination. What the film calls lying others might well call faith.

What then is implied by the presentation of faith as a "lie"? This perspective may be offensive to viewers for whom religious faith, specifically, the belief in life after death, is important. The comedic genre of the film, however, should caution us against attaching too much existential importance to its claims that faith in the unseen is but a lie to assuage the fear of mortality, and that the Bible is simply a human fabrication imputed to a fictional "Man in the Sky." The film is above all intended to entertain, and its humor lies in the inversion of conventional values around lying and truth-telling. At the same time, this film demonstrates the extent to which Hollywood has departed from the conventions of the Bible epic, and the Production Code, for which (primarily Christian) faith was an unassailable principle.

The Bible and the bad guy

Lying may be a transgression, but it is not always considered "evil" in the same sense as, say, murder. As we have already seen, there is a commonplace tendency to confer authority and attribute moral "goodness" on those who know the Bible, and justify their actions or attitudes on biblical grounds. Even those characters who are portrayed as too rigid in their interpretation and application of biblical injunctions, such as the prison guard in *Dead Man Walking* and the preachers in *Inherit the Wind* and *Footloose* can be seen as "good" even if one deplores the lack of nuance in their ethical positions considerably. Similarly, we can accept the fundamental goodness of flawed characters such as Andy Dufresne (*Shawshank Redemption*), and Walt Kowalski (*Gran Torino*), even as we recognize that they, like us, do not always behave ethically.

But since the disappearance of the Production Code, many films have challenged the commonplace positive associations between the Bible and ethics, by portraying "bad guys" who justify their behavior on biblical grounds, and sometimes even depicting them as Christ-figures. These are not ordinary flawed human beings who transgress on occasion but are more or less ethically motivated. No, these are mobsters, gangsters, gunslingers, indeed, criminals of all types.

Perhaps the least troubling are films in which the "bad guys" who cite scripture are critical, at least occasionally, of their own criminality, thereby allowing viewers to entertain the hope of their eventual reform. Quentin Tarantino plays skillfully upon this desire in his 1994 film *Pulp Fiction*, in which a hit man, Jules, habitually recites a (fake) version of Ezekiel 25:17 just before shooting his victim at point blank range. In the film's final sequence, Jules meditates upon that "biblical" speech as he declares his intention to leave the life of crime. Like his partner Vince, we may question Jules' chances for success – the fabricated nature of the passage itself implies that perhaps his repentance is equally false – but at the very least he refrains from shooting at the petty thief sitting across the dinner table from him at that moment. In *Dead Man Walking*, Matt Poncelet arrives at an ethical position of responsibility at the end of his life, because of the tremendous effort that Sister Helen has expended as his spiritual advisor.

3:10 to Yuma *(2007)*

More problematic, and more interesting, are those criminals who cite the scriptures in support of their unethical and unlawful activities. *The Godfather* trilogy (1972, 1974, 1990) explores the spiritual and ethical descent of Michael Corleone from an idealistic young man determined to chart a course outside the family business to the fearsome Don of his "family." The films make ample use of Catholic ritual and symbols, and prompt numerous comparisons with biblical stories, particularly the primordial family of Genesis.[25] The contradiction between their activities and their adherence to certain elements of Catholic faith and tradition contributes to the tension that gives these films their power.

The mafia families operate according to an ethical code even as they commit their crime.[26] Other criminals strike out on their own, in their ethics as in their activities. One such man is the outlaw Ben Wade, in *3:10 to Yuma*.

Plot summary

This film is a remake of the 1957 movie which in turn was an adaptation of Elmore Leonard's 1953 short story by the same name.[27] The setting is a poor ranch in Arizona, shortly after the end of the Civil War. The struggling rancher, Dan Evans, an injured Civil War veteran, owes money to his landlord, Mr. Hollander. Mr. Hollander is attempting to force Evans into penury so that he can sell off the land to the railroad company for a big profit. In the opening scene, the Evans family is awoken by Hollander's men, as they set fire to the Evans' barn. The fire destroys the barn as well as their stored animal feed, and threatens their livestock. The next morning, as they attempt to round up their escaped cattle, Evans and his two young sons stumble upon the infamous Ben Wade and watch, in fascinated horror, as Wade and his gang ambush a Pinkerton stagecoach, kill most of the passengers, and make off with the loot. When Wade realizes that he has been spotted, he does not kill Evans and his sons, as one might have expected. Instead, he takes their horses and then tells Ben where he will find them the next day. Wade heads to Bisbee to celebrate at the local saloon. Shortly thereafter, Evans arrives to confront Hollander. Evans finds Wade in the saloon and detains him long enough to be captured. The cash-strapped Evans volunteers to join the small group charged with delivering Wade to Contention, where they will put him on the 3:10 train to Yuma Territorial Prison.

In the face of almost insurmountable obstacles, Evans does eventually deliver Wade to Contention, where Wade boards the 3:10 train to Yuma. But in a last-minute, heart-wrenching scene, Evans is killed by Wade's right hand man, Charlie Prince – a ruthless, sadistic, but fanatically loyal follower. Wade turns on Charlie, kills him and the rest of his own gang, then climbs quietly onto the train. By this point the viewer knows Wade well enough to be suspicious of his docile behavior. Sure enough, as the train leaves the station, Wade whistles for his horse, which canters after the train – ready to provide a quick getaway at the first opportunity.

Themes

The main plot of the film concerns Dan Evans' extraordinary efforts to get Ben Wade to the 3:10 train from Contention to Yuma. The journey however provides the backdrop for an exploration of ethics developed through plot, characterization, and the use of the Bible. In the course of this exploration, two other subplots come into play. One subplot concerns the developing relationship between Dan and Ben. In his own way, Ben is a charismatic fellow who has a well-honed ability to gain people's confidence, often, but not always, for the purposes of exploiting them. But early on he takes a liking to Dan and his sons, perhaps because of Dan's skill as a sharpshooter, his ability to negotiate a good deal for himself, and his poker face (which he deployed to detain Ben in the saloon long enough to be arrested). Dan's resistance to Ben's overtures begins to soften only at the end of the journey, during the tense hours they spend in a hotel room in Contention waiting for the train, and then breaks down altogether as they make a run for it under intense fire from Charlie Prince and the gang.

The second subplot is the relationship between Dan and his 14-year-old son William. William has a romanticized adolescent view of outlaws, fed by the adventure stories he reads in bed by candlelight. When he meets a real-life outlaw he is both fascinated and repulsed. He is fascinated by Ben's colorful life and reputation, his strength and his decisiveness, and repulsed because of his continual and blatant flouting of the law and of human decency including the respect for human life. At the same time, William is disappointed in his father, and critical of his father's weaknesses, his softness of speech and demeanor, the setbacks he has suffered, his war injury, and his failure to provide well for his family. Dan's decision to take part in the trip is motivated not only by dire financial need but also a desire to redeem himself in his son's eyes. Ben Wade, a keen observer of human behavior and relationships, inserts himself into this situation, in ways that impact directly on the viewers' assessment of his ambiguous ethical status.

Preacher Wade

The Bible is instrumental in developing the first subplot. Ben knows his scriptures and he quotes twice from the book of Proverbs. The first time is in the Bisbee saloon. As the outlaws drink to their lucrative stage coach robbery, Charlie Prince proposes a toast: "Here's to the four who were lost in battle. And here's to the Boss, who had to say goodbye to Tommy Darden [one of their own men whom Wade himself killed] today. And that's too bad." In reply, Wade quotes Proverbs 13:3: "He that keepeth his mouth keepeth his life. He that opens his lips too wide shall bring on his own destruction."[28] One outlaw responds "Amen," but Wade does not let the matter go. In extreme close-up, he stares into Charlie's face and continues, "Tommy was weak. Tommy was stupid. Tommy is dead." Charlie's amen is "I'll drink to that" and they all drink up. Was Tommy's death then a fitting punishment for talking too much? Not surprisingly, Wade omits the previous verse: "From the fruit of their words good persons eat good things, but the desire of the treacherous is for wrongdoing" (Proverbs 13:2), which would have condemned his own behavior.

The second occasion occurs the evening before Evans and the others set out for Contention with their prisoner. For reasons of logistics and security, the men gather at Evans' ranch. The contrast between the rough outlaw and the genteel family emerges as they sit awkwardly together at the dinner table. After grace is said and the meal begun, Dan's younger son boasts to Wade about his father Dan's shooting prowess. Dan quietly corrects his son: "Shooting an animal's a lot different than, uh, shooting a man, son." But Ben quickly interjects, "No, it isn't. Not in my opinion." He gestures at one of the men charged with taking him to prison. "We could ask Byron [a Pinkerton guard who is in charge of getting Wade to Contention] here. Now, Byron, he's killed dozens of people: men and women and children, miners, Apache." Byron protests: "Not a soul taken didn't deserve what it got." Ben responds: "Every way of man is right in his own eyes, Byron" and then states: "The Lord ponders the heart. Proverbs 21" (Proverbs 21:2). Ben looks over with an almost shy – or is it sly? – smile at Dan's wife, as if to say: how bad a fellow can I be if I'm able to cite the scripture? Yet neither the Evans family, nor we the viewers, are taken in. Byron, of course, has merely articulated the narrow and vengeful moral vision that Ben himself had expressed back at the saloon: that it is right and just to mete out punishments to the people that deserve them – according to our own ethical norms. Ben draws attention to the idiosyncratic nature of Byron's own ethical code, a criticism that could just as easily be aimed at Ben himself.

While the film does not have any other explicit biblical quotations, the Bible continues to come up in conversation, as well as in the film's visual vocabulary. Ben and Byron continue to bait one another as they travel along. On the first night, Ben killed Tucker, Hollander's henchman and the man who had set fire to the Evans' barn. Dan is disturbed by Tucker's death, and asks Ben: "Why'd you kill Tucker? Why not me? Or Butterfield?" "Well," answers Ben, "Tucker took my horse. Did you like him, Dan?" Dan says no. Ben continues, "He told me he burnt down your barn." Dan responds, "He was an asshole, but wishing him dead and killing him are two different things." Here Dan is expressing the mature ethical response, distinguishing between desire and action. Ben clearly does not see things that way, and indeed, we suspect that Ben killed Tucker primarily to avenge the harm done to Dan. "Your conscience is sensitive," he says to Dan. "I don't think it's my favorite part of you."

At this point, Byron Butterfield, the lead man in the convoy, steps in to prevent further conversation between Dan and Ben. "You wanna talk to somebody," he tells Ben, "Talk to me." Ben protests,

> I don't like talking to you, Byron.... I just don't find you that interest-ing.... You ever read another book in your life, Byron, besides the Bible? ... [he turns to Dan to say:] Byron acts pious. Few years ago, when he was under contract to Central, I seen him and a bunch of other Pinks [Pinkerton Security company agents] mow down 32 Apache women and children.

Byron protests: "Renegades gunning down railroad men and their families. Picking 'em off the road one by one. Scalping 'em." Ben continues:

> There was young ones running around crying and screaming. No more than three years old. And his boys shot 'em all then pushed 'em into a ditch. Some of them was still crying. But I guess Byron figured that Jesus wouldn't mind. Apparently Jesus don't like the Apache.

Ben is not objecting to the killing *per se*, but to the fact that Byron's actions were motivated by racism.

Strictly speaking, of course, Ben is on the wrong side of the ethical divide, just as he is on the wrong side of the law. So says Byron, who relishes Ben's comeuppance: "Keep on talking all the way to Yuma, right up them steps, to the rope, straight to Hell." But Ben does not see it that way. "Day I die, Byron, I'm getting sprung from Hell." This is not necessarily an assertion of his fundamental goodness, so much as a confidence that he can get himself out of most uncomfortably "hot" situations.

Ben's knowledge of the Bible is revealed as the film builds to its climax. He and Dan are sitting in a hotel room in Contention, waiting for the train to Yuma to pull into the station. Dan is extremely tense about the barrage of fire that will surely greet them as they run from the hotel to the train station. Ben, by contrast, is calmly sketching on the frontispiece of a Bible.[29] As he is drawing, Ben asks: "You ever read the Bible, Dan?" Without waiting for an answer he continues,

> I read it one time. I was eight years old. My daddy just got hisself killed over a shot of whiskey, and my mama said, "We're going back East to start over." So she gave me a Bible, sat me down in the train station, told me to read it. She was gonna get our tickets. Well, I did what she said. I read that Bible from cover to cover. It took me three days. She never came back.

As he tells this story, he continues to look down as he sketches, but afterwards, he raises his eyes slowly to meet Dan's. Immediately the clock strikes 3, and Dan says, "It's time." The story explains Ben's knowledge of the Bible (or at least the Book of Proverbs), and also, if obliquely, hints at neglect and loneliness. Yet his sidelong glance at Dan, assessing the impact of his confession, implies that even at this tense moment, he is still trying to garner some sympathy that may prove helpful at a future point in time.

Ben's story contributes to the breakdown of Dan's defences against him. When they finally finish the dangerous run from the hotel to the tiny Contention train station, Dan shares a confidence of his own. "You said I was stubborn," he tells Ben, "for keeping my family on a dying ranch. It's my [younger] son Mark.... He got tuberculosis when he was two. The doctor said he'd die if he didn't have a dry climate, so ..." Ben interrupts him, "Why are you telling me this?" Dan answers, with a bit of a smile, "I don't know. I guess I just wanted you to know that I ain't stubborn is all." They chuckle, the way friends do. Despite himself, Dan cares that Ben understand him the way that he wishes to be understood. The camera cuts briefly and quickly to Yuma station and a brief but powerful shot of a pole with a sign across it, like the cross awaiting its victim. Ben then responds to Dan, "Well, as long as we're making confessions ... I've been to Yuma Prison before. Twice. Escaped twice, too." This may be mere braggadocio but it might also be an indirect response to Dan's move toward friendship, silently conveying the message that in delivering Ben to the train, Dan does not have to feel that he is betraying a friend. What can be done twice can be done a third time.

Christ-figures?

It seems obvious that while Ben quotes the Bible, it is Dan, and his family, who live by it. The film's exploration of ethics, however, brings another set of Bible-related considerations into play: Christ imagery. In many ways, Dan is a good candidate as a Christ-figure. His appearance – slight build, shoulder length brown hair, short beard – evokes the stereotypical Christ of the movies. He has lost a foot in battle, apparently – so brags his younger son Mark – in defence of the country's capital city. He treats everyone, even Ben Wade, with respect, and actively fosters these values in his children. He has sacrificed much in order to provide the ailing Mark with a dry climate and medications.

And yet, the film's abundant Christ-imagery points in the direction of Ben Wade as the Christ-figure. Ben's sudden appearance in various locales prompts holy exclamations. When Ben escapes briefly from his minders and turns up at an encampment of railroad workers, he is spotted by one Mr. Boles, who exclaims, "Holy Christ! … That's him!" Of course, "Holy Christ" is an expletive that can simply express shock and surprise. But in this instance, it is reinforced by a visual image, for when Dan and the others catch up, they find Ben hanging from a pole, and his captors preparing to torture him. The image evokes the scourging of Jesus and for a brief moment allows us a glimpse of Ben Wade as a persecuted savior figure. They escape, and as they do so, Boles closes out the scene with another holy exclamation: "God dammit!"

Even more striking are the crosses that are part of numerous mise-en-scènes: a striking landscape shot that bears an eerie resemblance to Golgotha as portrayed in numerous Jesus-movies (Figure 8.1), the view of the Contention train station (Figure 8.2) from the point of view of an outlaw waiting for Ben and Dan to emerge.

These crosses are evocative but do not directly point in Ben's direction. Not so with the crosses prominent in the movie's final scene (Figure 8.3).

Ben is finally on the train. He has just handed over his gun and ammunition to the conductor and taken a seat on the bench. Yet in Hollywood's lexicon, this shot identifies him as a Christ-figure, by seating him immediately in front of a window that looks more like the cross of a church than the window of a train.

Figure 8.1 Golgotha, *3:10 to Yuma.*

Figure 8.2 Train Station Cross, *3:10 to Yuma.*

Figure 8.3 Jesus Christ, Ben Wade, *3:10 to Yuma.*

Is this final image to be read sincerely or ironically? Ben's blatant disregard for property and human life suggests this image is ironic. When asked outright by Ben about the number of people he has killed and the number of families he has destroyed, he admits, "Quite a few." But he does not repent, nor does he seem to regret killing his follower Tommy Darden, or Mr. Boles' brother, or anyone else. Whereas he sharply condemns Byron for killing innocent women and children, many of them Apaches, he justifies the murders he has committed on the grounds that the victims deserved to die. This justification is symbolized by his gun – a big black pistol emblazoned with a large silver cross – called "The Hand of God" (Figure 8.4).

The phrase "hand of God" appears in 16 verses in the King James Version. Some of these refer to Jesus' exaltation at "right hand of God" (Mark 16:19; Acts 2:33; Acts 7:55; Acts 7:56; Romans 8:34; Colossians 3:1; Hebrews 10:12; 1 Peter 3:22). Other passages refer positively to the benefits bestowed by the hand of God (2 Chron. 30:12; Ecclesiastes 2:24, 9:1).

More directly relevant however are a number of passages that use the "hand of God" to describe the source of suffering. In 1 Samuel 5:11 the

Figure 8.4 The Hand of God, *3:10 to Yuma.*

Philistines want the ark of the God of Israel removed from the town of Ekron, "for there was a deadly destruction throughout all the city; the hand of God was very heavy there" (KJV). Job tells his wife and his friends that his troubles are caused by the "hand of God" (Job 2:10, 19:21, cf. 27:11). 1 Peter 5:6 expresses this idea less directly, promising that those who humble themselves "under the mighty hand of God" will be exalted in due course. In this context, Ben's use of the "hand of God" pistol exemplifies his self-understanding as God's avenger who cuts down those who deserve to die. Nowhere is this clearer than in the final scene. Dan has delivered Ben to the train, but is shot down, and then murdered, with glee, by Charlie Prince, who clearly believes that in doing so he has saved his boss from a potential death sentence. Ben jumps off the train. Charlie throws him the "hand of God" along with an ammunition belt. Ben looks down at the gun, offering us a close-up of the "hand of God" pistol (see Figure 8.4) resting in his own hand. He then shoots Charlie Prince and all of his own gang members. He then looks Charlie in the eye as he finishes him off, as he had done to Tommy Darden before him.

Ben's self-appointed role as the "hand of God" may seem inauthentic and highly problematic from both a spiritual and ethical standpoint. The big silver cross on the pistol handle serves only to accentuate the distance between Ben's actions and those of Christ, no matter what the ethical status of Ben's victims. But in other respects, it is not quite so easy to dismiss the idea of Ben as a Christ-figure.

At one point on the journey, Ben tries to tell Dan that his son William reminds him of himself as a young man. Dan rejects the implication: "He's gonna be nothing like you, Wade. William's got a head start on the path of decency." Wade responds: "Yeah, that's why I don't mess around with doing anything good, Dan. You do one good deed for somebody ... I imagine it's habit-forming. Something decent. See that grateful look in their eyes, imagine it makes you feel like Christ hisself." Yet Ben's self-described wickedness, like his self-appointed role as the avenger, does not quite ring true. We have already seen him behave decently, in his first encounter with Dan, when he did not touch Dan's cattle, did not steal his horses, and offered him money for the time he lost when his path crossed Ben's. William recognizes that Ben is not all bad. Indeed, the true villain of the film is not Ben but the greedy Mr. Hollander, who by squeezing the life out of Dan's ranch, and his soul, sets in motion the events that lead to Dan's death.

However one perceives Ben's deeds throughout the film, his final act is one of grace. Evans' son William has witnessed Ben and Dan's bloody race from the hotel to the train station, rejoiced when he saw Ben climb onto the train, and then observed, with horror, Charlie's deadly assault on his father and Ben's revenge. He now realizes that Ben is free to escape. With his father bleeding to death on the ground, no one can force Ben to get back on that train. Yet, as he kneels over his father, he reassures him: "You done it, Pa. You done it. You got him on the train." William then stands up and points his gun at Ben, who just stands there, unarmed, waiting. William could kill him if he chooses. But William cannot bring himself to do it. It seems that his father, and not Ben, was right after all: it is harder to shoot a man than it is to shoot an animal. William has made his choice between Ben and Dan, and chosen righteousness over vengeance. But in his final act of kindness and grace, Ben boards the train, hands over his pistol, and sits down. The cross behind him shows the truth of his earlier statement: it is true, then, that one decent act "makes you feel like Christ Hisself" and in that fleeting moment, who is to say you are not? Through this act Ben has put in the final stitch that repairs the relationship between Dan and William. William sees that Dan has delivered his quarry. He has not only remained an ethical human being in the process, but also, perhaps (who can say?), acted as a role model of ethics and human decency for Wade himself. William can perhaps even see Dan as a Christ-figure, as suggested by the sketch in the hotel room after Dan and Ben have left for the station. On the title page which announces the book as "The Holy Bible ... New Testament," Ben has sketched Dan as he sits in the hotel room waiting for 3 p.m., as if it is Dan that is the subject not only of the drawing but of the book itself.

Ben's Christ moment on the train is palpable but fleeting. Wade immediately whistles for his horse. When and how Ben will escape we do not know, but there is no doubt that escape he will. This too, however, can be seen as good thing. Dan would not have wanted Wade's execution on his own conscience, or that of his son. And if the raids on Pinkerton stage coaches begin again, well, that is not our concern.

The use of Christ imagery, even if ironic, underscores the ethical ambivalence of the film, as does Ben's penchant for Proverbs. This ambivalence however does not undermine either the importance of the Bible, or of ethical behavior. Rather, it serves to break down the stark contrast between good and evil, or "good guy" and "bad guy" that are common conventions in the Western movie genre.

Bible and unredeemable evil

Not all Bible-citing villains are so easily redeemed as the gunslinger Ben Wade. The film canon abounds with villains who cite scripture to justify truly horrific deeds. Indeed, Bible quotation is a feature of numerous horror and exorcism films. In the classic Stephen King film *Carrie* (1976, 2002),[30] the main character is an abusive mother whose shame about giving birth to an illegitimate child is based on an obsessive reading of the Bible. In her hands the Bible also becomes an instrument of abuse. When her daughter wants to go to her school prom, the mother screams a curse: "As Jezebel fell from the tower, let it be with you … And the dogs came and licked up the blood. It's in the Bible!" The protagonist of the 1999 movie *Resurrection*, a serial killer named Demus, descends from Judas Iscariot. He is determined to atone for Judas' sin by "reconstructing" Jesus' body from the body parts of his murder victims, named Peter, James, John, Andrew, Matthew, Mark, and Thomas. Using the biblical verses that the killer has left behind, the detective solves the case just before the final intended victim – a baby to be born to a mother named Mary – can be killed.[31]

Film noir

Film noir is another genre in which scripture-quoting villains can be found. The 1955 film *Night of the Hunter* is based on the 1953 novel by David Grubb, which itself was based on the true story of Harry Powell who was executed for killing two widows and three children in Clarksburg, West Virginia. The film is set in rural America during the depression. The protagonist is an itinerant preacher named Harry Powell who dupes, marries, and then murders rich elderly widows. While serving a prison term for theft, his cell mate, Ben Harper, talks in his sleep about a large sum of money hidden in his house, and recites the phrase " … a child shall lead them" (Isa. 11:6) as a clue to the money's whereabouts. Ben is executed for his crimes, but Powell is released. He now seeks out Harper's widow Willa as his next victim, and gains the confidence of her children. Powell uses the Bible to manipulate his victims, especially the children, and to reflect on his mission. He sees his flick knife as an instrument of divine retribution, citing Matthew 10:34, in which Jesus declares: "I come not to bring peace but a sword." He is certain that God does not mind the killings, because "Your book is full of killings" but he knows that God, like Harry, despises women and womanly things, for "a strange woman is a narrow pit" (Prov. 23:27). After Willa's death, the children are rescued by a saintly but tough woman Rachel who also cites scripture – about the pure in heart, for example (Matt. 5:8, 6:29) – not to justify murder but to comfort the children.[32]

Another film noir scripture-quoting villain is Max Cady, who torments Sam Bowden and his family in the truly terrifying 1991 version of *Cape Fear* (dir. Martin Scorsese).[33] This movie is a remake of the 1962 film about a convicted rapist who serves his sentence and then persecutes the public defender in his case, who, he believes, purposefully withheld evidence about the sex life of his victim that might have acquitted him. Sam's attempts to keep Cady at a distance, and then to keep him from harming his family erode his own moral sensibilities, so that by the end of the film he has sunk nearly as low as Cady – he fights, threatens, and attempts to entrap and then kill his adversary.

Scorsese pulls out all the stops, using music, color, camera angles, and editing to unsettle and deeply frighten the viewer. Within the dialog itself, however, it is the villain's use of the Bible that is most disturbing.[34] To be sure, Cady is not the only one to cite scripture in this film. Sam's lawyer, for example, hopes that Mr. Bowden will have his revenge on Cady "just as God arose to judgment to save all the meek of the earth" (cf. Matt. 5:5) and flatters the judge who has granted a restraining order against Cady that "King Solomon could not have adjudicated more wisely, your honour" (cf. 1 Kgs 3).[35]

But it is Cady who draws upon the Bible most frequently and most authoritatively, thereby legitimating his own twisted vengeance as a fulfillment of scripture. Cady "embodies" scripture, for his body is tattooed with biblical quotations of divine vengeance coupled with the need for patience: "Vengeance is Mine" (Rom. 12:19), "My Time is at Hand" (Matt. 26:18), "The Lord is the Avenger" (1 Thess 4:6), "I have put my trust in the Lord God, in him will I trust" (Ps. 91:2), – and "My time is not yet come" (John 7:6, 7:8). Cady sees his experiences in prison as equivalent to Paul's imprisonment, referring to Galatians 3; he gains the trust of Sam's moody teenage daughter by urging her to forgive her parents "for they know not what they do" (Luke 23:34). As Sam's lawyer wryly remarks, "I don't know whether to look at him or read him."

Suggestive as these quotations are, the key to Cady's self-understanding, and the plot of the movie, is to be found in a cryptic comment that he makes to Sam: "Check out the Bible, counsellor, the book between Esther and Psalms." Sam, far less familiar with the Bible than Cady, discovers the book of Job, which he summarizes for his terrified wife: "God took away everything he had, even his children." Leigh understands that Cady is their Satan and that they are about to be tested to the limits, not of their faith in God, but of their endurance. In the end, Cady dies and the family endures, but in regaining their lives, the Bowdens also recognize that they have forever lost their innocence.

The Girl with the Dragon Tattoo *(2011)*

Plot summary

More recently, the scripture-quoting villain has surfaced in *The Girl with the Dragon Tattoo*, adapted from the 2005 novel by Stieg Larrson.[36] An out-of-favor journalist, Mikael Blomkvist, has been hired by the wealthy patriarch of the Vanger dynasty to learn the fate of his niece, Harriet Vanger, who went missing from the family's remote Swedish island estate 40 years earlier. Mikael prevails upon Vanger to engage Lisbeth Salander, a talented and eccentric computer hacker, to help with the investigation. Mikael and Salander link Harriet's disappearance to a strange and seemingly random set of murders that took place in Sweden from the late 1940s to the mid-1960s. Eventually they learn that Harriet is living elsewhere under a false identity, and that the perpetrator of the murders was her brother Martin, who had inherited a nasty predilection for torture, sexual abuse, and murder from his Nazi-sympathizing father Gottfried.

The Bible as prop

An aspect of Harriet's life that puzzled her family was her increasing interest in the Bible. This interest was sudden, and quite at odds with her secular upbringing. The Vanger family attributed Harriet's sudden obsession to a newly found adolescent piety, or to a deep unhappiness. Harriet's cousin Anita commented:

> I never saw it myself, but you could tell something was going on. One day she'd be withdrawn. The next she'd be putting on makeup and wearing the tightest sweater she had to school. The next she'd be studying a Bible like a nun – no Vanger was ever religious – can you imagine? Obviously, she was very unhappy.

Perhaps, then, Harriet rebelled against her family, by running off or even committing suicide.

Bible quotation

Blomkvist takes this analysis of Harriet's behavior seriously. At night, alone in his cottage, he leafs through Harriet's Bible, and, at random, comes upon a passage in the Letter to the Hebrews, that is read out in the film by the young Harriet in voice-over: "Faith is the assurance of things hoped for, the evidence of things not seen. Through faith we understand that the world was created by the word of God – and that what is seen was not made of things that are visible" (Heb. 11:1–3).[37] Mikael sets the Bible down and rubs his eyes, exhausted and depressed.

It turns out, however, that the Bible is a key not to teenage rebellion but to the mysterious deaths of several young women, and it is these deaths, rather than teenage angst, that was at the core of Harriet's troubled state of mind. The mystery is uncovered by another Bible-reading young woman, Blomkvist's own daughter, Pernilla. Like Harriet, she was raised in a secular family, and she too had begun reading the Bible. She drops in on her father briefly en route to the Light of Life Bible camp. Her growing faith puzzles her father, but he accepts it. As she boards the train after her brief visit, she says, cryptically: "Don't go too hard on the Catholics." He has no idea what she is talking about. She explains: "The article you're writing." He is still puzzled. She continues: "The Bible quotes on your desk." Still mystified, he says goodbye and returns to his cottage. He looks through the papers on his desk, and then sees the photocopy of the last page of Harriet's address book. The book contains a list of five names, with numbers following them: Magda 32016 Sara 32109 R.J. 30114 R.L. 32027 Mari 32018. The names are biblical (except for R.L. which is as yet unknown), but also common-place. All along he has assumed that these are phone numbers, which he has been unable to trace. With his daughter's parting comments still in his mind, he starts looking through Harriet's Bible. All the numbers begin with the number 3, so he turns to the third book of the Bible, Leviticus, which, as he now notices, is slightly dog-eared. He reads Leviticus 1:14, which again is read in voice-over by the young Harriet: "If a dove is the sinner's offering, the priest shall wring off its head, cleave its wings, and burn it upon the altar."

The code, as it turns out, refers to biblical verses that describe gruesome executions to be carried out in particular circumstances. These passages too are read as a voice-over by the young Harriet. The first is Leviticus 21:9: "The daughter of any priest who profanes herself by playing the harlot, pro-fanes her father, and shall be burned with fire;" next is Leviticus 20:27: "A woman who is a medium or sorcerer shall be put to death by stoning." Third is Leviticus 4:32–34, for which Pernilla joins Harriet in the voice-over: "If a man's offering is a lamb, it shall be a female without blemish. He shall lay his hand upon its head, slaughter it, empty its blood on the base of the altar, and he shall be forgiven."

In the meantime, Lisbeth has been searching through newspaper reports of women who died in unusual ways, and she has matched the victims with the verses. She presents her findings to Mikael, "The five cases from Har-riet's list. And five more she missed – three I'm sure about." Blomkvist is shocked: "five more," he asks? She explains: "Rebecca was the first, like you thought ... M.H., is Mari Holmberg, a prostitute in Kalmar, murdered in 1954. Leviticus verse 20, line 18." Blomkvist reads the fourth quotation: "If a man lies with a woman having her sickness, he has made naked her fountain and she has uncovered the fountain of her blood." Salander explains the connection: "She was raped and stabbed, but the cause of death was suffocation with a sanitary napkin. R.L. Rakel Lunde, 1957 ... Clean-ing woman and part-time palm reader, tied up with a clothesline, gagged, raped, head crushed with a rock", in other words, in accordance with Leviticus 20:27. Salander continues: "Sara Witt, 1964. Daughter of a pastor. Tied to her bed, raped, charred in the fire that burned down her house," matching the punishment of the priest's daughter described in Leviticus 21:9. Next is "Magda Lovisa Sjoberg, 1960, found in a barn, stabbed and raped with farm tools. A cow in the next stall with its throat slit, its blood splashed on her, hers on it." Blomkvist reads the fifth and final verse from Leviticus: "Leviticus 20:16 – "If a woman lies with any beast, you shall kill the woman and the beast, their blood is upon them." Salander then describes the death of Lea Persson, 1962, "Found by her sister in their pet shop – raped, beaten. The killer uncaged the animals, smashed the aquariums. There was a parakeet inside her; Leviticus 26:21/22." Next is "Eva Gustavsson, 1960. A runaway. Raped, strangled, a burnt pigeon tied around her neck. Lena Andersson, 1967, a student. Raped, stabbed, decapitated –" Finally Mikael stops her. "I'm not done," Lisbeth protests. But he says, "It's all right, we're looking for a serial murderer ... But what does it have to do with a 16-year-old girl on an island?" Salander concludes: "She was looking for him, too."

The final piece of evidence: all of the names are biblical, and all of the victims are Jewish, suggesting a Nazi murderer, and pointing therefore to someone within the Vanger family itself, for "If there's one thing the Vangers have more than their share of, it's Nazis." Harriet herself is found, alive and well, and fills in the missing pieces of the story. The film comes to a suspenseful, and deadly, climax as Mikael and Lisbeth confront the killer.

The Devil and scripture

The behavior of the Nazi Vangers, like that of Cady, Powell, Wade, and others, is shocking because they use the "good book" to justify their own vile behavior. This association of the "devil" and the Bible, however, is not a new one that emerged in western culture only after the strictures of the Hays Production Code were eased in the late 1950s. In fact, it appears in Matthew's accounts of Jesus' temptation, in which Jesus and Satan engage in a Bible-quoting contest a good deal more antagonistic than the sparring match between Sister Helen Prejean and the prison guard in *Dead Man Walking*.

> The tempter came and said to him, "If you are the Son of God, command these stones to become loaves of bread." But he answered, "It is written, 'One does not live by bread alone, but by every word that comes from the mouth of God.'" Then the devil took him to the holy city and placed him on the pinnacle of the temple, saying to him, "If you are the Son of God, throw yourself down; for it is written, 'He will command his angels concerning you,' and 'On their hands they will bear you up, so that you will not dash your foot against a stone.'" Jesus said to him, "Again it is written, 'Do not put the Lord your God to the test.'" Again, the devil took him to a very high mountain and showed him all the kingdoms of the world and their splendor; and he said to him, "All these I will give you, if you will fall down and worship me." Jesus said to him, "Away with you, Satan! for it is written, 'Worship the Lord your God, and serve only him.'" Then the devil left him, and suddenly angels came and waited on him.
>
> (Matt. 4:3–11)

In the first and third temptations, it is Jesus who quotes scripture at Satan, but in the middle one, it is Satan who cites scripture as support for his challenge to Jesus, quoting from Psalms 91:11–12.[38]

Of course, there are numerous feature films in which ethical issues loom large and yet from which the Bible or biblical quotation is absent. But where present, the biblical resonances add a dimension to the ethical presentation by raising the question of divine authority. These films can either support and build upon the widespread assumption that knowledge of scripture implies divine approval and ethical superiority, by presenting a "good" character as the scripture-quoting individual, or they can subvert and question that assumption, as in films in which the "devil quotes scripture." In contrast to DeMille's 1923 *The Ten Commandments*, and the numerous Passion Play movies that were so popular in the early decades of the cinema, modern feature films reflect, if not the "real world" as such, at least the ethical complexity of the world as we know it, including the equivocal role of the Bible in ethical discourse.

Notes

1 Stanley Leathes, *The Foundations of Morality: Being Discourses on the Ten Commandments with Special Reference to their Origin and Authority* (London: Hodder and Stoughton, 1882), iii.

2 Ibid., viii.

3 Charles Musser, "Passions and the Passion Play: Theatre, Film and Religion in America, 1880–1900," *Film History* 5, no. 4 (1 December 1993): 450.

4 Gregory D. Black, *Hollywood Censored: Morality Codes, Catholics, and the Movies* (Cambridge; New York: Cambridge University Press, 1994), 56–57.

5 Gregory D. Black, "Hollywood Censored: The Production Code Administration and the Hollywood Film Industry, 1930–40," *Film History* 3, no. 3 (1 January 1989): 167.

6 Ibid., 168.

7 www.artsreformation.com/a001/hays-code.html (accessed 10 May 2013).

8 www.artsreformation.com/a001/hays-code.html (accessed 10 May 2013).

9 As noted in chapter 1, however, the biblical epics, which were produced at the height of the Code's influence, often justified the violation of biblically based ethical injunctions even as they assert the ethical superiority of Israelite law to pagan practices. The most blatant examples are found in the film *David and Bathsheba*. King David patently disregards the injunctions against adultery and murder; he is punished for these transgressions: his infant son, born out of his adulterous relationship with Bathsheba, dies; his prophet Nathan is furious; and God subjects the land to a drought. But the film goes to some lengths to excuse or at least create sympathy for these transgressions by suggesting that they are not motivated by malice or inherent sinfulness but by his passionate love for Bathsheba; a further factor is the obvious lack of love between Uriah and Bathsheba. In the end, love conquers all. The film therefore walks a fine line between moral offense and romantic entertainment.

10 For details and full text, see http://productioncode.dhwritings.com/Code_1966.html (accessed 10 May 2013).

11 Stephen Prince, *Savage Cinema: Sam Peckinpah and the Rise of Ultraviolent Movies* (Austin: University of Texas Press, 1998), 12–14. Andrew J. Rausch, *Turning Points in Film History* (New York: Citadel Press, 2004), 162–70.

12 On changes in movie ratings systems, see Matthew Bernstein, *Controlling Hollywood: Censorship and Regulation in the Studio Era* (New Brunswick, NJ: Rutgers University Press, 1999). Stephen Farber, *The Movie Rating Game* (Washington, DC: Public Affairs Press, 1972).

13 There is a voluminous bibliography on the Bible and ethics. See, for example, Richard Elliott Friedman and Shawna Dolansky, *The Bible Now* (New York: Oxford University Press, 2011); Richard B. Hays, *The Moral Vision of the New Testament: Community, Cross, New Creation: A Contemporary Introduction to New Testament Ethics* (San Francisco, CA: HarperSanFrancisco, 1996); Mark F. Rooker and E. Ray Clendenen, *The Ten Commandments: Ethics for the Twenty-First Century* (Nashville, TN: B & H Academic, 2010). On the use of the Bible to both support and condemn capital punishment, see Lloyd R. Bailey, *Capital Punishment: What the Bible Says* (Nashville, TN: Abingdon Press, 1987); Gardner C. Hanks, *Capital Punishment and the Bible* (Scottdale, PA: Herald Press, 2002); Millard Lind, *The Sound of Sheer Silence and The Killing State: The Death Penalty and the Bible* (Telford, PA: Cascadia Pub. House, 2004).

14 Gary A. Phillips and Danna Nolan Fewell, "Ethics, Bible, Reading As If," *Semeia* 77 (1997): 2.

15 W. Gunther Plaut and David E. Stein, *The Torah: A Modern Commentary* (New York: Union for Reform Judaism, 2005), 488. This basic role of the Ten Commandments is the basis of the ten-part television series *The Decalogue* (1989) by Polish film director Krzysztof Kieślowski that explores ethical issues in contemporary Poland.

16 The "golden rule" is attributed not only to Jesus but also to Hillel, a Pharisaic rabbi, who reportedly said, "That which is hateful to you, do not do to your fellow. That is the whole Torah; the rest is the explanation; go study." See Babylonian Talmud, Shabbat 31a, and Matthew 7:12; Luke 6:31.

17 The film was remade in 2011.

18 This verse seems to speak specifically about a legal situation of false testimony but which is often generalized to refer to speaking falsely in any situation.

19 See *Big Fat Liar* (2002), *40 Days and 40 Nights* (2002), *Meet the Robinsons* (2007), television series (*M★A★S★H* – The tooth shall set you free), and even video games (e.g., *Red Dead Redemption*, where one of the missions is called "The Truth Shall Set you Free").

20 For discussion of this film, see Jeffrey L. Staley, "Reading 'This Woman' Back into John 7:1–8:59: Liar Liar and the 'Pericope Adulterae' in Intertextual Tango," in *Those Outside: Noncanonical Readings of Canonical Gospels*, ed. George Aichele and Richard G. Walsh (New York: T & T Clark International, 2005), 85–107.

21 On life after death in world religions, see Hiroshi Obayashi, *Death and Afterlife: Perspectives of World Religions* (New York: Greenwood Press, 1992); Alan F. Segal, *Life after Death: A History of the Afterlife in the Religions of the West* (New York: Doubleday, 2004); Mircea Eliade, *Death, Afterlife, and Eschatology: A Thematic Source Book of the History of Religions* (New York: Harper & Row, 1974).

22 On stuttering in general, and Moses' stuttering in particular, see Marc Shell, *Stutter* (Cambridge, MA: Harvard University Press, 2005), 102–36.

23 See Numbers 11–12.

24 See Ace Collins, *Stories Behind the Hymns that Inspire America: Songs that Unite our Nation* (Grand Rapids, MI: Zondervan, 2003), 83–88.

25 See John R. May, "The Godfather Films: Birth of a Don, Death of a Family," in *Image and Likeness: Religious Visions in American Film Classics*, ed. John R. May (New York: Paulist Press, 1991), 65–75.

26 See, for example, "Police Discover Mafia's 'Ten Commandments' After Arresting Godfather," *Mail Online*, www.dailymail.co.uk/news/article-492449/Police-discover-Mafias-Ten-Commandments-arresting-Godfather.html (accessed 27 February 2013).

27 Elmore Leonard, *Three-Ten to Yuma: And Other Stories* (New York: Harper, 2006).
28 "Those who guard their mouths preserve their lives; those who open wide their lips come to ruin" (Proverbs 13:3).
29 It is not clear whether Ben had carried this Bible with him, or whether he found it in the hotel room. The Gideons organization did not begin placing Bibles in hotel rooms until 1908. See www.gideons.org/AboutUs/OurHistory.aspx (accessed 19 March 2013).
30 Another remake is due to be released in October 2013. www.imdb.com/title/tt1939659 (accessed 27 February 2013).
31 These analyses and descriptions are taken from Mary Ann Beavis, "'Angels Carrying Savage Weapons': Uses of the Bible in Contemporary Horror Films," *Journal of Religion and Film* 7 no. 2 (2003). www.unomaha.edu/jrf/Vol7No2/angels.htm (accessed 10 May 2013). See also Beavis, "Pseudapocrypha."
32 For detailed analysis, see Tom Aitken, "Night of the Hunter (1955)," in *Bible and Cinema: Fifty Key Films*, ed. Adele Reinhartz (New York: Routledge, 2012), 192–96.
33 See Reinhartz, "Magnolia and the Plague of Frogs (Exodus)."
34 The use of the Bible is absent from the 1962 original film.
35 In an ironic intertextual move, Cady's lawyer is played by Gregory Peck, the actor who played Sam Bowden in the 1962 film.
36 There is also a 2009 Swedish production of this film; my comments refer to the 2011 American production.
37 Biblical quotations in this section are transcribed from the 2011 film.
38 The idea of a villain who quotes scripture is attested in English literature from the time of Shakespeare onwards. Two of the most prominent examples are to be found in *The Merchant of Venice*, in which Antonio declares of Shylock that "The devil can cite Scripture for his purpose. An evil soul producing holy witness Is like a villain with a smiling cheek" (Act I, scene 3, line 93); and Charles Dickens' 1843 novel *Martin Chuzzlewit* in which the narrator declares: Is any one surprised at Mr. Jonas making such a reference to such a book for such a purpose? Does any one doubt the old saw that the Devil (being a layman) quotes Scripture for his own ends? Charles Dickens, *The Life and Adventures of Martin Chuzzlewit: In Two Volumes*, vol. 1 (London: Chapman and Hall, 1866), 266.

9 "In those days"

Destruction and redemption

In May of 2011, Christian radio broadcaster Harold Camping prophesied "without any shadow of doubt" that a massive earthquake would hit the Earth on 21 May. True believers would be swept up to heaven and the rest of humanity destroyed.[1] On 22 May, headlines read: "Apocalypse not right now: 'Rapture' end of world fails to materialize."[2] No doubt some took the prophecy seriously, though it provided amusement for a few, among them, New York mayor Michael Bloomberg. As one newspaper reported,

> Bloomberg – who is Jewish and, according to Camping's prophecy, therefore unlikely to be beamed up to sit alongside Jesus in heaven – said on his weekly radio show yesterday that he would partially suspend parking restrictions in New York if the world ended today.

Predictions of world-wide disasters and visions of a miserable and/or illustrious future on or off planet Earth have been recorded for millennia, and are associated with a worldview and genre of literature known as apocalypticism.[3] Apocalypticism is a prominent paradigm in religious systems that have their origins in the Middle East, from the ancient world to the present. The term "apocalypse" derives from the Greek *apokalypsis* (Ἀποκάλυψις), meaning "revelation." The revelations concern cosmic events, ideas, or prophecies that could not have been known except by divine revelation. Works belonging to this genre usually describe the visions, dreams, or other types of encounters between an individual and God or God's agents.

In the Jewish and Christian traditions, the first major work in the genre is the biblical book of Daniel, dated to the late second century BCE. The Gospels have apocalyptic sections, such as Mark 13 and parallels. The most famous and most influential New Testament representative being the Book of Revelation, also known as the Apocalypse of John.[4] The genre is also very well attested in ancient bodies of literature outside the canon, such as 4 Ezra, 2 Baruch, and the books of Enoch.[5]

The apocalyptic works associated with Judaism and Christianity often reflect a dualistic worldview that posits an absolute opposition between the forces of good and evil. Embedded in this worldview is a narrative that describes the corruption and eventual destruction of the present world order on all planes – physical, social, political, architectural. The destruction comes about through a cosmic battle between Good – sometimes represented by or associated with God – and Evil – sometimes represented by or associated with Satan or the Devil. Survivors of the destruction experience the return to an era of peace, prosperity, and goodness, often through the intervention of a human savior figure. Apocalyptic narratives are therefore both linear – in that they move from a starting point to an end point – and cyclical – in that they result in a return to primordial beginnings. Cosmic, fantastic, and ahistorical as they often are, apocalyptic stories nevertheless directly reflect the values, events, fears, and aspirations of their own time and place.

Film genre

Apocalyptic literature is often thought to be a cultural response to human helplessness in the face of disaster and the interpretation of that disaster in light of the relationship between humanity and God or the cosmos. The turn to the apocalyptic is not limited to the ancient Near East, but can be documented, at least in Europe and European-influenced societies, down to the present.[6] In recent decades, the Vietnam war, the social transformations, including the civil rights and feminist movements of the 1960s to the present, the turn of the millennium, the terrorist attacks of 11 September 2001, as well as profound concerns about the environment, global warming, and AIDS and other epidemics, have all been reflected in apocalyptic literature, film, art, and television.[7] Kirsten Moana Thompson argues that these cultural products express a well-established American apocalyptic tradition, which blends providential and messianic elements in Puritan Calvinism. These elements can be traced from science fiction films of the Cold War era, through science fiction and demonic films in the 1970s, which expressed social conservatism under Reagan in the 1980s, and

> reached a hysterical peak in the nineties in a cycle of horror, disaster, and science-fiction films explicitly focused on the approaching millennium. After 9/11, this dread took new forms with anxieties about the rise of Islamic fundamentalism and terrorism from within.[8]

The apocalyptic label seems rather straightforward; if most reviewers or audiences do not know much about the meaning of the term, its history and its characteristics, they nevertheless easily place movies portraying end of the world scenarios into this category. Charles P. Mitchell's useful anthology, *A Guide to Apocalyptic Cinema*, for example, defines an apocalyptic movie simply as "a motion picture that depicts a credible threat to the continuing existence of humankind as a species or the existence of Earth as a planet capable of supporting human life," Mitchell distinguishes apocalyptic movies from related genres such as post-apocalyptic movies, which concentrate "on survivors of a catastrophic event struggling to re-establish a livable society" but do not portray the event that led to humanity's extinction or near-extinction within the film itself.[9] He groups the 50 films he reviews according to the type of "life extinction" events they feature: religious or supernatural; celestial collision; solar or orbital disruption; nuclear war and radioactive fallout; germ warfare or pestilence; alien device or invasion; scientific miscalculation; and miscellaneous, such as vampirism, geological anomaly, or "nature in revolt."[10]

John Martens takes a more expansive approach; in his view, apocalyptic films portray a cosmic battle between the forces of Good (God) and Evil (Satan), in which Good eventually triumphs. In some films this battle has been foretold by sacred scriptures or other prophetic texts, but only certain people are aware of the coming destruction and therefore have the responsibility for halting it. The stories often involve both messianic and anti-messianic figures.[11] Martens distinguishes among five main categories of apocalyptic film: traditional apocalyptic, which relies explicitly on actual Jewish and Christian apocalyptic texts and uses religious, usually Christian, imagery; alien apocalyptics, in which aliens (usually) attempt to destroy or enslave humanity and whose intensions for humanity and the earth are utterly evil; post-apocalyptic dystopias in which some humans survive the apocalypse but must attempt to rebuild human society in an atmosphere of futility and hopelessness; technological apocalypses, in which natural or technological disasters, such as nuclear war, constitute the threat to human life; and, finally, futuristic apocalypses, in which human life is hopeless and opportunities diminished.[12]

Conrad Ostwalt, however, takes serious issue with the way in which this cinematic genre has been analyzed. In his view, the decisive element is the presence of divine power or oversight. He argues that in the apocalyptic paradigm, "it is divine intervention into the apocalyptic drama that allows the end of history to be meaningful. A vision of the end of the world without a sovereign reality beyond the world results in nihilism, and this is the outcome the apocalyptic drama wishes to avoid."[13] In his view, those end-of-the-world films that do not presume the presence of a divine power should not be considered apocalyptic in the full sense of the term. For this reason, Ostwalt distinguishes between (a) traditional apocalyptic films, such as *The Seventh Sign* (1988), and *The Rapture* (1991), which are based on the traditional Jewish–Christian apocalyptic literary genre; and (b) secular apocalyptic films, such as *Deep Impact* (1998) and *Armageddon* (1998) which incorporate disaster and cosmic themes but attribute the resolution to human effort rather than divine intervention.[14] Secular apocalyptic films often make use of science fiction tropes, and frequently avoid complete destruction.[15]

Ostwalt criticizes the tendency to classify apocalyptic films and to see apocalyptic themes everywhere.

Just because a film has a sacrificial character this does not necessarily make that character a Christ-figure, and just because a film has an end-of-the-world scenario this does not make that film an apocalyptic film. Such reductionism does not fully appreciate the intricacies of the apocalyptic tradition and is not helpful for theology, religious studies, or cultural criticism. It is at this point that religious studies and theology can serve to inform the popular appropriation of the apocalyptic label.[16]

The example Ostwalt cites is *Armageddon*. The title of this film is taken from Revelation 16:14–16, and refers to the site of the final battle between good and evil that ushers in the apocalyptic age. But because the biblical reference is not developed in the film, and there is no theological reflection and no ultimate victory of goodness, the film should not be considered apocalyptic in the true sense of the term.

My own definition of apocalyptic film is more expansive, and certainly less theological, perhaps because my interest is in "Bible and film" rather than "religion and film" or "theology and film." While it is true that *Armageddon* and biblical titles often include no explicit theological reflection, the very fact that they draw upon biblical language, names or imagery, however briefly, makes them witnesses to the varied use and role of the Bible in film and in contemporary society more generally. As Thompson has noted, the films often described as apocalyptic frequently have affinities with horror, science fiction, film noir, vampire movies, and other genres.[17] I would add that there is a permeability in the boundaries between one genre and another, as well as considerable variety in the ways in which the genre conventions are employed and deployed. In this chapter, I will focus on a few examples of apocalyptic and post-apocalyptic films, not for the sake of defining the genre but simply to discern their use of the Bible.[18]

Conventions

Like the epics of the 1940s and 1950s, recent large-scale apocalyptic and post-apocalyptic movies provide filmmakers with the potential for grandeur and a return to the grand scale, sound, and spectacle of the epic era. The wonders of technology allow filmmakers to create spectacular explosions, collisions, and other cosmic events in space and on earth, wild and wonderful vistas through which spaceships can sail, scenes of epic desolation and destruction, and casts of thousands, as needed.

Even those movies that Ostwalt would term secular apocalypses abound in biblical language and imagery. The most important biblical connections, however, are the cosmic settings of these films, and the overall narrative paradigm that moves from impending doom, to catastrophe and destruction, and concludes, or, at least, hints at, the promise of restoration. This paradigm is evident not only in ancient apocalyptic texts such as Daniel and Revelation, but in the books of the prophets as well. Isaiah 10:16–19 describes the destruction:

16   Therefore the Sovereign, the LORD of hosts, will send wasting sickness among his stout warriors, and under his glory a burning will be kindled, like the burning of fire.
17   The light of Israel will become a fire, and his Holy One a flame; and it will burn and devour his thorns and briers in one day.
18   The glory of his forest and his fruitful land the LORD will destroy, both soul and body, and it will be as when an invalid wastes away.
19   The remnant of the trees of his forest will be so few that a child can write them down.

This dire prophecy is followed by the promise of restoration, not for the entire nation, but for a remnant. In this restored time, Israel will have repented from her idolatry in order to "lean," once again, on the God of Israel alone.

20   On that day the remnant of Israel and the survivors of the house of Jacob will no more lean on the one who struck them, but will lean on the LORD, the Holy One of Israel, in truth.
21   A remnant will return, the remnant of Jacob, to the mighty God.
22   For though your people Israel were like the sand of the sea, only a remnant of them will return. Destruction is decreed, overflowing with righteousness.
23   For the Lord GOD of hosts will make a full end, as decreed, in all the earth.
(Isa. 10:16–23)

Apocalyptic films share this destruction–restoration paradigm, even though not all movies reproduce the full narrative. Some are concerned primarily with an impending apocalypse, perhaps as a consequence of an environmental disaster brought on by human exploitation of the world's natural resources. Others focus on the disaster as such, as well as on efforts to avert it, whether successful or not. And there are those that concentrate primarily on the aftermath, and efforts to rebuild. This chapter will look at examples of all three categories, though, as noted earlier, without an attempt to draw firm boundaries among them.

Pre-Apocalyptic movies

Avatar *(2009)*

Plot summary

James Cameron's American epic science fiction film portrays a future time – the twenty-second century – when the earth is running low on natural resources after centuries of irresponsible exploitation. A ruthless corporation,

RDA, is engaged in efforts to exploit the resources of a far-off moon not only to avert the apocalypse, but to become rich. Pandora, a moon in the Alpha Centauri star system, has a supply of a precious mineral called unobtainium.[19] RDA's efforts to mine this mineral are thwarted by Pandora's poisonous atmosphere, and by its human-like and highly intelligent population. The Na'vi are ten-foot high blue-colored figures who live at one with nature and worship the mother goddess Eywa, whose headquarters are a large and ancient sacred tree. Unobtainium is unobtainable except by conquering the Na'vi, destroying the tree, and disabling Eywa.

Between the Na'vi and RDA stands a group of scientists, employed by RDA but opposed to the corporation's goals and methods. The scientists have discovered a way to match human beings to their genetically compatible avatars. This matching allows their bodies to remain safe in a special pod in the lab, while their consciousness controls a Na'vi body that can move freely in Pandora's atmosphere. The catch is that the avatars must return periodically to their pods to replenish their oxygen, otherwise they will die.

The protagonist, Jake Sully, is a former marine who became a paraplegic during active combat duty. His presence on the scientific team is due not to any prior scientific training or particular expertise but to the death of his twin brother, a scientist. Because of their identical DNA, Jake can take over the avatar that had been matched to his brother. Although the rest of the team, especially the principal scientist, Dr. Grace Augustine, are initially wary, he earns their trust when he becomes deeply involved with the Na'vi leadership; the leader's daughter, Neytiri, falls in love with him, and the Na'vi welcome him as one of their own.

Jake's success on Pandora, however, is also noticed by the RDA's head of security, who promises to restore Jake's mobility in exchange for intelligence that will enable RDA to vanquish the Na'vi and mine the unobtainium. Jake initially agrees but as he becomes more deeply involved with the Na'vi and with Neytiri, he begins to see how devastating the RDA plan will be to all that he has come to love. A clash ensues; the corporation attacks, and after much destruction and numerous Na'vi deaths, Jake and the Na'vi warriors drive the RDA away. In the course of this action, however, Jake runs out of oxygen, and he hovers close to death, until Neytiri, who knows of his human identity, saves him. All humans, except for a chosen few, are sent back to earth. Jake is transferred into his avatar permanently; he gains his true love and his mobility, and the threat to the Na'vi is gone forever.

Biblical elements

The biblical elements in this film are legion. The chief scientist is named Grace Augustine and Jake's pod is called Beulah, an allusion to the prophecy in Isaiah 62:4 that the land shall no longer be Desolate but shall be called "Beulah … for the LORD delighteth in thee, and thy land shall be married" (KJV). This name foreshadows the transformation that Jake will experience

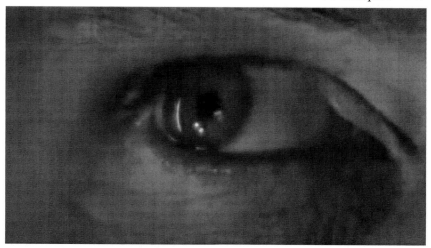

Figure 9.1 Jake's human eye, *Avatar*.

through association with the Na'vi. Pandora is a type of Eden, where people live in harmony with each other and with the land. The film contrasts Pandora with earth – Pandora as a wonderful natural environment filled with beauty and natural resources, and the earth as a place of desolation that has been mined and exploited nearly unto death.

The real contrast, however, is between the human beings who have exploited the earth's resources and set themselves up as the masters of the natural world, and the Na'vi who live in meaningful communication with the natural world. This environmental motif recalls Genesis 1:26–28, in which God gives humankind "dominion" (according to the King James Version) or stewardship (in more contemporary interpretations) over the natural world. It also recalls the role of trees, both the permitted ones, and the forbidden tree of the Knowledge of Good and Evil, the eating from which, according to Christian thought, was the original sin. Unlike Adam and Eve, the Na'vi are not cautioned to stay away from the tree. Rather, they draw sustenance and knowledge from it, as it is the home of their goddess Eywa and the source of their knowledge of all life, including good and evil.[20]

The biblical frame of reference is signaled by numerous visual and thematic references, such as the connection between sight and insight.

When the Na'vi greet each other, they say, "I see you," which means: I see you for who you really are. On the other hand, the machines that are used to attack the Na'vi have mechanical eyes; the machines lose their power to destroy when Jake disables these eyes at the climax of the film. This theme echoes numerous New Testament passages that use physical sight as a metaphor for spiritual insight, such as John 9:39, in which Jesus says: "I came into this world for judgment so that those who do not see may see, and those who do see may become blind."

Perhaps the most striking theme is rebirth. For the Na'vi, "every person is born twice. The second time is when you earn your place among the people, forever." The theme of rebirth echoes John 3:3: "Most assuredly, I say to you, unless one is born again, he cannot see the kingdom of God" (New King James Version). But the Na'vi have their own, risky and not always successful, method of bringing people back to life. When Grace is badly injured in the conflict against RDA, the Na'vi implore Eywa, the Great Mother, on her behalf but it is too late. Nevertheless, Grace dies at peace, for, as she tells Jake, "I'm with her, Jake, she's real." Soon Jake too is in danger, for the battle has delayed his return to a controlled environment. Neytiri finds him and manages to hook him up to the oxygen he needs, holding him in a *pietà* pose as he gradually returns to his human body. But Jake has had enough of life as a disabled man, and he has seen enough to know that he must live as a Na'vi from now on. To do so, he must die in this life and be brought back to life on Pandora. Neytiri presides over this risky process, but at last, in extreme close up, we see his eyes open.

This ending recalls Paul's description of the spiritual body that believers acquire "at the last trumpet" (1 Cor. 15:52), when "this perishable body puts on imperishability, and this mortal body puts on immortality" and "death is swallowed up in victory" (1 Cor. 15:54). Jake has left behind his disabled earthly body to take on a perfect, strong, and vital Na'vi body.

This film, however, cannot be reduced to a Christian parable of salvation; the name of the planet, Pandora, for example, comes from Greek mythology, and is best known from the phrase "Pandora's box" which, once opened, allows all manner of chaos and evil into the world. In Greek the name means "all giving," but Hesiod interpreted it as "all-gifted" and constructed a narrative around it in his *Theogony* and *Work and Days*; the end message of the latter, however, is a message of hope, which is certainly germane to the film.[21]

Apocalyptic movies

The movie *Avatar* implies a coming apocalypse without showing it. We turn now to two 1998 films that focus on imminent disasters: *Deep Impact* and *Armageddon*. The prominence of disaster films in the 1990s has been linked to anxiety about the turn of the millennium, an anxiety also expressed in the "real life" fears that all computers would cease to function when their internal clocks rolled over to 1/1/00.[22] The Y2K catastrophe did not materialize, but these films became classics of the apocalyptic genre.[23]

Deep Impact *(1998)*

Plot summary

Deep Impact has been called a celestial collision film (Mitchell), technological disaster movie (Martens), and a secular apocalypse (Ostwalt).[24] It is all these things, but it is also an example of the cinematic use of the Bible to express certain "big" ideas and themes. On a starry spring night in 1998, a group of teens in Richmond, Virginia, are outdoors gazing at the night sky through telescopes. One of the young people, Leo Biederman, spots an object that, he is convinced, is neither star nor planet. He sends his findings to an astronomer, Marcus Wolf, who determines that the unknown object is a comet. Unless drastic measures are taken, the comet will soon collide with the earth and destroy everyone and everything on it. As he races to alert the authorities, Wolf's car collides with a truck, and he is killed. The story resumes a year later, when an MSNBC reporter, Jenny Lerner, comes across some references to "Ellie" in connection with the resignation of the United States Secretary of the Treasury. Initially she assumes that Ellie is the name of a woman, but she soon learns that "E.L.E." stands for an "Extinction-Level Event." Jenny's discovery forces the hand of the United States President, Tom Beck, who announces the impending disaster to the world. He reassures the world that a plan is in place. Together with Russia, the United States has been building a spacecraft called *The Messiah*, which will take a special team, led by Captain Spurgeon Tanner, to destroy the comet before it hits the earth.

The plan is put into place. Tanner's team reaches the comet and buries nuclear bombs deep within it. But the resulting explosion merely splits the comet into two smaller rocks, each one large enough to destroy the world.

Time for Plan B. The United States has built a vast system of underground shelters, called Noah's Ark, which has room for one million people. Here is the classic, and dreadful dilemma: whom to choose for survival, and on what grounds? Two hundred thousand individuals – among them scientists, engineers, and artists – are pre-selected as their skills and talents will be needed in the post-apocalyptic reconstruction. The remaining 800,000 are to be chosen by lottery.

One comet fragment lands in the Atlantic Ocean near Bermuda and results in a giant tsunami affecting the Atlantic coasts of North and South America, Europe, and Africa. New York and many other cities are destroyed and thousands die. To avoid the impact of the other comet, the crew on the severely damaged spaceship embarks on a suicide mission. *The Messiah* will enter the comet, where they will detonate the remaining nuclear missiles, and themselves. The comet breaks into pieces which burn up in the earth's atmosphere. Humanity (the remnant!) is spared.

Biblical quotations

Biblical paradigms of destruction and restoration are explicitly evoked in the names given to the vehicles of salvation: the spaceship (*The Messiah*) and the underground bunker system (*Noah's Ark*). *The Messiah*'s captain, Spurgeon Tanner, is nicknamed the Fish, an ancient symbol of Christ.[25] Like its biblical prototype, Noah's Ark contains not only enough people to restore the human race, but also animals, seeds, and seedlings.[26]

The visual vocabulary of the film reinforces the flood and Christ paradigms. Extravagant flood imagery accompanies the first tsunami, recalling the scope and scale of the primordial flood. The promise of restoration is expressed by the use of light; although the spectacular destruction of the comet means the death of *The Messiah* – and its crew who sacrificed themselves so that others may live – it also signals the salvation of the fortunate remnant. The salvific aspect of the paradigm is underscored by the camera, which returns us at this climactic point to the young Leo, who watches the comet disintegrate. In the final frames of the movie, the waters recede and the president announces the beginning of the restoration (cf. Ezek. 32:7, 22; Rev. 8:12; 18:23; 21:23–24). These images of flood and then light trace the fundamental biblical narrative paradigm that underlies the film's plot as a whole.

Yet there is an element missing from the film's deployment of the flood and messianic paradigms. In contrast to the biblical flood, the disaster caused by the Wolf-Biederman comet is not morally freighted. It reflects no judgment on humankind, nor divine regret at having created such an evil species (Genesis 6:5–6). Exclusion from the ark is a matter of talent and circumstance, not ethics, lifestyle, or religious faith. For Ostwalt, the presence of religious imagery and symbolism and the absence of a divine dimension may be "the most telling comment on our secular society's appropriation of religion – while our culture is substantively secular, we legitimize it with a facade of religion."[27]

But the film's juxtaposition of religious and secular elements can also be seen, more productively, as an expression of a tension between faith and secularism, a theme that has persisted in Hollywood Bible movies from the golden age of the epics to the present day. This tension comes to the fore in the White House press conference after the survival plan has been announced. Jenny challenges the president: "In fact, isn't it true, sir, that not everyone in your administration is convinced that the '*Messiah*' will save us?" Of course in the immediate context she is referring to the spacecraft *Messiah*, but the statement can just as easily be heard as a broad statement about the increasingly diverse American population. In this film, however, as in the Bible and sword-and-sandal movies, Christian faith trumps atheism. In the president's address to the world, the president acknowledges this diversity. Nevertheless, he says, "I still want to offer a prayer for our survival," and then recites the priestly blessing: "The LORD bless you and keep you; the LORD make his face to shine upon you, and be gracious to you; the LORD lift up his countenance upon you, and give you peace" (Num. 6:24–26). The recitation identifies the president (played by Morgan Freeman, a familiar Hollywood savior figure[28]) as the High Priest of the modern world, a quasi-religious leader presiding over universal rituals that he hopes will lead to the salvation of all humanity. Although Russia, now no longer the Red Menace, is a full participant in this American-led plan, the president's speech still conveys the anti-atheist, even anti-communist stance so deeply entrenched in Hollywood Bible movies.

Another thematic undercurrent concerns ageism. Before embarking on the mission, Spurgeon's much-younger teammates complain about being led by such an old man and even mock him to his face. As the mission progresses, however, and difficulties arise, they turn to him as to a father. By the end, they fully appreciate his extraordinary leadership and altruism, and find themselves ready and willing to die with him (cf. John 11:16). In this way, their relationship to Spurgeon resembles, and indeed improves upon, that of Jesus' disciples to their master. Whereas Jesus' disciples fall short – they fall asleep during his darkest hour – Spurgeon's teammates rise to the challenge.

A second point at which age arises is in the profile of those who are eligible to enter Noah's Ark. With the exception of those who have special talents or high political roles, those over 50 are not eligible for the lottery. As a result, Jenny's mother elegantly but resolutely takes her own life, and Jenny faces the flood head on in the company of her father. Having relinquished her own place on the ark, she too is a savior figure, albeit on a smaller and more immediate plane than the crew of *The Messiah*. Although Tanner's crew overcomes their ageism, the moral dimensions of the decision to exclude the over-50 population from the Ark is not questioned; indeed, youth is glorified in the resolution of the plot which points to the creation and nurturing of new life, represented by Leo, his teenage wife, and her infant brother who are the harbingers of a new generation.

Finally, the film promotes an eschatological vision of international cooperation between former enemies in the aftermath of the Cold War and the belief that the ties that bind all people together must override national considerations. Nevertheless, as in the Cold War epics, it is the United States that takes the lead in ridding the world of a global menace. While America is not able to avert this natural disaster entirely, it provides the best leadership possible to ensure humanity's survival and to oversee the process of restoration and reconstruction. The goal is to return to how things were before – the continuation of "our" way of life – while granting that this will mean different things in the different nations as they rebuild. The alliance between the United States and Russia may be seen as a post–Cold War counterpoint to the biblical epics such as *The Ten Commandments* (1956) in which the Soviet Union is the enemy of freedom and democracy. Appearing before 9/11 and the wars in Afghanistan and Iraq, the film gives expression to a fragile optimism that existed only briefly, between the end of the Cold War and the threat of worldwide terrorism.

Armageddon *(1998)*

Plot summary

Armageddon appeared the same year as *Deep Impact*, with which it shares its narrative structure and many specific elements. In contrast to *Deep Impact*, however, the film situates its story explicitly in the history of the planet and its inhabitants. The film's introduction features a voice-over narration by Charlton Heston and shows the destruction of the dinosaurs caused by the impact of a large asteroid on the earth 65 million years ago. Fast forward to the more recent past, when the Space Shuttle Atlantis has been destroyed by a meteor shower, which has also bombarded New York City, the East Coast of the United States, and Finland. A bigger disaster is yet to come, however: a giant asteroid that will collide with earth in 18 days. NASA hires Harry Stamper, the world's best deep-sea oil driller, to lead a team that, as in *Deep Impact*, will implant a nuclear device into the asteroid. Russia, France, and Japan are also partners in this mission. Harry comes to NASA with his daughter Grace, who, against Harry's wishes, is in a relationship with one of the young drillers on his oil rig, A. J. Frost. Harry gathers an eccentric but highly skilled crew of oil drillers, who will carry out the mission under his leadership.

The team is divided between the shuttles, whose names − *Freedom* and *Independence* − express not only the goals of the mission but also deeply-rooted American values. In orbit, the shuttles dock with a Russian space station manned by Lev Andropov to refuel with liquid oxygen. During the transfer, however, a fire breaks out. Lev and A. J. escape but their shuttle, the *Independence*, crashes into the asteroid as the mission is resumed and the team members are presumed dead. The *Freedom*, meanwhile, successfully lands on the asteroid, but in the wrong location, requiring the team to drill through iron instead of soft matter. As time runs out, the NASA mission leader, Truman, disobeys the order to detonate the nuclear weapon remotely, which would have exploded the asteroid but also killed the shuttle team. The world panics but the crew of the *Freedom* are cheered by a small miracle: A. J., Lev, and another team member, "Bear," have survived after all, and they arrive just in time to help. NASA agrees to delay remote detonation to allow the team to continue its work. But as the asteroid moves closer to the earth, it heats up and creates a rock storm that damages the remote trigger of the nuclear weapon. Harry volunteers to stay behind to trigger the bomb manually. He and A. J. reconcile, and Harry gives his blessing to A. J.'s marriage to Grace. Harry says an emotional goodbye to Grace, and then, at the last possible moment, detonates the bomb, saves the world, and dies in glory.

Bible quotations

Like *Deep Impact*, *Armageddon* signals its biblical paradigms with numerous explicit references. Harry's daughter, Grace, shows grace to her father by taking steps to repair their troubled relationship, and he, in turn, bestows grace on her in his last words. A. J., Lev, and Bear experience a resurrection, at least, so it must have seemed to Harry and their teammates, when they reappeared after the destruction of their shuttle. Harry is a Christ-figure. A highly skilled craftsman, if not a carpenter, he gathers a quirky crew of equally skilled "disciples" who follow him to the bitter end. The NASA specialist who guides the mission is named Truman; he shows himself to be a true man – a "mentsch" – in his courageous decision to disobey his superiors by refusing to detonate the nuclear bomb. In doing so he grants the team more time to do their work and he minimizes the loss of human life.

Most obviously, as Truman himself notes, the name Armageddon itself stems from the Hebrew name *har megiddo*, the Mountain of Megiddo. Megiddo is mentioned 12 times in the Hebrew Bible[29] but it acquires eschatological significance in the book of Revelation 16:14–16, which refers to the demonic spirits who assembled for battle "on the great day of God the Almighty" at "the place that in Hebrew is called Harmagedon." Based on Revelation, Armageddon has been popularized in millennialist thinking as the location where the final war between the forces of good and evil will take place, and, more generally, as a metaphor for the final destruction, however and wherever it might occur.[30] Only in this last sense is it an appropriate title for a space disaster film such as this one, for, as in *Deep Impact*, there is no moral or religious dimension to the impending destruction, no evil force or army of demons but rather an impersonal cosmic body that through sheer bad luck will intersect with the earth unless it can be stopped.

Like *Deep Impact*, *Armageddon* expresses a post–Cold War political and ideological agenda in which America is joined by Russia, as well as by France and Japan, in a cooperative technological endeavour to save the world. America's leadership is expressed in the words embroidered on the patch that Harry asks A. J. to give to Truman once it is all over: "Freedom for all mankind."

But whereas *Deep Impact* privileges Christian faith, *Armageddon* envisages a future in which all religions can co-exist equally, along with no religion at all. This image is expressed most forcefully in the final frames of the film, in which the camera pans over celebrations around the world, taking place in churches, mosques, and temples, as well as in towns and cities all around the world. These two films, and others like them, explicitly express the anxieties, hopes, and values of their era. In their use of the Bible, and their epic scope, imagery, and music, they are reminiscent of the Bible movies of the golden age of the epic. Although their story lines are fictional, their view of America as a champion of world freedom is the same, even if the enemy and the mode of battle – cooperative deployment of science and technology – have changed.

Post-apocalyptic movies

In contrast to *Deep Impact* and *Armageddon*, post-apocalyptic movies tend to be critical of America and ideological trends – imperialism, consumerism – often associated with it. These films forego the spectacular special effects of apocalyptic films but at the same time they engage in a critique of human behavior, most often greed and environmental exploitation. Alongside this critique, however, they often convey some degree of optimism regarding the potential of the world, and humankind, to repair itself and one another. This section will discuss just a few of the many entries in this category that use biblical quotations or allusions to develop their characters, plot, and themes.

Blade Runner *(1982)*

Plot summary

Blade Runner is loosely based on Philip K. Dick's 1968 novel *Do Androids Dream of Electric Sheep?*[31] The film is set in a dark, rainy, and degraded Los Angeles in 2019. Most of the human beings have left the city for "off world" locations where their every need is taken care of by genetically engineered humanoid robots called replicants. To most observers, replicants are virtually indistinguishable from human beings, except that they have a short life span of four years, and they are banned from the earth.

The protagonist is a retired police officer, Rick Deckard, who has a stellar reputation as a "Blade Runner" – an officer who hunts and "retires" (kills) renegade replicants. The authorities have ordered Deckard to come out of retirement for one final mission: to "retire" four Nexus 6 replicants who have escaped to earth. But how does he identify the replicants, who look and behave like human beings? As he prepares for his mission, Deckard visits the headquarters of the Tyrell Corporation, which manufacture the replicants. There he meets Tyrell's assistant Rachael; he determines that she is an experimental model, Nexus 7. Rachael is initially unaware of her own identity as a replicant; she believes herself to be human because she has memories. In reality, however, these memories are not hers but have been implanted in her consciousness. Deckard falls in love with Rachael. He "retires" three of the four escaped Nexus 6 replicants, named Zhora, Leon, and Pris. Roy Batty, the leader of the renegades, is more difficult to track down. The climax of the film is a dramatic confrontation between Roy and Deckard; Roy has vanquished Deckard. Deckard is seconds away from falling to his death when Roy saves him, and quietly dies. Deckard returns to his own apartment to find Rachael; in the director's cut, they leave the apartment block and head together into an unknown future.

Biblical allusions

Blade Runner borrows heavily from science fiction, in its exploration of technology, spaceships, and robotic intelligence, as well as from film noir, in its overall dismal and dark mood, its air of dread and foreboding, and the run-down urban setting. The film has virtually no verbal biblical quotation. One possible exception is the name of the protagonist's love interest. Jack Boozer, Jr., has drawn a connection between Rachael the replicant and the biblical Rachel, one of the wives of the patriarch Jacob, first introduced in Genesis 29: "Generous Rachael, like her Old Testament namesake, stands for an alternative and more humanized direction of technological aspiration, her 'escape' with Deckard represents only a metaphorical possibility of revised positioning in the world created by Man."[32] Yet the biblical connection is tenuous and indirect at best.

The visual vocabulary of the film, however, alludes directly to the para-digms of creation and destruction in the book of Genesis.[33] The persistent rain, while paying homage to the film noir genre, also recalls the biblical story of the flood. This association is reinforced in the final scene by the dove that Roy brings to his final confrontation with Deckard, and then releases. The dove symbolizes the spirit of life that ebbs from Roy Batty as he expires at the end of the film, but it also raises the hope of some sort of restoration beyond the final credits. Also evoked is the Tower of Babel, in the architecture of the Tyrell Corporation. The Tyrell offices, located at the pinnacle of the futuristic ziggurat, can be reached only by spaceship. Only such a tower could properly match the hubris of Tyrell's entire enterprise: to create a species of slaves that has human traits but a limited life span. Once perfected, the species will be so humanlike that almost no one can tell the difference, but, Tyrell believes, it will remain incapable of autonomy and therefore also of posing a challenge to Tyrell's control.

The key question in the film is that of Genesis: what is it that makes a being human? The essential and irreducible elements of humankind are extraordinarily difficult to define, but their existence seems irrefutable. When God decides that "It is not good that the man should be alone; I will make him a helper as his partner" (Gen. 2:18), God soon learns that the man's need for partnership cannot be met by any of the animals of the field or birds of the air, but only through a creature like himself, created from his very self: "This at last is bone of my bones and flesh of my flesh" (Gen. 2:19–23).

The boundaries between the human and the synthetic – and the question of whether, or how, human beings can create a human being without enga-ging in the biological processes of reproduction – have long preoccupied filmmakers. The classic example is the 1931 film Frankenstein, adapted loosely from Mary Shelley's novel *Frankenstein; or, The Modern Prometheus*, which first appeared in 1818. Both novel and film depict the ultimate failure of the scientist Dr. Frankenstein's attempts to animate a human being pieced together from the bits and pieces of dead humans stolen from the cemetery. *Blade Runner's* Dr. Tyrell is much more successful; his replicants look, sound, and act like human beings; they have strength and also intelligence. As one of the renegades declares, following Descartes, "I think therefore I am." She *is*, but is she therefore human?

At the outset, the film posits a specific if often elusive distinction between humans and replicants: humans are capable of empathy; replicants are not. The capacity for empathy is closely related to the presence, or absence, of memories, not merely the ability to remember but the possession of personal memories. The only way to identify a replicant, therefore, is to find out whether he or she is capable of empathy. To this end, the police have developed the so-called Voight-Kampff test, which measures respondents' capacity for empathy by gauging their eye movements as they respond to questions. Yet in the case of Rachael, the experimental Nexus 7 replicant model, it takes Deckard more than a hundred questions to determine that she is indeed a replicant. She does better on this test than the Nexus 6 replicants because she in fact has memories, albeit artificial ones that have been implanted in her consciousness at the time that she was manufactured, and which are reinforced by photographs.

Of course there are other differences. Replicants do not have human parents; the corporation brought them into being. And replicants live for a maximum of four years. To Tyrell's regret, he has not succeeded in eliminating desire, and a love of life, from the replicant's consciousness. Batty brings all of these points to Tyrell's attention in his final, violent confrontation with his maker. Batty comes to Tyrell to demand more life. In an attempt to mollify him, Tyrell calls him "The best of all possible replicants. We're proud of our prodigal son …". Roy acknowledges that "It's not an easy thing to meet your maker," playing on Tyrell as creator and acknowledging his impending death. Then he briefly considers Tyrell his father confessor: "I have done questionable things" but Tyrell doesn't play along, instead he continues his attempt to flatter Batty: "Also extraordinary things. Revel in your time." Tyrell misreads the desperation of this "prodigal son" who has come home not to reconcile with his father but to wrest what he wants out of him, or else kill him. Roy completes the sequence: "Nothing the God of bio-mechanics wouldn't let you into heaven for." Roy then kisses Tyrell (as a prodigal son would his father? As a betraying disciple would his savior?) then crushes his skull and gouges out his eyes.

Throughout, however, the film challenges, indeed explodes, this presumed duality between human and replicant, and thereby creates uncertainty in the viewer. As Boozer notes,

> Because the replicants seem as real as any of the other characters, the viewer's dilemma initially takes on the crisis orientation of the police. The film virtually forces the spectator to mistrust the conventional reading of living things represented on, and by way of, the screen … since the outlaw replicants are fully identified on video early in the film, the issue is not a detective game of character appearance and reality; it becomes a crisis of the collapse of any meaningful distinction between the two.[34]

As in *Avatar*, the central theme of this film – can we trust what we see? – is reinforced by visual metaphors pertaining to sight and insight. Eyes, real and artificial, in all shapes and sizes, appear at the crucial turning points in the story.[35]

Related to the theme of vision is the use of glass, especially glass windows. One can see through glass, but one cannot touch or otherwise reach what one sees unless that glass shatters, as it does numerous times in this film especially at moments of conflict and death.

Each of the three main characters – Deckard, Rachael, and Batty – challenges the dichotomy between human and replicant. Initially there is no reason to doubt Deckard's humanness. His job is to "retire" replicants and he

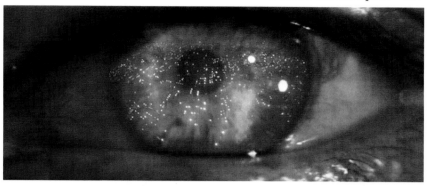

Figure 9.2 Human eye or replicant? *Blade Runner.*

is as fully human as any human film character can be. But as Rachael notices, there are photographs around his apartment that are very similar to the ones that she has been given to support her (false) memories. Once it occurs to the viewer that Deckard may – unbeknownst to himself – be a replicant, some of the dialog begins to ring ironically. As they head into their final confrontation, Roy taunts Deckard: "Aren't you the good man? Show me what you're made of." After Roy's death, Deckard's partner Gaff, compliments him: "You've done a man's job, sir." Yet Roy was not "retired" by Deckard but by his own actions. If Deckard was indeed a replicant, then perhaps we might say that, like the biblical patriarch Jacob (Gen. 32:25–31), he had to wrestle with an angel in order to become a man.[36] Deckard himself points out that in some ways, blade runners are like the replicants they are meant to hunt down: neither was supposed to have feelings.[37] Yet the question of Deckard's humanity is left unresolved, a mystery that can be pondered after the final credits have rolled.

Rachael too challenges the human–replicant dichotomy. There is no doubt that she is a replicant, and initially it would seem that this makes her completely "other" despite her humanoid qualities. As David Desser comments, Rachael is the classic *femme fatale* of film noir; her hair is pinned up and her wardrobe echoes the classic 1940s padded-shoulder wardrobe of Joan Crawford. "Her links with the *noir* era of filmmaking are further stressed by the saxophone music on the soundtrack … iconography automatically makes Rachael suspect – a potential spider woman, the woman-as-temptress, our fallen mother, Eve."[38] However, as she develops her relationship with Deckard, and acknowledges the powerful emotion of love, she is transformed from an automaton to a natural, sensual, beautiful woman, symbolized most clearly when she lets her hair down in Deckard's apartment. Gaff too points to the blurring of the distinction between human and replicant when he remarks about Rachael, "It's too bad she won't live, but then again, who does?"

Roy too is unquestionably a replicant. But as with Rachael, his portrayal raises questions about the boundaries between replicants and human beings. Roy has superhuman strength and ruthlessness, but he is also capable of love, as evident in his obvious grief when his replicant lover, Pris, is "retired." Roy is also the "angel" with whom Deckard wrestles, for, paraphrasing William Blake's poem, *America: A Prophecy*, he anticipates the fatal outcome of his fall from the high building where their confrontation takes place: "Fiery the angels fell; deep thunder rolled around their shores; burning with the fires of Orc."[39] What he and his followers want is more life; powerful and beautiful as they are, they are slaves, relegated to off-world sites where they serve humans in various predetermined capacities, yet able to see very clearly their own potential for a longer and full existence. Batty wants Deckard to understand him, that is, to empathize with his situation. As he literally holds Deckard's life in his hands, he tells him: "Quite an experience to live in fear, isn't it? That's what it is to be a slave." At the end he laments, "I've seen things you people wouldn't believe. Attack ships on fire off the shoulder of Orion. I watched C-beams glitter in the darkness at Tan Hauser Gate. All those moments will be lost in time like tears in rain. Time to die." In voice-over, Deckard then comments: "I don't know why he saved my life. Maybe in those last moments he loved life more than he ever had before. Not just his life, anybody's life, my life. All he'd wanted were the same answers the rest of us want. Where did I come from? Where am I going? How long have I got? All I could do was sit there and watch him die." If Roy truly loved all life, including that of his pursuer, then he also had empathy, and emotion that went far beyond his own aspirations and desires.

In their final battle it is not only Deckard who showed his humanity, but also Roy. Or perhaps it is more than humanity. The dove that Roy releases when he dies alludes to the dove that signals the end of the primordial flood (Gen. 8:9–11). But it also recalls the traditional symbolism of the dove as the holy spirit settled upon the young Mary as she conceived Jesus (Luke 1:35), on Jesus at the baptism (Luke 3:22) and which is released again at Jesus' death (Mark 15:13). The symbolism is based on John 1:32, in which John the Baptist testifies: "I saw the Spirit descending from heaven like a dove, and it remained on him." One would hardly see Roy as a Jesus figure, and yet his possession of the dove, and its release at his death, calls forth this comparison despite all evidence to the contrary.

WALL-E *(2008)*

Plot summary

WALL-E too elides the distinction between the human and the synthetic, but because such elision is conventional in children's books and movies (the

Toy Story franchise, for example), it does not raise the same existential questions. Nor does it project the same bleak mood, despite the obvious devastation of its landscape, due to its vivid color and its unambiguously positive ending.

The year is 2110, and the earth has become a giant landfill site. The consumerist, wasteful behavior that rendered the earth uninhabitable was exploited and abetted by large multinational corporations such as Buy 'N Large (BnL). The BnL billboards that dot the landscape advertise five-year cruises in outer space – "the final fun-teer" – but we soon learn that these are not holidays but forced and permanent evacuations.

The earth's only occupants are a small robot and his cockroach pal. The robot is WALL-E, or rather, *a* WALL-E: a Waste Allocation Load Lister Earth Class. He spends his days methodically picking up garbage and compacting it into bricks, which he piles up neatly. But WALL-E has a daily routine. After work, he comes home, feeds his pet bug, and rocks himself to sleep. He hordes the "treasures" that he finds in the trash, the detritus of a species that is not his own, and displays nostalgia for a world, a society, and an era, that he did not experience. His most prized possessions are an old VCR and television, on which he watches the 1964 musical *Hello Dolly* for entertainment, comfort, and companionship in his lonely world. A resourceful little robot, he has not only figured out how to use many of his treasures but also how to repair them, and himself, as need arises.

Another of WALL-E's treasures is a seedling, a miracle of perseverance and hope in a waste-ridden world that has quashed all other forms of natural life. One day, as WALL-E is going about his daily business, he is astonished to see a spaceship land nearby. Out of this spaceship pops one small white, egg-shaped robot. WALL-E is intrigued. This small robot's behavior and appearance imply female gender, and he soon learns that she is EVE. As an Extraterrestrial Vegetation Evaluator, she is programed to seek out any remaining plant life and take it back to the mother ship.

WALL-E, romantic robot that he is, falls in love at first sight. He takes her home to show her his treasures. Upon sensing the seedling, however, she stores it within her "body," which automatically signals the spaceship, called the Axiom, to return for her. WALL-E hitches a ride, and they learn that the Axiom is the "cruise" ship to which humankind has been evacuated. Contrary to all promises, the BnL corporation had no intention of returning the humans to earth. Through years of enforced inactivity, poor nutrition, away from the pull of gravity, these humans have become obese, shapeless, and weak. In fact, by catering to their desire for mindless entertainment, junk food, and inactivity, the corporation has rendered its "guests" barely recognizable as human beings. A battle with the two small robots and the overseers of the megacorporation ensues. WALL-E is mortally wounded, but he and EVE force the ship to return to earth. EVE takes WALL-E's body home repairs – resurrect, restoring – him his consciousness and his lost memories. The human beings rejoice at their return to earth, they plant the seedlings that begin its restoration, and regain their own humanity.

Bible quotations

The biblical connections here are more explicit than in *Blade Runner*, if also less nuanced. EVE, as her name implies, is the agent of new life, the fitting partner for WALL-E; her egg-shaped body protects and gestates the seedling, which glows inside her. Although she initially behaves as programed, she becomes an agent and free-thinker under WALL-E's influence and in their shared mission to rescue the world and its rightful inhabitants. The eschatological vision is of a return to the Garden of Eden, or at least, a world in which all living things can flourish. This message is underscored by the visuals that accompany the closing credits which take us quickly through a tour of human creativity and art. This motif echoes Genesis 1:29 in which God tells the first humans: "See, I have given you every plant yielding seed that is upon the face of all the earth, and every tree with seed in its fruit; you shall have them for food." A second obvious biblical motif is death and resurrection, as experienced by WALL-E. He is restored by EVE – the agent of new life – but it is only when his memory is restored that he becomes fully himself.

Children of Men *(2006)*

Plot summary

Like *WALL-E, Children of Men* envisions the creation of new life, though its story and film style are much darker in mood. Loosely adapted from P. D. James' 1992 novel *The Children of Men*, the film is set in England in 2027, some two decades after the world's human population has inexplicably become infertile. As the film opens, the youngest living person has died, plunging the country, and the protagonist, Theo Faron, into despair. Theo fears for humankind, but also mourns his own son who died in infancy. Exactly what led to the collapse of global society is never stated. England, apparently the last country that has any resources left at all, has become a martial state. Illegal immigrants from Italy, Germany, and other parts of the world, flood its borders only to be labelled "foogies" (refugees) and herded into concentration camps where they are brutalized by the police. The plot revolves around a terrorist group called The Fishes, led by Theo's ex-wife, Julian. She conscripts Theo to help Kee, a young – and pregnant – West African "foogie," escape the United Kingdom by boat to a sanctuary run by a group called the Human Project so that her baby will be safe. The plan succeeds, but not without much despair, pain, and bloodshed.

Biblical quotations and allusions

The expression "children of men" appears several times in the King James translation of the Hebrew Bible. In Psalm 90, the psalmist declares:

> Lord, thou hast been our dwelling place in all generations. Before the mountains were brought forth, or ever thou hadst formed the earth and the world, even from everlasting to everlasting, thou art God. Thou turnest man to destruction; and sayest, Return, ye children of men.... For we are consumed by thine anger, and by thy wrath are we troubled. Thou hast set our iniquities before thee, our secret sins in the light of thy countenance.
>
> (Ps. 90:1–8)

Psalm 115:16 points out that "The heaven, even the heavens, are the LORD'S: but the earth hath he given to the children of men" (KJV) These psalms provide two different hypotheses with regard to the destruction of the world; in the film, it would appear that the world is not destroyed by God to punish human iniquity, as Psalm 90 might suggest, but rather by human beings, to whom God had handed over the responsibility for and stewardship of the world (see also Gen. 1:26–28).

The biblical connection is reinforced by the names of some of the characters. "Theo" is the Greek term for God. While Theo is certainly fallible, he is the mediator both in the creator of Kee's child – her safe delivery midst the most dire conditions of the refugee camp – and her salvation. He sprinkles the baby girl with some water, thereby performing a baptism of sorts, if in the name of hygiene, and gets them both safely to the boat, dying just before they reach safety.

Other characters include Luke and Simon, who are leaders of The Fishes. The name of this group evokes Christ, but this association functions ironically given the Fishes' disdain for human life, including that of Kee and her child, whom they had claimed to cherish. The film also has two Mary figures: a midwife named Miriam, perhaps reminiscent of Moses' sister Miriam who in some post-biblical Jewish interpretations was a midwife,[40] and a gypsy woman named Marichka who helps Theo, Kee, and the new baby escape by boat.

Kee herself evokes both the Virgin Mary and Mary Magdalene. She is very young, previously unknown, and unexpectedly pregnant with a child fathered by an unknown father. When asked about the father, Kee jokes: "Whiffet! I'm a virgin. Nah! Be great, though, wouldn't it? Fuck knows. I don't know half the wankers' names." As in Matthew, the birth of this child puts both the baby and its mother in physical danger, not only from the unhygienic conditions in which the child must be born – a stable in Matthew, a refugee camp, in the film – but from those who feel threatened or wish to take advantage of the unusual birth (Herod; the Fishes).

But most important, the birth of the child is an event of earth-shattering importance, and heralded as the first step in the salvation of humankind. The miraculous nature of the pregnancy and its salvific potential are underscored by the change in extradiegetic music in the scene in which Kee reveals her pregnancy to Theo. The music is heavenly, like sacred church music. When he sees her swollen belly, Theo exclaims: "Jesus Christ!" He tells Luke, "She's pregnant!" Luke responds: "Yeah, I know. It's a miracle, innit?" though his faintly sarcastic tone of voice suggests that he is more annoyed by the burden than awed by the miracle. Jasper, Theo's old friend, who helps Theo and Kee escape the Fishes, tells Kee: "Your baby is the miracle the whole world has been waiting for." When Jasper and Kee say goodbye, their hands almost touch, evoking the image of God touching Adam in the Sistine Chapel, though Jasper looks more like John Lennon than Michelangelo's image of the divine. After the baby is born, Theo repeats: "Oh my God!"

Kee's newborn daughter, like the infant Jesus, has a transformative effect on those around her. The child is born in a refugee camp, which Theo and Kee have entered, as per Jasper's directions. He has arranged for a rowboat to take them out to the ship *Tomorrow* which in turn would transport them to the Human Project. The other inhabitants are persecuted, hungry, exhausted, and without hope. To make matters worse, factions within the camp have staged a revolt, and the Fishes have arrived in pursuit of Theo, Kee, and the baby, and are shooting everyone in their way. Midst the mayhem, the baby's cry is heard. The fighting stops. All are overcome by the miracle of new life. One woman sings a song; others reach out to touch the baby reverently. The moment ends as quickly as it began, and the killing starts again. Badly wounded, Theo hustles Kee, and the child onto the rowboat; they row away into the misty water, and as Theo dies, Kee exclaims joyfully: "The boat! The boat! We are safe now!" But Theo can no longer hear her. The movie ends on this note that mingles sadness at Theo's death with hope at new life, and a new beginning for humanity.

Book of Eli *(2010)*

Plot summary

The films discussed thus far portray apocalyptic destruction and the hope for a new earth and new life. *The Book of Eli*, by contrast, is concerned with the post-apocalyptic restoration of human culture and its legacy of books and knowledge. *The Book of Eli* is set in the Midwest, in an unspecified future time, 30 years after a nuclear event has wreaked havoc on America. The setting recalls the dusty, dirty, lawless towns and deserts of the Western film genre. The same is true of the social order. In the absence of a well-functioning legal and political system, it is the unscrupulous men and women with guns, food, and, especially, water, that rule the day. As in the Westerns, marauders and outlaws abound, but this post-apocalyptic society sinks far below the Wild West, for cannibalism is rife.

The main character is a mysterious nomad named Eli, on a westward mission to deliver a mysterious book to a safe location. Eli has superb survival skills, and although he kills when necessary, he adheres to a strict ethical code. He arrives in a particularly rundown town owned by a man named Carnegie. Carnegie has big plans, but he is also obsessed with one desire: to gain access to a book, which, he believes, will give him the power to realize his ambition of domination. Eli stays overnight in a room upstairs from Carnegie's bar. Carnegie's blind mistress, Claudia, gives him food and Carnegie sends Claudia's beautiful young daughter, Solara, to seduce Eli and pry information from him. To Solara's relief, Eli does not touch her, but he does share his food with her. She learns that he has a book – perhaps even *the* book that Carnegie is seeking. Instead of turning Eli in, however, she allies herself with him, and, against his better judgment, he allows her to accompany him to the West Coast.

As they proceed on their journey, the viewer comes to realize two things: that Eli's book is the Bible, or rather, a copy of the King James translation of the Bible, and Eli is completely blind. After many adventures, Eli loses his copy of the Bible to Carnegie's men. Carnegie pries open the lock on the book's cover, only to learn that it is written in Braille. Claudia can read Braille but refuses to read it to him, and so its secrets of how to gain power are lost to him forever. Meanwhile Eli and Solara continue to the West Coast until they arrive at the Golden Gate Bridge. They row out to Alcatraz, where they find a group of survivors who have dedicated themselves to replenishing the library of great books destroyed in the apocalypse. Eli's physical copy of the Bible is lost, but he has memorized it, and is able to dictate it verbatim. The resulting book – *The Holy Bible* – is printed and placed reverently on the bookshelf between copies of the Hebrew scriptures and the Qu'ran. Eli dies and Solara heads home, bringing Eli's few treasures with her.

The Bible as actor

As in many other films, the biblical associations are created in the first instance by the names of one or more characters. The name Eli alludes to Elijah who, as a prophet, is a divinely sent messenger. Like Elijah, Eli obeys words that he has heard. Although the film, unlike the Bible (cf. 1 Kings 17:8), does not identify the source of those words, the mission suggests a divine connection. And this film, like *Avatar* and *Blade Runner*, plays on the metaphor of sight and insight. As in the Gospel of John, those who are blind can see the truth (Eli, and, to a lesser extent, Claudia) whereas those who claim to see (Carnegie) are in fact blind.

In this film, however, the Bible is not merely a source of imagery, language, theology, and narrative. The question of the Bible's absence and presence is the major focus of the plot. The conflict between the hero, Eli, and the villain, Carnegie, revolves around who can possess the Bible, and what it means to do so. Carnegie craves the Bible, for he views it – falsely – as a means to manipulate others and gain power. Eli protects the Bible, reads it nightly, inscribes its words upon his heart; these divine word have shaped his moral life and given his life a purpose.

The essential difference between Carnegie and Eli is illustrated by Carnegie's speech upon learning that Eli's book is in fact the book he has been looking for.

> You know, I've been searching for a book like that one for years. All I've ever wanted was to bring the word of God to these poor unfortunates here. To shine its light upon them and give them something in this wretched world that they could believe in. Something to live for! It's why I built this town, did you know that? All we've been missing is the word to show us the way. And now, praise the Lord, you've brought it to us.

Carnegie then tries to wheedle Eli into sharing the book, insincerely offering himself as a partner to what he supposes is Eli's mission:

> It's not right to keep that book hidden away, all to yourself. The word is meant to be shared with others. It's meant to be spread! Isn't that what you want? I could help you do that. You and me, we could do it together.

Eli, though blind, sees through Carnegie, and evades him at this point. Though he eventually loses his copy of the Bible to Carnegie, this loss is not a victory for Carnegie, for he is blind to its beauty, and its content, written in Braille, is still hidden from him. Eli, on the other hand, does not need to possess the physical copy of the Bible in order to have it. He has become a living Bible, enabling it to be printed and thereby become a resource for the world's restoration.

Eli as Christ-figure

Whereas Eli sets out on his mission alone, he picks up a companion, one might say a disciple, Claudia's daughter Solara, whose name recalls the sun (*sol*). She might be described as a reluctant Mary Magdalene figure. Sent against her will to seduce Eli and pry his secret from him, she is saved from transgression by Eli himself. Not only does he "save" her purity, but he also saves her from Carnegie's clutches, and, even more, he teaches her to know and value the Bible as he does. His mission becomes hers, and she becomes essential to its successful completion. Solara might also be compared to the Samaritan woman whom Jesus meets at the well in John 4. Just as the

Samaritan woman offered fresh water to Jesus, so does Solara refresh Eli with water from Carnegie's secret reserve. Just as it is Jesus who provides the eternal life-giving water to the Samaritan woman (John 4:10), so it is Eli who in the end transforms Solara's life, as she carries on his mission after his death.

In the final scene of the film, Eli recites 2 Timothy 4:7 in voice-over: "I have fought the good fight, I have finished the race ..." The verse ends in a way that would be appropriate to Eli as well: "I have kept the faith."

Conclusion

Like other movies in the category of "Bible in film," apocalyptic films use the Bible as a source of quotations, allusions, and images, as well as an on-screen object. In their overall style, their grand scale, their music, and their spectacular special effects, apocalyptic movies resemble the biblical epics. And, like the epics, they often convey a worldview that is firmly centered on the United States as the leader in the efforts to free the world of this cosmic threat. Even as they criticize materialism, consumerism, and environmental exploitation, many also convey optimism regarding the potential of humankind to repair the world, and themselves. In that sense, the question of whether they are "religious" or "secular" is besides the point. Ostwalt is certainly correct that these films do not engage explicitly with the powerful religious visions of Revelation and other ancient apocalypses. Yet while they may not focus explicitly on the divine role in the narrative of the last days, they have much in common with those ancient stories. Most obvious of these is the narrative paradigm, which moves from destruction to restoration, and the centrality of a savior figure, who mediates the restoration, or at least the possibility thereof. Even more important, they help viewers experience the fragility of human existence on the planet, the mutual responsibility of human beings, the terrifying fear of cosmic destruction, and the life-giving hope of restoration.

Notes

1 "Doomsayers predict apocalypse now." www.telegraph.co.uk/news/worldnews/northamerica/usa/8525047/Doomsayers-predict-apocalypse-now.html, 20 May 2011 (accessed 4 April 2012).

2 www.telegraph.co.uk/news/religion/8527582/Apocalypse-not-right-now-Rapture-end-of-world-fails-to-materialise.html (accessed 4 April 2012).

3 Ibid. A similar media frenzy took place in December 2012, due to the apparent prediction of the Mayan calendar that the world would end on 21 December 2012. For an explanation, see www.timeanddate.com/calendar/mayan.html (accessed 10 May 2013).

4 On importance of Revelation for popular culture representations, see Ostwalt, "Apocalyptic," 368.

5 For a comprehensive introduction to apocalyptic literature, see John J. Collins, *The Apocalyptic Imagination: An Introduction to Jewish Apocalyptic Literature* (Grand Rapids,

MI: William B. Eerdmans, 1998); Greg Carey, *Ultimate Things: An Introduction to Jewish and Christian Apocalyptic Literature* (St. Louis, MO: Chalice Press, 2005).

6 See the essays in Abbas Amanat and Magnus Thorkell Bernhardsson, *Imagining the End: Visions of Apocalypse from the Ancient Middle East to Modern America* (London; New York: I. B. Tauris, 2002).

7 Kirsten Moana Thompson, *Apocalyptic Dread: American Film at the Turn of the Millennium* (Albany, NY: State University of New York Press, 2007), 1–2.

8 Ibid., 2.

9 Charles P. Mitchell, *A Guide to Apocalyptic Cinema* (Westport, CT: Greenwood Press, 2001), xi.

10 Ibid., xii–xv.

11 John W. Martens, *The End of the World: The Apocalyptic Imagination in Film and Television* (Winnipeg, MB: J. Gordon Shillingford, 2003), 89–90.

12 Ibid., 91–93. Atomic bomb movies would come under Martens' fourth category. For a study of these movies as a separate genre, see Jerome Franklin Shapiro, *Atomic Bomb Cinema: The Apocalyptic Imagination on Film* (New York: Routledge, 2002).

13 Ostwalt, "Apocalyptic," 368.

14 Ibid., 371.

15 Ibid., 376. See also Ostwalt, "Armageddon at the Millennial Dawn."

16 Ostwalt, "Apocalyptic," 376.

17 Thompson, *Apocalyptic Dread*, 9–12.

18 On science fiction as a genre, and its overlap with apocalyptic and other types of films considered in this chapter, see Keith M. Johnston, *Science Fiction Film: A Critical Introduction* (Oxford; New York: Berg, 2011). On the role of martyrdom in apocalyptic film, see Laura Copier, *Preposterous Revelations: Visions of Apocalypse and Martyrdom in Hollywood Cinema 1980–2000* (Sheffield: Sheffield Phoenix Press, 2012).

19 The Alpha Centauri star system has been much studied by astronomers. See "A Family Portrait of the Alpha Centauri System – VLT Interferometer Studies the Nearest Stars," www.eso.org (accessed 16 December 2012), www.eso.org/public/news/eso0307. This star system is the setting of numerous science fiction novels, television series, and movies, such as M. John Harrison, *The Centauri Device* (Garden City, NY: Doubleday, 1974) and William Barton and Michael Capobianco, *Alpha Centauri* (New York: Avon Books, 1997). See Thomas Elsaesser, "James Cameron's *Avatar*: Access for All," *New Review of Film and Television Studies* 9, no. 3 (1 September 2011): 249. Television series include *Lost in Space* (1965–68), and episodes of *Star Trek: The Original Series* (episode entitled "Metamorphosis" [1967]) and *Doctor Who* (*The Curse of Peladon* [1972] and *The Monster of Peladon* [1974]). Movies include *Lost in Space* (1998), *Imposter* (2002), and *Transformers* (2007).

20 Thomas Elsaesser notes that "The peace-loving natives – compiled from a mélange of Native American, African, Vietnamese, Iraqi and other cultural fragments – are like the peace-loving natives you've seen in a hundred other movies. They're tall, muscular and admirably slender. They walk around nearly naked. They are phenomenal athletes and pretty good singers and dancers." Elsaesser, "James Cameron's *Avatar*," 249. Alessio and Meredith comment that the film falls into the stereotypical characterization of native people as "little children of the forest." Dominic Alessio and Kristen Meredith, "Decolonising James Cameron's Pandora: Imperial History and Science Fiction," *Journal of Colonialism and Colonial History* 13, no. 2 (2012): http://muse.jhu.edu/journals/journal_of_colonialism_and_colonial_history/v013/13.2.alessio.html (accessed 10 May 2013).

21 For analysis of the important, and ambiguous, role of Hope in Hesiod's work, see Jenny Strauss Clay, *Hesiod's Cosmos* (Cambridge; New York: Cambridge University Press, 2003), 103.

22 Y2K anxiety is evident not only in films but in numerous books, magazine articles, and news reports. See, for example, Dick Lefkon, *Year 2000: Best Practices for Y2K*

Millennium Computing (Upper Saddle River, NJ: Prentice Hall, 1998). Book titles themselves reflect the apocalyptic scenario, such as Minda Zetlin, *Surviving the Computer Time Bomb: How to Plan for and Recover from the Y2K Explosion* (New York: AMACOM, 1999). For more sober analysis, see Stephen Feinstein, *The 1990s from the Persian Gulf War to Y2K* (Berkeley Heights, NJ: Enslow Publishers, 2001).

23 This is a major focus throughout Thompson, *Apocalyptic Dread*.

24 Mitchell, *A Guide to Apocalyptic Cinema*, 48. Martens, *The End of the World*, 92. Conrad Eugene Ostwalt, *Secular Steeples: Popular Culture and the Religious Imagination* (Harrisburg, PA: Trinity Press International, 2003), 173.

25 Fish are associated with Jesus, for example, in Luke 5:1–11 and John 21, which describe a miraculous catch of fish. The use of fish as a symbol for Christ, however, is generally attributed to the fact that the Greek word for fish is an acronym for "Jesus Christ God's Son Savior." George Ferguson, *Signs & Symbols in Christian Art* (New York: Oxford University Press, 1954), 18. In the film, however, it is also possible to associate the "Fishes" with "Fascists," just as "Foogies" are associated with "Refugees."

26 Though not explicitly mentioned in Genesis, the reference to restoring agriculture implies that seeds were included on the biblical ark as well (Gen. 8:22).

27 Ostwalt, "Armageddon at the Millennial Dawn," para. 11.

28 See *Evan Almighty* (2007) and *Bruce Almighty* (2003).

29 Joshua 12:21, 17:11; Judges 5:19, 1 Kings 4:12, 9:15; 2 Kings 9:27, 23:29; 1 Chronicles 7:29, 2 Chronicles 35:22, and Zechariah 12:11.

30 For an exploration of the language of contemporary apocalyptic discourse, see Stephen D. O'Leary, *Arguing the Apocalypse: A Theory of Millennial Rhetoric* (New York: Oxford University Press, 1998).

31 There are seven versions of the film, made for different markets. The differences are most pronounced in the ending. The present study is based on the Director's Cut. For details on the making of the film and its versions, see Paul Sammon, *Future Noir: The Making of Blade Runner* (New York: HarperPrism, 1996).

32 Jack Boozer, Jr., "Crashing the Gates of Insight: Blade Runner," in *Retrofitting Blade Runner: Issues in Ridley Scott's Blade Runner and Philip K. Dick's Do Androids Dream of Electric Sheep?* ed. Judith Kerman (Bowling Green, OH: Bowling Green State University Popular Press, 1991), 225–26.

33 Judith Kerman, "Post-Millennium Blade Runner," in *The Blade Runner Experience: The Legacy of a Science Fiction Classic*, ed. Will Brooker (London; New York: Wallflower, 2005), 31–39.

34 Boozer, "Crashing the Gates of Insight," 214.

35 Ibid.

36 Kerman, "Post-Millennium Blade Runner," 35.

37 David Desser, "The New Eve: The Influence of Paradise Lost and Frankenstein on Blade Runner," in *Retrofitting Blade Runner: Issues in Ridley Scott's Blade Runner and Philip K. Dick's Do Androids Dream of Electric Sheep?* ed. Judith Kerman (Bowling Green, OH: Bowling Green State University Popular Press, 1991), 60.

38 Ibid.

39 The original is "Fiery the angels rose, and as they rose deep thunder roll'd. Around their shores: indignant burning with the fires of Orc." William Blake, *America: Poem*, ed. Paul Peter Piech (Bushey Heath, Herts.: Taurus Press of Willow Dene, 1977), 216.

40 See Jonathan Cohen, *The Origins and Evolution of the Moses Nativity Story* (Leiden; New York: Brill, 1993), 93.

10 Conclusion: "my heart is glad, and my soul rejoices"

Cinema and transcendence

More than a century has passed since the 1897 Horitz Play thrilled and delighted its first audiences. Since that time, the Bible has become a movie star in its own right, appearing in countless features in numerous genres, from the biblical epic to the apocalyptic disaster movie. It has been drawn into the Cold War and the debates over gender roles, civil rights, and capital punishment. It has pledged its support for America's role as the champion of freedom and democracy at home and abroad, but also provided a paradigm for critiquing the army bureaucracy and ethos. Above all, it has demonstrated its ongoing relevance to history, culture, and the human experience.

The Bible that appears on the silver screen is not the same one that worshippers encounter in synagogues and churches, or that scholars and students grapple with in the classroom or the library. In the first place, Hollywood's Bible is not nearly as extensive as the Jewish or Christian scriptures. It consists of only a selection of biblical books: Genesis, Exodus, Samuel and Kings, Esther, Ruth and Job, the Gospels, and Revelation, supplemented by snippets from the Psalms, the Prophets, and the Letters of Paul. Second, the cinematic scriptures are clothed in layers of artistic, musical, dramatic, liturgical, and theological reflection and interpretation. Indeed, one may question whether, for example, it is truly the historical, or even the biblical, Jesus that is the subject of the Jesus-movies, or rather, the culturally constructed Jesus that has developed over centuries of representation. Finally, Hollywood's Bible – in its partial and culturally shaped form – is above all the Christian Bible. Even when it draws on books that are also present in the Jewish Scriptures, Hollywood presents them as "Old Testament" and not as "Hebrew Bible," that is, as looking ahead to, and completed by, the New Testament and the coming of Christ.

Not surprisingly, then, the Hollywood Bible is often used to imply the normativity of Christian faith in American society. The epics show that the faithful triumph over atheists, and that prayer leads to abundance. Later films often refrain from presenting an explicitly Christian message, but traces can be detected beneath the surface, particularly in films that draw upon the Bible to reflect on the law, ethics, gender, race, politics, and other aspects of American society. Even films that are entirely free of such biblical undercurrents never-theless draw upon the Bible to promote personal and social values such as hope, altruism, generosity, tolerance of difference, and responsibility toward the other, and to society as a whole.

Transcendence

Whatever else the Bible may be – a source of narrative, a foundation for ethics – it is first and foremost a record of how an ancient people gave expression to their belief in the existence of an unseen reality alongside, above, or beyond the world of daily life. For Moses, the first encounter, of many, occurred at Horeb, where the startled shepherd saw a "flame of fire out of a bush" and realized that "the bush was blazing, yet it was not con-sumed" (Exod. 3:2). This encounter set in motion a series of events that involved all Israelites, who experienced the divine as a force that "bore [them] on eagles' wings" (Exod. 19:4) out of Egypt and, eventually, to the "promised land." Some three months after the exodus from Egypt, God came to meet the people on Mount Sinai, an event so momentous that it was signalled by "thunder and lightning, as well as a thick cloud on the mountain, and a blast of a trumpet so loud that all the people who were in the camp trembled" (Exodus 19:16).

Other encounters are much quieter, individual experiences. Moses in Exodus 33:17–23. The young Samuel, lying down to sleep in the temple near his mentor Eli, heard a voice call "Samuel, Samuel," and it took him some time to realize that it was God, not Eli, calling to him (1 Sam. 3:1–18). Elijah is told to "Go out and stand on the mountain before the LORD, for the LORD is about to pass by." But how to recognize the Lord? Elijah waited without knowing what he was waiting for. "Now there was a great wind, so strong that it was splitting mountains and breaking rocks in pieces before the LORD, but the LORD was not in the wind; and after the wind an earth-quake, but the LORD was not in the earthquake; and after the earthquake a fire, but the LORD was not in the fire; and after the fire a sound of sheer silence" – and in the silence, what the King James Version poetically called the "still small voice" – was the Lord (1 Kgs. 19:11–12).

In a later era, the prophet Isaiah described his terrifying encounter with the divine:

> In the year that King Uzziah died, I saw the Lord sitting on a throne, high and lofty; and the hem of his robe filled the temple. Seraphs were in attendance above him; each had six wings: with two they covered their faces, and with two they covered their feet, and with two they flew. And one called to another and said: "Holy, holy, holy is the LORD of hosts; the whole earth is full of his glory." The pivots on the thresholds shook at the voices of those who called, and the house filled with smoke. And I said: "Woe is me! I am lost, for I am a man of unclean lips, and I live

among a people of unclean lips; yet my eyes have seen the King, the
LORD of hosts!"

(Isaiah 6:1–5)[1]

Some centuries after Isaiah, the Hellenistic Jewish philosopher Philo of Alexandria vividly describes the ecstatic experiences that he gave up when he
entered public life:

> There was once a time when, devoting my leisure to philosophy and to the
> contemplation of the world and the things in it, I reaped the fruit of excel-
> lent, and desirable, and blessed intellectual feelings, being always living among
> the divine oracles and doctrines, on which I fed incessantly and insatiably, to
> my great delight, never entertaining any low or grovelling thoughts, nor ever
> wallowing in the pursuit of glory or wealth, or the delights of the body, but I
> appeared to be raised on high and borne aloft by a certain inspiration of the
> soul, and to dwell in the regions of the sun and moon, and to associate with
> the whole heaven, and the whole universal world.[2]

A few decades later, the Synoptic Gospels (Matthew, Mark, and Luke),
describe a small group experience, in which

> Jesus took with him Peter and James and John, and led them up a high
> mountain apart, by themselves. And he was transfigured before them,[3]
> and his clothes became dazzling white, such as no one on earth could
> bleach them.[4] And there appeared to them Elijah with Moses, who were
> talking with Jesus.
>
> (Mark 9:2–4)

According to the Gospels, not only the disciples but all believers could transcend their present lives, in the present and in the eschatological future. The
Synoptic Gospels (Matthew, Mark, and Luke) refer to this unseen reality as
the kingdom of God or the kingdom of heaven, and they have Jesus utter
numerous parables – short symbolic stories, that paint the kingdom of heaven
both as highly desirable and highly attractive:

> The kingdom of heaven is like treasure hidden in a field, which someone
> found and hid; then in his joy he goes and sells all that he has and buys
> that field. Again, the kingdom of heaven is like a merchant in search of
> fine pearls; on finding one pearl of great value, he went and sold all that
> he had and bought it.
>
> (Matt. 13:44–46)

In a similar vein, the author of the Gospel of John promises believers rebirth
as children of God (John 1:13), and an eternal dwelling place in God's house
(John 14:2).

These and other ancient texts describe moments of transcendence or com-munication with the divine, a sense of life's infinite possibilities, a life beyond the mundane. For some people, the liturgy, ritual, and the Bible itself can mediate such experiences; for others, moments of transcendence – moments that take us outside the realm of everyday experience in powerful and trans-formative ways – are less closely connected to our religious beliefs and prac-tices, but are more amorphously and inchoately experienced as happiness, love, compassion, or humility, a sense of our own small place in the universe, cosmos, or "the scheme of things." Such moments can simply "happen" but they too can be mediated, by art, music, literature, and, yes, film.

Respite from the mundane

Most people seek moments of respite from the mundane, when we may take a break from daily life. As Robert Bellah puts it, "one of the first things to be noticed about the world of daily life is that *nobody can stand to live in it all the time.* ... All of us leave the world of daily life with considerable frequency...." (emphasis in original).[3] For one thing, we spend between six and eight hours of every day sleeping, which also means that we dream; dreams are free from the chronological, geographical, and physical constraints that control our experi-ences in daily life. Aside from sleep, however, we regularly participate in activities – watching television, listening to music, reading a novel – that by their absorbing nature in effect remove us from our daily lives. The major reason we spend so much time at these activities, suggests Bellah, is precisely because they divert us from our mundane existence.[4]

As we have seen throughout this book, films quote from, or allude to the Bible at least in part to attribute universal, perhaps even divinely ordained meanings to their characters and the stories. Few films, however, succeed in drawing us in to that broader, cosmic dimension. Those that do succeed in creating a transcendent experience for the viewer do not use the Bible alone, but draw on images and music that, together with the Bible, and the cine-matographic, narrative, editorial, and other skills of the filmmakers, combine to give us respite from the everyday, and help us also to see the mundane in new ways.

Transcendence and subjectivity

We all respond to films out of our own experiences, perceptions, likes, and dislikes.[5] For this reason, it is not at all unusual to find differing assessments of the same movie. The 2011 film, *The Mill and the Cross*, based on a 1996 essay by Michael Francis Gibson, was both reviled and applauded by reviewers. The film is a cinematic exploration of, or, better, meditation on, Peter Bruegel the Elder's 1564 painting *The Procession to Calvary*.[6] Like many of Bruegel's works, this painting is crowded with characters – approximately 500 of them – and frenetic with activity. The film takes us into the lives of 12 of them, in meticulous detail. The film is set not in the time of Jesus but in Bruegel's own time and place, sixteenth-century Flanders, in which the role of the Romans is played by the soldiers of the Spanish occupation, who ruthlessly persecuted the Flemish Protestants.

In *Film Journal International*, Doris Toumarkine complimented the director for creating a "haunting film experience" and describes it as a powerful, memorable, and "jaw-dropping spectacle."[7] Even more effusive was Graham Leggat, who called the film "a miracle of technology in the service of the artistic imagination [that] transports its viewers into the living, breathing world of Pieter Bruegel's dense frieze of Christ's passion." In his view, "The painting literally comes to life in this spellbinding film, its wondrous scenes entering the viewer like a dream enters a sleeping body."[8] Yet not all were delighted by this film. In his review for the *Hollywood Reporter*, Neil Young called the film "an ambitious but frustratingly flat attempt to explore, analyze and dramatize a masterpiece of 16th-century art."[9] Carrie Rickey, film critic for the *Philadelphia Inquirer*, described the film as "visually ravishing and narratively dry." She concluded that "the movie rewards the patient viewer by putting her into the artist's shoes. But rather than bring to life Bruegel's 'The Procession to Calvary,' Majewski's deliberate pace sucks the air out of it."[10]

Transcendence and emotion

Although different films will engender, or fail to engender, an experience of transcendence, for different viewers, it is also clear that filmmakers aspire to take viewers through particular emotional experiences. As Carl Plantinga stresses, "The experience of emotion is one of the principal motivations for the viewing of movies."[11]

Cinematic storytellers count on audiences to bring their own emotions to the movies.[12] At the same time, they elicit emotions and responses from their audiences through a set of techniques and features that are fundamental to the film medium itself. These include narrative structure and character development, as well as the use of technology, such as 3D, and camera work to bring the viewer into the movie. Many of these emotional experiences are pre-structured and predictable responses to identifiable conventions.[13] The grandeur of the Bible epics, for example, was intended to thrill audiences, and audience response suggests that it often succeeded. The emotions solicited by different conventions and genres occur as temporal processes, unfolding over time as the film itself unfolds.[14] Plantinga draws attention to the role of character and character engagement in engendering emotion. He defines character engagement as "the trajectory of mental activities and responses viewers have in relation to film characters."[15] These may include antipathy, conflict, and indifference. Most powerful, however, is sympathy:

> Most classical Hollywood films encourage strong sympathy for one or
> more characters. This sympathy is pleasurable in itself, but it also ensures

strong emotional responses, since when the audience cares deeply about a character, it also has deeper concerns about the unfolding narrative. And deeper concerns often lead to stronger emotions.[16]

Conventions and transcendence

Films also however draw on techniques that are used by other forms of art; Bellah refers to these techniques as iconic, musical, poetic, narrative, and conceptual representation.[17] Above all, movies draw on the human fascination with narrative; by both nature and nurture, we are easily drawn into stories that are not our own but become our own vicariously.[18]

The Bible recounts the incursion of God into human space, the visits of visionaries into God's heavenly domains, and the many words that God addressed directly to the prophets and indirectly to the people as a whole. It uses symbolic language – eagles' wings, the light, the word – and describes spectacular events such as a burning bush and fluttering cherubim, natural but awe-inspiring occurrences such as clouds, smoke, and thunder, and the sometimes equally terrifying experience of sheer silence – the still small voice – to signify and express the Divine and inspire awe in its readers or listeners.

The Bible epics of the 1950s and 1960s attempt to represent these events faithfully, and literally, using the special effects that were state of the art at the time and the well-worn conventions that are understood to represent God or God's domain, such as big sky, big scenery, and big music. While these cinematic sequences may have inspired awe at the time, they do not always foster the emotion or experience of transcendence. Two reasons may be suggested. One is that despite their spectacular, epic nature, such scenes treat the audience purely as spectators; they do not invite them into the film to become vicarious participants. This is due at least in part to the fact that the experiences depicted emphatically did not and could not happen to us: we are none of us Moses or Jesus. Second, these conventions became the characteristics of stereotypes and clichés, drawing attention not to the divine they are meant to signify but to their own ubiquitous nature as signifiers of the divine. They distract us from their meaning by drawing our attention to their very nature as clichés. By contrast, the transcendent is called forth when we are surprised, startled out of our scripted responses by something unexpected either on the representational or narrative levels.

Plot

Some films, such as *The Shawshank Redemption*, draw attention to the contrast between the mundane and the transcendent by engaging the viewer in the interplay between two worlds: the "real world" – Shawshank Prison – and the world outside the confines of the mundane – the Pacific coast,.[19] The hero moves between these two worlds, and is fundamentally transformed in the process.[20] Andy seeks not only to transcend the walls that confine him but also to promise transcendence to his fellow inmates, even if they do not physically escape with him.

One such attempt takes place on a sunny May afternoon. Andy and some of his friends have had the extraordinary good fortune to be chosen for a short job outside the prison walls, tarring a factory roof. Andy overhears a conversation among the guards, and learns that the meanest of them all, Hadley, has inherited the sum of $35,000 that he would like to hide from the long arm of the IRS. Andy, taking his life into his hands, suggests that Hadley bestow that money as a gift to his wife. Such a gift would be tax free. Andy offers to set up the gift, for a payment of three beers for each of his "co-workers." To the shock of all concerned, including Hadley himself, the guard agrees, and the prisoners have a few moments of feeling like free men again.

Music

The Shawshank Redemption depicts a second, even more astonishing moment of transcendence. After trying for years, Andy acquires a large supply of books and recordings for the prison library. He locks the guard into the bathroom, and places a recording of a Mozart aria on the record player, and hooks up the loudspeaker. As the beautiful music soars above the prison walls, the inmates look up in the heavens in astonishment at the heavenly sounds. Red, the narrator and Andy's friend, remembers:

> I tell you those voices soared higher and farther than anybody dares to dream ... It was like ... some beautiful bird flapped into our drab little cage and made those walls dissolve away. And, for the briefest of moments, every last man at Shawshank felt free. It pissed the warden off something awful. Andy got two weeks in the hole for that little stunt.[21]

Music is an important element in Pasolini's *The Gospel According to Saint Matthew*. By juxtaposing image and sound, Pasolini takes us unexpectedly into the emotional lives of the young Mary and Joseph. As the opening credits scroll, the primary soundtrack is the joyous and down-to-earth Gloria section of the African Mass, entitled *Missa Luba*. In the *Missa Luba*, the text of the Latin Mass is set to a score based on traditional Congolese songs, arranged by a Belgian Franciscan Friar, Guido Haazen, and recorded in 1958 by a Congolese children's choir. The *Missa Luba* is followed by the more traditional, and familiar, Bach's *St. Matthew Passion* (BWV 244) No. 68: "Wir setzen uns mit Tränen nieder" (We sit down with tears), marking the change to a more sombre, sorrowful mood. The music then falls silent as the movie opens with a beautifully framed close up of the very pregnant Mary, modelled after Piero della Francesca's fresco painting *Madonna del parto* (1459–67), and slowly and carefully reveals Joseph's dismay, and his departure. As he rests, conflicted and tormented, in the village, the sound suddenly stops again. Joseph opens his eyes with a start to see an angel in a flowing white robe, who reassures him that the child is from the Holy Spirit. The angel instructs Joseph to return and marry Mary, and name the child Jesus (Matt. 1:20–21). The Gloria of the *Missa Luba* sounds forth again; as he hurries home, Mary allows herself to smile, tentatively at first, then broadly, as the camera again cuts back and forth between them. Pasolini has created a small drama of loss and restoration of trust. The music, together with the masterful camerawork and the allusions to Piero della Francesca's beautiful art, transform this first chapter of the Gospel of Matthew from a story of divine revelation to a story of love between Mary and Joseph, and turns the mood from sadness to exultation. In this way, Pasolini transcends the boundaries of the Gospel account without changing any of the words, and implies that human love – between Mary and Joseph – may transcend even the divine love that engendered the child in Mary's womb.

The transcendent moments in *Jesus of Montreal* are also created by the interplay between music and image, in this case, in the architectural spaces that begin and end the film. As the opening credits roll, the camera takes us into the beautiful dome of St. Joseph's Oratory, the highest spot in the entire city, in which musicians and two soloists are rehearsing the second-last movement of Pergolesi's *Stabat Mater* in front of gorgeous stained glass windows. In the final scene, we encounter these two singers again, this time accompanied only by a tinny ghetto blaster, as they sit on their knees and hope for handouts from passers-by. The backdrop this time is not the majestic stained glass of the Oratory but a huge advertisement for "Wild Man perfume," featuring the head of the actor who at the outset of the film heralded Daniel's arrival on the Montreal theater scene. How far they have fallen! Yet even at this final point, reminiscent of Jesus' tomb, the camera scrolls endlessly upwards, taking us from the depths of the grave to the heavenly heights of resurrection as the final credits roll.

Son of Man *(2006)*

Plot summary

A recent South African movie, *Son of Man*, transposes Jesus, his family, his disciples, and his enemies from first-century Palestine to twenty-first century "Judea," a fictional country somewhere in Africa in which an outside, hostile leadership runs a military state, supported by a local elite, terrorizing ordinary individuals in order to keep power in an orderly manner. Jesus instigates a movement of non-violent resistance to the regime, and gains a huge following. Like his first-century counterpart, he is executed by the authorities but his family and followers carry on the work that he had begun, inspired by his example and the quiet force of his extraordinary

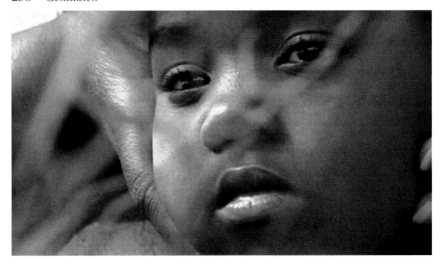

Figure 10.1 Baby Jesus gazes on the slaughter of the innocents, *Son of Man*.

personality. In fusing a contemporary story with the plot and characters of the ancient Gospel story, the movie merges the literal and allegorical levels of its own narrative.

The film begins with the temptation scene, when Jesus is just coming of age as a young man, and then returns to the story of the Nativity, here told not as a pastoral encounter between Mary (Luke) or Joseph (Matthew) with an angel, but as an epiphany in the midst of unbearable violence. The young woman Mary comes upon a school in which dozens of children have been massacred. The perpetrators are still on the premises, and to avoid detection, she lies down among the dead children and pretends to be dead herself. When the perpetrators leave, an angel appears to her and tells her that she will have a son. The angel, and the other child angels who accompany him, are both linked and contrasted with the young children whose bodies are not yet cold.

Mary and the other villagers leave their homes to escape the military forces that surround their village, but they are assaulted on the way and many of the children brutally murdered before their eyes (see the "slaughter of the innocents," Matt. 2:16). Jesus is spared, for Mary and Joseph had hidden with him as soon as they sensed danger. Peering out from the bushes, Mary had initially covered her son's eyes, but she then uncovered them so that he could take in the full measure of the oppressors' cruelty. It is this viewing – this gaze – that set the boy on the path to non-violent resistance.

The film follows him through to young adulthood, as he gathers his followers, and, to his own surprise, performs miracles, which are broadcast to his people through eloquent wall paintings. Jesus saves Mary Magdalene from

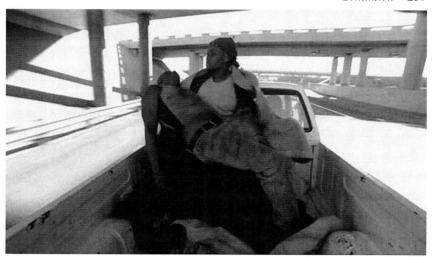

Figure 10.2 The *Pietà, Son of Man.*

stoning; she becomes a disciple alongside the other men and women he has gathered, and she is the one who welcomes his mother Mary when she arrives to join the group. Judas is initially a disciple like all the others, but marked by his own experience as a child soldier forced to kill on command. He finds it hard to relinquish his gun, and in the end, he betrays Jesus as Judas does in every iteration of the Jesus story. In this case he does so by providing video recordings of Jesus' speeches and activities to the local authorities, named Caiaphas and Annas, whom the foreign dictator (Pilate) has tacitly authorized to make Jesus disappear. These recordings are meant to provide evidence of Jesus' treason.

Moments of transcendence

The moments of transcendence occur most powerfully in the final scenes of the film, which overturn the conventional story of Jesus' crucifixion. Jesus has been killed by the henchmen of the regime and buried in an unmarked grave, but Mary and his closest followers find him and dig him up. Mary rides in the back of a pickup truck, her dead son laid out across her knees in the classic *pietà* pose.

One might expect his mother and followers to rebury him with dignity, but the opposite occurs: they put him up on a cross. Instead of nailing him to the crossbeam, they tie his hands with a red ribbon. At this point, astonishment has already set in, due to the striking departure from the Gospel narratives. To reverse the death and the crucifixion: that is a stunning, even blasphemous, movie.

People make a determined pilgrimage to the site. Mary is calm, sad, and resigned. She and a handful of Jesus' followers look down from the platform

Figure 10.3 Crucifixion and resistance, *Son of Man*.

at the gathering crowds below. Then the camera zooms in for an extreme close-up, as she closes her eyes and begins to sing mournfully: "The land is covered in darkness." One by the one other voices pick up the tune, and one starts a harmony. The sound becomes stronger and stronger, as more women, then also men, join in. As the crowds now sing together, they swarm the platform. Mary is now standing tall, her crucified son elevated on the cross behind her. The crowds dance, clap their hands; the dirge has changed to a "toyi-toyi" – song and dance of protest[22] – becoming more and more defiant, but still peaceful. An army helicopter hovers overhead; the camera cuts to an army vehicle headed for the singing and dancing protesters. The soldiers rush the platform, their leader shouting "I'm going to give you five minutes to disperse." Many do leave, but there are still dozens of men and women singing and dancing on the platform. Suddenly shots are heard; people scream, the chanting stops. Will the soldiers gun the protesters down? That is what we might expect, given the pervasive violence, from the massacre which opens the film to the surreptitious killing and burial of Jesus himself.

But no. After a moment of paralysis, Mary, who had been crouched down on the platform like everyone else, slowly stands up. Her back still to the camera, she looks over her shoulder at the soldiers behind her, and then at her son hanging on the cross beside her. She moves slowly toward the soldiers.

The others also slowly rise to their feet. The guns are still aimed at them, but they are silent now. Mary plants her legs shoulder width apart in the utter silence, then she begins again: "The land is covered in darkness." The followers all join in and this time the energy builds quickly and powerfully,

Figure 10.4 Resurrection, *Son of Man.*

as they toyi-toyi. They look directly into the camera, placing us, the spectators, in the subject position of the soldiers. But we too can only be silent in the face of their determination and the power of their protest. The camera zooms in on Mary and the others at the front of the group, then cuts quickly to a folk painting on a fence, depicting her son on the cross as the followers dance.

There is near silence; any ambient noise is muted. The camera then cuts to a barren hill, shadow, and a new song – "The sun in Spring will rise over the mountain, today we are united" – but one which has appeared numerous times in the film to this point, as a marker of Jesus' movement and the hope it provided. The shadow falls over a crater in the barren earth, a shadow of an adult soon joined by many smaller shadows. The song of hope grows stronger, and we see that the person making the shadow is Jesus, now restored to life triumphant, in the company of playful and joyful child angels. They run up the hill toward the now-empty platform and the now-empty cross, a heavenly choir met with ululation.

Jesus looks back at the camera and raises his arm in joy and triumph. The movie is over. A scrolled text now appears, proclaiming the dignity and divinity of all human beings: "And God said let us make man in our image after our likeness," (Gen. 1:26; KJV). The credits roll, to every day scenes from the townships.[23]

Despite the deviation of this ending from the Gospel Passion narratives, the film evokes the Gospel of John by showing the cross as an instrument not of death but of exaltation. The tension of this last scene, and its joyful resolution brings home to many the message of Christ as a champion of the oppressed, but also, even more powerfully, the power of hope and the ability of faith, song, and dance to unite people and give them strength in the face of adversity.

Filming transcendence

In these films, moments of transcendence are fleeting, and secondary to the main themes. We turn now to two films in which transcendence is a major theme, and which therefore, through a broad range of techniques, attempt to draw the viewer into that experience in a sustained way.

Babette's Feast *(1987)*

Plot summary

The Danish film *Babette's Feast*, based on a story by Isak Dinesen (Karen Blixen), is set in the late nineteenth century, in a tiny village in Jutland, Denmark. It focuses on two elderly sisters, Martine and Filippa, whose father had founded a very strict, ascetic Christian sect. In the story's "present time" the sisters are anticipating the hundredth anniversary of their father's birth, which they plan to commemorate with their tiny, aging, and increasingly querulous flock. Surprisingly – given the severeness and austerity of their surroundings and their religious asceticism – they employ a housekeeper, Babette, who serves them and the congregation. In a lengthy flashback, we learn of the foreign suitor that each sister turned away when they were young. Martine's wealthy beau was a handsome but dissipate soldier, Lorens Löwenhielm; he departed abruptly after deciding that he could not live the sort of life to which she was committed. Filippa's admirer was the famous Parisian opera singer Achille Papin, who was dazzled by her voice and her beauty, offered her singing lessons, and fell in love. She put an end to the romance, uncomfortable with his attentions, and disturbed by the romantic content of the repertoire. Both sisters remained, contentedly enough, in their small village, and took on the leadership of their sect after their father's death.

Babette appeared some 35 years after the young men's departure, during a dark and stormy night, exhausted and bedraggled. She carried little but a letter of introduction from Papin. The letter explained that Babette was fleeing Paris after the murder of her husband and son at the hands of Gaston Alexandre Auguste, Marquis de Galliffet, during the violent repression of the Paris Commune in the spring of 1871, and that she "knows how to cook."

After 14 years of service to the sisters, for room and board, Babette receives a letter from France: she has won 10,000 francs in the Paris lottery. She asks permission to prepare a dinner to celebrate their father's centenary, at her own expense. Despite their misgivings – food is for sustenance, not enjoyment – the sisters agree. Preparations are complex, and the results delectable. On the menu: "Potage à la Tortue" (turtle soup); "Blinis Demidoff au

Caviar" (buckwheat cakes with caviar and sour cream); "Caille en Sarcophage avec Sauce Perigourdine" (quail in puff pastry shell with foie gras and truffle sauce); a salad featuring Belgian chicory and walnuts in a vinaigrette; and "Les Fromages" featuring blue cheese, papaya, figs, grapes, pineapple, and pomegranate. Dessert: "Savarin au Rhum avec des Figues et Fruits Glacées" (rum sponge cake with figs and glacéed fruits). This sumptuous meal is accompanied by the most exquisite, and expensive, wines and champagnes, including an 1845 Clos de Vougeot, and an 1860 Veuve Clicquot, and all is served on beautiful china dishes and crystal stemware. The meal is attended by the small community and, unexpectedly, by Lorens Löwenhielm. The sisters reluctantly accept that Babette will now leave them and return to Paris. But she stays; the meal has consumed her entire winnings, and in any case they are now her family.

Biblical quotations

Given the Christian faith of the sisters and their community, the presence of biblical quotations is hardly surprising. Lorens Löwenhielm, now almost 50 years older and wiser, quotes Ecclesiastes 1:2 – "Vanity of vanities … vanity of vanities! All is vanity" – as he dresses for dinner, expressing regret for the choices he made as an ambitious and foolish young man. During the meal itself, one of the elderly parishioners greets the dessert – the mounds of fresh grapes and figs – by quoting Numbers 13:23:

> And they [the spies sent by Moses on a reconnoitering mission to the Promised land] came to the Wadi Eshcol, and cut down from there a branch with a single cluster of grapes, and they carried it on a pole between two of them. They also brought some pomegranates and figs.

Babette herself is a Christ-figure; the camera focuses frequently on the cross she wears around her neck.[24] Just as the crowds marveled when Jesus multiplied the loaves and fishes, so do the sisters remark with surprise that since Babette came they have more money. On one level the reason is obvious: Babette is shrewd and she drives a hard bargain with the local grocer and fishermen. But from the sisters' perspective, the bounty that she provides is a mysterious gift.

The messianic banquet

But the experience of transcendence is not found in the biblical quotations or the characterization of Babette. It is found in the feast itself, a messianic banquet not only for those who partake but for those who watch it being lovingly prepared, served, and enjoyed. The association of abundant, luxurious, exotic food and drink with a future but coming age of peace and reconciliation is attested in biblical texts, post-biblical Jewish sources, and early

Christian texts. Isaiah 25:5–6 assures us that "on that day" and "on this mountain" the LORD of hosts will make for all peoples a "feast of rich food, a feast of well-aged wines, of rich food filled with marrow, of well-aged wines strained clear." Isaiah 55:1–2 picks up the theme again, by calling on "everyone who thirsts, come to the waters; and you that have no money, come, buy and eat! Come, buy wine and milk without money and without price.... eat what is good, and delight yourselves in rich food." This is precisely the offer that Babette makes to the sisters and their small flock.

According to Proverbs 9, Lady Wisdom connects the eating of fine, abundant food, with spiritual maturity:

> She has slaughtered her animals, she has mixed her wine, she has also set her table.[3] She has sent out her servant-girls, she calls from the highest places in the town,[4] "You that are simple, turn in here!" To those without sense she says,[5] "Come, eat of my bread and drink of the wine I have mixed.[6] Lay aside immaturity, and live, and walk in the way of insight.
>
> (Prov. 9:2–6)

While these passages specify bread and wine, the pseudepigraphic book 2 Baruch adds a number of exotic items to the menu, promising that "it shall come to pass when all is accomplished that was to come to pass in those parts, that the Messiah shall then begin to be revealed.[4] And Behemoth shall be revealed from his place and Leviathan shall ascend from the sea, those two great monsters which I created on the fifth day of creation, and shall have kept until that time; and then they shall be for food for all that are left." The giant turtle who gives his life for Babette's sublime turtle soup may be more charming in appearance than we usually imagine the monsters Behemoth and Leviathan, but they are all related. 2 Baruch continues by promising unimaginable abundance:

> The earth also shall yield its fruit ten thousandfold and on each vine there shall be a thousand branches, and each branch shall produce a thousand clusters, and each cluster produce a thousand grapes, and each grape produce a cor of wine.
>
> (2 Baruch 29:3)

The theme of the messianic banquet also underlies the Wedding at Cana (John 2:1–12), in which the chief steward praises the bridegroom for the excellence and abundance of the wine that appeared after the initial batch had run out (2:10). In all four gospels Jesus multiplies loaves and fishes to feed hungry crowds that run into the thousands (Matt. 14:13–21, 15:32–39; Mark 6:31–44, 8:1–9; Luke 9:10–17; John 6:5–15). These miracle stories highlight Jesus' miraculous abilities but also suggest the abundance that will be ours in a future, perfect world.[25] The same message is conveyed by the banquet parables in the Gospel of Luke (Luke 14, 15, 22).

But the biblical meal to which *Babette's Feast* most obviously alludes is the Last Supper that Jesus shared with his disciples before his death. In both cases, the guests numbered 12, and both occasions were momentous. The moods are very different, however; whereas the Last Supper is sombre and marked by the recognition that one of those at the table is about to betray Jesus and lead to his death, *Babette's Feast* is joyous and welcomes a guest rather than banishes a betrayer. Whereas Jesus is present at the Last Supper to speak directly to his followers, Babette is absent from the table. The meaning of her artistic and spiritual achievement is provided by Lorens Löwenhielm, the outsider to the community. Only he truly understands who she is and the heavenly grandeur of what she is providing, though he has never met her and does not set eyes on her at any point during the meal. Perhaps he is best understood as an evangelist. He can see, more clearly than those among whom she lives, who exactly it is that has provided this feast for them to enjoy, and is therefore able to convey what she can teach them about how to live in the world and in the spirit.

Transcendence

The film is transcendent on a number of different planes. Diegetically, that is, within the narrative world created by the film, Babette's feast is a vehicle through which the small community can transcend its own narrow vision of Christian piety. Babette herself does not set out to critique or undermine their asceticism. On the contrary, she does her best to adapt to the much simpler cooking style of the community. But the feast that she prepares requires them to go far outside their comfort zone, into a sphere that they anticipate with horror and fear. But their fear turns to joy during the experience itself, due to the inherent pleasures of good food, drink, and companionship, and the sense of special occasion, and, most important, they realize that abundance is not a barrier but, on the contrary, a path toward the divine, when it is prepared and consumed in the spirit of selfless love. The meal is truly a foretaste of the world to come, of the Jerusalem about which they sing on a daily basis. Like prayer and music, the meal helps them transcend the bonds of this earthly life, at least for an evening, and to see what awaits them in that other, future dimension. In doing so, the meal allows them to overcome their squabbling and to set aside age-old regrets and resentments, and become a loving community again.

Extra-diegetically, that is, for the viewer, this movie transcends the usual norms of realistic films to create a different viewing experience. The abundance and luxurious nature of the meal is matched, indeed, enhanced, cinematically by the abundant and close attention paid to all phases of preparation. Although we do not see the purchase or ordering of the food, we watch as it comes ashore and is carried to the sisters' home. We look on as the food is prepared, arranged and then served. The scenes are long and slow, featuring extreme close-ups of Babette's hands as she works. The transformative nature of the meal is further emphasized by the use of color. Whereas the first half of the film is in the sombre greys and browns that convey the simplicity and severity of the sisters' lifestyle, the second half of the film, devoted to the Feast, are in riotous colour, a feast for the eyes that allows viewers to experience vicariously the feast for the palate that Babette has prepared.

The Tree of Life *(2011)*

Plot summary

A far more unusual film is director Terrence Malick's strange and intense *The Tree of Life*. This film is a coming-of-age story of sorts, set primarily in Texas in the 1950s and 1960s. But this genre description does not begin to do justice to the complexity of the film, which truly defies description or synopsis.[26] The plot outline is easily recounted. Early in the film, a mother and father in Texas receive word that one of their three sons, a soldier, has died, perhaps in battle, though this is not stated.[27] This opening leads us to expect a film about the ways in which the parents and remaining two sons come to terms with, or fail to come to terms with, the untimely and sudden death of a loved one. And in a sense, the film is indeed about this process of grief and acceptance, as seen particularly through the eyes of the oldest brother, Jack, and the parents, Mr. and Mrs. O'Brien (their first names are never revealed, though we come to know them intimately).

But this brief description does not begin to convey what this movie is about, or, more precisely, what it feels like to watch it. The film's structure is non-linear: we are introduced to the family and its tragedy, then treated to a 20-minute visual and musical meditation on the creation of the world and the origins and evolution of life. This is followed by Jack's coming-of-age story in "the traditional family where father rules, mother loves, and Oedipus stirs."[28] Much of the film consists of Jack's flashbacks to their childhood, within the home of their empathetic mother and loving but overly strict father, and outside in the bucolic fields and streams, the three brothers together, apart, and with their friends. These flashbacks focus on those moments of both grace and cruelty that are part of family relationships. Interspersed are occasional "present day" moments of the adult, mature Jack, and his life as a successful architect. These scenes underline the contrast between Jack's present life, bound by the steel and cement structures which he builds, in which he works, and in which he lives, and the leafy green environment in which he grew up. The film concludes with a second vision, this time of a future or perhaps present alternate universe where all our loved ones will be together in one place. Jack and his mother reunite with his dead brother, the younger selves of his family, of himself, and many others. As we watch, caught up in this moment of grace, we are unsure as to whether this is "real" or Jack's dream or vision (or both real and a vision).

This final scene brings to a powerful climax the emotions and impressions that have been building up since the first frame. The story can be described variously, even within the same review, for example, as the "story of a single life drawn upward to God" but also as "the story of two contrary motions: a soul being drawn into the mystery of God's grace in the midst of the downward pull of human nature."[29] Kristen Scharold notes that:

> The final scenes of the film are not a vision of the afterlife (Jack never dies) but rather a highly abstract rendering of the experience of stepping into faith. After nearly two and a half hours of recounting the tuggings of grace, *The Tree of Life* attempts to capture the moment of reconciliation with God. As Sean Penn walks through the symbolic desert, admitting how he has long wandered through the world, the viewer sees him pass through a door where he meets his younger self. Time is split by eternity. Jack finds himself reunited with his family on the sands of a reflective beach. All the strands of Jack's memory that brought him to faith are there: love, suffering, beauty, his childhood, his father, his brother, his mother. Incredibly, the viewer hears the words, "I give you my Son." This is the climax of belief. And when the camera leaves Jack's mind and views him again from the outside, the only indication of change is the mysterious smile on Sean Penn's face as he stands outside his office. But that is enough.[30]

Mrs. O'Brien gives God back her son. This is her moment of reconciliation with God; in an act of unsurpassable grace, she forgives God for taking her son by freely giving him back. In the end Jack too chooses grace, a choice he could only have made by nature, that is, by the scars that he bears due to his father's harsh love, and the apparent indifference of God and the universe to the immense tragedy that has defined his adult life.

The way of nature and the way of grace

The theme of the movie is announced early on, by Mrs. O'Brien. She recalls:

> The nuns taught us there were two ways through life – the way of nature and the way of grace. You have to choose which one you'll follow.... Grace doesn't try to please itself. Accepts being slighted, forgotten, disliked. Accepts insults and injuries.... Nature only wants to please itself. Get others to please it too. Likes to lord it over them. To have its way. It finds reasons to be unhappy when all the world is shining around it. And love is smiling through all things.... The nuns taught us that no one who loves the way of grace ever comes to a bad end.

In this film, Mrs. O'Brien represents the way of grace – loving, tolerant, all-embracing, forgiving. Mr. O'Brien represents the way of nature – attempting to control others, to dominate a recalcitrant earth into yielding produce, and to bully stubborn and sometimes fearful children into obedience. Yet he too loves his children and occasionally shows it. In the aftermath of his son's death, he recognizes that perhaps he was too hard on his children. Perhaps after all the way of nature must give way to the way of grace. He acknowledges: "I wanted to be loved because I was great; A big man. I'm nothing. Look at the glory around us; trees, birds. I lived in shame. I dishonored it all, and didn't notice the glory. I'm a foolish man." Here nature seems to be negative, but even in these words, Mr. O'Brien shows us a different side of nature: its glory.

Indeed, nature is essential to the way of grace that Mrs. O'Brien embodies. Mrs. O'Brien reflects on grace as she swings idly on the swing hung between sun dappled trees. It may be obvious that grace is the better way, but what the film shows is the inextricability of these two paths, the appeal and the dangers of both, and therefore the difficulty in choosing between them. It is this same struggle that defines Jack's path to adulthood, and that seems to be resolved for him only in his final beatific vision of life everlasting. Early in the film, Jack whispers: "Brother. Mother. It was they who led me to your door." He later acknowledges: "Mother, father, always you wrestle inside me, always you will."

Technique and transcendence

The experience of transcendence is fostered by a number of specific cinematic techniques. The plot line itself – in which a man comes to an acceptance of his life and some sort of perception of a larger mystery and reality beyond his own life (perhaps God) – encourages us to follow this path. The dialog is also important, particularly the whispered questions, insights, phrases, reactions, of Jack and his mother, which sound like petitions, conversations, or arguments with God. The use of voice-over is particularly effective, for it evokes not only the notion of prayer or at least communication with an all-powerful being, but also intimacy with the viewer. Mrs. O'Brien and Jack are whispering their deepest thoughts and questions right in our ears, making us feel that we are the ones to whom they are addressed and from whom they expect answers. But we don't have answers to these existential questions; that being the case, they must be addressed to a greater being, a God, who in theory does know more than we do.

The images are also central to this film's impact on the viewer. The first visual meditation portrays the swirling cosmos in the moment before creation, and the dinosaurs roaming the forests, but also a father's wonder at the tiny foot of his new born child, and that child's loving gaze at his mother, and his horror when his friend drowns in a swimming pool. The film itself is framed, beginning and end, with a single flickering flame (coincidentally, also the final image in *Babette's Feast*). As A. O. Scott notes in his review,

At the beginning and the conclusion – alpha and omega – we gaze on a flickering flame that can only represent the creator. Not Mr. Malick (who prefers to remain unseen in public) but the elusive deity whose presence in the world is both the film's overt subject and the source of its deepest, most anxious mysteries.[31]

As in Pasolini's film, music is central to the experience. The film's soundtrack features a "playlist" of approximately 37 pieces, including works or parts of works by François Couperin, Bach, Berlioz, Brahms, Smetana, Mahler, Holst, Górecki, and Tavener, woven together with some original music by Alexandre Desplat.[32] The music is not only extra-diegetic – musical accompaniment that presumably is not "heard" by the characters in the movie – but also diegetic. Music is important for understanding the character of Mr. O'Brien, a superb but frustrated pianist who also tries, in a heavy-handed and joyless way, to make music a part of his children's lives. His passion leads to a strict requirement for silence at the dinner table, so that full attention can be given to the recording that he has chosen for the family to hear at the meal. Scott concludes that the film itself is like a musical composition; its four sections are more like movements of a musical piece "than the conventional 'acts' of a screenplay." Like great music, the film proceeds by layering and recasting themes rather than by telling a linear narrative.

> And it depends on the contrapuntal arrangement of contrasting ideas: time and eternity; past and present; masculine and feminine; innocence and experience. And, perhaps above all, human and divine.[33]

Biblical quotations

And speaking of the divine: the Bible has no small role to play in the way in which this film exerts its power, its magic, over the audience. As in most of the other films that we have looked at, the use of the Bible is overt, direct, explicit. It begins in the first frames, with a scrolling text from Job 38:4, 7: "Where were you when I laid the foundations of the earth? ... When the moving stars sang together, and all the sons of God shouted for joy?" Only after seeing and thinking about the film, and feeling its power and resonances, does the tremendous aptness of this epigraph become clear. The situation of Job is evoked elsewhere in the film. Most obviously, the O'Brien family experiences the depths of loss and tragedy of Job, if not in quantity then certainly in quality. Like Job, Jack and his mother interrogate God, seriously, persistently, until some reconciliation is achieved. The book of Job is also the subject of the sermon that Father Haynes preaches after the boy's death.

In the context of the book of Job, these words in 38:4,7 are part of God's speech in the whirlwind, which chastises Job for questioning the source and purpose of his misfortunes. But in the film, the interrogative form, and the large, searching, almost pleading tone are echoed through the voice-overs of Jack and Mrs. O'Brien, which run as a refrain throughout the entire film. It is as if the suffering ones – the Job figures – question God, and not the other way around. Second, it evokes the time before creation, as a time of perfect joy and harmony between God and God's creation, cavorting in the cosmos. This same era is visualized in the 20-minute extravaganza tracing the creation of the world and the evolution of living creatures. In this way, the quotation, like the visual meditation, reminds Job, and all humankind, of their smallness in the face of the vastness and eternity of the cosmos. Third, it evokes the emotions of joy and wonder that are integral to the "way of grace," the followers of which will never die.

In her period of deep mourning after her son's death, Mrs. O'Brien whispers the words from Psalms 22:11: "Be not far from me for trouble is near." And as the young Jack struggles with his impulses, and the guilt over his cruelty to his younger brother, he thinks, "What I want to do, I can't do. I do what I hate," the quintessential human struggle described so vividly by the apostle Paul in Romans 7:15. Our struggles may seem unique to us, just as Jack's do to him, but the Pauline quotation points out that the struggle between the way of nature and the way of grace is a fact of human existence.

Most obvious, and perhaps also most important, however, is the film's title itself. The tree of life is first mentioned in Genesis 2:9: "Out of the ground the LORD God made to grow every tree that is pleasant to the sight and good for food, the tree of life also in the midst of the garden, and the tree of the knowledge of good and evil." The tree is mentioned twice more in Genesis, both times in connection with the eventual expulsion of the primordial couple from the Garden of Eden or paradise. Genesis 3:22 introduces the notion of mortality: "Then the LORD God said, 'See, the man has become like one of us, knowing good and evil; and now, he might reach out his hand and take also from the tree of life, and eat, and live forever.'" Genesis 3:24 describes the primordial couple's expulsion from the garden, and the need to protect the tree of life from human interference: "He drove out the man; and at the east of the garden of Eden he placed the cherubim, and a sword flaming and turning to guard the way to the tree of life."

Genesis treats the tree of life as a highly desirable, divinely created tree that is forbidden to mere mortals. It takes on a much more positive, and metaphorical, meaning in the Book of Proverbs. Proverbs 3:18 describes Wisdom as "a tree of life to those who lay hold of her; those who hold her fast are called happy." In Jewish tradition wisdom in this verse became equated with the Torah, and this verse is sung liturgically at the moment that the Torah is returned to the ark after having been read during communal prayer. Elsewhere in Proverbs, the tree of life is associated with happiness or positive behaviors or values. Proverbs 11:30 describes the fruit of the righteous as the tree of life, which however can be destroyed by violence; Proverbs 13:12 declares that "Hope deferred makes the heart sick, but a desire fulfilled is a tree of life," while Proverbs 15:4 states that "A gentle tongue is a tree of life, but perverseness in it breaks the spirit." In these verses, the tree of life is that which is positive and life-giving.

The association of the tree of life and paradise, Eden and God's primordial creation, returns in the book of Revelation, in which the *eschaton*, that time after the present world order has passed away, is described as a return to paradise. Revelation 22:2 states that "the river of the water of life" runs "through the middle of the street of the city. On either side of the river is the tree of life with its twelve kinds of fruit, producing its fruit each month; and the leaves of the tree are for the healing of the nations." Revelation 2:7 promises that "everyone who conquers" will receive "permission to eat from the tree of life that is in the paradise of God." In other words, life is the overcoming of mortality or death. Revelation 22:14 promises that "those who wash their robes … will have the right to the tree of life and may enter the city by the gates." By the same token, Revelation 22:19 threatens that "if anyone takes away from the words of the book of this prophecy, God will take away that person's share in the tree of life and in the holy city, which are described in this book."

The Tree of Life holds within it these different meanings and nuances of the biblical tree of life. Its images evoke the primordial creation and ascribe it to God, who, as Mrs. O'Brien tells her young children, lives in the sky. R. L.'s death ruptures the family just as the introduction of mortality ruptured Eden. The desire of Jack and his parents to regain spiritual and emotional equilibrium after their tragedy is akin to a return to paradise, a return that is envisioned in the final scenes of the film. The Proverbs passages describe the way of grace that Mrs. O'Brien tries to teach her children, a way that includes love for all creation, goodness, positive desires, and a gentle tongue.

Certainly film, as a highly absorbing entertainment medium, allows us to escape our own thoughts, concerns, worries, preoccupations, at least for a time. But movies can also – at times – transport us so far from our daily lives that we experience transcendence; like Philo, we soar above the world as we know it, and glimpse, even if only for a moment, the possibility of a world beyond our own, one that can add meaning to our own mundane lives.

Notes

1 See also *The Testament of Abraham*, www.newadvent.org/fathers/1007.htm (accessed 10 May 2013).
2 Philo, *On the Special Laws* III, 1–6. (www.earlychristianwritings.com/yonge/book29.html [accessed 10 May 2013). See also Dream of Scipio. 6.16: "When I gazed in every direction from that point, all else appeared wonderfully beautiful. There were stars which we never see from the earth, and they were all much larger than we have ever imagined … The starry spheres were much larger than the earth; indeed the earth itself seemed to me so small that I was scornful of our empire, which covers only a single point, as it were, upon its surface."

3 Robert Neelly Bellah, *Religion in Human Evolution: From the Paleolithic to the Axial Age* (Cambridge, MA: Belknap Press of Harvard University Press, 2011), 3.

4 Ibid.

5 Carl R. Plantinga, *Moving Viewers: American Film and the Spectator's Experience* (Berkeley, CA: University of California Press, 2009), 5. For a phenomenological analysis of transcendence in "spiritual" or "religious" films, see Vivian Sobchack, "Embodying Transcendence: On the Literal, the Material, and the Cinematic Sublime," *Material Religion: The Journal of Objects, Art and Belief* 4, no. 2 (2008): 194–203.

6 Michael Gibson, *The Mill and the Cross: Peter Bruegel's "Way to Calvary"* (Lausanne: Editions Acatos, 2000).

7 www.filmjournal.com/filmjournal/content_display/reviews/specialty-releases/e3i4829807a140cf52df9c006f9067dc8a9 12 September 2011 (accessed 29 May 2012).

8 http://fest11.sffs.org/films/film_details.php?id=61 (accessed 29 May 2012).

9 www.hollywoodreporter.com/review/mill-cross-berlin-review-97627 (accessed 29 May 2012).

10 Posted 22 September 2011, www.philly.com/philly/columnists/carrie_rickey/20110923_The_restaging_of_how_a_painting_came_to_be.html (accessed 29 May 2012).

11 Plantinga, *Moving Viewers*, 5.

12 Ibid.

13 Ibid., 78.

14 Ibid., 80.

15 Ibid., 111.

16 Ibid.

17 Bellah, *Religion in Human Evolution*, 21–43.

18 On the role of narrative in human nature and experience, see Jonathan Gottschall, *The Storytelling Animal: How Stories Make us Human* (Boston, MA: Houghton Mifflin Harcourt, 2012).

19 Another obvious example is *The Truman Show* in which a character is trapped inside a television show and finally escapes. See Adele Reinhartz, "The Truman Show and the Great Escape from Paradise (Genesis)," in *Scripture on the Silver Screen* (Louisville, KY: Westminster John Knox Press, 2003), 5–23.

20 See Ibid.; Adele Reinhartz, "The Shawshank Redemption and the Redemption That Lies Within (1 Corinthians)," *Scripture on the Silver Screen* (Louisville, KY: Westminster John Knox Press, 2003), 129–43.

21 Birds are used throughout the film as a symbol of freedom. For example, Brooks, the old convict, has a bird named Jake whom he cares for, and then releases immediately before he himself is released on parole. During the scene in which Andy plays a recording of a Mozart aria, birds are seen flying above the prison yard. For further discussion, see Robert Jewett, "A Problematic Hope for the Shamed in The Shawshank Redemption," in *Saint Paul Returns to the Movies: Triumph over Shame* (Grand Rapids, MI: William B. Eerdmans, 1999), 168.

22 The toyi-toyi is a rhythm used to convey political dissent and express the desire for human rights and justice. It is "characterized by regular beats produced by a stationary but vigorous dance, and punctuated by a simple pattern of off-beats articulated by political watchwords." Ian Peddie, *Popular Music and Human Rights* (Farnham, Surrey, England; Burlington, VT: Ashgate, 2011), 40.

23 For more detailed analyses of this wonderful film, see Richard Walsh, Jeffrey L. Staley, and Adele Reinhartz, ed., *Son of Man: An African Jesus Film*, Bible in the Modern World 52 (Sheffield: Sheffield Phoenix Press, 2013).

24 See S. D. Giere, "Babette's Feast (1987)," in *Bible and Cinema: Fifty Key Films*, ed. Adele Reinhartz (New York: Routledge, 2012), 18–23, and Baugh, *Imaging the Divine*, 137–45.

25 The Feeding of the 5,000 appears in all four canonical Gospels (Matt. 14:13–21, Mark 6:31–44, Luke 9:10–17, and John 6:5–15). "The Feeding of the 4,000" is reported by Mark 8:1–9 and Matthew 15:32–39.

26 It is almost impossible to write about this film. Stone comments that "After seeing the film for a third time, I believe that any verbal interpretation, right or wrong, could not be aesthetically faithful to Malick's visual masterpiece." Alan A. Stone, "The Tree of Life (Review)," *Journal of Religion and Film* 15, no. 2 (October 2011): 5. http://www.unomaha.edu/jrf/Vol15no2/Reviews/StoneTreeLife.html (accessed 10 May 2013).

27 Some have suggested that the brother was modeled on Malick's own brother, who suffered from severe depression and committed suicide, www.thepointmag.com/2011/reviews/terrence-malicks-song-of-himself (accessed 10 May 2013).

28 Stone, "The Tree of Life (Review)."

29 Kristen Scharold, "The Tree of Life (Review)," *Books and Culture*, 29 June 2012, www.booksandculture.com/articles/webexclusives/2011/june/treelife.html (accessed 10 May 2013).

30 Ibid.

31 A. O. Scott, "The Tree of Life (Review)," *The New York Times*, 26 May 2011, http://movies.nytimes.com/2011/05/27/movies/the-tree-of-life-from-terrence-malick-review.html?pagewanted=print (accessed 10 May 2013).

32 Culture Monster, "Terrence Malick's 'Tree of Life': The Classical Music Factor," *LA Times*, n.d., http://latimesblogs.latimes.com/culturemonster/2011/07/tree-of-life-terrence-malick.html (accessed 10 May 2013) for the list and some MP3s.

33 A. O. Scott, "Fugue for History and Memory," *The New York Times*, 30 December 2011, sec. Movies/Awards Season, www.nytimes.com/2012/01/01/movies/awardsseason/a-o-scott-on-the-musical-movement-of-the-tree-of-life.html?ref=awardsseason (accessed 10 May 2013).

Bibliography

"A Family Portrait of the Alpha Centauri System – VLT Interferometer Studies the Nearest Stars." www.eso.org (accessed 16 December 2012). www.eso.org/public/news/eso0307.

Aitken, Tom. "Night of the Hunter (1955)." In *Bible and Cinema: Fifty Key Films*, edited by Adele Reinhartz, 192–96. New York: Routledge, 2012.

Alessio, Dominic and Kristen Meredith. "Decolonising James Cameron's Pandora: Imperial History and Science Fiction." *Journal of Colonialism and Colonial History* 13, no. 2 (2012). http://muse.jhu.edu.proxy.bib.uottawa.ca/journals/journal_of_colonialism_and_colonial_history/v013/13.2.alessio.html (accessed 10 May 2013).

Altman, Rick. *Silent Film Sound*. New York: Columbia University Press, 2004.

Amanat, Abbas and Magnus Thorkell Bernhardsson. *Imagining the End: Visions of Apocalypse from the Ancient Middle East to Modern America*. London; New York: I. B. Tauris, 2002.

Anker, Roy M. *Catching Light: Looking for God in the Movies*. Grand Rapids, MI: W. B. Eerdmans, 2004.

Arbitron. *The Arbitron Cinema Advertising Study: Appointment Viewing by Young, Affluent, Captive Audiences*, n.d. www.adbay.com/downloads/Arbitron_Cinema_Study.pdf (accessed 9 May 2013).

Arnheim, Rudolf. *Film Essays and Criticism*. Madison, WI: University of Wisconsin Press, 1997.

Arterbury, A. E. "Abraham's Hospitality among Jewish and Early Christian Writers: A Tradition History of Gen 18:1–16 and Its Relevance for the Study of the New Testament." *Perspectives in Religious Studies* 30, no. 3 (2003): 359–76.

Auerbach, Erich. *Mimesis: The Representation of Reality in Western Literature*. Princeton, NJ: Princeton University Press, 1953.

Augustine, *The City of God*. Trans. Marcus Dods. From Nicene and Post-Nicene Fathers, First Series, vol. 2, ed. Philip Schaff. Buffalo, NY: Christian Literature Publishing Co., 1887. Rev. ed. by Kevin Knight. www.newadvent.org/fathers/120116.htm (accessed 10 May 2013).

Babington, Bruce and Peter William Evans. *Biblical Epics: Sacred Narrative in the Hollywood Cinema*. Manchester; New York: Manchester University Press; St. Martin's Press, 1993.

Bach, Alice. *Biblical Glamour and Hollywood Glitz*. Atlanta, GA: Scholars Press, 1996.

Bahrani, Shahriar. *The Kingdom of Solomon*. Drama, History, 2010. www.imdb.com/title/tt1706450 (accessed 9 May 2013).

Bailey, Lloyd R. *Capital Punishment: What the Bible Says*. Nashville, TN: Abingdon Press, 1987.

Bakker, Freek L. *The Challenge of the Silver Screen: An Analysis of the Cinematic Portraits of Jesus, Rama, Buddha and Muhammad.* Studies in Religion and the Arts v. 1. Leiden; Boston, MA: Brill, 2009.

Balentine, Samuel E. *Prayer in the Hebrew Bible: The Drama of Divine-human Dialogue.* Overtures to Biblical Theology. Minneapolis, MN: Augsburg Fortress, 1993.

Barton, William and Michael Capobianco. *Alpha Centauri.* New York: Avon Books, 1997.

Baugh, Lloyd. *Imaging the Divine: Jesus and Christ-Figures in Film.* Communication, Culture & Theology. Kansas City, MO: Sheed & Ward, 1997.

Baugh, Scott L. *Latino American Cinema: An Encyclopedia of Movies, Stars, Concepts, and Trends.* Santa Barbara, CA: Greenwood, 2012.

Beavis, Mary Ann. "'Angels Carrying Savage Weapons': Uses of the Bible in Contemporary Horror Films," *Journal of Religion and Film* 7 (2003), www.unomaha. edu/jrf/Vol7No2/angels.htm (accessed 10 May 2013).

——. "Pseudapocrypha: Invented Scripture in Apocalyptic Horror Films." In *Reel Revelations*, edited by John Walliss and Lee Quinby, 75–90. Sheffield: Phoenix, 2010.

Bellah, Robert Neelly. *Religion in Human Evolution: From the Paleolithic to the Axial Age.* Cambridge, MA: Belknap Press of Harvard University Press, 2011.

Belton, John. "Introduction." In *Movies and Mass Culture*, 1–22. Rutgers Depth of Field Series. New Brunswick, NJ: Rutgers University Press, 1996.

Benshoff, Harry M. *America on Film: Representing Race, Class, Gender, and Sexuality at the Movies.* Malden, MA: Blackwell Pub., 2004.

Bercovitch, Sacvan. *The Puritan Origins of the American Self.* New Haven, CT: Yale University Press, 1975.

——. "The Biblical Basis of the American Myth." In *The Bible and American Arts and Letters*, edited by Giles B. Gunn, 219–29. Philadelphia, PA; Chico, CA: Fortress Press; Scholars Press, 1983.

——. *The Rites of Assent: Transformations in the Symbolic Construction of America.* New York: Routledge, 1993.

Berlin, Adele and Maxine Grossman. *The Oxford Dictionary of the Jewish Religion.* Oxford University Press, 2011.

Bernstein, Matthew. *Controlling Hollywood: Censorship and Regulation in the Studio Era.* New Brunswick, NJ: Rutgers University Press, 1999.

Bien, Peter. "Nikos Kazantzakis's Novels on Film." *Journal of Modern Greek Studies* 18, no. 1 (2000): 161–69.

Birch, Bruce C. "The Arts, Midrash, and Biblical Teaching." *Teaching Theology and Religion* 8, no. 2 (2005): 114–22.

Birnbaum, Ellen. *The Place of Judaism in Philo's Thought: Israel, Jews, and Proselytes.* Brown Judaic Studies no. 290. Atlanta, GA: Scholars Press, 1996.

Black, Gregory D. "Hollywood Censored: The Production Code Administration and the Hollywood Film Industry, 1930–40." *Film History* 3, no. 3 (1 January 1989): 167–89.

——. *Hollywood Censored: Morality Codes, Catholics, and the Movies.* Cambridge; New York: Cambridge University Press, 1994.

Blake, William. *America: Poem.* Edited by Paul Peter Piech. Bushey Heath, Herts.: Taurus Press of Willow Dene, 1977.

Blomberg, Craig. *Jesus and the Gospels: An Introduction and Survey.* Nashville, TN: Broadman & Holman, 1997.

Bondanella, Peter E. *A History of Italian Cinema*. New York: Continuum International Pub. Group, 2009.

Boozer, Jack Jr. "Crashing the Gates of Insight: Blade Runner." In *Retrofitting Blade Runner: Issues in Ridley Scott's Blade Runner and Philip K. Dick's Do Androids Dream of Electric Sheep?* edited by Judith Kerman, 212–29. Bowling Green, OH: Bowling Green State University Popular Press, 1991.

Bordwell, David and Kristin Thompson. *Film Art: An Introduction*. New York: The McGraw-Hill Companies, 1997.

Bowersock, Glen W. "Helena's Bridle and the Chariot of Ethiopia." In *Antiquity in Antiquity: Jewish and Christian Pasts in the Greco-Roman World*, edited by Gregg Gardner and Kevin Lee Osterloh, 383–93. Tübingen: Mohr Siebeck, 2008.

Bradford, Roark. *Ol' Man Adam An' His Chillun Being The Tales They Tell About The Time When The Lord Walked The Earth Like A Natural Man*. New York: Harper, 1928.

Brant, Jo-Ann A. *Dialogue and Drama: Elements of Greek Tragedy in the Fourth Gospel*. Peabody, MA: Hendrickson Publishers, 2004.

Brintnall, Kent L. *Ecce Homo: The Male-Body-in-Pain as Redemptive Figure*. Chicago, IL: University of Chicago Press, 2011.

Britt, Brian M. *Rewriting Moses: The Narrative Eclipse of the Text*. Journal for the Study of the Old Testament 402. London: New York: T & T Clark International, 2004.

Brooks, Peter. *Reading for the Plot: Design and Intention in Narrative*. New York: Alfred A. Knopf, 1984.

Brown, Dan. *The Da Vinci Code: A Novel*. New York: Doubleday, 2003.

Brown, Raymond Edward. *The Gospel According to John*. Garden City, NY: Doubleday, 1966.

Brunette, Peter. *Roberto Rossellini*. New York: Oxford University Press, 1987.

Budge, E. A. *The Queen of Sheba and Her Only Son Menyelek (I) Being the Book of the Glory of Kings, Kebra Nagast*, 2000. www.yorku.ca/inpar/kebra_budge.pdf (accessed 12 May 2013).

Burnett, Ron. *Explorations in Film Theory: Selected Essays from Ciné-Tracts*. Bloomington, IN: Indiana University Press, 1991.

Burnham, John C. "American Medicine's Golden Age: What Happened to It?" In *Sickness and Health in America: Readings in the History of Medicine and Public Health*, edited by Judith Walzer Leavitt and Ronald L. Numbers, 284–94. Madison, WI: University of Wisconsin Press, 1978.

Byron, John. *Recent Research on Paul and Slavery*. Recent Research in Biblical Studies. Sheffield: Sheffield Phoenix Press, 2008.

Calvino, Italo. *If on a Winter's Night a Traveler*. Vol. 1. New York: Harcourt Brace Jovanovich, 1981.

Campbell, Joseph. *The Hero with a Thousand Faces*, edited by Northrop Frye. Bollingen Series, 17. New York: Pantheon Books, 1949.

Carey, Greg. *Ultimate Things: An Introduction to Jewish and Christian Apocalyptic Literature*. St. Louis, MO: Chalice Press, 2005.

Carroll, Noël. "The Future of Allusion: Hollywood in the Seventies (And Beyond)." *October* 20, Spring (1982): 51–81.

——. *Interpreting the Moving Image*. Cambridge; New York, NY: Cambridge University Press, 1998.

——. "The Problem with Movie Stars." In *Photography and Philosophy: Essays on the Pencil of Nature*, edited by Scott Walden, 248–64. Malden, MA: Blackwell Pub., 2008.

Chancey, Mark. *The Bible and Public Schools.* http://faculty.smu.edu/mchancey/public_schools.htm (accessed 25 January 2012).

Christianson, Eric S., Peter Francis, and William R. Telford, eds. *Cinéma Divinité: Religion, Theology and the Bible in Film.* London: SCM, 2005.

Clanton, Dan. "'Here, There, and Everywhere': Images of Jesus in American Popular Culture." In *The Bible In/and Popular Culture: Creative Encounter,* edited by Elaine Mary Wainwright and Philip Leroy Culbertson, 41–60. Society of Biblical Literature Semeia Studies. Leiden; Boston, MA: Brill, 2010.

Clay, Jenny Strauss. *Hesiod's Cosmos.* Cambridge, UK; New York: Cambridge University Press, 2003.

Clifton, N. Roy. *The Figure in Film.* Newark, NJ; London: University of Delaware Press; Associated University Presses, 1983.

Cohen, Arthur A. *The Myth of the Judeo-Christian Tradition.* New York: Harper & Row, 1969.

Cohen, Jonathan. *The Origins and Evolution of the Moses Nativity Story.* Leiden; New York: Brill, 1993.

Collins, Ace. *Stories Behind the Hymns that Inspire America: Songs that Unite our Nation.* Grand Rapids, MI: Zondervan, 2003.

Collins, Jim, Hilary Radner, and Ava Collins. *Film Theory Goes to the Movies.* New York: Routledge, 1993.

Collins, John J. *The Apocalyptic Imagination: An Introduction to Jewish Apocalyptic Literature.* Grand Rapids, MI: William B. Eerdmans, 1998.

Connelly, Marc. *Voices Offstage: A Book of Memoirs.* Chicago, IL: Holt, Rinehart & Winston, 1968.

Copier, Laura. *Preposterous Revelations: Visions of Apocalypse and Martyrdom in Hollywood Cinema 1980–2000.* Sheffield: Sheffield Phoenix Press, 2012.

Corley, Kathleen E. and Robert L. Webb, eds. *Jesus and Mel Gibson's The Passion of the Christ: The Film, the Gospels and the Claims of History.* London; New York: Continuum, 2004.

Cornelius, Michael G. *Of Muscles and Men: Essays on the Sword and Sandal Film.* Jefferson, NC: McFarland & Company, Inc., Publishers, 2011.

——. "Introduction," in *Of Muscles and Men: Essays on the Sword and Sandal Film,* edited by M. G. Cornelius. Jefferson, NC: McFarland & Company, Inc., Publishers, 2011.

Creed, Barbara. *Pandora's Box: Essays in Film Theory.* Victoria: Australian Centre for the Moving Image, 2004.

Cullmann, Oscar. "The Infancy Gospels." In *New Testament Apocrypha. Volume I: Gospels and Related Writings,* edited by Wilhelm Schneemelcher and Robert MacLachan Wilson, 421–37. Cambridge; Louisville, KY: Westminster – J. Knox Press, 1991.

Culture Monster. "Terrence Malick's 'Tree of Life': The Classical Music Factor." *LA Times,* n.d. http://latimesblogs.latimes.com/culturemonster/2011/07/tree-of-life-terrence-malick.html (accessed 10 May 2013).

Custen, George Frederick. *Bio/pics: How Hollywood Constructed Public History.* New Brunswick, NJ: Rutgers University Press, 1992.

Dargis, Manohla and A. O. Scott. "The History in 'Lincoln,' 'Argo' and 'Zero Dark Thirty'." *The New York Times,* 22 February 2013, sec. Movies/Awards Season. www.nytimes.com/2013/02/23/movies/awardsseason/the-history-in-lincoln-argo-and-zero-dark-thirty.html (accessed 9 May 2013).

Davis, John. *The Landscape of Belief: Encountering the Holy Land in Nineteenth-Century American Art And Culture*. Princeton, NJ: Princeton University Press, 1996.

Deacy, C. R. "Reflections on the Uncritical Appropriation of Cinematic Christ-Figures: Holy Other or Wholly Inadequate?" *Journal of Religion and Popular Culture* 13, no. 1, June 2006, http://utpjournals.metapress.com/content/m033q25567093k82/?p=44defd2357804dd18d19ca19a8200488&pi=0 (accessed 9 May 2013).

DelFattore, Joan. *The Fourth R: Conflicts over Religion in America's Public Schools*. New Haven, CT: Yale University Press, 2004.

DeMille, Cecil B. *The Autobiography of Cecil B. DeMille*. Englewood Cliffs, NJ: Prentice-Hall, 1959.

Desser, David. "The New Eve: The Influence of Paradise Lost and Frankenstein on *Blade Runner*." In *Retrofitting Blade Runner: Issues in Ridley Scott's Blade Runner and Philip K. Dick's Do Androids Dream of Electric Sheep?* edited by Judith Kerman, 53–65. Bowling Green, OH: Bowling Green State University Popular Press, 1991.

Dickens, Charles. *The Life and Adventures of Martin Chuzzlewit: In Two Volumes*. Vol. 1. London: Chapman and Hall, 1866.

Dickinson, John Alexander and Brian J. Young. *A Short History of Quebec*. Montreal; Ithaca, NY: McGill-Queen's University Press, 2003.

DiMare, Philip C. *Movies in American History: An Encyclopedia*. Santa Barbara, CA: ABC-CLIO, 2011.

Edelman, Marsha Bryana. *Discovering Jewish Music*. Philadelphia, PA: Jewish Publication Society, 2003.

Eilberg-Schwartz, Howard. *God's Phallus and Other Problems for Men and Monotheism*. Boston: Beacon Press, 1994.

Eisen, Ute E. *Women Officeholders in Early Christianity: Epigraphical and Literary Studies*. Collegeville, MN: Liturgical Press, 2000.

Eisenberg, Ronald L. *The JPS Guide to Jewish Traditions*. Philadelphia, PA: Jewish Publication Society, 2004.

Eliade, Mircea. *Death, Afterlife, and Eschatology: A Thematic Source Book of the History of Religions*. New York: Harper & Row, 1974.

Elis, Niv. "The Film That Launched a Thousand Court Cases." *Moment Magazine*, 2010. www.oldsite.momentmag.net/datetalk/ten_commandments.html (accessed 9 May 2013).

Elsaesser, Thomas. "James Cameron's Avatar: Access for All." *New Review of Film and Television Studies* 9, no. 3 (1 September 2011): 247–64.

Elster, Janice. *Women's Public Legal Roles as Judges and Witnesses in the Bible and Early Rabbinic Literature*. Cincinnati, OH: Hebrew Union College-Jewish Institute of Religion, 2007.

Everett-Green, Robert. "How Survivor's Mark Burnett Gathered Believers for His Epic Bible Miniseries." *The Globe and Mail*. http://globeandmail.tumblr.com/post/44278962176/how-survivors-mark-burnett-gathered-believers-for-his (accessed 1 March 2013).

Exum, J. Cheryl. *Fragmented Women: Feminist (Sub)Versions of Biblical Narratives*. Valley Forge, PE: Trinity Press International, 1993.

——. *The Bible in Film – the Bible and Film*. Leiden; Boston, MA: Brill, 2006.

——. *Retellings: The Bible in Literature, Music, Art and Film*. Leiden; Boston, MA: Brill, 2007.

Farber, Stephen. *The Movie Rating Game*. Washington, DC: Public Affairs Press, 1972.

Fea, John. *Was America Founded as a Christian Nation? A Historical Introduction*. Louisville, KY: Westminster John Knox Press, 2011.

Feinstein, Stephen. *The 1990s from the Persian Gulf War to Y2K.* Berkeley Heights, NJ: Enslow Publishers, 2001.

Feldman, Louis H. "Josephus' Portrait of Moses," *The Jewish Quarterly Review* 82, no. 3/4 (1992): 285–328.

——. "Josephus' Portrait of Moses: Part Two," *The Jewish Quarterly Review* 83, no. 1/2 (1992): 7–50.

——. "Josephus' Portrait of Moses: Part Three," *The Jewish Quarterly Review* 83, no. 3/4 (1993): 301–30.

——. *Philo's Portrayal of Moses in the Context of Ancient Judaism.* Notre Dame, IN: University of Notre Dame Press, 2007.

Ferguson, George. *Signs & Symbols in Christian Art.* New York: Oxford University Press, 1954.

First Amendment Center. "The Bible and Public Schools: A First Amendment Guide." n.d. www.firstamendmentcenter.org/madison/wp-content/uploads/2011/03/bible_guide_graphics.pdf (accessed 9 May 2013).

Fischoff, Stuart, Joe Antonio, and Diane Lewis. "Favorite Films and Film Genres as a Function of Race, Age, and Gender." *Journal of Media Psychology* 3, no. 1 (1998). www.calstatela.edu/faculty/sfischo/media3.html (accessed 9 May 2013).

Fredriksen, Paula. *Augustine and the Jews: A Christian Defense of Jews and Judaism.* New York: Doubleday, 2008.

Freedman, H. and Maurice Simon, trans. *The Midrash Rabbah*, vol. 2. London: Soncino Press, 1977.

Friedman, Richard Elliott, and Shawna Dolansky. *The Bible Now.* New York: Oxford University Press, 2011.

Gabler, Neal. *An Empire of Their Own: How the Jews Invented Hollywood.* New York: Crown Publishers, 1988.

Garrett, Greg. *Holy Superheroes! Exploring the Sacred in Comics, Graphic Novels, and Film.* Rev. and expanded. Louisville, KY: Westminster John Knox Press, 2008.

Garver, Eugene. "The Ten Commandments: Powerful Symbols and Symbols of Power." *Law, Culture and the Humanities* 3, no. 2 (2007): 205–24.

Gauvreau, Michael. *The Catholic Origins of Quebec's Quiet Revolution, 1931–1970.* Montreal, QC: McGill-Queen's University Press, 2005.

Gehring, Wes D. *Parody as Film Genre: "Never Give a Saga an Even Break."* Westport, CT: Greenwood Press, 1999.

Gibson, Michael. *The Mill and the Cross: Peter Bruegel's "Way to Calvary."* Lausanne: Editions Acatos, 2000.

Giere, S. D. "Babette's Feast (1987)." In *Bible and Cinema: Fifty Key Films*, edited by Adele Reinhartz, 18–23. New York: Routledge, 2012.

Ginzberg, Louis. *Legends of the Jews.* Philadelphia, PA: Jewish Publication Society, 1909–38.

——. *Legends of the Jews: Notes.* Vol. 2. Hildesheim [u.a.]: Olms, 2000.

Glasser, Brian. *Medicinema: Doctors in Films.* Oxford; New York: Radcliffe Pub., 2010.

Glaude, Eddie S. *Exodus! Religion, Race, and Nation in Early Nineteenth-century Black America.* Chicago, IL: University of Chicago Press, 2000.

Goldman, Vivien. *The Book of Exodus: The Making and Meaning of Bob Marley and the Wailers' Album of the Century.* New York: Three Rivers Press, 2006.

Gonthier, David. *American Prison Film since 1930: From The Big House to The Shawshank Redemption.* Lewiston, NY: Edwin Mellen Press, 2006.

Goodacre, Mark. "Do You Think You're What They Say You Are? Reflections on Jesus Christ Superstar," *Journal of Religion and Film* 3, no. 1 (1999): 1–13.

Gorak, Jan. *Canon vs. Culture: Reflections on the Current Debate.* New York: Garland, 2001.

Gottlieb, Jack. *Funny, It Doesn't Sound Jewish: How Yiddish Songs and Synagogue Melodies Influenced Tin Pan Alley, Broadway, and Hollywood.* Albany, NY: State University of New York Press in association with the Library of Congress, 2004.

Gottschall, Jonathan. *The Storytelling Animal: How Stories Make us Human.* Boston, MA: Houghton Mifflin Harcourt, 2012.

Gourley, Catherine. *Gidgets and Women Warriors: Perceptions of Women in the 1950s and 1960s.* Images and Issues of Women in the Twentieth Century. Minneapolis, MN: Twenty-First Century Books, 2008.

Grant, Barry Keith. *Film Genre: From Iconography to Ideology.* Short Cuts 33. London; New York: Wallflower, 2007.

———. *Film Genre Reader IV.* Austin, TX: University of Texas Press, 2012.

Grindon, Leger. *Shadows on the Past: Studies in the Historical Fiction Film.* Philadelphia: Temple University Press, 1994.

Gunn, David M. "Bathsheba Goes Bathing in Hollywood: Words, Images, and Social Locations." *Semeia* 74 (1996): 75–101.

Gutjahr, Paul C. *An American Bible: A History of the Good Book in the United States, 1777–1880.* Stanford, CA: Stanford University Press, 1999.

———. "The Letter(s) of the Law: Four Centuries of Typography in the King James Bible." In *Illuminating Letters: Typography and Literary Interpretation,* edited by Paul C. Gutjahr and Megan Benton, 19–44. Amherst, MA: University of Massachusetts Press, 2001.

Hall, Sheldon. *Epics, Spectacles, and Blockbusters: A Hollywood History.* Contemporary Approaches to Film and Television Series. Detroit, MI: Wayne State University Press, 2010.

Hamilton, Marybeth. "Goodness Had Nothing To Do With It: Censoring Mae West." In *Movie Censorship and American Culture,* edited by Francis G. Couvares, 187–211. Washington, DC: Smithsonian Institution Press, 1996.

Hamlin, Hannibal and Norman W. Jones. *The King James Bible after 400 Years: Literary, Linguistic, and Cultural Influences.* Cambridge; New York: Cambridge University Press, 2010.

Hanks, Gardner C. *Capital Punishment and the Bible.* Scottdale, PA: Herald Press, 2002.

Harlow, John. "Biblical Films May Spark Epic Controversy." *The Ottawa Citizen.* Ottawa, Canada, 12 March 2013, sec. Arts & Life, p. C7.

Harries, Dan. *Film Parody.* London: BFI Pub., 2000.

Harrington, Daniel J. "Palestinian Adaptations of Biblical Narratives and Prophecies: The Bible Rewritten." In *Early Judaism and Its Modern Interpreters,* edited by Robert A. Kraft and George W. E. Nickelsburg, 239–47. Philadelphia, PA: Fortress Press, 1986.

Harris, David. "America and Israel are Inseparable," *Der Tagesspiegel,* 26 May 2011. www.ajc.org/site/apps/nlnet/content3.aspx?c=7oJILSPwFfJSG&b=8566343&ct=12476627 (accessed 9 May 2013).

Harrison, M. John. *The Centauri Device.* Garden City, NY: Doubleday, 1974.

Hays, Richard B. *The Moral Vision of the New Testament: Community, Cross, New Creation: A Contemporary Introduction to New Testament Ethics.* San Francisco, CA: HarperSanFrancisco, 1996.

Heimlich, Evan Samuel. "Divination by 'The Ten Commandments': Its Rhetorics and their Genealogies." Thesis, University of Kansas, Lawrence, 2007.

Helm, Zach. *Stranger Than Fiction: The Shooting Script*. New York: Newmarket Press, 2006.

Herzog, Jonathan P. *The Spiritual-Industrial Complex: America's Religious Battle Against Communism in the Early Cold War*. New York: Oxford University Press, 2011.

Higashi, Sumiko. *Cecil B. DeMille and American Culture: the Silent Era*. Berkeley, CA: University of California Press, 1994.

Hirsch, Foster. *The Hollywood Epic*. South Brunswick, NJ: Barnes, 1978.

Hogue, Peter. "A Man Escaped." *Film Comment* 35, no. 3 (June 1999): 44–48.

Horsley, Richard A. "Paul and Slavery: A Critical Alternative to Recent Readings." *Semeia* 83–84 (1998): 153–200.

Hunt, Steven A. "And the Word Became Flesh – Again? Jesus and Abraham in John 8:31–59." In *Perspectives on our Father Abraham: Essays in Honor of Marvin R. Wilson*, edited by Steven A. Hunt, 81–109. Grand Rapids, MI: W. B. Eerdmans Pub. Co., 2010.

Hutcheon, Linda. *A Theory of Adaptation*. New York: Routledge, 2006.

Idelsohn, A. Z. "The Kol Nidre Tune." *Hebrew Union College Annual* 8 (1931): 493–509.

Jensen, Morten Hørning. *Herod Antipas in Galilee: The Literary and Archaeological Sources on the Reign of Herod Antipas and its Socio-Economic Impact on Galilee*. Tübingen: Mohr Siebeck, 2006.

Jewett, Robert. "A Problematic Hope for the Shamed in *The Shawshank Redemption*." In *Saint Paul Returns to the Movies: Triumph over Shame*, 162–78. Grand Rapids, MI: William B. Eerdmans, 1999.

Johnson, David L. "The Case for Empirical Assessment of Biblical Literacy in America." In *The Bible and the University*, edited by C. Stephen Evans and David L. Jeffrey. The Scripture and Hermeneutics Series v. 8, pp. 240–52. Grand Rapids, MI: Zondervan, 2007.

Johnson, Elizabeth A. *Truly Our Sister: A Theology of Mary in the Communion of Saints*. New York: Continuum, 2003.

Johnston, Keith M. *Coming Soon: Film Trailers and the Selling of Hollywood Technology*. Jefferson, NC: McFarland, 2009.

——. *Science Fiction Film: A Critical Introduction*. Oxford; New York: Berg, 2011.

Jordan, Mark D., and Kent L Brintnall. "Mel Gibson, Bride of Christ." In *Mel Gibson's Bible: Religion, Popular Culture, and The Passion Of The Christ*, edited by Timothy K. Beal and Tod Linafelt, 81–87. Chicago, IL: University of Chicago Press, 2006.

Kalinak, Kathryn Marie. *Film Music: A Very Short Introduction*. Very Short Introductions. New York: Oxford University Press, 2010.

Keller, Rosemary Skinner, Rosemary Radford Ruether, and Marie Cantlon, eds. *Encyclopedia of Women and Religion in North America*. Vol. 1. Bloomington, IN: Indiana University Press, 2006.

Kerman, Judith. "Post-Millennium Blade Runner." In *The Blade Runner Experience: The Legacy of a Science Fiction Classic*, edited by Will Brooker, 31–39. London; New York: Wallflower, 2005.

Kindem, Gorham Anders. *The International Movie Industry*. Carbondale, IL: Southern Illinois University Press, 2000.

King, Stephen. "Rita Hayworth and the Shawshank Redemption." In *Different Seasons*. New York: Viking Press, 1982.

Kinnard, Roy and Tim Davis. *Divine Images: A History of Jesus on the Screen*. New York, NY: Carol Pub. Group, 1992.

Klocke, Astrid. "Subverting Satire: Edgar Hilsenrath's Novel *Der Nazi und der Friseur* and Charlie Chaplin's Film *The Great Dictator*." *Holocaust and Genocide Studies* 22, no. 3 (1 December 2008): 497–513.

Knust, Jennifer Wright. "Too Hot to Handle? A Story of an Adulteress and the Gospel of John." In *Women of the New Testament and Their Afterlives*, edited by Christine E Joynes, 143–63. Sheffield: Sheffield Phoenix Press, 2009.

Kozloff, Sarah. *Invisible Storytellers: Voice-Over Narration in American Fiction Film*. Berkeley, CA: University of California Press, 1988.

Kozlovic, Anton. "The Structural Characteristics of the Cinematic Christ-figure." *Journal of Religion and Popular Culture* 8, no. 1 (2004): 38.

——. "The Construction of a Christ-figure within the 1956 and 1923 Versions of Cecil B. DeMille's *The Ten Commandments*." *Journal of Religion and Film* 10, no. 1 (2006).

Kraemer, Ross Shepard. *Unreliable Witnesses: Religion, Gender, and History in the Greco-Roman Mediterranean*. New York: Oxford University Press, 2011.

Kreitzer, L. Joseph. *The New Testament in Fiction and Film: On Reversing the Hermeneutical Flow*. Sheffield: JSOT Press, 1993.

——. *The Old Testament in Fiction and Film: On Reversing the Hermeneutical Flow*. Sheffield: Sheffield Academic Press, 1994.

——. *Pauline Images in Fiction and Film: On Reversing the Hermeneutical Flow*. Sheffield: Sheffield Academic Press, 1999.

——. *Gospel Images in Fiction and Film: On Reversing the Hermeneutical Flow*. London; New York: Sheffield Academic Press, 2002.

Kronish, Amy and Costel Safirman. *Israeli Film: a Reference Guide*. Westport, CT: Praeger, 2003.

Kunzler, Michael. *The Church's Liturgy*. London; New York: Continuum, 2001.

Lakoff, George. *Moral Politics: How Liberals and Conservatives Think*. Chicago, IL: University of Chicago Press, 2002.

Lassner, Jacob. *Demonizing the Queen of Sheba: Boundaries of Gender and Culture in Postbiblical Judaism and Medieval Islam*. Chicago Studies in the History of Judaism. Chicago, IL: University of Chicago Press, 1993.

Lawrence, John Shelton and Robert Jewett. *The Myth of the American Superhero*. Grand Rapids, MI: W. B. Eerdmans, 2002.

Leathes, Stanley. *The Foundations of Morality: Being Discourses on the Ten Commandments with Special Reference to their Origin and Authority*. London: Hodder and Stoughton, 1882.

Leff, Leonard J. and Jerold Simmons. *The Dame in the Kimono: Hollywood, Censorship, and the Production Code from the 1920s to the 1960s*. New York: Grove Weidenfeld, 1990.

Lefkon, Dick. *Year 2000: Best Practices for Y2K Millennium Computing*. Upper Saddle River, NJ: Prentice Hall, 1998.

Leonard, Elmore. *Three-Ten to Yuma: And Other Stories*. New York: Harper, 2006.

Lev, Peter. *Transforming the Screen, 1950–1959*. Berkeley, CA: University of California Press, 2006.

Lierman, John. *The New Testament Moses: Christian Perceptions of Moses and Israel in the Setting of Jewish Religion*. Tübingen: Mohr Siebeck, 2004.

Lind, Millard. *The Sound of Sheer Silence and The Killing State: The Death Penalty and the Bible*. Telford, PA: Cascadia Pub. House, 2004.

Lyden, John. *The Routledge Companion to Religion and Film*. London; New York: Routledge, 2009.

McAlister, Melani. *Epic Encounters: Culture, Media, and U.S. Interests in the Middle East Since 1945*. Berkeley, CA: University of California Press, 2005.

McKenna, George. *The Puritan Origins of American Patriotism*. New Haven, CT: Yale University Press, 2007.

Madigan, Kevin and Carolyn Osiek. *Ordained Women in the Early Church: A Documentary History*. Baltimore, MD: Johns Hopkins University Press, 2005.

Malamud, Margaret. "Swords-and-Scandals: Hollywood's Rome during the Great Depression." *Arethusa* 41, no. 1 (2008): 157–83.

Malone, Peter. *Movie Christs and Antichrists*. New York: Crossroad, 1990.

Mancoff, Debra N. and David Roberts. *David Roberts: Travels in Egypt and the Holy Land*. San Francisco, CA: Pomegranate, 1999.

Marsh, Clive. *Cinema and Sentiment: Film's Challenge to Theology*. Milton Keynes; Waynesboro, GA: Paternoster Press, 2004.

Martens, John W. *The End of the World: The Apocalyptic Imagination in Film and Television*. Winnipeg, MB: J. Gordon Shillingford, 2003.

Martin, Joel W. and Conrad Eugene Ostwalt, eds. *Screening the Sacred: Religion, Myth, and Ideology in Popular American Film*. Boulder, CO: Westview Press, 1995.

Mast, Gerald and Marshall Cohen, eds. *Film Theory and Criticism: Introductory Readings*. New York: Oxford University Press, 1974.

May, John R. "The Godfather Films: Birth of a Don, Death of a Family." In *Image and Likeness: Religious Visions in American Film Classics*, edited by John R. May, 65–75. New York: Paulist Press, 1991.

Medved, Michael. *Hollywood vs. America: Popular Culture and the War on Traditional Values*. New York, NY; Grand Rapids, MI: HarperCollins; Zondervan, 1992.

Meeks, Jack D. "From the Belly of the HUAC: The Red Probes of Hollywood, 1947–52," 2009. http://hdl.handle.net/1903/9140 (accessed 9 May 2013).

Meier, John P. *A Marginal Jew: Rethinking the Historical Jesus. Volume 4, Law and Love*. New Haven, CT: Doubleday, 2009.

Mellinkoff, Ruth. *The Mark of Cain*. Berkeley, CA: University of California Press, 1981.

Mendelson, Alan. *Philo's Jewish Identity*. Brown Judaic Studies no. 161 Atlanta, GA: Scholars Press, 1988.

Miles, Margaret R. *Seeing and Believing: Religion and Values in the Movies*. Boston, MA: Beacon Press, 1996.

Mitchell, Charles P. *A Guide to Apocalyptic Cinema*. Westport, CT: Greenwood Press, 2001.

Monaco, Paul. *A History of American Movies: A Film-by-Film Look at the Art, Craft, and Business of Cinema*. Lanham, MD: Scarecrow Press, 2010.

Moore, George Foot. "Christian Writers on Judaism." *The Harvard Theological Review* 14, no. 3 (1 July 1921): 197–254.

Morgan, David. *The Sacred Gaze: Religious Visual Culture in Theory and Practice*. Berkeley, CA: University of California Press, 2005.

Mulvey, Laura. "Visual Pleasure and Narrative Cinema." *Screen* 16, no. 3 (1975): 6–18.

Musser, Charles. "Passions and the Passion Play: Theatre, Film and Religion in America, 1880–1900." *Film History* 5, no. 4 (1 December 1993): 419–56.

Nadel, Alan. "God's Law and the Wide Screen: The Ten Commandments as Cold War 'Epic'." *PMLA* 108, no. 3 (1 May 1993): 415–30.

Neve, Brian. *Film and Politics in America: A Social Tradition*. London; New York: Routledge, 1992.

Nickelsburg, George W. E. "The Bible Rewritten and Expanded." In *Jewish Writings of the Second Temple Period*, edited by Michael E. Stone, 89–156. Assen, Netherlands: Van Gorcum, 1984.

Nulman, Macy. *The Encyclopedia of Jewish Prayer: Ashkenazic and Sephardic Rites.* Northvale, NJ: Jason Aronson, 1993.

Obayashi, Hiroshi. *Death and Afterlife: Perspectives of World Religions.* New York: Greenwood Press, 1992.

O'Connor, Kathleen. "Humour, Turnabouts and Survival in the Book of Esther." In *Are we Amused? Humour about Women in the Biblical Worlds*, edited by Athalya Brenner, 52–64. London; New York: T & T Clark International, 2003.

O'Leary, Cecilia Elizabeth. *To Die For: The Paradox of American Patriotism.* Princeton, NJ: Princeton University Press, 1999.

O'Leary, Stephen D. *Arguing the Apocalypse: A Theory of Millennial Rhetoric.* New York: Oxford University Press, 1998.

Olson, Roger E. *The SCM Press A-Z of Evangelical Theology.* London: SCM, 2005.

Ostwalt, Conrad Eugene. "Armageddon at the Millennial Dawn." *The Journal of Religion and Film* 4, no. 1 (2000). www.unomaha.edu/jrf/armagedd.htm (accessed 10 May 2013).

——. *Secular Steeples: Popular Culture and the Religious Imagination.* Harrisburg, PA: Trinity Press International, 2003.

——. "Apocalyptic." In *The Routledge Companion to Religion and Film*, edited by John Lyden, 368–83. London; New York: Routledge, 2009.

Paley, Michael. "The Hollywood Midrash." *Jewish Folklore and Ethnology Review* 16, no. 1 (1994): 34–37.

Panofsky, Erwin. "Style and Medium in the Motion Pictures." In *Film Theory and Criticism: Introductory Readings*, edited by Gerald Mast and Marshall Cohen, 151–69. New York: Oxford University Press, 1974.

Pearson, Roberta A. "Biblical Movies." In *Encyclopedia of Early Cinema*, edited by Richard Abel, 68–71. London: Taylor & Francis, 2005.

Peddie, Ian. *Popular Music and Human Rights.* Farnham; Burlington, VT: Ashgate, 2011.

Petersen, Anders Klostergaard. "Rewritten Bible as a Borderline Phenomenon – Genre, Textual Strategy, or Canonical Anachronism?" In *Flores Florentino: Dead Sea Scrolls and Other Early Jewish Studies in Honour of Florentino Garcia Martinez*, edited by A. Hilhorst, Eibert J. C. Tigchelaar, and Emile Puech, 285–306. Leiden: Brill, 2007.

Petersen, David L. "The Bible in Public View." In *Foster Biblical Scholarship: Essays in Honor of Kent Harold Richards*, edited by Frank Ritchel Ames and Charles William Miller, 117–33. Atlanta, GA: Society of Biblical Literature, 2010.

Phillips, Gary A. and Danna Nolan Fewell. "Ethics, Bible, Reading As If." *Semeia* 77 (1997): 1–21.

Philo. *Philo: In Ten Volumes (and Two Supplementary Volumes).* Translated by F. H. Colson, G. H. Whitaker, and Ralph Marcus. Vol. 6. Cambridge, MA; London: Harvard University Press: W. Heinemann, 1966.

Phy-Olsen, Allene. *The Bible and Popular Culture in America.* Philadelphia, PA; Chico, CA: Fortress Press; Scholars Press, 1985.

Pipolo, Tony. *Robert Bresson: A Passion for Film.* Oxford; New York: Oxford University Press, 2010.

Plantinga, Carl R. *Moving Viewers: American Film and the Spectator's Experience.* Berkeley, CA: University of California Press, 2009.

Plaut, W. Gunther and David E. Stein. *The Torah: A Modern Commentary.* New York: Union for Reform Judaism, 2005.

"Police Discover Mafia's 'Ten Commandments' After Arresting Godfather." *Mail Online.* www.dailymail.co.uk/news/article-492449/Police-discover-Mafias-Ten-Commandments-arresting-Godfather.html (accessed 27 February 2013).

Prime, Rebecca. "Cloaked in Compromise: Jules Dassin's Naked City." In *Tender Comrades: A Backstory of the Hollywood Blacklist,* edited by Patrick McGilligan and Paul Buhle, 142–51. New York: St. Martin's Press, 1997.

Prince, Stephen. *Savage Cinema: Sam Peckinpah and the Rise of Ultraviolent Movies.* Austin, TX: University of Texas Press, 1998.

Prothero, Stephen R. *American Jesus: How the Son of God Became a National Icon.* New York: Farrar, Straus, and Giroux, 2003.

Quinones, Ricardo J. *The Changes of Cain: Violence and the Lost Brother in Cain and Abel Literature.* Princeton, NJ: Princeton University Press, 1991.

Raboteau, Albert J. "African Americans, Exodus, and the American Israel." In *African-American Christianity: Essays in History,* edited by Paul E. Johnson, 1–17. Berkeley, CA: University of California Press, 1994.

Rausch, Andrew J. *Turning Points in Film History.* New York: Citadel Press, 2004.

Redles, David. *Hitler's Millennial Reich: Apocalyptic Belief and the Search for Salvation.* New York: New York University Press, 2005.

Reinhartz, Adele. "Jesus as Prophet: Predictive Prolepses in the Fourth Gospel." *Journal for the Study of the New Testament* 11, no. 36 (1989): 3–16.

——. *Befriending the Beloved Disciple: A Jewish Reading of the Gospel of John.* New York: Continuum, 2001.

——. *Scripture on the Silver Screen.* Louisville, KY: Westminster John Knox Press, 2003.

——. "The Happy Holy Family in the Jesus Film Genre." In *On the Cutting Edge: The Study of Women in Biblical Worlds: Essays in Honor of Elisabeth Schüssler Fiorenza,* edited by Jane Schaberg, Alice Bach, and Esther Fuchs, 123–42. New York: Continuum, 2004.

——. "History and Pseudo-History in the Jesus Film Genre." In *The Bible in Film – and The Bible and Film,* edited by J. Cheryl Exum, 1–17. Leiden: Brill, 2006.

——. *Jesus of Hollywood.* Oxford; New York: Oxford University Press, 2007.

——. "Playing with Paradigms: The Christ-Figure Genre in Contemporary Film." *Australian Religious Studies Review* 21, no. 3 (2008): 298–317.

——. "'Rewritten Gospel': The Case of Caiaphas the High Priest." *New Testament Studies* 55, no. 2 (2009): 160–78.

——. "The Jesus Movies." In *The Continuum Companion to Religion and Film,* edited by William L. Blizek, 211–22. London; New York: Continuum, 2009.

——. *Caiaphas the High Priest.* Columbia, MO: University of South Carolina Press, 2011.

——. *The Bible and Cinema: Fifty Key Films.* New York: Routledge, 2012.

——, ed. *The Bible and Film: Fifty Key Films.* London; New York: Routledge, 2013.

Richardson, Michael. *Surrealism and Cinema.* Oxford; New York: Berg, 2006.

Rohdie, Sam and Pier Paolo Pasolini. *The Passion of Pier Paolo Pasolini.* Bloomington, IN; London: Indiana University Press; British Film Institute, 1995.

Rollins, Peter C. and John E. O'Connor. *Why We Fought: America's Wars in Film and History.* Film & History. Lexington, KY: University Press of Kentucky, 2008.

Rooker, Mark F. and E. Ray Clendenen. *The Ten Commandments: Ethics for the Twenty-First Century.* Nashville, TN: B & H Academic, 2010.

Rosenberg, Joel. "What You Ain't Heard Yet: The Languages of *The Jazz Singer.*" *Prooftexts* 22, no. 1/2 (2002): 11–54.

Ross, Steven J. *Working-class Hollywood: Silent Film and the Shaping of Class in America.* Princeton, NJ: Princeton University Press, 1999.

Ruether, Rosemary Radford. *Faith and Fratricide: The Theological Roots of Anti-Semitism.* New York: Seabury Press, 1974.

Runions, Erin. *How Hysterical: Identification and Resistance in the Bible and Film.* New York: Palgrave Macmillan, 2003.

Salisbury, Joyce E. *Encyclopedia of Women in the Ancient World.* Santa Barbara, CA: ABC-CLIO, 2001.

Sammon, Paul. *Future Noir: The Making of Blade Runner.* New York: HarperPrism, 1996.

Sanders, E. P. *Paul and Palestinian Judaism: A Comparison of Patterns of Religion.* Philadelphia, PA: Fortress Press, 1977.

Sandmel, Samuel. "Philo's Knowledge of Hebrew: The Present State of the Problem," *Studia Philonica* 5(1978): 107–12.

Scharold, Kristen. "The Tree of Life (Review)." *Books and Culture,* 29 June 2012. www.booksandculture.com/articles/webexclusives/2011/june/treelife.html (accessed 10 May 2013).

Schatz, Thomas. *Hollywood Genres: Formulas, Filmmaking, and the Studio System.* Philadelphia, PA: Temple University Press, 1981.

Schiffman, Harold F. *Linguistic Culture and Language Policy.* London; New York: Routledge, 2002.

Schrader, Paul. *Transcendental Style in Film: Ozu, Bresson, Dreyer.* Berkeley, CA: University of California Press, 1972.

Schrecker, Ellen. *The Age of McCarthyism: A Brief History with Documents.* Boston, MA: Bedford Books of St. Martin's Press, 1994.

Schroeder, Caroline T. "Ancient Egyptian Religion on the Silver Screen: Modern Anxieties About Race, Ethnicity, and Religion." *Journal of Religion and Film* 7, no. 2 (2003). www.unomaha.edu/jrf/Vol7No2/ancienteqypt.htm (accessed 12 May 2013).

Scott, A. O. "Fugue for History and Memory." *The New York Times,* 30 December 2011, sec. Movies/Awards Season. www.nytimes.com/2012/01/01/movies/award sseason/a-o-scott-on-the-musical-movement-of-the-tree-of-life.html?ref=awardsseason (accessed 12 May 2013).

——. "The Tree of Life (Review)." *The New York Times,* 26 May 2011. http://movies.nytimes.com/2011/05/27/movies/the-tree-of-life-from-terrence-malick-review.html?pagewanted=print (accessed 10 May 2013).

Scott, Allen J. "Hollywood and the World: The Geography of Motion-Picture Distribution and Marketing." *Review of International Political Economy* 11, no. 1 (2004): 33–61.

Scott, Bernard Brandon. *Hollywood Dreams and Biblical Stories.* Minneapolis, MN: Fortress Press, 1994.

Segal, Alan F. *Life after Death: A History of the Afterlife in the Religions of the West.* New York: Doubleday, 2004.

Segrave, Kerry. *American Films Abroad: Hollywood's Domination of the World's Movie Screens from the 1890s to the Present.* Jefferson, NC: McFarland, 1997.

Shakespeare, William. *The Merchant of Venice.* Edited by E. F. C. Ludowyk. Cambridge: Cambridge University Press, 1964.

Shapiro, James S. *Oberammergau: The Troubling Story of the World's Most Famous Passion Play.* New York: Pantheon Books, 2000.

Shapiro, Jerome Franklin. *Atomic Bomb Cinema: The Apocalyptic Imagination on Film*. New York: Routledge, 2002.

Shell, Marc. *Stutter*. Cambridge, MA: Harvard University Press, 2005.

Shepherd, David, ed. *Images of the Word: Hollywood's Bible and Beyond*. Atlanta, GA: Society of Biblical Literature, 2008.

Sheppard, William Anthony. *Revealing Masks: Exotic Influences and Ritualized Performance in Modernist Music Theater*. Berkeley, CA: University of California Press, 2001.

Shiloah, Amnon. *Jewish Musical Traditions*. Detroit, MI: Wayne State University Press, 1992.

Short, K. R. M. "Chaplin's 'The Great Dictator' and British Censorship, 1939." *Historical Journal of Film, Radio and Television* 5, no. 1 (1 March 1985): 85–108.

Sklar, Robert. *Movie-Made America: A Cultural History of American Movies*. New York: Vintage Books, 1994.

Sleeper, Jim. "AMERICAN BRETHREN: Hebrews and Puritans." *World Affairs* 172, no. 2 (31 December 2009): 46–60.

Slotkin, Richard. *Gunfighter Nation: The Myth of the Frontier in Twentieth-century America*. Oklahoma paperbacks ed. Norman, OK: University of Oklahoma Press, 1998.

Smith, Gary. *Epic Films: Casts, Credits and Commentary on over 350 Historical Spectacle Movies*. 2 ed. Jefferson, MO: McFarland, 2004.

Sobchack, Vivian. "'Surge and Splendor': A Phenomenology of the Hollywood Historical Epic." *Representations* 29, Winter (1990): 24–49.

———. "Embodying Transcendence: On the Literal, the Material, and the Cinematic Sublime." *Material Religion: The Journal of Objects, Art and Belief* 4, no. 2 (2008): 194–203.

Solomon, Jon. *The Ancient World in the Cinema*. New Haven, CT: Yale University Press, 2001.

Staley, Jeffrey L. "Reading 'This Woman' Back into John 7:1–8:59: Liar Liar and the 'Pericope Adulterae' in Intertextual Tango." In *Those Outside: Noncanonical Readings of Canonical Gospels*, edited by George Aichele and Richard G. Walsh, 85–107. New York: T & T Clark International, 2005.

Staley, Jeffrey L. and Richard G. Walsh. *Jesus, the Gospels, and Cinematic Imagination: A Handbook to Jesus on DVD*. Louisville, KY: Westminster John Knox Press, 2007.

Steffen, Therese Frey. "Introduction to Part II." In *The Civil Rights Movement Revisited: Critical Perspectives on the Struggle for Racial Equality in the United States*, edited by Patrick B. Miller, Therese Frey Steffen, and Elisabeth Schäfer-Wünsche, 83–86. Lit; Distributed in North America by Transaction Publishers, 2001.

Stern, Richard C., Clayton N. Jefford, and Guerric DeBona. *Savior on the Silver Screen*. New York: Paulist Press, 1999.

Sternberg, Meir. *The Poetics of Biblical Narrative: Ideological Literature and the Drama of Reading*. Bloomington, IN: Indiana University Press, 1985.

Stolzman, Henry, Tami Hausman, and Daniel Stolzman. *Synagogue Architecture in America: Faith, Spirit and Identity*. Mulgrave, Vic.; Woodbridge: Images; ACC Distribution, 2004.

Stone, Alan A. "The Tree of Life (Review)." *Journal of Religion and Film* 15, no. 2 (October 2011): 5.

Stone, Bryan P. *Faith and Film: Theological Themes at the Cinema*. St. Louis, MO: Chalice Press, 2000.

Tatum, W. Barnes. *Jesus at the Movies: A Guide to the First Hundred Years*. Rev. and expanded. Santa Rosa, CA: Polebridge Press, 2004.

——. *Jesus at the Movies: A Guide to the First Hundred Years and Beyond.* 3rd Edition. Santa Rosa, CA: Polebridge Press, 2013.

Telford, William R. "Jesus and Women in Fiction and Film." In *Transformative Encounters: Jesus and Women Re-Viewed*, edited by Ingrid R. Kitzberger, 353–91. Leiden; Boston, MA: Brill, 2000.

——. "Through a Lens Darkly: Critical Approaches to Theology and Film." In *Cinéma Divinité: Religion, Theology and the Bible in Film*, edited by Eric S. Christianson, Peter Francis, and William R. Telford, 15–43. London: SCM, 2005.

Thistlethwaite, Susan. "Mel Makes a War Movie." In *Perspectives on The Passion of the Christ: Religious Thinkers and Writers Explore the Issues Raised by the Controversial Movie*, 127–45. New York: Miramax Books, 2004.

Thompson, Kirsten Moana. *Apocalyptic Dread: American Film at the Turn of the Millennium.* Albany, NY: State University of New York Press, 2007.

Trachtenberg, Joshua. *The Devil and the Jews: The Medieval Conception of the Jew and Its Relation to Modern Antisemitism.* New Haven, CT; London: Yale University Press, 1943.

Tuck, Stephen. "Black Protest During the 1940s: The NAACP in Georgia." In *The Civil Rights Movement Revisited: Critical Perspectives on the Struggle for Racial Equality in the United States*, edited by Patrick B. Miller, Therese Frey Steffen, and Elisabeth Schäfer-Wünsche, 61–81. Lit; Distributed in North America by Transaction Publishers, 2001.

Unterseher, Lisa A. *The Mark of Cain and the Jews: Augustine's Theology of Jews and Judaism.* Gorgias Dissertations 39. Piscataway, NJ: Gorgias Press, 2009.

Uris, Leon M. *Exodus.* Garden City, NY: Doubleday, 1958.

Valdes, Mario. "The Black Wiseman in European Symbolism." *Journal of African Civilizations* 3, no. 1 (1981): 67–85.

Verdon, Timothy and Filippo Rossi. *Mary in Western Art.* New York: In Association with Hudson Mills Press, 2005.

Volkan, Vamik D. and Norman Itzkowitz. *Turks and Greeks: Neighbours in Conflict.* Huntingdon: Eothen Press, 1994.

Von Doviak, Scott. *Hick Flicks: The Rise and Fall of Redneck Cinema.* Jefferson, NC: McFarland, 2005.

Wainwright, Elaine Mary, and Philip Leroy Culbertson. *The Bible In/and Popular Culture: Creative Encounter.* Society of Biblical Literature Semeia Studies. Leiden; Boston, MA: Brill, 2010.

Walker, Alison Tara. "The Sounds of Silents: Aurality and Medievalism in Benjamin Christensen's Häxan." In *Mass Market Medieval: Essays on the Middle Ages in Popular Culture*, edited by David W. Marshall, 42–56. Jefferson, NC: McFarland & Co., 2007.

Walsh, Richard. "The Passion as Horror Film: St. Mel of the Cross." *Journal of Religion and Popular Culture* 20 (Fall 2008). http://utpjournals.metapress.com/content/yl64p102j8875102/?p=cdc1bc5701a44398aad21363705ad0be&pi=1 (accessed 12 May 2013).

Walsh, Richard G. *Reading the Gospels in the Dark: Portrayals of Jesus in Film.* Harrisburg, PA: Trinity Press International, 2003.

Walsh, Richard G., Jeffrey L. Staley, and Adele Reinhartz, eds. *Son of Man: An African Jesus Film.* Bible in the Modern World 52. Sheffield: Sheffield Phoenix Press, 2013.

Warren, Hillary. *There's Never Been a Show Like Veggie Tales: Sacred Messages in a Secular Market.* Lanham, MD: AltaMira Press, 2005.

Wassen, Cecilia. *Women in the Damascus Document.* Atlanta, GA: Society of Biblical Literature, 2005.

Weisberg, Dvora E. "The Widow of Our Discontent: Levirate Marriage in the Bible and Ancient Israel." *Journal for the Study of the Old Testament* 28, no. 4 (2004): 403.

———. *Levirate Marriage and the Family in Ancient Judaism.* Waltham, MA; Hanover, NH: Brandeis University Press; University Press of New England, 2009.

Weisenfeld, Judith. *Hollywood Be Thy Name: African American Religion in American Film, 1929–1949.* Berkeley, CA: University of California Press, 2007.

Wenzel, Uwe. "Blacks and Interracial Cooperation: African American Interest Groups and the Fight for Civil Rights from the 1930s to the 1950s." In *The Civil Rights Movement Revisited: Critical Perspectives on the Struggle for Racial Equality in the United States,* edited by Patrick B. Miller, Therese Frey Steffen, and Elisabeth Schäfer-Wünsche, 39–60. Lit; Distributed in North America by Transaction Publishers, 2001.

White, Eric Walter. *Benjamin Britten: His Life and Operas,* ed. John Evans, 2d ed. Berkeley, CA: University of California Press, 1983.

Withalm, Gloria. "The Self-Reflexive Screen: Outlines of a Comprehensive Model." In *Self-Reference in the Media,* edited by Winfried Nöth and Nina Bishara, 125–42. Berlin; New York: Mouton de Gruyter, 2007.

Woloch, Nancy. *Women and the American Experience.* 4th ed. Boston, MA: McGraw-Hill, 2006.

Wood, Michael. *America in the Movies: Or, "Santa Maria, It Had Slipped My Mind."* New York: Basic Books, 1975.

Wright, Melanie Jane. *Moses in America: The Cultural Uses of Biblical Narrative.* American Academy of Religion Cultural Criticism Series. Oxford; New York: Oxford University Press, 2003.

———. *Religion and Film: An Introduction.* London; New York: I. B. Tauris; Distributed in the US by Palgrave Macmillan, 2007.

Wyke, Maria. *Projecting the Past: Ancient Rome, Cinema, and History.* The New Ancient World. New York: Routledge, 1997.

Zakai, Avihu. *Exile and Kingdom: History and Apocalypse in the Puritan Migration to America.* Cambridge; New York: Cambridge University Press, 1992.

Zetlin, Minda. *Surviving the Computer Time Bomb: How to Plan for and Recover from the Y2K Explosion.* New York: AMACOM, 1999.

Index of ancient sources

Bible

Hebrew Bible/Old Testament

Index of modern authors

Film index

Subject index

www.routledge.com/religion

Also available...

Bible and Cinema:
Fifty Key Films

Edited by Adele Reinhartz

Series: *Routledge Key Guides*

Movies which have drawn inspiration from the Bible, either directly or indirectly, have been extremely popular since the earliest days of cinema. *Bible and Cinema: Fifty Key Films* introduces a wide range of those movies, which are among the most important, critically-acclaimed and highest-grossing films of all time, including:

- The King of Kings
- Ben-Hur
- The Passion of the Christ
- Frankenstein
- Close Encounters of the Third Kind
- 2001: A Space Odyssey
- Apocalypse Now
- Monty Python's Life of Brian.

Written by a team of international scholars, the fifty entries discuss the Biblical stories, characters or motifs depicted in each film making this book the ideal guide for anyone interested in the long-standing relationship between the Bible and film.

2012 | 276 Pages | PB: 978-0-415-67719-6 | HB: 978-0-415-67720-2
Learn more at: www.routledge.com/9780415677196

Available from all good bookshops

www.routledge.com/religion

Also available...

The Routledge Companion to Religion and Film

Edited by John Lyden

Series: *Routledge Religion Companions*

"A young field – the study of religion and film – has come of age with the publication of this wonderful volume...this book illuminates how religions have responded to films, how films have responded to religions, and how we might best go about interpreting what this reveals about our culture." *– Joel Martin, University of Massachusetts, USA*

The Routledge Companion to Religion and Film brings together a lively and experienced team of contributors to introduce key topics in religion and film and to investigate the ways in which this exciting discipline is developing. Divided into four parts, the *Companion*:

- analyzes the history of the interaction of religion and film, through periods of censorship as well as appreciation of the medium
- studies religion in film, examining how the world's major religions, as well as postcolonial, Japanese and new religions, are depicted by and within films
- uses diverse methodologies to explore religion and film, such as psychoanalytical, theological and feminist approaches, and audience reception
- analyzes religious themes in film, including redemption, the demonic, Jesus or Christ-figures, heroes and superheroes
- considers films as diverse as *The Passion of the Christ*, *The Matrix*, *Star Wars* and *Groundhog Day*.

2010 | 506 Pages | PB: 978-0-415-60187-0 | HB: 978-0-415-44853-6
Learn more at: www.routledge.com/9780415601870

Available from all good bookshops

www.routledge.com/religion

Also available...

Screening the Afterlife:
Theology, Eschatology, and Film

By Christopher Deacy

"Chris Deacy is a theologian who knows how to look at film. This is among the best books yet published that evidences a robust two-way dialogue between serious theology and Hollywood films."
– Robert K. Johnston, Fuller Theological Seminary, USA

Screening the Afterlife is a unique and fascinating exploration of the 'last things' as envisaged by modern filmmakers. Drawing on a range of films from *Flatliners* and *What Dreams May Come* to *Working Girl* and *The Shawshank Redemption*, it offers the first comprehensive examination of death and the afterlife within the growing field of religion and film. Topics addressed include:

• the survival of personhood after death
• the language of resurrection and immortality
• Near-Death Experiences and Mind-Dependent Worlds
• the portrayal of 'heaven' and 'hell'.

Students taking courses on eschatology will find this a stimulating and thought provoking resource, while scholars will relish Deacy's theological insight and understanding.

2011 | 188 Pages | PB: 978-0-415-57259-0 | HB: 978-0-415-57258-3
Learn more at: www.routledge.com/9780415572590

Available from all good bookshops

www.routledge.com/religion

Also available...

The Religion and Film Reader

The Religion and Film Reader

Edited by Jolyon Mitchell

and S. Brent Plate

"This is a highly intelligent and thought-provoking collection of work exploring the relationship between religion and film"
- David Murphy, *University of Stirling, UK*

Edited by leading experts in the field, *The Film and Religion Reader* brings together key writings in this exciting and dynamic discipline. In over sixty interviews, essays and reviews from numerous directors, film critics and scholars, it offers the most complete survey of the field to date.

The Reader is organized into thematic and chronological sections, each with an introduction by the editors:

- The dawn of cinema: advocates and detractors
- The birth of film theory: realism, formalism, and religious vision
- Global perspectives: filmmakers and critics
- Theological and Biblical approaches to analysing film
- Recent reflections on the relation between religion and film.

This anthology brings together a wealth of material in a student-friendly format, making it an invaluable resource for courses within theology and religious studies.

2007 | 496 Pages | PB: 978-0-415-40495-2 | HB: 978-0-415-40494-5
Learn more at: www.routledge.com/9780415404952

Available from all good bookshops

www.routledge.com/religion

Also available...

Theology Goes to the Movies

An Introduction to Critical
Christian Thinking

By Clive Marsh

"By starting from issues explored in particular films, the book helps to
ground theological debates in relation to human questions and
experience. This really helps to bring the discipline of theology alive, and
I wish this book had been available when I was a theology student."
– *Gordon Lynch, University of Birmingham, UK*

Drawing a comparison between religion and cinema-going, *Theology Goes
to the Movies* examines a range of contemporary films in relation to key
theological concepts. Cinema as a religion-like activity is explored through
cognitive, affective, aesthetic and ethical levels, identifying the religious
aspects in the social practice of cinema-going.

Written by a leading expert in the field, this text analyses:
- The role of cinema and Church in Western culture
- The power of Christian symbols and images within popular culture
- Theological concepts of humanity, evil and redemption, eschatology
  and God.

2007 | 198 Pages | PB: 978-0-415-38012-6 | HB: 978-0-415-38011-9
Learn more at: www.routledge.com/9780415380126

Available from all good bookshops

Taylor & Francis

eBooks

ORDER YOUR FREE 30 DAY INSTITUTIONAL TRIAL TODAY!

FOR LIBRARIES

Over 22,000 eBook titles in the Humanities, Social Sciences, STM and Law from some of the world's leading imprints.

Choose from a range of subject packages or create your own!

Benefits for **you**

▶ Free MARC records
▶ COUNTER-compliant usage statistics
▶ Flexible purchase and pricing options

Benefits for your **user**

▶ Off-site, anytime access via Athens or referring URL
▶ Print or copy pages or chapters
▶ Full content search
▶ Bookmark, highlight and annotate text
▶ Access to thousands of pages of quality research at the click of a button

For more information, pricing enquiries or to order a free trial, contact your local online sales team.

UK and Rest of World: **online.sales@tandf.co.uk**
US, Canada and Latin America:
e-reference@taylorandfrancis.com

www.ebooksubscriptions.com

 ALPSP Award for BEST eBOOK PUBLISHER 2009 Finalist

 Taylor & Francis **eBooks**
Taylor & Francis Group

A flexible and dynamic resource for teaching, learning and research.

791.4368
R 371 B

131171

4486002

3 4711 00226 2162

LINCOLN CHRISTIAN UNIVERSITY